6th Workshop on Computational Approaches to Subjectivity, Sentiment and Social Media Analysis (WASSA 2015)

Held at EMNLP 2015

Lisbon, Portugal
17 September 2015

ISBN: 978-1-5108-1189-8

Printed from e-media with permission by:

Curran Associates, Inc.
57 Morehouse Lane
Red Hook, NY 12571

proceedings.com

Some format issues inherent in the e-media version may also appear in this print version.

Printed by Curran Associates, Inc. (2015)

Association for Computational Linguistics
209 N. Eighth Street
Stroudsburg, Pennsylvania 18360

Phone: 1-570-476-8006
Fax: 1-570-476-0860

acl@aclweb.org

Additional copies of this publication are available from:

Curran Associates, Inc.
57 Morehouse Lane
Red Hook, NY 12571 USA
Phone: 845-758-0400
Fax: 845-758-2634
Email: curran@proceedings.com
Web: www.proceedings.com

EMNLP 2015

6TH WORKSHOP ON COMPUTATIONAL APPROACHES TO SUBJECTIVITY, SENTIMENT AND SOCIAL MEDIA ANALYSIS WASSA 2015

Workshop Proceedings

17 September 2015
Lisbon, Portugal

Preface

Emotions are an important part of our everyday lives. However, until quite recently, human affect was regarded in a dual manner - positively, for its regulatory power and negatively, as a sort of a "weakness" of the human spirit, that should ideally be rational, logical, *thinking* in a very matter of fact and consequence-based fashion.

Recent discoveries in Neuropsychology and the possibilities opened by the functional Magnetic Resonance Imaging have made it clear that emotions play a very important role for the well-functioning of the human body, both psychologically, as well as physically.

Apart from the importance emotions have for each human being individually, research in Social Psychology and disciplines such as Marketing, Mass-media Communication or Political Science, has shown time and time again that the emotional discourse, its content - in words with affective connotation and the combination thereof - is of paramount difference between the success and failure of social actions, consumer products or political candidates.

Given that nowadays messages with (sometimes) high emotional connotations are so easily shared using Social Media platforms and that their high volume makes manual sifting mostly impossible, the automatic processing of Subjectivity, Sentiment and Emotions in texts, especially in Social Media contexts is highly relevant.

Bearing these observations in mind, the aim of the 6th Workshop on Computational Approaches to Subjectivity, Sentiment and Social Media Analysis (WASSA 2015) was to continue the line of the previous editions, bringing together researchers in Computational Linguistics working on Subjectivity and Sentiment Analysis and researchers working on interdisciplinary aspects of affect computation from text. Starting with 2013, WASSA has extended its scope and focus to Social Media phenomena and the impact of affect-related phenomena in this context. The past two editions have shown important breakthroughs in dealing with the challenges of these types of texts, in monolingual, multilingual and cross-domain contexts.

WASSA 2015 was organized in conjunction to EMNLP 2015: the Conference on Empirical Methods in Natural Language Processing, on September 17, 2015, in Lisboa, Portugal.

For this year's edition of WASSA, we received a total of 48 submissions, from universities and research centers all over the world, out of which 8 were accepted as long and another 16 as short papers. Each paper has been thoroughly reviewed by at least 2 members of the Program Committee. The accepted papers were all highly assessed by the reviewers, the best paper receiving an average punctuation (computed as an average of all criteria used to assess the papers) of 4.8 out of 5.

The main topics of the accepted papers are related to challenges in dealing with language and domain diversity in Social Media - the creation and evaluation of resources for subjectivity, sentiment and emotion resources for Twitter mining, but also the use of the particular structure of Social Media texts to improve the sentiment and subjectivity classification. Additionally, articles presenting valuable work concentrating on building lexica for this field demonstrate that there is still a high requirement to develop such resources, taking into account deeper levels of annotations that are inspired by theories in Psychology. Finally, some articles deal with the issue of sentiment visualization and the use of such tools to improve the performance of automatic systems for emotion detection and classification.

This year's edition has again shown that the topics put forward to discussion by WASSA are of high interest to the research community and that the papers chosen to be debated in this forum bring an important development to the SSA research area.

We would like to thank the EMNLP 2015 Organizers and Workshop Chairs for the help and support at the different stages of the workshop organization process. We are also especially grateful to the Program Committee members and the external reviewers for the time and effort spent assessing the papers. We would like to extend our thanks to our invited speaker – Dr. Zornitsa Kozareva - for accepting to deliver the keynote talk, opening a new path of collaboration between two very closely-linked topics - emotions and metaphors.

Secondly, we would like to express our gratitude for the official endorsement we received from SIGSEM - the ACL Special Interest Group on Computational Semantics, SIGWAC - the Special Interest Group of the Association for Computational Linguistics (ACL) on Web as Corpus, SIGANN - the ACL Special Interest Group for Annotation - and SIGNLL - ACL's Special Interest Group on Natural Language Learning.

We would like to express our gratitude to Yaniv Steiner, who created the WASSA logo and to the entire Europe Media Monitor team at the European Commission Joint Research Centre, for the technical support they provided.

Alexandra Balahur, Erik van der Goot, Piek Vossen and Andrés Montoyo

WASSA 2015 Chairs

Organizers:

Alexandra Balahur
European Commission Joint Research Centre
Institute for the Protection and Security of the Citizen

Erik van der Goot
European Commission Joint Research Centre
Institute for the Protection and Security of the Citizen

Piek Vossen
University of Amsterdam
Department of Language, Literature and Communication

Andrés Montoyo
University of Alicante
Department of Software and Computing Systems

Program Committee:

Nicoletta Calzolari, CNR Pisa (Italy)
Erik Cambria, University of Stirling (U.K.)
Veronique Hoste, University of Ghent (Belgium)
Dirk Hovy, University of Copenhagen (Denmark)
Ruben Izquierdo Bevia - Vrije Universiteit Amsterdam (The Netherlands)
Manfred Klenner, University of Zuerich (Switzerland)
Roman Klinger, University of Bielefeld (Germany)
Gerard Lynch, University College Dublin (Ireland)
Isa Maks - Vrije Universiteit Amsterdam (The Netherlands)
Diana Maynard - University of Sheffield (U.K.)
Saif Mohammad, National Research Council (Canada)
Karo Moilanen, University of Oxford (U.K.)
Günter Neumann, DFKI (Germany)
Constantin Orasan, University of Wolverhampton (U.K.)
Viktor Pekar, University of Wolverhampton (U.K.)
Jose-Manuel Perea-Ortega, University of Extremadura (Spain)
Paolo Rosso, Technical University of Valencia (Spain)

Josef Steinberger, Charles University Prague (The Czech Republic)
Mike Thelwall, University of Wolverhampton (U.K.)
Dan Tufis, RACAI (Romania)
Alfonso Ureña, University of Jaén (Spain)
Janyce Wiebe - University of Pittsburgh (U.S.A.)
Michael Wiegand, Saarland University (Germany)
Taras Zagibalov, Brantwatch (U.K.)

Invited Speaker:

Dr. Zornitsa Kozareva, Yahoo!

Table of Contents

Workshop Program

Thursday, September 17, 2015

09:00–09:05 Opening Remarks

09:05–09:40 Invited talk

Multilingual Affect Polarity and Valence Prediction in Metaphors
Zornitsa Kozareva

09:40–10:30 Session 1: Multilingual Sentiment Analysis in Social Media

09:40–10:10 *Sentiment Analysis on Monolingual, Multilingual and Code-Switching Twitter Corpora*
David Vilares, Miguel A. Alonso and Carlos Gómez-Rodríguez

10:10–10:30 *Connotation in Translation*
Marine Carpuat

10:30–11:00 *Coffee Break*

11:00–12:30 Session 2: The Influence of Context for Sentiment Analysis in Social Media

11:00–11:30 *Enhanced Twitter Sentiment Classification Using Contextual Information*
Soroush Vosoughi, Helen Zhou and deb roy

11:30–12:00 *Your Sentiment Precedes You: Using an author's historical tweets to predict sarcasm*
Anupam Khattri, Aditya Joshi, Pushpak Bhattacharyya and Mark Carman

12:00–12:30 *Optimising Agile Social Media Analysis*
Thomas Kober and David Weir

12:30–14:00 *Lunch Break*

Thursday, September 17, 2015 (continued)

14:00–15:30 Session 3: Beyond Review Mining

14:00–14:30 *Utilizing review analysis to suggest product advertisement improvements*
Takaaki Tsunoda, Takashi Inui and Satoshi Sekine

14:30–15:00 *Towards Opinion Mining from Reviews for the Prediction of Product Rankings*
Wiltrud Kessler, Roman Klinger and Jonas Kuhn

15:00–15:30 *Classification of deceptive opinions using a low dimensionality representation*
Leticia Cagnina and Paolo Rosso

15:30–16:00 ***Coffee Break***

16:00–17:20 Session 4: Lexicon Generation and Visualisation for Sentiment Analysis

16:00–16:30 *Extending effect annotation with lexical decomposition*
Josef Ruppenhofer and Jasper Brandes

16:30–17:00 *Analysing domain suitability of a sentiment lexicon by identifying distributionally bipolar words*
Lucie Flekova, Daniel Preoţiuc-Pietro and Eugen Ruppert

17:00–17:20 *Imagisaurus: An Interactive Visualizer of Valence and Emotion in the Roget's Thesaurus*
Saif Mohammad

17:20–17:30 ***Break***

Thursday, September 17, 2015 (continued)

17:30–19:20 Session 5: Posters

Personality Traits on Twitter—or—How to Get 1,500 Personality Tests in a Week
Barbara Plank and Dirk Hovy

Negation Scope Detection for Twitter Sentiment Analysis
Johan Reitan, Jørgen Faret, Björn Gambäck and Lars Bungum

A Linguistically Informed Convolutional Neural Network
Sebastian Ebert, Ngoc Thang Vu and Hinrich Schütze

How much does word sense disambiguation help in sentiment analysis of micropost data?
Chiraag Sumanth and Diana Inkpen

Predicting Ratings for New Movie Releases from Twitter Content
Wernard Schmit and Sander Wubben

Beyond Sentiment: Social Psychological Analysis of Political Facebook Comments in Hungary
Márton Miháltz, Tamás Váradi, István Csertő, Éva Fülöp, Tibor Pólya and Pál Kővágó

Verb-centered Sentiment Inference with Description Logics
Manfred Klenner

Mining HEXACO personality traits from Enterprise Social Media
Priyanka Sinha, Lipika Dey, Pabitra Mitra and Anupam Basu

Opinion Holder and Target Extraction for Verb-based Opinion Predicates – The Problem is Not Solved
Michael Wiegand, Marc Schulder and Josef Ruppenhofer

Synthetic Text Generation for Sentiment Analysis
Umar Maqsud

Detecting speculations, contrasts and conditionals in consumer reviews
Maria Skeppstedt, Teri Schamp-Bjerede, Magnus Sahlgren, Carita Paradis and Andreas Kerren

Using Combined Lexical Resources to Identify Hashtag Types
Credell Simeon and Robert Hilderman

Thursday, September 17, 2015 (continued)

Sentiment Classification via a Response Recalibration Framework
Phillip Smith and Mark Lee

19:20–19:30 Closing discussion - "Where do we go from here?"

Multilingual Affect Polarity and Valence Prediction in Metaphors

Dr. Zornitsa Kozareva – Yahoo!

Abstract: Understanding metaphor rich texts like "*Her lawyer is a shark*", "*Time is money*", "*We need to construct a strong argument*" and the affect associated with them is a challenging problem, which has been of interest to the research community for a long time. One crucial challenge is to build an automated system that can identify the polarity and valence associated with metaphors and create multilingual platform for that. In this talk, I will introduce the task of multilingual sentiment analysis of metaphors and will present novel algorithms that integrate affective, perceptual and social processes with stylistic and lexical information. Finally, by running evaluations on datasets in English, Spanish, Farsi and Russian, I will show that the method is portable and works equally well when applied to different languages.

Proceedings of the 6th Workshop on Computational Approaches to Subjectivity, Sentiment and Social Media Analysis (WASSA 2015), page 1,
Lisboa, Portugal, 17 September, 2015.

Sentiment Analysis on Monolingual, Multilingual and Code-Switching Twitter Corpora

David Vilares, Miguel A. Alonso and Carlos Gómez-Rodríguez
Grupo LyS, Departamento de Computación, Universidade da Coruña
Campus de A Coruña s/n, 15071, A Coruña, Spain
{david.vilares, miguel.alonso, carlos.gomez}@udc.es

Abstract

We address the problem of performing polarity classification on Twitter over different languages, focusing on English and Spanish, comparing three techniques: (1) a monolingual model which knows the language in which the opinion is written, (2) a monolingual model that acts based on the decision provided by a language identification tool and (3) a multilingual model trained on a multilingual dataset that does not need any language recognition step. Results show that multilingual models are even able to outperform the monolingual models on some monolingual sets. We introduce the first code-switching corpus with sentiment labels, showing the robustness of a multilingual approach.

1 Introduction

Noisy social media, such as Twitter, are especially interesting for *sentiment analysis* (SA) and *polarity classification* tasks, given the amount of data and their popularity in different countries, where users simultaneously publish opinions about the same topic in different languages (Cambria et al., 2013a; Cambria et al., 2013b). Some expressions are written in different languages, making the polarity classification harder. In this context, handling texts in different languages becomes a real need. We evaluate three machine learning models, considering Spanish (*es*), English (*en*) and its multilingual version, English-Spanish (*en-es*):

1. *Multilingual approach (en-es model)*: A model does not need to recognise the language of the text. The *en* and *es* training and development corpora are merged to train an unique *en-es* sentiment classifier.
2. *Monolingual approach (en and es models)*: The ideal case where the language of the text is known and the right model is executed. Each language model is trained and tuned on a monolingual corpus.
3. *Monolingual pipeline with language detection (pipe model)*: Given an unknown text, we first identify the language of the message through `lang.py` (Lui and Baldwin, 2012). The output language set was constrained to Spanish and English to make sure every tweet is classified and guarantee a fair comparison with the rest of the approaches. The training was done in the same way as in the monolingual approach, as we know the language of the texts. `Lang.py` is just needed for evaluation. The language is predicted, the corresponding monolingual classifier is called and the outputs are joined to compare them to the gold standard.

The approaches are evaluated on: (1) an English monolingual corpus, (2) a Spanish monolingual corpus (3) a multilingual corpus which combines the two monolingual collections and (4) a code-switching (Spanish-English) corpus, that is introduced together with this paper.

2 Related work

The problem of multilingual polarity classification has already been addressed from different perspectives, such as monolingual sentiment analysis in a multilingual setting (Boiy and Moens, 2009), cross-lingual sentiment analysis (Brooke et al., 2009) or multilingual sentiment analysis (Balahur and Turchi, 2014). Banea et al. (2010) shows that including multilingual information can improve by almost 5% the performance of subjectivity classification in English. Davies and Ghahramani (2011) propose a language-independent model for sentiment analysis of Twitter messages, only relying on emoticons; that outperformed a *bag-of-words* Naive Bayes approach.

Proceedings of the 6th Workshop on Computational Approaches to Subjectivity, Sentiment and Social Media Analysis (WASSA 2015), pages 2–8,
Lisboa, Portugal, 17 September, 2015.

Cui et al. (2011) consider that not only emoticons, but also character and punctuation repetitions are language-independent emotion tokens. A different way of evaluating multilingual SA systems is posed by Balahur et al. (2014). They translate the English SemEval 2013 corpus (Nakov et al., 2013) into Spanish, Italian, French and German by means of machine translation (MT) systems. The resulting datasets were revised by non-native and native speakers independently, finding that the use of machine translated data achieves similar results as the use of native-speaker translations.

3 Multilingual sentiment analysis

Our goal is to compare the performance of supervised models based on *bag-of-words*, often used in SA tasks. We trained our classifiers using a L2-regularised logistic regression (Fan et al., 2008).

3.1 Feature Extraction

We apply Natural Language Processing (NLP) techniques for extracting linguistic features, using their total occurrence as the weighting factor (Vilares et al., 2014). Four atomic sets of features are considered:

- *Words (W)*: Simple statistical model that counts the frequencies of words in a text.
- *Lemmas (L)*: Each term is lemmatised to reduce sparsity, using lexicon-based methods that rely on the Ancora corpus (Taulé et al., 2008) for Spanish and Multext (Ide and Véronis, 1994) and a set of rules[1] for English.
- *Psychometric properties (P)*: Emotions, psychological concepts (e.g. *anger*) or topics (e.g. *job*) that commonly appear in messages. We rely on the LIWC dictionaries (Pennebaker et al., 2001) to detect them.
- *Part-of-speech tags (T)*: The grammatical categories were obtained using the Stanford Maximum Entropy model (Toutanova and Manning, 2000). We trained an *en* and an *es* tagger using the Google universal PoS tagset (Petrov et al., 2011) and joined the Spanish and English corpora to train a combined *en-es* tagger. The aim was to build a model that does not need any language detection to tag samples written in different languages, or even code-switching sentences. Table 1 shows how the three taggers work on a real code-switching sentence from Twitter, illustrating how the *en-es* tagger effectively tackles them. The accuracy of the *en* and *es* taggers was 98.12%[2] and 96.03% respectively. The multilingual tagger obtained 98.00% and 95.88% over the monolingual test sets.

These atomic sets of features can be combined to obtain a rich linguistic model that improves performance (Section 4).

3.2 Contextual features

Syntactic features

Dependency parsing is defined as the process of obtaining a dependency tree given a sentence. Let $S = [s_1 s_2 ... s_{n-1} s_n]$ be a sentence[3] of length *n*, where s_i indicates the token at the ith position; a *dependency tree* is a graph of binary relations, $G = \{(s_j, m_{jk}, s_k)\}$, where s_j and s_k are the *head* and *dependent* tokens, and m_{jk} represents the syntactic relation between them. To obtain such trees, we trained an *en*, *es* and an *en-es* parser (Vilares et al., 2015b) using MaltParser (Nivre et al., 2007). In order to obtain competitive results for a specific language, we relied on MaltOptimizer (Ballesteros and Nivre, 2012). The parsers were trained on the Universal Dependency Treebanks v2.0 (McDonald et al., 2013) and evaluated against the monolingual test sets. The Labeled Attachment Score (LAS) of the Spanish and English monolingual parsers was 80.54% and 88.35%, respectively. The multilingual model achieved a LAS of 78.78% and 88.65% (significant improvement with respect to the monolingual model, using Bikel's randomised parsing evaluation comparator and $p < 0{,}05$). Figure 1 shows an example how the *en*, *es* and *en-es* parsers work on a code-switching sentence.

In the next step, words, lemmas, psychometric properties and PoS tags are used to extract *enriched generalised triplet* features (Vilares et al., 2015a). Let (s_j, m_{ij}, s_k) be a triplet with $s_j, s_k \in W$ and a generalisation function, $g : W \rightarrow \{W, L, P, T\}$, a *generalised triplet* is defined as $(g(s_j), m_{ij}, g(s_k))$.

[1] http://sourceforge.net/p/zpar/code/HEAD/tree/src/english/morph/aux_lexicon.cpp

[2] Note that Toutanova and Manning reported 97.97% on the Penn Treebank tagset, which is bigger than the Google Universal tagset (48 vs 12 tags).

[3] An artificial token s_0, named ROOT, is usually added for technical reasons.

	El	Cafe	Colombiano	taking	over	Newcastle	with	its	three	best
es	DET	NOUN	ADJ	X	X	X	X	X	X	X
en	NOUN	NOUN	NOUN	VERB	PTR	NOUN	ADP	PRON	NUM	ADJ
es-en	DET	NOUN	ADJ	VERB	ADP	NOUN	ADP	PRON	NUM	ADJ

Table 1: Performance of taggers on a code-switching sentence from Twitter: *adjective* (ADJ), *prepositions* and *postpositions* (ADP), *determinant* (DET), *noun* (NOUN), *particles* (PTR) *pronoun* (PRON), *verb* (VERB) and *other category* (X)

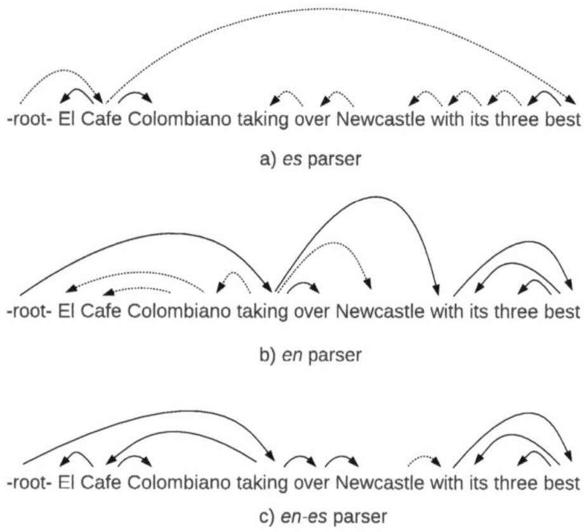

Figure 1: Example with the *en*, *es* and *en-es* dependency parsers. Dotted lines represent incorrectly-parsed dependencies

N-gram features

N-gram features capture shallow structure of sentences, identifying local relations between words (e.g. *'not good'* becomes *'not_good'*).

4 Experimental framework

The proposed sets of features and models are evaluated on standard monolingual corpora, taking accuracy as the reference metric. These monolingual collections are then joined to create a multilingual corpus, which helps us compare the performance of the approaches when tweets come from two different languages. An evaluation over a code-switching test set is also carried out.

4.1 Monolingual corpora

Two corpora are used to compare the performance of monolingual and multilingual models:

- *SemEval 2014 task B* corpus (Rosenthal et al., 2014): A set of English tweets[4] split into a training (8,200 tweets), development (1,416) and a test set[5] (5,752). Each tweet was manually classified as *positive*, *none* or *negative*.
- *TASS 2014* corpus (Román et al., 2015): A corpus of Spanish tweets containing a training set of 7,219 tweets. We split it into a new training and a development set (80:20). Two different test sets are provided: (1) a *general test set* of 60,798 tweets that was made by pooling and (2) a small test-set of 1,000 manually labelled tweets, named *1K test set*. The tweets are labelled with *positive*, *none*, *negative* and *mixed*, but in this study the *mixed* class was treated as *none*, following the same criteria as in SemEval 2014.

4.2 Multilingual corpora

These two test sets were merged to create a synthetic multilingual corpus. The aim was to compare the multilingual and the monolingual approach with language detection under this configuration. The unbalanced sizes of the test sets result in a higher performance when correctly classifying the majority language. We do not consider that as a methodological problem, but rather as a challenge of monitoring social networks in real environments, where the number of tweets in each language is not necessarily balanced.

4.3 Code-switching corpus

We created a polarity corpus with code-switching tweets based on the training collection[6] (*en-es*) presented by Solorio et al. (2014). Each word in the corpus is labelled with its language, serving as the starting point to obtain a collection of multilingual tweets. We first filtered the tweets containing both Spanish and English words, obtaining 3,062 tweets. Those were manually labelled by three annotators according to the SentiStrength strategy, a

[4]Due to Twitter restrictions some of the tweets are not available anymore, so the corpus statistics may vary slightly from those of other researchers that used the corpus.

[5]It also contained short texts coming from SMS and messages from LiveJournal, that we removed as they are out of the scope of this study.

[6]The test set was not released for the research community.

dual score *(p,n)* from 1 to 5 where *p* and *n* indicate the positive and the negative sentiment (Thelwall et al., 2010). Krippendorf's alpha coefficient indicated an inter-annotator agreement from 0.629 to 0.664 for negative sentiment and 0.500 to 0.693 for positive sentiment. To obtain the final score, we applied an average strategy with regular round: if $p > n$ then the tweet is labelled as *positive*, if $p < n$ then it is labelled as *negative* and otherwise it is labelled as *none*. After the transformation to the trinary scheme, we obtained a corpus where: the *positive* class represents the 31.45% of the corpus, the *negative* one represents a 25.67% and the remaining 42.88% belongs to the *none* class.

To the best of our knowledge, this is the first code-switching corpus with sentiment annotations.[7], which presents several challenges. It is an especially noisy corpus, were many grammatical errors occur in each tweet. There is also an overuse of subjective clauses and abbreviations (e.g. *'lol'*, *'lmao'*, ...) whose subjectivity was considered a controversial issue by the annotators. Finally, a predominant use of English was detected (`lang.py` classified 59.29% of the tweets as English). We believe this is because the Solorio et al. (2014) corpus was collected by downloading tweets for people from Texas and California.

5 Experimental results

5.1 Results on the English corpus

Features	en	pipe	en-es
Words (W)	**66.72**	66.71	66.22
Lemmas (L)	**66.74**	66.71	66.48
Psychometric (P)	62.52	**62.53**	61.47
PoS-tags (T)	51.82	51.80	**52.03**
Bigrams of W	60.99	61.00	**61.47**
Bigrams of L	61.75	**61.77**	61.32
Bigrams of P	**61.32**	**61.32**	60.41
Triplets of W	56.40	56.38	**57.84**
Triplets of L	58.69	58.67	**59.16**
Triplets of P	**58.26**	58.24	57.60
Combined (W,P,T)	68.52	**68.58**	68.48
Combined (L,P,T)	**68.43**	68.38	68.34
Combined (W,P)	68.72	**68.74**	68.52
Combined (L,P)	**68.57**	68.53	68.32

Table 2: Accuracy (%) on the SemEval 2014

Table 2 shows the performance of the three models on the SemEval test set. The differences between the monolingual model and the monolingual pipeline with language detection are tiny. This is due to the high performance of `lang.py` on this corpus, where only 6 tweets were misclassified as Spanish tweets. Despite of this issue, the *en-es* classifier performs very competitively on the English monolingual test sets, and the differences with respect to the *en* model range from 0.2 to 1.05 percentage points. With certain sets of features, consisting of triplets, the multilingual model even outperforms both monolingual models, reinforcing the validity of this approach.

Features	1K test set			General test set		
	es	pipe	en-es	es	pipe	en-es
Words (W)	**56.60**	56.50	54.60	64.39	64.35	**64.59**
Lemmas (L)	56.40	56.30	**56.60**	64.45	64.48	**64.57**
Psychometric (P)	**54.70**	**54.70**	53.10	58.77	58.69	**59.50**
PoS-tags (T)	**48.90**	48.80	41.70	49.44	**49.49**	47.72
Bigrams of W	**52.90**	52.70	52.10	58.37	58.41	**58.66**
Bigrams of L	**54.00**	53.90	52.20	58.73	58.74	**59.29**
Bigrams of P	46.00	46.00	**47.00**	51.30	51.26	**53.22**
Triplets of W	**52.40**	52.20	44.60	54.26	54.41	**54.96**
Triplets of L	**54.40**	54.40	46.30	56.06	56.09	**56.38**
Triplets of P	**45.80**	**45.80**	47.50	50.00	49.44	**52.34**
Combined (W,P,T)	**60.00**	59.90	59.10	**66.43**	66.34	66.34
Combined (L,P,T)	**61.40**	**61.40**	59.20	**66.18**	66.10	66.12
Combined (W,P)	59.10	59.20	**59.60**	66.27	66.18	**66.28**
Combined (L,P)	59.80	**59.90**	59.30	**65.95**	65.89	65.92

Table 3: Accuracy (%) on the TASS test sets

5.2 Results on the Spanish corpus

With respect to the evaluation on the TASS 2014 corpus, the tendency seems to remain on the TASS 2014-1k, as illustrated in Table 3. It general terms the *es* model obtains the best results, followed by the *pipe* and the *en-es* models. In this version of the corpus, the system misclassified 17 of the manually labelled tweets, and the impact of the monolingual model with language detection is also small. Results obtained on the TASS 2014 general set give us more information, since a significant number of tweets from this collection (842) were classified as English tweets. Some of these tweets actually were short phrases in English, some presented code-switching and some others were simply misclassified. Under this configuration, the multilingual model outperforms monolingual models with most of the proposed features. This suggests that multilingual models present advantages when messages in different languages need to be analysed.

Experimental results allow us to conclude that the multilingual models proposed in this work are a competitive option when applying polarity classification to a medium where messages in different

[7]Freely available in `grupolys.org/software/CS-CORPORA/cs-en-es-corpus-wassa2015.txt`

Features	pipe	en-es	pipe	en-es
Words (W)	**64.93**	64.20	64.55	**64.71**
Lemmas (L)	**65.03**	64.76	64.66	**64.72**
Psychometric (P)	**61.17**	60.02	59.03	**59.66**
PoS-tags (T)	**51.28**	50.23	**49.69**	48.11
Bigrams of W	59.55	**59.84**	58.63	**58.90**
Bigrams of L	**60.40**	59.73	59.00	**59.46**
Bigrams of P	**58.65**	58.08	52.19	**53.88**
Triplets of W	**55.65**	55.54	54.57	**55.21**
Triplets of L	**57.93**	56.92	56.31	**56.62**
Triplets of P	**56.08**	55.84	50.25	**52.81**
Combined (W,P,T)	**67.07**	66.85	**66.52**	**66.52**
Combined (L,P,T)	**67.17**	66.75	66.28	**66.30**
Combined (W,P)	**67.08**	66.97	66.39	**66.47**
Combined (L,P)	**67.03**	66.75	66.11	**66.12**

Table 4: Accuracy (%) on the multilingual test set

Features	en	es	pipe	en-es
Words (W)	**55.65**	47.65	52.74	54.87
Lemmas (L)	55.68	48.66	53.00	**56.37**
Psychometric (P)	53.04	43.63	50.69	**53.69**
PoS-tags (T)	**45.07**	39.32	44.71	43.17
Bigrams of W	54.31	47.45	51.67	**54.34**
Bigrams of L	55.03	48.92	52.16	53.63
Bigrams of P	**49.48**	40.46	46.08	46.86
Triplets of W	**52.55**	36.54	45.95	50.72
Triplets of L	**52.97**	44.68	48.99	50.42
Triplets of P	**48.14**	40.59	45.72	45.98
Combined (W,P,T)	**59.18**	48.27	56.53	58.52
Combined (L,P,T)	58.55	49.67	56.07	**59.11**
Combined (W,P)	58.72	49.90	56.40	**58.82**
Combined (L,P)	58.85	50.82	56.07	**59.34**

Table 5: Accuracy (%) on the code-switching set

languages might appear. The results are coherent across different languages and corpora, and also robust on a number of sets of features. In this respect, for contextual features the performance was low in all cases, due to the small size of the employed training corpus. Vilares et al. (2015a) explain how this kind of features become useful when the training data becomes larger.

5.3 Results on a synthetic multilingual corpus

Table 4 shows the performance both of the multilingual approach and the monolingual pipeline with language detection when analysing texts in different languages. On the one hand, the results show that using a multilingual model is the best option when Spanish is the majority language, probably due to a high presence of English words in Spanish tweets. On the other hand, combining monolingual models with language detection is the best-performing approach when English is the majority language. The English corpus contains only a few Spanish terms, suggesting that the advantages of having a multilingual model cannot be exploited under this configuration.

5.4 Results on the code-switching corpus

Table 5 shows the performance of the three proposed approaches on the code-switching test set. The accuracy obtained by the proposed models on this corpus is lower than on the monolingual corpora. This suggests that analysing subjectivity on tweets with code-switching presents additional challenges. The best performance (59.34%) is obtained by the *en-es* model using lemmas and psychometric properties as features. In general terms, atomic sets of features such as words, psychometric properties or lemmatisation, and their combinations, perform competitively under the *en-es* configuration. The tendency remains when the atomic sets of features are combined, outperforming the monolingual approaches in most cases.

The pipeline model performs worse on the code-switching test set than the multilingual one for most of the sets of features. These results, together with the ones obtained on the monolingual corpora, indicates that a multilingual approach like the one proposed in this article is more robust on environments containing code-switching tweets and tweets in different languages. The *es* model performs poorly, probably due to the smaller presence of Spanish words in the corpus. The annotators also noticed that Spanish terms present a larger frequency of grammatical errors than the English ones. Surprisingly, the *en* model performed really well in many of the cases. We hypothesise this is due to the higher presence of English phrases, that made it possible to extract the sentiment of the texts in many of the cases.

6 Conclusions

We compared different machine learning approaches to perform multilingual polarity classification in three different environments: (1) where monolingual tweets are evaluated separately, (2) where texts in different languages need to be analysed and (3) where code-switching texts appear. The proposed approaches were: (a) a purely monolingual model, (b) a simple pipeline which used language identification techniques to determine the language of unseen texts (c) a multilingual model trained on a corpus that joins the two monolingual corpora. Experimental results reinforces the robustness of the multilingual approach under the three configurations.

Acknowledgments

This research is supported by the Ministerio de Economía y Competitividad (FFI2014-51978-C2) and Xunta de Galicia (R2014/034). The first author is funded by the Ministerio de Educación, Cultura y Deporte (FPU13/01180).

References

A. Balahur and M. Turchi. 2014. Comparative experiments using supervised learning and machine translation for multilingual sentiment analysis. *Computer Speech and Language*, 28(1):56–75, January.

A. Balahur, M. Turchi, R. Steinberger, J. M. Perea-Ortega, G. Jacquet, D. Kucuk, V. Zavarella, and A. E. Ghali. 2014. Resource Creation and Evaluation for Multilingual Sentiment Analysis in Social Media Texts. In Nicoletta Calzolari (Conference Chair), Khalid Choukri, Thierry Declerck, Hrafn Loftsson, Bente Maegaard, Joseph Mariani, Asuncion Moreno, Jan Odijk, and Stelios Piperidis, editors, *Proceedings of the Ninth International Conference on Language Resources and Evaluation (LREC'14)*, Reykjavik, Iceland, May. European Language Resources Association (ELRA).

M. Ballesteros and J. Nivre. 2012. MaltOptimizer: an optimization tool for MaltParser. In *Proceedings of the Demonstrations at the 13th Conference of the European Chapter of the Association for Computational Linguistics*, pages 58–62. Association for Computational Linguistics.

C. Banea, R. Mihalcea, and J. Wiebe. 2010. Multilingual Subjectivity: Are More Languages Better? In Chu-Ren Huang and Dan Jurafsky, editors, *COLING 2010. 23rd International Conference on Computational Linguistics. Proceedings of the Conference*, volume 2, pages 28–36, Beijing, August. Tsinghua University Press.

E. Boiy and M. Moens. 2009. A machine learning approach to sentiment analysis in multilingual Web texts. *Information Retrieval*, 12(5):526–558, October.

J. Brooke, M. Tofiloski, and M. Taboada. 2009. Cross-Linguistic Sentiment Analysis: From English to Spanish. In *Proceedings of the International Conference RANLP-2009*, pages 50–54, Borovets, Bulgaria. ACL.

E. Cambria, D. Rajagopal, D. Olsher, and D. Das. 2013a. Big social data analysis. *Big data computing*, pages 401–414.

E. Cambria, B. Schuller, B. Liu, H. Wang, and C. Havasi. 2013b. Knowledge-based approaches to concept-level sentiment analysis. *IEEE Intelligent Systems*, (2):12–14.

A. Cui, M. Zhang, Y. Liu, and S. Ma. 2011. Emotion Tokens: Bridging the Gap Among Multilingual Twitter Sentiment Analysis. In Mohamed Vall Mohamed Salem, Khaled Shaalan, Farhad Oroumchian, Azadeh Shakery, and Halim Khelalfa, editors, *Information Retrieval Technology. 7th Asia Information Retrieval Societies Conference, AIRS 2011, Dubai, United Arab Emirates, December 18-20, 2011. Proceedings*, volume 7097 of *Lecture Notes in Computer Science*, pages 238–249. Springer, Berlin and Heidelberg.

A. Davies and Z. Ghahramani. 2011. Language-independent Bayesian sentiment mining of {Twitter}. In *The 5th SNA-KDD Workshop'11 (SNA-KDD'11)*, San Diego, CA, August. ACM.

R. Fan, K. Chang, C. Hsieh, X. Wang, and C. Lin. 2008. LIBLINEAR: A library for large linear classification. *The Journal of Machine Learning Research*, 9:1871–1874.

N. Ide and J. Véronis. 1994. Multext: Multilingual text tools and corpora. In *Proceedings of the 15th conference on Computational linguistics-Volume 1*, pages 588–592. Association for Computational Linguistics.

M. Lui and T. Baldwin. 2012. langid.py: An off-the-shelf language identification tool. In *Proceedings of the ACL 2012 system demonstrations*, pages 25–30. Association for Computational Linguistics.

R. McDonald, J. Nivre, Y. Quirmbach-Brundage, Y. Goldberg, D. Das, K. Ganchev, K. Hall, S. Petrov, Hao Zhang, O. Täckström, C. Bedini, N. Castelló, and J. Lee. 2013. Universal Dependency Annotation for Multilingual Parsing. In *Proceedings of the 51st Annual Meeting of the Association for Computational Linguistics*, pages 92–97. Association for Computational Linguistics.

P. Nakov, S. Rosenthal, Z. Kozareva, V. Stoyanov, A. Ritter, and T. Wilson. 2013. SemEval-2013 Task 2: Sentiment Analysis in Twitter. In *Second Joint Conference on Lexical and Computational Semantics (*SEM), Volume 2: Seventh International Workshop on Semantic Evaluation (SemEval 2013)*, pages 312–320, Atlanta, Georgia, June. ACL.

J. Nivre, J. Hall, J. Nilsson, A. Chanev, G. Eryigit, S. Kübler, S. Marinov, and E. Marsi. 2007. MaltParser: A language-independent system for data-driven dependency parsing. *Natural Language Engineering*, 13(2):95–135.

J. W. Pennebaker, M. E. Francis, and R. J. Booth. 2001. Linguistic inquiry and word count: LIWC 2001. *Mahway: Lawrence Erlbaum Associates*, page 71.

S. Petrov, D. Das, and R. McDonald. 2011. A universal part-of-speech tagset. *arXiv preprint arXiv:1104.2086*.

J. Román, E. Martínez-Cámara, J. García-Morera, and Salud M. Jiménez-Zafra. 2015. TASS 2014-The Challenge of Aspect-based Sentiment Analysis. *Procesamiento del Lenguaje Natural*, 54:61–68.

S. Rosenthal, P. Nakov, A. Ritter, and V. Stoyanov. 2014. Semeval-2014 task 9: Sentiment analysis in Twitter. In *Proceedings of The 8th International-Workshop on Semantic Evaluation (SemEval 2014)*, pages 411–415.

T. Solorio, E. Blair, S. Maharjan, S. Bethard, M. Diab, M. Gohneim, A. Hawwari, F. AlGhamdi, J. Hirschberg, A. Chang, and P Fung. 2014. Overview for the first shared task on language identification in code-switched data. In *Proceedings of The First Workshop on Computational Approaches to Code Switching*, pages 62–72, Doha, Qatar. Association for Computational Linguistics.

M. Taulé, M. A. Martí, and M. Recasens. 2008. AnCora: Multilevel Annotated Corpora for Catalan and Spanish. In Nicoletta Calzolari, Khalid Choukri, Bente Maegaard, Joseph Mariani, Jan Odjik, Stelios Piperidis, and Daniel Tapias, editors, *Proceedings of the Sixth International Conference on Language Resources and Evaluation (LREC'08)*, pages 96–101, Marrakech, Morocco.

M. Thelwall, K. Buckley, G. Paltoglou, D. Cai, and A. Kappas. 2010. Sentiment Strength Detection in Short Informal Text. *Journal of the American Society for Information Science and Technology*, 61(12):2544–2558, December.

K. Toutanova and C. D Manning. 2000. Enriching the knowledge sources used in a maximum entropy part-of-speech tagger. In *Proceedings of the 2000 Joint SIGDAT conference on Empirical methods in natural language processing and very large corpora: held in conjunction with the 38th Annual Meeting of the Association for Computational Linguistics-Volume 13*, pages 63–70.

D. Vilares, M. Hermo, M. A. Alonso, C. Gómez-Rodríguez, and Y. Doval. 2014. LyS : Porting a Twitter Sentiment Analysis Approach from Spanish to English. In *Proceedings og The 8th International-Workshop on Semantic Evaluation (SemEval 2014)*, pages 411–415.

D. Vilares, M. A Alonso, and C. Gómez-Rodríguez. 2015a. On the usefulness of lexical and syntactic processing in polarity classification of Twitter messages. *Journal of the Association for Information Science Science and Technology*, 66:1799–1816.

D. Vilares, M. A. Alonso, and C. Gómez-Rodríguez. 2015b. One model, two languages: training bilingual parsers with harmonized treebanks. *arXiv*, 1507.08449 [cs.CL].

Connotation in Translation

Marine Carpuat
Department of Computer Science
University of Maryland
College Park, MD, USA
marine@cs.umd.edu

Abstract

We present a pilot study analyzing the connotative language found in a bilingual corpus of French and English headlines. We find that (1) manual annotation of connotation at the word-level is more reliable than using segment-level judgments, (2) connotation polarity is often, but not always, preserved in reference translations produced by humans, (3) machine translated text does not preserve the connotative language identified by an English connotation lexicon. These lessons will helps us build new resources to learn better models of connotation and translation.

1 Introduction

Subtle shades of meaning beyond surface meaning are receiving increasing attention in Natural Language Processing. Recognizing that even words that are objective on the surface can reveal sentiment of the writer or evoke emotions in readers, Feng et al. (2013) show that the connotation of words can be induced from corpora in an unsupervised fashion, and that the learned connotation polarity of words is useful for sentiment analysis tasks. While such connotation resources only exist for English at the moment, sentiment and subjectivity analysis (Pang and Lee, 2008) increasingly addresses other languages (Banea et al., 2011).

This leads us to ask whether connotation can also be studied in the cross-lingual and multilingual setting. Modeling and detecting differences of connotation across languages would have many applications, e.g., enabling comparison of social media discussions in different languages. But since connotation is a more subtle form of meaning, with cultural and emotional associations, it is not clear to what extend we can expect it to be preserved in translation. On the one hand, we expect correct translations to preserve the meaning of the source: this is the key assumption underlying alignment algorithms in statistical machine translation (Brown et al., 1990), as well as the use of translations to capture the meaning of words in lexical semantics (Resnik and Yarowsky, 1999; Callison-Burch, 2007; Apidianaki, 2009; Carpuat, 2013, among others). On the other hand, cross-lingual structural divergences (Dorr, 1994) might introduce subtle but unavoidable shifts in meaning as part of the translation process.

In this short paper, we report on a pilot study on connotation and translation, using human and machine translated text, and manual as well as automatic tagging of connotative language. We will see that connotation is often, but not always, preserved in translation. This suggests that new models will be needed to represent, predict and use word connotation in more than one language.

2 Defining connotation

We adopt the notion of word connotation defined, and used, by Feng et al. (2013). Connotation refers to "an idea or feeling that a word invokes in addition to its literal or primary meaning [or denotation]." Words with positive connotation describe "physical objects or abstract concepts that people generally value, cherish or care about", while words with negative connotation "describe physical objects or abstract concepts that people generally disvalue or avoid".

As a result, connotation can be evoked by words that do not express sentiment (either explicitly or implicitly), and that would be considered neutral in a sentiment analysis or opinion mining task. For instance, the nouns "life" and "home" are annotated as objective in SentiWordNet (Baccianella et al., 2010), while they carry a positive connotation according to the definition above.

3 Study conditions

Languages: We choose French and English as tar-

Proceedings of the 6th Workshop on Computational Approaches to Subjectivity, Sentiment and Social Media Analysis (WASSA 2015), pages 9–15,
Lisboa, Portugal, 17 September, 2015.

get languages, as these are resource-rich languages and machine translation between them can be achieved with reasonably high quality (Callison-Burch et al., 2009; Bojar et al., 2013).

Domain: We collect text from the Global Voices[1] website Unlike more traditional news sources, Global Voices content is produced by a community of volunteers who curate, verify and translate trending news emerging from social media or blogs. We crawled Global Voices to collect articles that are translations of each other. This study focuses on headlines from these articles: we anticipate that headlines are good candidates for studying connotative language since they aim to provide a concise summary of a news story, and are often written to capture the attention of readers.

Size: We work with a sample of 245 parallel headlines, and study the connotation in each language using both automatic and manual analysis.

4 Does machine translation preserve connotative language?

We start our analysis of connotation using fully automatic means: machine translation and an automatically induced connotation lexicon. We use the lexicon to tag connotative words in both human-produced English, and machine-translated English. If machine translation preserves connotation, we expect to find a high overlap between connotative words in machine translated text and the human-produced reference, and we expect the connotation polarity to remain the same.

4.1 Marking connotative language

We use the English connotation lexicon[2] to tag connotative language. We run the Stanford part-of-speech tagger on all our English examples (Toutanova et al., 2003), and tag word and part-of-speech pairs that are found in the lexicon with their polarity (i.e. negative, positive or neutral). [3]

For instance, in the example "Guinea-Bissau: Citizen Frustration and Defiance in Face of Turmoil", the connotation lexicon detects one word with positive connotation ("citizen_NN") and three words with negative connotation ("frustration_NN", "defiance_NN" and "turmoil_NN").

[1] https://globalvoicesonline.org/about/

[2] http://www3.cs.stonybrook.edu/~ychoi/connotation/data/connotation_lexicon_a.0.1.csv

[3] Words that are out of the vocabulary of the connotation lexicon are considered neutral in this experiment.

This broad-coverage lexicon was automatically induced from raw text, based on the intuition that connotation can be propagated to the entire vocabulary based on co-occurrences with a small set of seed connotative predicates of known polarity. For instance, the arguments of "enjoy" are typically positive, while those of "suffer" are typically negative. Follow-up work showed that connotation can be associated with fine-grained word senses(Kang et al., 2014), but we limit our analysis of connotation at the word level at this stage.

4.2 Machine translation systems

We produce automatic translations of the French headlines into English using two different machine translation systems.

First, we use Google Translate, since this free online system is known to achieve good translation quality in a variety of domains for French to English translation. Second, we build a system using publicly available resources, to complement the black-box Google Translate system. We use the hierarchical phrase-based machine translation model (Chiang, 2005) from the open-source cdec toolkit (Dyer et al., 2010), and datasets from the Workshop on Machine Translation.[4]

Google Translate achieves an uncased BLEU score (Papineni et al., 2002) of 20.13, and the cdec-based system 14.60. The lower score of the cdec system reflects the nature of its training data which is primarily drawn from parliament proceedings rather than news, as well as the difficulty of translating headlines. The translation quality is nevertheless reasonable, as illustrated by the randomly selected examples in Table 1.

4.3 Connotative words in human vs. machine-translated text

First, we note that connotative language is found in 89% of the original English examples and 92% of the machine-translated examples. This confirms our intuition that Global Voices headlines are a good source of connotative language.

Second, we compare the connotative language found in machine translated text to the connotative language found in the reference translations

[4] Our training set comprises more than two million segment pairs from Europarl and News Commentary data from www.statmt.org/wmt15, and our English language model is trained on the additional English news corpora. Translation hypotheses are scored using standard features, including a 4-gram language model. We tune using the MIRA algorithm.

	human references vs. machine translation
input	Visages de la crise et appels au secours
reference	Faces of the crisis and a cry for help
google	Faces of the crisis and calls for help
euro+news	faces of the crisis and calls to the rescue
input	Record de financement collectif pour un documentaire sur lindpendance de la Catalogne
reference	Crowdfunders Empty Pockets for Catalan Independence
google	Collective fundraising record for a documentary on the independence of Catalonia
euro+news	collective record funding for a documentary on catalonia s independence

Table 1: Machine translation output for two systems: (1) Google Translate (Google), and (2) a hierarchical phrase-based system trained on WMT data (euro+news).

Translation System	Google	euro+news
Do positive words overlap with references?		
Precision	42.35	56.13
Recall	30.03	53.87
Do negative words overlap with references?		
Precision	50.75	52.60
Recall	46.69	50.53
Do content words overlap with references?		
Precision	37.35	49.70
Recall	41.56	58.52

Table 2: Are connotative words in machine translation output found in reference translations?

produced by humans. We use Precision and Recall metrics to represent the overlap.

Table 2 shows that precision and recall are in the 40-50 range for connotative words, indicating that they are often not found in the reference. However, this happens less frequently for connotative words than for content words in general: precision with respect to the reference words is higher for connotative words (positive or negative) than for all content words.

Surprisingly, the translations obtained using our in-house system achieves a higher overlap with references despite having a lower translation quality according to BLEU. This might be explained by the nature of its training data which is presumably smaller and more homogeneous, resulting in translations that might be more literal at the cost of fluency, resulting in more matches for content words, and fewer matches for the higher order n-grams taken into account in BLEU.

4.4 Segment-level connotation analysis

Lastly, we use the polarity of the words to compute the dominant polarity of the entire headline. Following the sentiment analysis experiments of (Feng et al., 2013), the dominant polarity is defined as $pol(E) = argmax_{pol=pos,neg} \sum_{e \in E_{pol}} w_{E_{pol}}(e)$ where $w_{E_{pol}}(e) = 2$ if $e \in E_{pol}$ and e is a verb or an adjective; $w_{E_{pol}}(e) = 1$ if $e \in A$ and e has another part-of-speech. Based on this statistic, the dominant connotation of the reference English vs. machine translated English headlines only agree in 60% of the examples considered.

Translation System	Google	euro+news
Comparing MT to positive references		
Precision	54.34	54.34
Recall	30.86	28.73
Comparing MT to negative references		
Precision	62.40	50.40
Recall	75.72	76.82

Table 3: Comparing the dominant connotation of the entire machine translated segment to that of the reference for our two systems.

Taken together, these results suggest that machine translation does not preserve connotative language accurately, even for an "easy" language pair such as as French-English. This differs from prior work on sentiment analysis which suggests that even imperfect machine translation can be good enough to port systems from e.g., English to Arabic dialects (Salameh et al., 2015), or to project labels of subjectivity from English into Romanian and Spanish (Banea et al., 2008).

However, our study of connotation differs from prior work in two important ways: (1) as defined in Section 2, *connotation* refers to meaning that is evoked or associated with a word, while *sentiment or subjectivity* tends to be more explicit. So we expect connotation shifts to be more subtle. (2) our study focuses on *word* connotation, while prior cross-lingual analyses have focused on sentiment/subjectivity at the *segment* level, and are therefore expected to be more tolerant of machine translation errors.

5 Human connotation judgments on human-translated examples

We now turn to manual evaluation of connotation expressed in French and English using manually translated data.

5.1 Defining an annotation scheme

We collect human judgments for the connotation of a given headline. Each annotator is asked whether the language used in the headline implies (1) something positive, (b) something negative, (c) both, or (d) neither (neutral), according to the definition of connotation and its polarity from Section 2. Annotations were produced by native speakers independently for each language, using two different schemes and sets of instructions.

Segment-level 3-way annotation At first, annotators were asked to mark whether the dominant connotation of each segment (i.e. the complete headline) is positive, negative, or neutral. This task was inspired by prior segment-level annotation schemes used for annotating more overt emotion and its polarity in news headlines (Strapparava and Mihalcea, 2007). The inter-annotator agreement (Cohen, 1960) was poor between the two versions of the English annotations, and even worse between annotations of French and English text (see Table 4).

Kappa	en 3a	en 3b	fr 3a
en 3a	100	67.20	55.20
en 3b	67.20	100	55.31

Table 4: Inter-annotator agreement for segment-level 3-way annotation of connotation (positive vs. negative vs. neutral)

Bag-of-words 4-way annotation We then redefined the annotation scheme to discriminate between language that is neutral and language that contains both positive and negative connotations. This yields a set of four labels. We call this annotation "bag-of-words" because it simply indicates whether there exists words in the segment with negative or positive connotation, instead of attempting to assign a single dominant connotation label to the entire segment. This schemes results in higher agreement as measured by Kappa score (Cohen, 1960), both within and across languages (see Table 5).

Kappa	en 4a	en 4b	fr 4a	fr 4b
en 4a	100	73.79	71.08	70.35
en 4b	73.79	100	73.54	72.28
fr 4a	70.35	72.28	100	80.07

Table 5: Inter-annotator agreement for bag-of-word 4-way annotation of connotation (positive vs. negative vs. both vs. neutral)

The "both" category allows annotators to avoid difficult decisions for the confusing examples where positive and negative words are observed in

Label	Example
neu	Russia: Online Cooperation as an Alternative for Government?
pos	Russie : la collaboration en ligne comme nouvelle forme de gouvernance ?
neg	China: Wiping Sweat Gate
neu	Chine : le commissaire politique essuie la sueur du front des policiers
pos	China: The Most Awesome Train Door
neu	Chine : Métro de Pékin, attention à la fermeture des portes !
neu	Nicaragua: Opposition Youth Affected by Hacktivism
neg	Nicaragua : Les jeunes de lopposition victimes de piratage informatique

Table 6: Agreement within and Disagreement across languages: negative (neg); positive (pos); both (both); neutral (neu)

the same examples (see Table 7). The agreement within languages remains higher across languages.

5.2 Agreement within and across languages

While we expect the annotation task to be difficult, we found that agreements are more frequent than disagreements both within and across languages.

In fact, all four annotations are identical for 71% of examples, which suggests that the majority of the headlines are not ambiguous. Such examples of agreement can be found in Table 7. English annotations disagree for 16.8% of examples; while French annotations disagree only for 12.30%.

5.3 Disagreement within and across languages

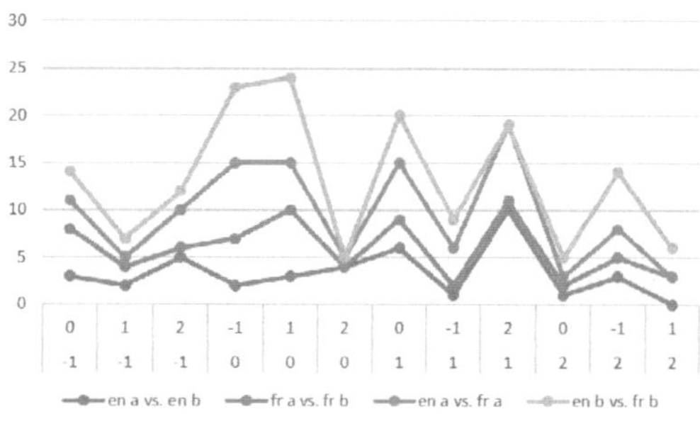

Figure 1: Disagreement in pairwise comparison of annotations: the x axis represents disagreement for each label pair (-1 = negative; 1 = positive; 2 = both; 0 = neutral), the y axis represents the number of observed examples.

Figure 1 summarizes the disagreements observed within English and French annotation, as

Label	Example
neg	Uganda: Government Quiet as Famine Takes Toll
neg	Ouganda : Le gouvernement garde le silence sur la famine
pos	Mexico: Indigenous Long-Distance Runner Wins International Race
pos	Mexique : Une femme de la tribu Tarahumara remporte une course internationale
both	Spain: 12M, a Ray of Sun in the Midst of the Crisis
both	Espagne : Le premier anniversaire des Indignés, un rayon de soleil en pleine crise
neu	China: Graduate thesis or practical training?
neu	Chine : Vaut-il mieux avoir une thèse ou une formation pratique ?

Table 7: Agreement within and across languages.

well as across languages. We observe that there are fewer disagreements between monolingual annotations than across languages. The most frequent confusion is between "positive" or "both" in monolingual, while confusions between "neutral" and "positive" as well as "neutral" and "negative" increase in cross-lingual comparisons.

For a small number of examples (4.5%), French and English annotations are internally consistent within each language but disagree across languages. This happens when one example is deemed neutral or considered to have both negative and positive polarity in one language, but is considered only positive or negative in the other. A sample of such examples is given in Table 6. The differences are due to a number of factors. In the most extreme case, we have an idiomatic expressions with a strong connotation polarity, such as the English suffix "Gate" used to denote a political scandal (derived from "Watergate"). This suffix does not have a direct equivalent in French, and the translation loses the strong negative connotation present in the English. More frequently, key words that convey connotation are translated with words that have a weaker connotation (e.g. the strongly negative "victimes" becomes the more neutral "affected", the positive sounding "serendipity" is dropped from the French version of the headline.)

6 Automatic predictions vs. human labels

Finally, we compare the automatic predictions based on the connotation lexicon from Section 4 to the manual annotation of connotation collected in Section 5. To focus on the most reliable annotations, we only use the subset of examples where

reference	input	accuracy
fr	en	44.39
en	en	46.12
fr	mt	40.94
en	mt	37.93

Table 8: Connotation lexicon predictions on English headlines

intra-language annotations are consistent, which yields a smaller subset of 232 examples out of the initial 244. Furthermore, for each example, we compare the positive vs. negative connotation strengths from Section 4, so as to predict one of the four classes for each example.

A baseline predicting the most frequent class ("negative") would get an accuracy of 55%. So the main lesson of this comparison is that using the lexicon out of the box is not sufficient to replicate the decisions of human annotators. Nevertheless, it is reassuring that predictions based on the English headlines agree more with English annotations, while predictions based on machine translation of French agree more with manual annotations of the original French.

7 Discussion

We have studied the connotation of French and English headlines using both manual and automatic annotations and translations.

The manual annotation revealed that translations can diverge in connotation, even in manually translated parallel texts in closely related languages. This suggests that further cross-lingual studies should not use parallel corpora to project annotations blindly. Perhaps more importantly, we found that annotating connotation reliably requires working with a set of four categories ("positive", "negative", "both" or "neutral") to achieve better inter-annotator agreement. We will use these lessons to collect and annotate larger datasets with more annotators, and more languages.

As can be expected, simple lexicon-based predictors are far from sufficient to determine the dominant connotation of a segment. This is consistent with the observations of (Greene and Resnik, 2009) who developed syntactically motivated features for the analysis of implicit sentiment. Accordingly, we will focus on developing better models of connotation preservation and divergence across languages in the future.

References

Marianna Apidianaki. 2009. Data-driven semantic analysis for multilingual WSD and lexical selection in translation. In *Proceedings of the 12th Conference of the European Chapter of the ACL (EACL 2009)*, pages 77–85, Athens, Greece, March.

Stefano Baccianella, Andrea Esuli, and Fabrizio Sebastiani. 2010. SENTIWORDNET 3.0: An enhanced lexical resource for sentiment analysis and opinion mining. In *Proceedings of the seventh international conference on Language Resources and Evaluation (LREC)*.

Carmen Banea, Rada Mihalcea, Janyce Wiebe, and Samer Hassan. 2008. Multilingual subjectivity analysis using machine translation. In *Proceedings of the Conference on Empirical Methods in Natural Language Processing*, EMNLP '08, pages 127–135, Stroudsburg, PA, USA.

Carmen Banea, Rada Mihalcea, and Janyce Wiebe. 2011. Multilingual sentiment and subjectivity. *Multilingual Natural Language Processing*.

Ondřej Bojar, Christian Buck, Chris Callison-Burch, Christian Federmann, Barry Haddow, Philipp Koehn, Christof Monz, Matt Post, Radu Soricut, and Lucia Specia. 2013. Findings of the 2013 Workshop on Statistical Machine Translation. In *Proceedings of the Eighth Workshop on Statistical Machine Translation*, pages 1–44, Sofia, Bulgaria, August.

Peter Brown, John Cocke, Stephen Della Pietra, Vincent Della Pietra, Frederik Jelinek, John Lafferty, Robert Mercer, and Paul Rossin. 1990. A statistical approach to machine translation. *Computational Linguistics*, 16:79–85.

Chris Callison-Burch, Philipp Koehn, Christof Monz, and Josh Schroeder. 2009. Findings of the 2009 Workshop on Statistical Machine Translation. In *Proceedings of the Fourth Workshop on Statistical Machine Translation*, pages 1–28, Athens, Greece, March.

Chris Callison-Burch. 2007. *Paraphrasing and Translation*. Ph.D. thesis, University of Edinburgh.

Marine Carpuat. 2013. A semantic evaluation of machine translation lexical choice. In *Proceedings of the 7th Workshop on Syntax, Semantics and Structure in Statistical Translation*, Atlanta, USA, May.

David Chiang. 2005. A hierarchical phrase-based model for statistical machine translation. In *Proceedings of the 43rd Annual Meeting of the Association for Computational Linguistics*, pages 263–270, Ann Arbor, Michigan.

Jacob Cohen. 1960. A coefficient of agreement for nominal scales. *Educational and Psychological Measurement*, 20 (1):37–46.

Bonnie J. Dorr. 1994. Machine translation divergences: A formal description and proposed solution. *Computational Linguistics*, 20(4):597–633.

Chris Dyer, Adam Lopez, Juri Ganitkevitch, Johnathan Weese, Ferhan Ture, Phil Blunsom, Hendra Setiawan, Vladimir Eidelman, and Philip Resnik. 2010. cdec: A decoder, alignment, and learning framework for finite-state and context-free translation models. In *Proceedings of the Association for Computational Linguistics (ACL)*.

Song Feng, Jun Seok Kang, Polina Kuznetsova, and Yejin Choi. 2013. Connotation lexicon: A dash of sentiment beneath the surface meaning. In *Proceedings of the 51st Annual Meeting of the Association for Computational Linguistics (Volume 1: Long Papers)*, pages 1774–1784, Sofia, Bulgaria, August.

Stephan Greene and Philip Resnik. 2009. More than words: Syntactic packaging and implicit sentiment. In *Proceedings of Human Language Technologies: The 2009 Annual Conference of the North American Chapter of the Association for Computational Linguistics*, NAACL '09, pages 503–511, Stroudsburg, PA, USA.

Jun Seok Kang, Song Feng, Leman Akoglu, and Yejin Choi. 2014. ConnotationWordNet: Learning connotation over the Word+Sense network. In *Proceedings of the 52nd Annual Meeting of the Association for Computational Linguistics (Volume 1: Long Papers)*, pages 1544–1554, Baltimore, Maryland, June.

Bo Pang and Lillian Lee. 2008. Opinion mining and sentiment analysis. *Found. Trends Inf. Retr.*, 2(1-2):1–135, January.

Kishore Papineni, Salim Roukos, Todd Ward, and Wei-Jing Zhu. 2002. BLEU: a method for automatic evaluation of machine translation. In *Proceedings of the 40th Annual Meeting of the Association for Computational Linguistics*, Philadelphia, PA, July.

Philip Resnik and David Yarowsky. 1999. Distinguising systems and distinguishing senses: New evaluation methods for word sense disambiguation. *Natural Language Engineering*, 5(2):113–133.

Mohammad Salameh, Saif Mohammad, and Svetlana Kiritchenko. 2015. Sentiment after translation: A case-study on arabic social media posts. In *Proceedings of the 2015 Conference of the North American Chapter of the Association for Computational Linguistics: Human Language Technologies*, pages 767–777, Denver, Colorado, May–June.

Carlo Strapparava and Rada Mihalcea. 2007. SemEval-2007 task 14: Affective text. In *Proceedings of the 4th International Workshop on Semantic Evaluations*, SemEval '07, pages 70–74.

Kristina Toutanova, Dan Klein, Christopher D. Manning, and Yoram Singer. 2003. Feature-rich part-of-speech tagging with a cyclic dependency network. In *Proceedings of the 2003 Conference of the North*

American Chapter of the Association for Computational Linguistics on Human Language Technology - Volume 1, NAACL '03, pages 173–180, Stroudsburg, PA, USA.

Enhanced Twitter Sentiment Classification Using Contextual Information

Soroush Vosoughi
The Media Lab
MIT
Cambridge, MA 02139
soroush@mit.edu

Helen Zhou
The Media Lab
MIT
Cambridge, MA 02139
hlzhou@mit.edu

Deb Roy
The Media Lab
MIT
Cambridge, MA 02139
dkroy@media.mit.edu

Abstract

The rise in popularity and ubiquity of Twitter has made sentiment analysis of tweets an important and well-covered area of research. However, the 140 character limit imposed on tweets makes it hard to use standard linguistic methods for sentiment classification. On the other hand, what tweets lack in structure they make up with sheer volume and rich metadata. This metadata includes geolocation, temporal and author information. We hypothesize that sentiment is dependent on all these contextual factors. Different locations, times and authors have different emotional valences. In this paper, we explored this hypothesis by utilizing distant supervision to collect millions of labelled tweets from different locations, times and authors. We used this data to analyse the variation of tweet sentiments across different authors, times and locations. Once we explored and understood the relationship between these variables and sentiment, we used a Bayesian approach to combine these variables with more standard linguistic features such as n-grams to create a Twitter sentiment classifier. This combined classifier outperforms the purely linguistic classifier, showing that integrating the rich contextual information available on Twitter into sentiment classification is a promising direction of research.

1 Introduction

Twitter is a micro-blogging platform and a social network where users can publish and exchange short messages of up to 140 characters long (also known as tweets). Twitter has seen a great rise in popularity in recent years because of its availability and ease-of-use. This rise in popularity and the public nature of Twitter (less than 10% of Twitter accounts are private (Moore, 2009)) have made it an important tool for studying the behaviour and attitude of people.

One area of research that has attracted great attention in the last few years is that of tweet sentiment classification. Through sentiment classification and analysis, one can get a picture of people's attitudes about particular topics on Twitter. This can be used for measuring people's attitudes towards brands, political candidates, and social issues.

There have been several works that do sentiment classification on Twitter using standard sentiment classification techniques, with variations of n-gram and bag of words being the most common. There have been attempts at using more advanced syntactic features as is done in sentiment classification for other domains (Read, 2005; Nakagawa et al., 2010), however the 140 character limit imposed on tweets makes this hard to do as each article in the Twitter training set consists of sentences of no more than several words, many of them with irregular form (Saif et al., 2012).

On the other hand, what tweets lack in structure they make up with sheer volume and rich metadata. This metadata includes geolocation, temporal and author information. We hypothesize that sentiment is dependent on all these contextual factors. Different locations, times and authors have different emotional valences. For instance, people are generally happier on weekends and certain hours of the day, more depressed at the end of summer holidays, and happier in certain states in the United States. Moreover, people have different baseline emotional valences from one another. These claims are supported for example by the annual Gallup poll that ranks states from most happy to least happy (Gallup-Healthways, 2014), or the work by Csikszentmihalyi and Hunter (Csikszentmihalyi and Hunter, 2003) that showed reported

Proceedings of the 6th Workshop on Computational Approaches to Subjectivity, Sentiment and Social Media Analysis (WASSA 2015), pages 16–24,
Lisboa, Portugal, 17 September, 2015.

happiness varies significantly by day of week and time of day. We believe these factors manifest themselves in sentiments expressed in tweets and that by accounting for these factors, we can improve sentiment classification on Twitter.

In this work, we explored this hypothesis by utilizing *distant supervision* (Go et al., 2009) to collect millions of labelled tweets from different locations (within the USA), times of day, days of the week, months and authors. We used this data to analyse the variation of tweet sentiments across the aforementioned categories. We then used a Bayesian approach to incorporate the relationship between these factors and tweet sentiments into standard n-gram based Twitter sentiment classification.

This paper is structured as follows. In the next sections we will review related work on sentiment classification, followed by a detailed explanation of our approach and our data collection, annotation and processing efforts. After that, we describe our baseline n-gram sentiment classifier model, followed by the explanation of how the baseline model is extended to incorporate contextual information. Next, we describe our analysis of the variation of sentiment within each of the contextual categories. We then evaluate our models and finally summarize our findings and contributions and discuss possible paths for future work.

2 Related Work

Sentiment analysis and classification of text is a problem that has been well studied across many different domains, such as blogs, movie reviews, and product reviews (e.g., (Pang et al., 2002; Cui et al., 2006; Chesley et al., 2006)). There is also extensive work on sentiment analysis for Twitter. Most of the work on Twitter sentiment classification either focuses on different machine learning techniques (e.g., (Wang et al., 2011; Jiang et al., 2011)), novel features (e.g., (Davidov et al., 2010; Kouloumpis et al., 2011; Saif et al., 2012)), new data collection and labelling techniques (e.g., (Go et al., 2009)) or the application of sentiment classification to analyse the attitude of people about certain topics on Twitter (e.g., (Diakopoulos and Shamma, 2010; Bollen et al., 2011)). These are just some examples of the extensive research already done on Twitter sentiment classification and analysis.

There has also been previous work on measuring the happiness of people in different contexts (location, time, etc). This has been done mostly through traditional land-line polling (Csikszentmihalyi and Hunter, 2003; Gallup-Healthways, 2014), with Gallup's annual happiness index being a prime example (Gallup-Healthways, 2014). More recently, some have utilized Twitter to measure people's mood and happiness and have found Twitter to be a generally good measure of the public's overall happiness, well-being and mood. For example, Bollen et al. (Bollen et al., 2011) used Twitter to measure the daily mood of the public and compare that to the record of social, political, cultural and economic events in the real world. They found that these events have a significant effect on the public mood as measured through Twitter. Another example would be the work of Mitchell et al. (Mitchell et al., 2013), in which they estimated the happiness levels of different states and cities in the USA using Twitter and found statistically significant correlations between happiness level and the demographic characteristics (such as obesity rates and education levels) of those regions.

In this work, we combined the sentiment analysis of different authors, locations, times and dates as measured through labelled Twitter data with standard word-based sentiment classification methods to create a context-dependent sentiment classifier. As far as we can tell, there has not been significant previous work on Twitter sentiment classification that has achieved this.

3 Approach

The main hypothesis behind this work is that the average sentiment of messages on Twitter is different in different contexts. Specifically, tweets in different spatial, temporal and authorial contexts have on average different sentiments. Basically, these factors (many of which are environmental) have an affect on the emotional states of people which in turn have an effect on the sentiments people express on Twitter and elsewhere. In this paper, we used this contextual information to better predict the sentiment of tweets.

Luckily, tweets are tagged with very rich metadata, including location, timestamp, and author information. By analysing labelled data collected from these different contexts, we calculated *prior* probabilities of negative and positive sentiments for each of the contextual categories shown below:

- The states in the USA (50 total).
- Hour of the day (HoD) (24 total).
- Day of week (DoW) (7 total).
- Month (12 total).
- Authors (57710 total).

This means that for every item in each of these categories, we calculated a probability of sentiment being positive or negative based on historical tweets. For example, if seven out of ten historical tweets made on Friday were positive then the prior probability of a sentiment being positive for tweets sent out on Friday is 0.7 and the prior probability of a sentiment being negative is 0.3. We then trained a Bayesian sentiment classifier using a combination of these prior probabilities and standard n-gram models. The model is described in great detail in the "Baseline Model" and "Contextual Model" sections of this paper.

In order to do a comprehensive analysis of sentiment of tweets across aforementioned contextual categories, a large amount of labelled data was required. We needed thousands of tweets for every item in each of the categories (e.g. thousands of tweets per hour of day, or state in the US). Therefore, creating a corpus using human-annotated data would have been impractical. Instead, we turned to distant supervision techniques to obtain our corpus. Distant supervision allows us to have noisy but large amounts of annotated tweets.

There are different methods of obtaining labelled data using distant supervision (Read, 2005; Go et al., 2009; Barbosa and Feng, 2010; Davidov et al., 2010). We used emoticons to label tweets as positive or negative, an approach that was introduced by Read (Read, 2005) and used in multiple works (Go et al., 2009; Davidov et al., 2010). We collected millions of English-language tweets from different times, dates, authors and US states. We used a total of six emoticons, three mapping to positive and three mapping to negative sentiment (table 1). We identified more than 120 positive and negative ASCII emoticons and unicode emojis[1], but we decided to only use the six most common emoticons in order to avoid possible selection biases. For example, people who use obscure emoticons and emojis might have a different base sentiment from those who do not. Using the six most commonly used emoticons limits this bias. Since there are no "neutral" emoticons, our dataset is limited to tweets with positive or negative sentiments. Accordingly, in this work we are only concerned with analysing and classifying the polarity of tweets (negative vs. positive) and not their subjectivity (neutral vs. non-neutral). Below we will explain our data collection and corpus in greater detail.

[1]Japanese pictographs similar to ASCII emoticons

Positive Emoticons	Negative Emoticons
:)	:(
:-)	:-(
:)	: (

Table 1: List of emoticons.

4 Data Collection and Datasets

We collected two datasets, one massive and labelled through distant supervision, the other small and labelled by humans. The massive dataset was used to calculate the prior probabilities for each of our contextual categories. Both datasets were used to train and test our sentiment classifier. The human-labelled dataset was used as a sanity check to make sure the dataset labelled using the emoticons classifier was not too noisy and that the human and emoticon labels matched for a majority of tweets.

4.1 Emoticon-based Labelled Dataset

We collected a total of 18 million, geo-tagged, English-language tweets over three years, from January 1st, 2012 to January 1st, 2015, evenly divided across all 36 months, using Historical PowerTrack for Twitter[2] provided by GNIP[3]. We created geolocation bounding boxes[4] for each of the 50 states which were used to collect our dataset. All 18 million tweets originated from one of the 50 states and are tagged as such. Moreover, all tweets contained one of the six emoticons in Table 1 and were labelled as either positive or negative based on the emoticon. Out of the 18 million tweets, 11.2 million (62%) were labelled as positive and 6.8 million (38%) were labelled as negative. The 18 million tweets came from $7,657,158$ distinct users.

[2]Historical PowerTrack for Twitter provides complete access to the full archive of Twitter public data.

[3]https://gnip.com/

[4]The bounding boxes were created using http://boundingbox.klokantech.com/

4.2 Human Labelled Dataset

We randomly selected 3000 tweets from our large dataset and had all their emoticons stripped. We then had these tweets labelled as positive or negative by three human annotators. We measured the inter-annotator agreement using *Fleiss' kappa*, which calculates the degree of agreement in classification over that which would be expected by chance (Fleiss, 1971). The *kappa* score for the three annotators was 0.82, which means that there were disagreements in sentiment for a small portion of the tweets. However, the number of tweets that were labelled the same by at least two of the three human annotator was 2908 out of of the 3000 tweets (96%). Of these 2908 tweets, 60% were labelled as positive and 40% as negative.

We then measured the agreement between the human labels and emoticon-based labels, using only tweets that were labelled the same by at least two of the three human annotators (the majority label was used as the label for the tweet). Table 2 shows the confusion matrix between human and emoticon-based annotations. As you can see, 85% of all labels matched ($\frac{1597+822}{1597+882+281+148} = .85$).

	Human-Pos	Human-Neg
Emot-Pos	1597	281
Emot-Neg	148	882

Table 2: Confusion matrix between human-labelled and emoticon-labelled tweets.

These results are very promising and show that using emoticon-based distant supervision to label the sentiment of tweets is an acceptable method. Though there is some noise introduced to the dataset (as evidenced by the 15% of tweets whose human labels did not match their emoticon labels), the sheer volume of labelled data that this method makes accessible, far outweighs the relatively small amount of noise introduced.

4.3 Data Preparation

Since the data is labelled using emoticons, we stripped all emoticons from the training data. This ensures that emoticons are not used as a feature in our sentiment classifier. A large portion of tweets contain links to other websites. These links are mostly not meaningful semantically and thus can not help in sentiment classification. Therefore, all links in tweets were replaced with the token "URL". Similarly, all mentions of usernames (which are denoted by the @ symbol) were replaced with the token "USERNAME", since they also can not help in sentiment classification. Tweets also contain very informal language and as such, characters in words are often repeated for emphasis (e.g., the word *good* is used with an arbitrary number of *o*'s in many tweets). Any character that was repeated more than two times was removed (e.g., *goooood* was replaced with *good*). Finally, all words in the tweets were stemmed using *Porter Stemming* (Porter, 1980).

5 Baseline Model

For our baseline sentiment classification model, we used our massive dataset to train a negative and positive n-gram language model from the negative and positive tweets.

As our baseline model, we built purely linguistic bigram models in Python, utilizing some components from NLTK (Bird et al., 2009). These models used a vocabulary that was filtered to remove words occurring 5 or fewer times. Probability distributions were calculated using Kneser-Ney smoothing (Chen and Goodman, 1999). In addition to Kneser-Ney smoothing, the bigram models also used "backoff" smoothing (Katz, 1987), in which an n-gram model falls back on an $(n-1)$-gram model for words that were unobserved in the n-gram context.

In order to classify the sentiment of a new tweet, its probability of fit is calculated using both the negative and positive bigram models. Equation 1 below shows our models through a Bayesian lens.

$$\Pr(\theta_s \mid W) = \frac{\Pr(W \mid \theta_s)\Pr(\theta_s)}{\Pr(W)} \qquad (1)$$

Here θ_s can be θ_p or θ_n, corresponding to the hypothesis that the sentiment of the tweet is positive or negative respectively. W is the sequence of ℓ words, written as w_1^ℓ, that make up the tweet. $\Pr(W)$ is not dependent on the hypothesis, and can thus be ignored. Since we are using a bigram model, Equation 1 can be written as:

$$\Pr(\theta_s \mid W) \propto \prod_{i=2}^{\ell} \Pr(w_i \mid w_{i-1}, \theta_s)\Pr(\theta_s) \qquad (2)$$

This is our purely linguistic baseline model.

6 Contextual Model

The Bayesian approach allows us to easily integrate the contextual information into our models. $\Pr(\theta_s)$ in Equation 2 is the prior probability of a tweet having the sentiment s. The prior probability ($\Pr(\theta_s)$) can be calculated using the contextual information of the tweets. Therefore, $\Pr(\theta_s)$ in equation 2 is replaced by $\Pr(\theta_s|C)$, which is the probability of the hypothesis given the contextual information. $\Pr(\theta_s|C)$ is the posterior probability of the following Bayesian equation:

$$\Pr(\theta_s \mid C) = \frac{\Pr(C \mid \theta_s)\Pr(\theta_s)}{\Pr(C)} \quad (3)$$

Where C is the set of contextual variables: $\{State, HoD, Dow, Month, Author\}$. $\Pr(\theta_s|C)$ captures the probability that a tweet is positive or negative, given the state, hour of day, day of the week, month and author of the tweet. Here $\Pr(C)$ is not dependent on the hypothesis, and thus can be ignored. Equation 2 can therefore be rewritten to include the contextual information:

$$\Pr(\theta_s \mid W, C) \propto \prod_{i=2}^{\ell} \Pr(w_i \mid w_{i-1}, \theta_s) \Pr(C \mid \theta_s)\Pr(\theta_s) \quad (4)$$

Equation 4 is our extended Bayesian model for integrating contextual information with more standard, word-based sentiment classification.

7 Sentiment in Context

We considered five contextual categories: one spatial, three temporal and one authorial. Here is the list of the five categories:

- The states in the USA (50 total) (spatial).
- Hour of the day (HoD) (24 total) (temporal).
- Day of week (DoW) (7 total) (temporal).
- Month (12 total) (temporal).
- Authors (57,710 total) (authorial).

We used our massive emoticon labelled dataset to calculate the average sentiment for all of these five categories. A tweet was given a score of -1 if it was labelled as negative and a score 1 if it was labelled as positive, so an average sentiment of 0 for a contextual category would mean that tweets in that category were evenly labelled as positive and negative.

7.1 Spatial

All of the 18 million tweets in our dataset originate from the USA and are geo-tagged. Naturally, the tweets are not evenly distributed across the 50 states given the large variation between the population of each state. Figure 1 shows the percentage of tweets per state, sorted from smallest to largest. Not surprisingly, California has the highest number of tweets ($2,590,179$), and Wyoming has the lowest number of tweets ($11,719$).

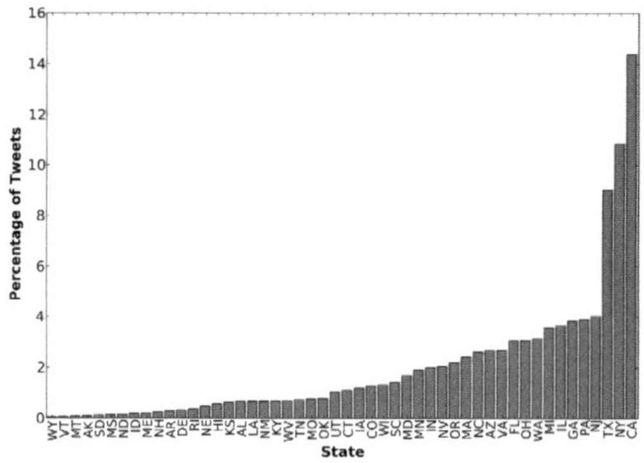

Figure 1: Percentage of tweets per state in the USA, sorted from lowest to highest.

Even the state with the lowest percentage of tweets has more than ten thousand tweets, which is enough to calculate a statistically significant average sentiment for that state. The sentiment for all states averaged across the tweets from the three years is shown in Figure 2. Note that an average sentiment of 1.0 means that all tweets were labelled as positive, -1.0 means that all tweets were labelled as negative and 0.0 means that there was an even distribution of positive and negative tweets. The average sentiment of all the states leans more towards the positive side. This is expected given that 62% of the tweets in our dataset were labelled as positive.

It is interesting to note that even with the noisy dataset, our ranking of US states based on their Twitter sentiment correlates with the ranking of US states based on the well-being index calculated by Oswald and Wu (Oswald and Wu, 2011) in their work on measuring well-being and life satisfaction across America. Their data is from the behavioral risk factor survey score (BRFSS), which is a survey of life satisfaction across the United States from 1.3 million citizens. Figure 3 shows this correlation ($r = 0.44$, $p < 0.005$).

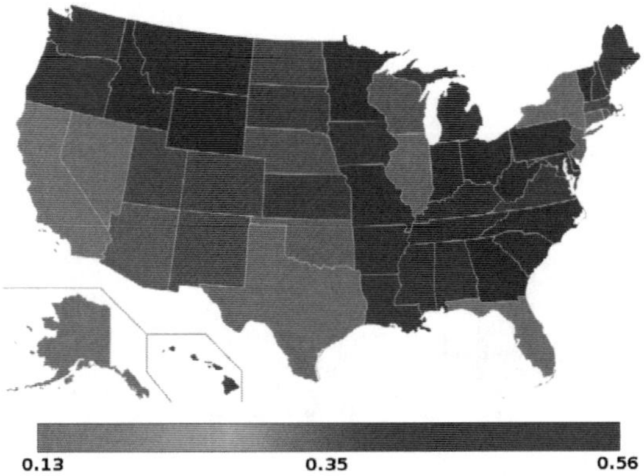

Figure 2: Average sentiment of states in the USA, averaged across three years, from 2012 to 2014.

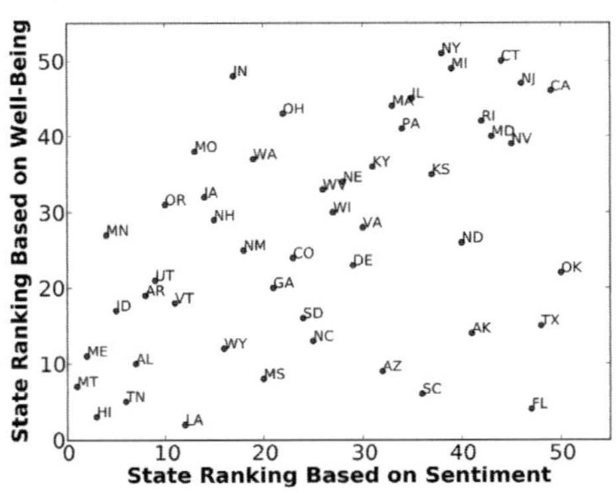

Figure 3: Ranking of US states based on Twitter sentiment vs. ranking of states based on their well-being index. $r = 0.44, p < 0.005$.

7.2 Temporal

We looked at three temporal variables: time of day, day of the week and month. All tweets are tagged with timestamp data, which we used to extract these three variables. Since all timestamps in the Twitter historical archives (and public API) are in the UTC time zone, we first converted the timestamp to the local time of the location where the tweet was sent from. We then calculated the sentiment for each day of week (figure 4), hour (figure 5) and month (figure 6), averaged across all 18 million tweets over three years. The 18 million tweets were divided evenly between each month, with 1.5 million tweets per month. The tweets were also more or less evenly divided between each day of week, with each day having somewhere between 14% and 15% of the tweets. Similarly, the tweets were almost evenly divided between each hour, with each having somewhere between 3% and 5% of the tweets.

Some of these results make intuitive sense. For example, the closer the day of week is to Friday and Saturday, the more positive the sentiment, with a drop on Sunday. As with spatial, the average sentiment of all the hours, days and months lean more towards the positive side.

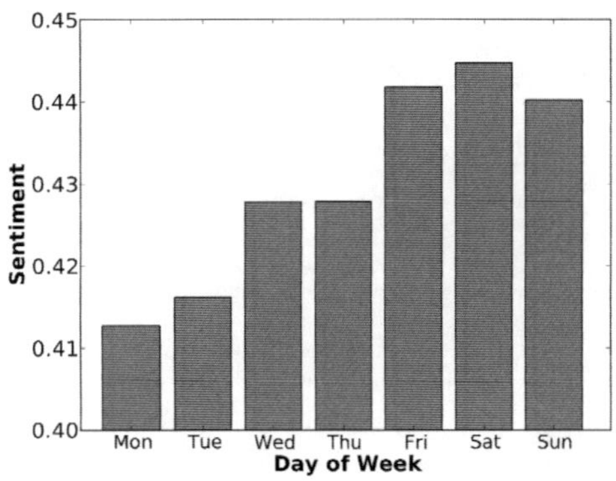

Figure 4: Average sentiment of different days of the week in the USA, averaged across three years, from 2012 to 2014.

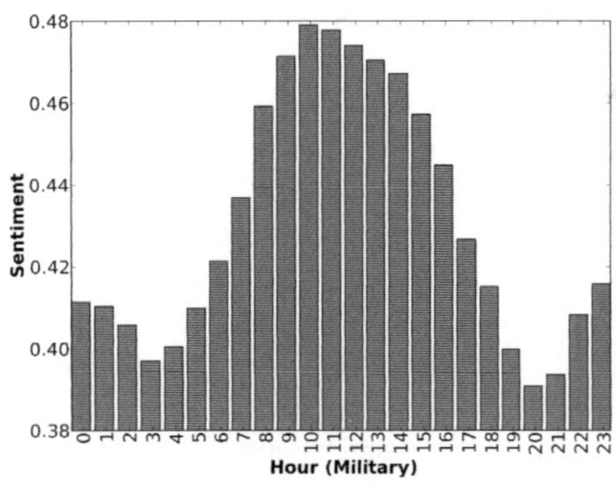

Figure 5: Average sentiment of different hours of the day in the USA, averaged across three years, from 2012 to 2014.

7.3 Authorial

The last contextual variable we looked at was authorial. People have different baseline attitudes, some are optimistic and positive, some are pessimistic and negative, and some are in between. This difference in personalities can manifest itself in the sentiment of tweets. We attempted to capture this difference by looking at the history of

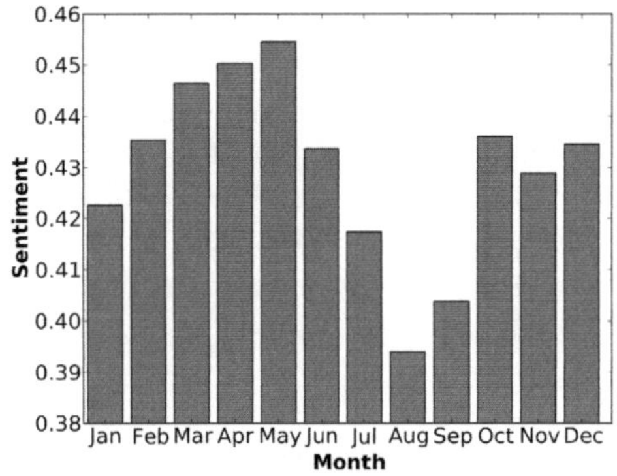

Figure 6: Average sentiment of different months in the USA, averaged across three years, from 2012 to 2014.

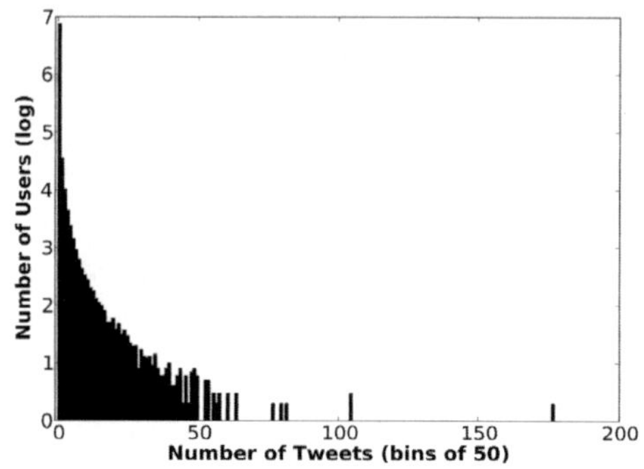

Figure 7: Number of users (logarithmic) in bins of 50 tweets. The first bin corresponds to number of users that have less than 50 tweets throughout the three years and so on.

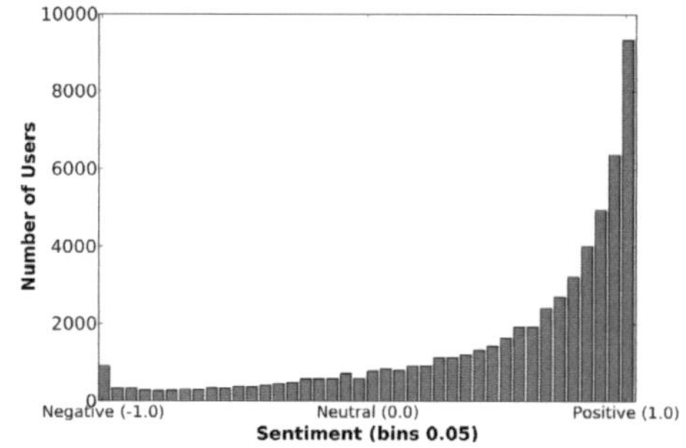

Figure 8: Number of users (with at least 50 tweets) per sentiment bins of 0.05, averaged across three years, from 2012 to 2014.

tweets made by users. The 18 million labelled tweets in our dataset come from 7,657,158 authors.

In order to calculate a statistically significant average sentiment for each author, we need our sample size to not be too small. However, a large number of the users in our dataset only tweeted once or twice during the three years. Figure 7 shows the number of users in bins of 50 tweets. (So the first bin corresponds to the number of users that have less than 50 tweets throughout the three year.) The number of users in the first few bins were so large that the graph needed to be logarithmic in order to be legible. We decided to calculate the prior sentiment for users with at least 50 tweets. This corresponded to less than 1% of the users (57,710 out of 7,657,158 total users). Note that these users are the most prolific authors in our dataset, as they account for 39% of all tweets in our dataset. The users with less than 50 posts had their prior set to 0.0, not favouring positive or negative sentiment (this way it does not have an impact on the Bayesian model, allowing other contextual variables to set the prior).

As it is not feasible to show the prior average sentiment of all 57,710 users, we created 20 even sentiment bins, from -1.0 to 1.0. We then plotted the number of users whose average sentiment falls into these bins (Figure 8). Similar to other variables, the positive end of the graph is much heavier than the negative end.

8 Results

We used 5-fold cross validation to train and evaluate our baseline and contextual models, ensuring that the tweets in the training folds were not used in the calculation of any of the priors or in the training of the bigram models. Table 3 shows the accuracy of our models. The contextual model outperformed the baseline model using any of the contextual variables by themselves, with state being the best performing and day of week the worst. The model that utilized all the contextual variables saw a 10% relative and 8% absolute improvement over the baseline bigram model.

Because of the great increase in the volume of data, distant supervised sentiment classifiers for Twitter tend to generally outperform more standard classifiers using human-labelled datasets. Therefore, it makes sense to compare the performance of our classifier to other distant supervised

Model	Accuracy
Baseline-Majority	0.620
Baseline-Bigram	0.785
Contextual-DoW	0.798
Contextual-Month	0.801
Contextual-Hour	0.821
Contextual-Author	0.829
Contextual-State	0.849
Contextual-All	**0.862**

Table 3: Classifier accuracy, sorted from worst to best.

classifiers. Though not directly comparable, our contextual classifier outperforms the distant supervised Twitter sentiment classifier by Go et al (Go et al., 2009) by more than 3% (absolute).

Table 4 shows the precision, recall and F1 score of the positive and negative class for the full contextual classifier (Contextual-All).

Class	Precision	Recall	F1 Score
Positive	0.864	0.969	0.912
Negative	0.905	0.795	0.841

Table 4: Precision, recall and F1 score of the full contextual classifier (Contexual-All).

9 Discussions

Even though our contextual classifier was able to outperform the previous state-of-the-art, distant supervised sentiment classifier, it should be noted that our contextual classifier's performance is boosted significantly by spatial information extracted through geo-tags. However, only about one to two percent of tweets in the wild are geo-tagged. Therefore, we trained and evaluated our contextual model using all the variables except for state. The accuracy of this model was 0.843, which is still significantly better than the performance of the purely linguistic classifier. Fortunately, all tweets are tagged with timestamps and author information, so all the other four contextual variables used in our model can be used for classifying the sentiment of any tweet.

Note that the prior probabilities that we calculated need to be recalculated and updated every once in a while to account for changes in the world. For example, a state might become more affluent, causing its citizens to become on average happier. This change could potentially have an effect on the average sentiment expressed by the citizens of that state on Twitter, which would make our priors obsolete.

10 Conclusions and Future Work

Sentiment classification of tweets is an important area of research. Through classification and analysis of sentiments on Twitter, one can get an understanding of people's attitudes about particular topics.

In this work, we utilized the power of distant supervision to collect millions of noisy labelled tweets from all over the USA, across three years. We used this dataset to create prior probabilities for the average sentiment of tweets in different spatial, temporal and authorial contexts. We then used a Bayesian approach to combine these priors with standard bigram language models. The resulting combined model was able to achieve an accuracy of 0.862, outperforming the previous state-of-the-art distant supervised Twitter sentiment classifier by more than 3%.

In the future, we would like to explore additional contextual features that could be predictive of sentiment on Twitter. Specifically, we would like to incorporate the topic type of tweets into our model. The topic type characterizes the nature of the topics discussed in tweets (e.g., breaking news, sports, etc). There has already been extensive work done on topic categorization schemes for Twitter (Dann, 2010; Sriram et al., 2010; Zhao and Jiang, 2011) which we can utilize for this task.

11 Acknowledgements

We would like to thank all the annotators for their efforts. We would also like to thank Brandon Roy for sharing his insights on Bayesian modelling. This work was supported by a generous grant from Twitter.

References

Luciano Barbosa and Junlan Feng. 2010. Robust sentiment detection on twitter from biased and noisy data. In *Proc. COLING 2010*, pages 36–44. Association for Computational Linguistics.

Steven Bird, Ewan Klein, and Edward Loper. 2009. *Natural language processing with Python*. O'Reilly Media, Inc.

Johan Bollen, Huina Mao, and Alberto Pepe. 2011. Modeling public mood and emotion: Twitter sentiment and socio-economic phenomena. In *Proc. ICWSM 2011*.

Stanley F Chen and Joshua Goodman. 1999. An empirical study of smoothing techniques for language modeling. *Computer Speech & Language*, 13(4):359–393.

Paula Chesley, Bruce Vincent, Li Xu, and Rohini K Srihari. 2006. Using verbs and adjectives to automatically classify blog sentiment. *Training*, 580(263):233.

Mihaly Csikszentmihalyi and Jeremy Hunter. 2003. Happiness in everyday life: The uses of experience sampling. *Journal of Happiness Studies*, 4(2):185–199.

Hang Cui, Vibhu Mittal, and Mayur Datar. 2006. Comparative experiments on sentiment classification for online product reviews. In *AAAI*, volume 6, pages 1265–1270.

Stephen Dann. 2010. Twitter content classification. *First Monday*, 15(12).

Dmitry Davidov, Oren Tsur, and Ari Rappoport. 2010. Enhanced sentiment learning using twitter hashtags and smileys. In *Proc. COLING 2010*, pages 241–249. Association for Computational Linguistics.

Nicholas A Diakopoulos and David A Shamma. 2010. Characterizing debate performance via aggregated twitter sentiment. In *Proc. SIGCHI 2010*, pages 1195–1198. ACM.

Joseph L Fleiss. 1971. Measuring nominal scale agreement among many raters. *Psychological bulletin*, 76(5):378.

Gallup-Healthways. 2014. State of american well-being. *Well-Being Index*.

Alec Go, Lei Huang, and Richa Bhayani. 2009. Twitter sentiment analysis. *Entropy*, 17.

Long Jiang, Mo Yu, Ming Zhou, Xiaohua Liu, and Tiejun Zhao. 2011. Target-dependent twitter sentiment classification. In *Proc. ACL 2011: Human Language Technologies-Volume 1*, pages 151–160. Association for Computational Linguistics.

Slava Katz. 1987. Estimation of probabilities from sparse data for the language model component of a speech recognizer. *Acoustics, Speech and Signal Processing, IEEE Transactions on*, 35(3):400–401.

Efthymios Kouloumpis, Theresa Wilson, and Johanna Moore. 2011. Twitter sentiment analysis: The good the bad and the omg! *Proc. ICWSM 2011*.

Lewis Mitchell, Morgan R Frank, Kameron Decker Harris, Peter Sheridan Dodds, and Christopher M Danforth. 2013. The geography of happiness: Connecting twitter sentiment and expression, demographics, and objective characteristics of place. *PloS one*, 8(5):e64417.

Robert J Moore. 2009. Twitter data analysis: An investor's perspective. http://techcrunch.com/2009/10/05/twitter-data-analysis-an-investors-perspective-2/. Accessed: 2015-01-30.

Tetsuji Nakagawa, Kentaro Inui, and Sadao Kurohashi. 2010. Dependency tree-based sentiment classification using crfs with hidden variables. In *Proc. NAACL-HLT 2010*, pages 786–794. Association for Computational Linguistics.

Andrew J Oswald and Stephen Wu. 2011. Well-being across america. *Review of Economics and Statistics*, 93(4):1118–1134.

Bo Pang, Lillian Lee, and Shivakumar Vaithyanathan. 2002. Thumbs up?: sentiment classification using machine learning techniques. In *Proc. EMNLP 2002-Volume 10*, pages 79–86. Association for Computational Linguistics.

Martin F Porter. 1980. An algorithm for suffix stripping. *Program: electronic library and information systems*, 14(3):130–137.

Jonathon Read. 2005. Using emoticons to reduce dependency in machine learning techniques for sentiment classification. In *Proceedings of the ACL Student Research Workshop*, pages 43–48. Association for Computational Linguistics.

Hassan Saif, Yulan He, and Harith Alani. 2012. Alleviating data sparsity for twitter sentiment analysis. CEUR Workshop Proceedings (CEUR-WS. org).

Bharath Sriram, Dave Fuhry, Engin Demir, Hakan Ferhatosmanoglu, and Murat Demirbas. 2010. Short text classification in twitter to improve information filtering. In *Proc. ACM SIGIR 2010*, pages 841–842. ACM.

Xiaolong Wang, Furu Wei, Xiaohua Liu, Ming Zhou, and Ming Zhang. 2011. Topic sentiment analysis in twitter: a graph-based hashtag sentiment classification approach. In *Proc. CIKM 2011*, pages 1031–1040. ACM.

Xin Zhao and Jing Jiang. 2011. An empirical comparison of topics in twitter and traditional media. *Singapore Management University School of Information Systems Technical paper series. Retrieved November*, 10:2011.

Your Sentiment Precedes You: Using an author's historical tweets to predict sarcasm

Anupam Khattri[1] **Aditya Joshi**[2,3,4]
Pushpak Bhattacharyya[2] **Mark James Carman**[3]
[1]IIT Kharagpur, India, [2]IIT Bombay, India, [3]Monash University, Australia
[4]IITB-Monash Research Academy, India
anupam.khattri@iitkgp.ac.in ,{adityaj, pb}@cse.iitb.ac.in
mark.carman@monash.edu

Abstract

Sarcasm understanding may require information beyond the text itself, as in the case of 'I absolutely love this restaurant!' which may be sarcastic, depending on the contextual situation. We present the first quantitative evidence to show that historical tweets by an author can provide additional context for sarcasm detection. Our sarcasm detection approach uses two components: a contrast-based predictor (that identifies if there is a sentiment contrast within a target tweet), and a historical tweet-based predictor (that identifies if the sentiment expressed towards an entity in the target tweet agrees with sentiment expressed by the author towards that entity in the past).

1 Introduction

Sarcasm[1] is defined as *'the use of remarks that clearly mean the opposite of what they say, made in order to hurt someone's feelings or to criticize something in a humorous way'*[2]. An example of sarcasm is *'Being stranded in traffic is the best way to start my week'*(Joshi et al., 2015). There exists a sentiment contrast between the phrases *'being stranded'* and *'best way'* which enables an automatic sarcasm detection approach to identify the sarcasm in this sentence.

Existing approaches rely on viewing sarcasm as a contrast in sentiment (Riloff et al., 2013; Maynard and Greenwood, 2014). However, consider the sentences *'Nicki Minaj, don't I hate her!'* or *'I love spending four hours cooking on a weekend!'*. The sarcasm is ambiguous because of a likely hyperbole in the first sentence, and because sentiment associated with 'four hours cooking' depends on how much the author/speaker likes cooking. Such sarcasm is difficult to judge for humans as well as an automatic sarcasm detection approach. Essentially, we need more context related to the author of these sentences to identify sarcasm within them.

The question we aim to answer in this paper is: '**What sentiment did the author express in the past about the entities in the tweet that is to be classified? Can this information help us understand if the author is being sarcastic?**' We present the first quantitative evidence to show that historical text generated by an author may be useful to detect sarcasm in text written by the author. In this paper, we exploit the timeline structure of twitter for sarcasm detection of tweets. To gain additional context, we explore beyond the tweet to be classified (called '**target tweet**'), and look up the twitter timeline of the author of the target tweet (we refer to these tweets as the '**historical tweets**'). Our method directly applies to discussion forums and review websites, where other posts or reviews by this author may be looked at.

The rest of the paper is organized as follows. Section 2 contains the related work. We present a motivating example in Section 3, and describe the architecture of our approach in Section 4. The experimental setup and results are in Sections 5 and 6. We present a discussion of challenges observed with the proposed historical tweet-based approach in Section 7, and conclude the paper in Section 8.

2 Related work

Sarcasm detection relies mostly on rule-based algorithms. For example, Maynard and Greenwood (2014) predict a tweet as sarcastic if the sentiment embedded in a hashtag is opposite to sentiment in the remaining text. Similarly, Riloff et al. (2013) predict a tweet as sarcastic if there is a sentiment contrast between a verb and a noun phrase.

[1]We use irony and sarcasm interchangeably in this paper, as has been done in past work. Sarcasm has an element of criticism, while irony may not.

[2]http://dictionary.cambridge.org/dictionary/british/sarcasm

Proceedings of the 6th Workshop on Computational Approaches to Subjectivity, Sentiment and Social Media Analysis (WASSA 2015), pages 25–30,
Lisboa, Portugal, 17 September, 2015.

Figure 1: A motivating example for our approach

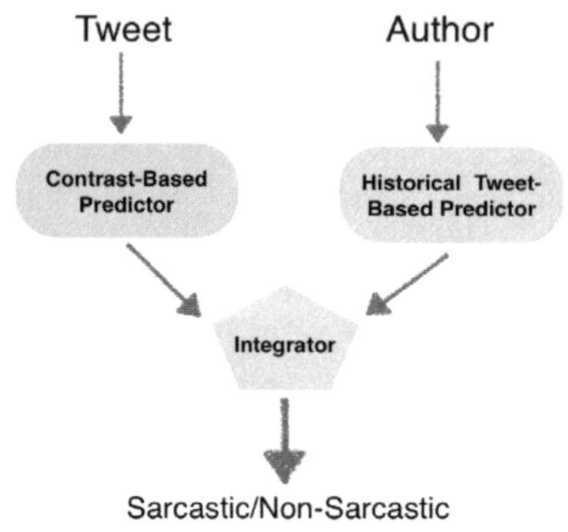

Figure 2: Architecture of our sarcasm detection approach

Similarly, supervised approaches implement sarcasm as a classification task that predicts whether a piece of text is sarcastic or not (Gonzalez-Ibanez et al., 2011; Barbieri et al., 2014; Carvalho et al., 2009). The features used include unigrams, emoticons, etc. Recent work in sarcasm detection deals with a more systematic feature design. Joshi et al. (2015) use a linguistic theory called context incongruity as a basis of feature design, and describe two kinds of features: implicit and explicit incongruity features. Wallace et al. (2015) uses as features beyond the target text as features. These include features from the comments and description of forum theme. In this way, sarcasm detection using ML-based classifiers has proceeded in the direction of improving the feature design, while rule-based sarcasm detection uses rules generated from heuristics.

Our paper presents a novel approach to sarcasm detection: '*looking at historical tweets for sarcasm detection of a target tweet*'. It is similar to Wallace et al. (2015) in that it considers text apart from the target text. However, while they look at comments within a thread and properties of a discussion thread, we look at the historical tweets by the author.

3 Motivating example

Existing approaches detect contrast in sentiment to predict sarcasm. Our approach extends the past work by considering sentiment contrasts beyond the target tweet. Specifically, we look at tweets generated by the same author in the past (we refer to this as '**historical tweets**'). Consider the example in Figure 1. The author USER1 wrote the tweet '*Nicki Minaj, don't I hate her?!*'. The author's historical tweets may tell us that he/she has spoken positively about Nicki Minaj in the past. In this case, we observe an additional tweet where the author describes having a good time at a Nicki Minaj concert. This additional knowledge helps to identify that although the target tweet contains the word '*hate*', it is sarcastic.

4 Architecture

Figure 2 shows the architecture of our sarcasm detection approach. It takes as input the text of a tweet and the author, and predicts the output as either sarcastic or non-sarcastic. This is a rule-based sarcasm detection approach that consists of three modules: (a) **Contrast-based Predictor**, (b) **Historical Tweet-based Predictor**, and (c) **Integrator**. We now describe the three modules in detail.

4.1 Contrast-based Predictor

This module uses only the target tweet. The contrast-based predictor identifies a sarcastic tweet using a sentiment contrast as given in Riloff et al. (2013). A contrast is said to occur if:

- **Explicit contrast**: The tweet contains one word of a polarity, and another word of another polarity. This is similar to explicit incongruity given by Joshi et al. (2015).
- **Implicit Contrast**: The tweet contains one word of a polarity, and a phrase of the other polarity. The implicit sentiment phrases are extracted from a set of sarcastic tweets as described in Tsur et al. (2010) Davidov et al. (2010). This is similar to implicit incongruity given by Joshi et al. (2015).

For example, the sentence '*I love being ignored.*' is predicted as sarcastic since it has a positive word '*love*' and a negative word '*ignored*'. We include rules to discount contrast across conjunctions like 'but' [3].

4.2 Historical Tweet-based Predictor

This module uses the target tweet and the name of the author. The goal of the historical tweet-based predictor is to identify if the sentiment expressed in the tweet does not match the historical tweets posted by the author. The steps followed are:

1. The sentiment of the target tweet is computed using a rule-based sentiment analysis system that we implemented. The system takes as input a sentence, and predicts whether it is positive or negative. It uses simple rules based on lookup in a sentiment word list, and rules based on negation, conjunctions (such as 'but'), etc. On Sentiment140 [4] corpus, our sentiment analysis system performs with an accuracy of 58.49%.
2. The target tweet is POS-tagged, and all NNP sequences are extracted as '**target phrases**'.
3. '**Target phrases**' are likely to be the targets of the sentiment expressed in the tweet. So, we *download only the historical tweets which contain the target phrases*[5].
4. The sentiment analysis system also gives the sentiment of the downloaded historical tweets. A majority voting-based sentiment in the historical tweets is considered to be the author's historical sentiment towards the target phrase.
5. This module predicts a tweet as sarcastic if the historical sentiment is different from the sentiment of the target tweet.

A target tweet may contain more than one target phrase. In this case, the predictor considers all target phrases, and predicts the tweet as sarcastic if the above steps hold true for any of the phrases. Possible lacunae in this approach are:

1. If the historical tweets contained sarcasm towards the target phrase, while the target tweet did not, the predictor will incorrectly mark the tweet as sarcastic.
2. If the historical tweets contained sarcasm towards the target phrase, and so did the target tweet, the predictor will incorrectly mark the tweet as non-sarcastic.
3. If an entity mentioned in the target tweet never appeared in the author's historical tweets, then no input from the historical tweet is considered.

4.3 Integrator

This module combines the predictions from the historical tweet-based predictor and the contrast-based predictor. There are four versions of the module:

1. **Only historical tweet-based**: This prediction uses only the output of the historical tweet-based predictor. This also means that if this author had not mentioned the target phrase in any of his/her tweets in the past, the tweet is predicted as non-sarcastic.
2. **OR**: If either of the two predictors marked a tweeet as sarcastic, then the tweet is predicted as sarcastic. If not, then it is predicted to be non-sarcastic.
3. **AND**: If both the predictors marked a tweet as sarcastic, then the tweet is predicted as sarcastic. If not, then it is predicted to be non-sarcastic.
4. **Relaxed-AND**: If both the predictors marked a tweet as sarcastic, then predict the tweet as sarcastic. If the historical tweet-based predictor did not have any tweets to look up (*i.e.,* the author had not expressed any sentiment towards the target in the past), then consider only the output of the contrast-based predictor.

5 Experimental Setup

For the contrast-based predictor, we obtain the implicit sentiment phrases as follows: (1) We download a set of 8000 tweets marked with #sarcasm, and assume that they are sarcastic tweets. These are not the same as the test tweets, (2) We extract 3-grams to 10-grams (1-gram represents a word) in these tweets, (3) We select phrases that occur at least thrice. This results in a set of 445 phrases. These phrases are used as implicit sentiment phrases for the contrast-based predictor.

For the historical tweet-based predictor, we first POS tag the sentence using Malecha and Smith

[3] For example, 'I like the movie but I dislike the cinema hall' does not count as a contrast, in terms of sarcastic expression

[4] http://help.sentiment140.com/for-students

[5] Twitter API allows access to the most recent 3500 tweets on a timeline. This is an additional limitation.

(2010). We then select NNP sequences[6] in the target tweet as the target phrase. Then, we download the complete timeline of the author using Twitter API [7], and select tweets containing the target phrase. The historical tweet-based predictor then gives its prediction as described in the previous section.

Both the predictors rely on sentiment lexicons: The contrast-based predictor needs sentiment-bearing words and phrases to detect contrast, while the historical tweet-based predictor needs sentiment-bearing words to identify sentiment of a tweet. We experiment with two lexicons:

1. Lexicon 1 (**L1**): In this case, we use the list of positive and negative words from Pang and Lee (2004).
2. Lexicon 2 (**L2**): In this case, we use the list of positive and negative words from Mohammad and Turney (2013).

Based on the two lexicons, we run two sets of experiments:

1. **Sarcasm detection with L1 (SD1)**: In this set, we use L1 as the lexicon for the two predictors. We show results for all four integrator versions (*Only historical tweet-based, AND, OR, Relaxed-AND*).
2. **Sarcasm detection with L2 (SD2)**: In this set, we use L2 as the lexicon for the two predictors. We show results for all four integrator versions (*Only historical tweet-based, AND, OR, Relaxed-AND*).

For all experiments, we use the test corpus given by Riloff et al. (2013). This is a manually annotated corpus consisting of 2278 tweets[8], out of which 506 are sarcastic.

6 Results

Tables 1 and 2 show Precision (P), Recall (R) and F-score (F) for SD1 and SD2 respectively. We compare our values with the best reported values in Riloff et al. (2013). This comparison is required because the test corpus that we used was obtained from them.

	P	**R**	**F**
Best reported value by Riloff et al. (2013)	0.62	0.44	0.51
Only Historical tweet-based	0.498	0.499	0.498
OR	0.791	**0.8315**	0.811
AND	0.756	0.521	0.617
Relaxed-AND	**0.8435**	0.81	**0.826**

Table 1: Averaged Precision, Recall and F-score of the SD1 approach for four configurations of the integrator

	P	**R**	**F**
Best reported value by Riloff et al. (2013)	0.62	0.44	0.51
Only Historical tweet-based	0.496	0.499	0.497
OR	0.842	**0.927**	**0.882**
AND	0.779	0.524	0.627
Relaxed-AND	**0.880**	0.884	**0.882**

Table 2: Averaged Precision, Recall and F-score of the SD2 approach for four configurations of the integrator

Table 1 shows that using only the historical tweet-based predictor, we are able to achieve a comparable performance (F-score of approximately 0.49 in case of SD1 and SD2 both) with the benchmark values (F-score of 0.51 in case of Riloff et al. (2013)). The performance values for 'Only historical tweet-based' are not the same in SD1 and SD2 because the lexicon used in predictors of the two approaches are different. This is obviously low because only using historical contrast is not sufficient.

The AND integrator is restrictive because it requires both the predictors to predict a tweet as sarcastic. In that case as well, we obtain F-scores of 0.617 and 0.627 for SD1 and SD2 respectively. Relaxed-AND performs the best in both the cases with F-scores of 0.826 and 0.882 for SD1 and SD2 respectively.

We experiment with two configurations SD1 and SD2, in order to show that the benefit of our approach is not dependent on the choice of lexicon. To understand how well the two captured the positive (*i.e.,* sarcastic tweets) class, we compare their precision and recall values in Table 3. We

[6] We also experimented with NN and JJ_NN sequences. However, the output turned out to be generic.

[7] `https://dev.twitter.com/overview/api`

[8] Some tweets in their original corpus could not be downloaded due to privacy settings or deletion.

observe that the positive precision is high in case of OR, AND, Relaxed-AND. The low precision-recall values in case of 'Only historical tweet-based' indicates that relying purely on historical tweets may not be a good idea. The positive precision in case of Relaxed-And is 0.777 for SD1 and 0.811 for SD2. The contrast within a tweet (captured by our contrast-based predictor) and the contrast with the history (captured by our historical tweet-based predictor) both need to be applied together.

7 Discussion

Our target phrases are only NNP sequences. However, by the virtue of the POS tagger[9] used, our approach predicts sarcasm correctly in following situations:

1. **Proper Nouns**: The tweet *'because **Fox** is well-balanced and objective?'* was correctly predicted as sarcastic because our predictor located a past tweet *'**Fox**'s World Cup streaming options are terrible'*.
2. **User Mentions**: User mentions in a tweet were POS-tagged as NNPs, and hence, became target phrases. For example, a target tweet was *'**@USERNAME** ooooh that helped alot'*, where the target phrase was extracted as @USERNAME. Our approach looked at historical tweets by the author containing '*@USERNAME*'. Thus, the predictor took into consideration how 'cordial' the two users are, based on the sentiment in historical tweets between them.
3. **Informal Expressions**: Informal expressions like 'Yuss' were tagged as NNPs. Hence, we were able to discover the common sentiment that were used in, by the author. The target tweet containing 'Yuss' was correctly marked as sarcastic.

However, some limitations of our approach are:

1. **The non-sarcastic assumption**: We assume is that the author has not been sarcastic about a target phrase in the past (because we assume that the historical tweets contain an author's 'true' sentiment towards the target phrase).
2. **Timeline-related challenges**: Obtaining the Twitter timeline of an author may not be straightforward. A twitter timeline may be private where the user adds his/her followers, and only these followers have access to the user's tweets. Twitter also allows change of twitter handle name because of which the timeline cannot be searched. In some cases, the twitter account was deactivated. Hence, we could not download the twitter timeline for 248 out of 2273 unique authors in our dataset.

	SD1 PP	SD1 PR	SD2 PP	SD2 PR
OHTB	0.218	0.073	0.215	0.063
OR	0.647	0.785	0.691	0.978
AND	0.727	0.047	0.771	0.053
Relaxed-AND	0.777	0.675	0.811	0.822

Table 3: Positive Precision (PP) and Recall (PR) for SD1 and SD2; OHTB: Only Historical tweet-based

8 Conclusion & Future Work

Past work in sarcasm detection focuses on target tweet only. We present a approach that predicts sarcasm in a target tweet using the tweet author's historical tweets. Our historical tweet-based predictor checks if the sentiment towards a given target phrase in the target tweet agrees to the sentiment expressed in the historical tweets by the same author. We implement four kinds of integrators to combine the contrast-based predictor (which works on the target tweet alone) and the historical tweet-based predictor (which uses target tweet and historical tweets). We obtain the best F-score value of 0.882, in case of SD2, where the contrast predictor uses a set of polar words from a word-emotion lexicon and phrases with implicit sentiment.

Our work opens a new direction to sarcasm detection: considering text written by an author in the past to identify sarcasm in a piece of text. With availability of such data in discussion forums or social media, sarcasm detection approaches would benefit from making use of text other than just the target text. Integration of historical text-based features into a supervised sarcasm detection framework is a promising future work.

[9]For example, some POS taggers have a separate tag for user mentions.

References

Francesco Barbieri, Horacio Saggion, and Francesco Ronzano. 2014. Modelling sarcasm in twitter, a novel approach. *ACL 2014*, page 50.

Paula Carvalho, Luís Sarmento, Mário J Silva, and Eugénio de Oliveira. 2009. Clues for detecting irony in user-generated contents: oh...!! it's so easy;-). In *Proceedings of the 1st international CIKM workshop on Topic-sentiment analysis for mass opinion*, pages 53–56. ACM.

Dmitry Davidov, Oren Tsur, and Ari Rappoport. 2010. Semi-supervised recognition of sarcastic sentences in twitter and amazon. In *Proceedings of the Fourteenth Conference on Computational Natural Language Learning*, pages 107–116. Association for Computational Linguistics.

Roberto Gonzalez-Ibanez, Smaranda Muresan, and Nina Wacholder. 2011. Identifying sarcasm in twitter: a closer look. In *Proceedings of the 49th Annual Meeting of the Association for Computational Linguistics: Human Language Technologies: short papers-Volume 2*, pages 581–586. Association for Computational Linguistics.

Aditya Joshi, Vinita Sharma, and Pushpak Bhattacharyya. 2015. Harnessing context incongruity for sarcasm detection. In *ACL-IJCNLP 2015*.

Gregory Malecha and Ian Smith. 2010. Maximum entropy part-of-speech tagging in nltk. *unpublished course-related report*.

Diana Maynard and Mark A Greenwood. 2014. Who cares about sarcastic tweets? investigating the impact of sarcasm on sentiment analysis. In *Proceedings of LREC*.

Saif M. Mohammad and Peter D. Turney. 2013. Crowdsourcing a word-emotion association lexicon. 29(3):436–465.

Bo Pang and Lillian Lee. 2004. A sentimental education: Sentiment analysis using subjectivity summarization based on minimum cuts. In *Proceedings of the 42nd annual meeting on Association for Computational Linguistics*, page 271. Association for Computational Linguistics.

Ellen Riloff, Ashequl Qadir, Prafulla Surve, Lalindra De Silva, Nathan Gilbert, and Ruihong Huang. 2013. Sarcasm as contrast between a positive sentiment and negative situation. In *Proceedings of the 2013 Conference on Empirical Methods in Natural Language Processing*, pages 704–714. Association for Computational Linguistics.

Oren Tsur, Dmitry Davidov, and Ari Rappoport. 2010. Icwsm-a great catchy name: Semi-supervised recognition of sarcastic sentences in online product reviews. In *ICWSM*.

Byron C Wallace, Do Kook Choe, and Eugene Charniak. 2015. Sparse, contextually informed models for irony detection: Exploiting user communities, entities and sentiment. In *ACL-IJCNLP 2015*.

Optimising Agile Social Media Analysis

Thomas Kober
Department of Informatics
University of Sussex
Brighton, UK
t.kober@sussex.ac.uk

David Weir
Department of Informatics
University of Sussex
Brighton, UK
d.j.weir@sussex.ac.uk

Abstract

Agile social media analysis involves building bespoke, one-off classification pipelines tailored to the analysis of specific datasets. In this study we investigate how the DUALIST architecture can be optimised for agile social media analysis. We evaluate several semi-supervised learning algorithms in conjunction with a Naïve Bayes model, and show how these modifications can improve the performance of bespoke classifiers for a variety of tasks on a large range of datasets.

1 Introduction

Natural Language Processing (NLP) on large social media datasets has emerged as a popular theme in the academic NLP community with publications ranging from predicting elections, e.g. (Tumasjan et al., 2010; Marchetti-Bowick and Chambers, 2012), to forecasting box-office revenues for movies, e.g. (Asur and Huberman, 2010) and anticipating the stock market, e.g. (Bollen et al., 2011; Si et al., 2013). More recently, Opinion Mining and Sentiment Analysis on large social media datasets have received an increasing amount of attention outside academia, where a growing number of businesses and public institutions seek to gain insight into public opinion. For example, companies are primarily interested in what is being said about their brand and products, while public organisations are more concerned with analysing reactions to recent events, or with capturing the general political and societal Zeitgeist. The social network Twitter has been a popular target for such analyses as the vast majority of tweets are publicly available, and easily obtainable via the Twitter API[1], which conveniently enables the harnessing of a large number of real-time responses to any user-defined keyword query.

In this paper we are concerned with what we call *agile social media analysis*, which is best illustrated with an example. Imagine that a political scientist wants to investigate reactions on Twitter to a speech given by British Prime Minister David Cameron the previous night. She uses an application which allows her to query the Twitter API in order to gather a dataset, and to interactively design classifiers, tailored to specific tasks. For her analysis, she starts searching for "Cameron", which inevitably will retrieve a large number of irrelevant tweets, e.g. those referring to Cameron Diaz. Her first goal therefore is to filter out all of those unrelated tweets, for which she requires a bespoke classifier that will only be used for *this single task*. In order to create such a classifier, she first needs to annotate a gold standard evaluation set which is randomly sampled from the initially retrieved tweets. While labelling the first few tweets for the evaluation set, she starts to build a picture of the range of topics being discussed on Twitter that night. She notices that a considerable proportion of tweets appears to be talking about David Cameron's personality. Many of the others appear to be about two specific topics mentioned in the speech: tax policy and the EU referendum. After training a classifier to perform relevancy classification, she therefore decides to create another one-off classifier to divide the relevant tweets into the three categories, "personality", "tax policy" and "EU referendum". To conclude her analysis, she creates three more bespoke classifiers to perform Sentiment Analysis on each of the three subsets *separately*.

A crucial aspect of performing agile social media analysis is the direct interaction with the data, through which the analyst gains a sense of what the discourse is about. It furthermore enables her to better tailor her analysis to the collected

[1] http://dev.twitter.com/

Proceedings of the 6th Workshop on Computational Approaches to Subjectivity, Sentiment and Social Media Analysis (WASSA 2015), pages 31–40,
Lisboa, Portugal, 17 September, 2015.

data. DUALIST introduced the framework which enables non-technical analysts to design bespoke classifiers by labelling documents and features through active learning, with only a few minutes of annotation effort (Settles, 2011; Settles and Zhu, 2012). Wibberley et al. (2013) and Wibberley et al. (2014) showed that the DUALIST architecture can successfully be used for performing ad-hoc analyses in an agile manner.

The remainder of this paper is organised as follows: in Section 2 we more generally introduce agile social media analysis, followed by the description of the datasets we use in our empirical evaluation in Section 3. Section 4 describes our approach alongside related work and Section 5 presents our experiments and discusses our findings. In Section 6 we give an overview of future work and we conclude this paper in Section 7.

2 Agile Social Media Analysis

When beginning an analysis the social scientist has no predetermined plan of the specific content of her investigation. The reason is that there is limited appreciation for what is being discussed in advance of engaging with the data. Therefore, the process of annotating a gold standard evaluation set and a training set to create bespoke classifiers, also serves the purpose of exploring the data space.

After collecting a text corpus from Twitter, the analyst typically creates a tailored multi-stage classification pipeline to organise the heterogenous mass of data. As explained in the introductory scenario, the first stage often involves filtering irrelevant tweets, since keyword queries are purposefully kept broad to minimise the risk of missing relevant aspects of a discussion. The following stages are completely dependent on the extracted content — target categories are not known upfront, but are determined while interacting with the data. Each stage in this pipeline requires the annotation of a gold standard evaluation set and the training of a bespoke classifier to perform the categorisation. The tweets for the gold standard set are randomly sampled from the available data, whereas the creation of the classifier is guided by active learning to accelerate the training process (Settles, 2009). The two kinds of labelling tasks have intrinsic beneficial side-effects that support the analyst's investigation. When annotating a gold standard set, the social scientist is able to explore the data and gather ideas for further analyses. The training of a bespoke classifier enables the analyst to quickly test whether the algorithm has the capability to divide the data into the target categories. This is possible because the system is able to provide instant feedback on how well the current classifier is performing on the evaluation set, and allows the social scientist to "fail fast". This has the benefit of being able to quickly define new target categories which better match the data.

From a Machine Learning perspective, agile social media analysis poses a number of distinct challenges. The labelled data for any classification task can contain a considerable amount of noise as the dataset is not labelled and validated by a team of experienced annotators in month-long efforts, but in short sessions by a single analyst. Furthermore, for most downstream classification tasks, the input dataset often is the product of one or more preceding classifiers. Therefore, there is no guarantee that a given tweet is actually relevant to the current analysis.

The small amount of labelled data together with the large amount of unlabelled data raise the issue of how to best make effective use of the vast number of unlabelled tweets. We investigate this problem from two complementing angles. On the one side we enhance our current semi-supervised learning algorithm with several simple modifications. On the other side, we compare the adjusted algorithms with various other semi-supervised learning algorithms that aim to leverage the information in the unlabelled data in a different way. We furthermore examine whether we can improve the classifier by extending its language model to include bigrams and trigrams.

3 Datasets

We evaluate our experiments on 24 Twitter datasets that have been collected by social scientists for a number of real-world analyses (Bartlett and Norrie, 2015; Bartlett et al., 2014b; Bartlett et al., 2014a). The Twitter datasets represent a diverse range of possible applications of agile social media analysis. Some are focused on "Twitcidents"[2] during political debates or speeches (*boocheer, cameron 1-3, clacton, clegg, debate 1-2, farage, immigr, miliband 1-2, salmond*). Three

[2]"A major incident provoking a firestorm of reactions on Twitter", see `http://www.urbandictionary.com/define.php?term=Twitcident`

datasets are concerned with reactions to the inquest following the death of Mark Duggan in London 2013 (*duggan 1-3*), and the remaining ones investigate topics such as the winter floods in many coastal regions in the South of England, throughout late 2013 and early 2014 (*flood 1-2*), misogyny (*misogyny, rape*), extremism (*isis 1-3*) and oil drillings in the arctic (*shell*). The Twitter datasets are drawn from different stages of the processing pipeline, which means that some datasets consist of the unprocessed tweets matching an initial keyword query while others have already been processed by one or more preceding steps in the pipeline. For example, the *shell* and *flood-1* datasets are the result of querying the Twitter API, whereas the *duggan-1* dataset has already been cleared of irrelevant tweets, and tweets only containing news links, in two separate preceeding stages of the processing pipeline. We furthermore evaluate our implementations on 2 commonly used NLP benchmark datasets, 20 Newsgroups (Lang, 1995), henceforth "*20news*", as an example Topic Classification dataset, and Movie Reviews (Maas et al., 2011), henceforth "*reviews*", as an example Sentiment Analysis dataset.

Table 1 highlights the extreme imbalance between labelled and unlabelled data and the corresponding differences in vocabulary size. In the Twitter datasets, $|V_{\mathcal{L}}|$ is usually one order of magnitude smaller than $|V_{\mathcal{L} \cup \mathcal{U}}|$. In comparison, the disparity in vocabulary size between labelled and unlabelled data in the *reviews* corpus is less than a factor of two. The difference is more extreme when looking at the actual amounts of labelled and unlabelled data, where the Twitter datasets often contain two orders of magnitude more unlabelled data than labelled data. Furthermore, the disparity in number of labelled documents between the Twitter datasets and the NLP benchmark corpora usually is one to two orders of magnitude. Where the *20news* dataset contains more than 10k labelled documents and the *reviews* dataset even 25k labelled instances, the Twitter datasets rarely contain more than a few hundred labelled tweets.

4 Approach & Related Work

The DUALIST architecture represents the general framework for performing agile social media analysis by combining active learning, semi-supervised learning, a Naïve Bayes text classifier and a graphical user interface into an application. A human annotator iteratively labels new tweets and terms in tweets which the active learning algorithm identifies as being most beneficial for annotation. The flexibility to label instances and individual words perhaps is the most important reason why effective classifiers can be created with only a few minutes of labelling effort. To leverage the collective information of the labelled and unlabelled data, DUALIST executes a single iteration of the Expectation-Maximization algorithm (Settles, 2011). In this paper we focus on the Naïve Bayes classifier and the semi-supervised learning algorithm and leave an investigation of the active learning component — and especially the feature labelling — for future work.

4.1 Naïve Bayes

Naïve Bayes fulfills the most important requirements for agile social media analysis: it is fast to train, proven to work well in the text domain despite its often violated independence assumptions, and is easily extensible with semi-supervised learning algorithms such as Expectation-Maximization due to its generative nature (Domingos and Pazzani, 1997; McCallum and Nigam, 1998; Nigam et al., 2000). The goal of classification is to find the class $c \in C$ that is most likely to have generated document d, which Naïve Bayes estimates as:

$$c = \underset{c \in C}{\operatorname{argmax}} P(c) \prod_{i=1}^{N_D} P(w_i \mid c) \qquad (1)$$

where $P(w_i \mid c)$ is the conditional probability of word w_i occurring in a document of class c, containing N_D words in a given labelled dataset $\mathcal{L}$.

4.2 Which Naïve Bayes?

There are several distinct flavours of the Naïve Bayes model, with different model types being better suited for some tasks and data characteristics than others. One major distinction is whether a Multinomial or Bernoulli event model is used. The former incorporates term frequency information into the model whereas the latter only uses term occurrence information. It has been shown that the Multinomial model usually performs better in the Topic Classification domain (McCallum and Nigam, 1998). However, Manning et al. (2008) highlight that the Bernoulli model tends to work better for short texts. Interestingly, a variant of the Multinomial event model that only uses binary

Name	$\mathcal{T}$	$\|C\|$	$\|\mathcal{L}\|$	$\|\mathcal{U}\|$	$\|V_{\mathcal{L}}\|$	$\|V_{\mathcal{L}\cup\mathcal{U}}\|$	**Name**	$\mathcal{T}$	$\|C\|$	$\|\mathcal{L}\|$	$\|\mathcal{U}\|$	$\|V_{\mathcal{L}}\|$	$\|V_{\mathcal{L}\cup\mathcal{U}}\|$
20news	TC	20	11314	-	130107	130107	*flood-1*	TC	2	530	116123	2176	72004
boo-cheer	SA	3	1665	436305	7092	104477	*flood-2*	TC	4	1615	39327	5043	25326
cameron-1	TC	2	205	33561	1491	33234	*immigr*	TC	2	210	425425	1098	171195
cameron-2	TC	4	320	867637	1317	294169	*isis-1*	SA	3	322	19378	2123	32242
cameron-3	SA	3	502	303868	1858	122372	*isis-2*	TC	2	827	107310	2549	51444
clacton	SA	3	930	147493	2785	59990	*isis-3*	TC	2	602	56928	1859	29287
clegg	SA	3	500	9597	3280	8349	*miliband-1*	SA	3	927	36335	3378	19728
debate-1	SA	3	306	31993	917	10987	*miliband-2*	SA	3	449	35786	2092	19785
debate-2	TC	5	123	31993	482	10984	*misogyny*	TC	2	215	119078	1131	89474
duggan-1	TC	3	475	86749	1376	26382	*rape*	TC	3	746	108044	3908	78757
duggan-2	TC	4	1086	53440	2609	15760	*reviews*	SA	2	25000	50000	74849	124255
duggan-3	TC	3	401	86749	1283	26385	*salmond*	SA	3	228	55899	1171	14464
farage	SA	3	2614	9794	5305	8349	*shell*	TC	2	221	50065	1196	60815

Table 1: Datasets: $\mathcal{T}$=Task, where TC=Topic Classification; SA=Sentiment Analysis; $|C|$ = number of labels; $\mathcal{L}$=Labelled data, $|\mathcal{L}|$=amount of Labelled data; $\mathcal{U}$=Unlabelled data, $|\mathcal{U}|$=amount of Unlabelled data; $|V_{\mathcal{L}}|$=Vocabulary size of the labelled data; $|V_{\mathcal{L}\cup\mathcal{U}}|$=Vocabulary size of the labelled and unlabelled data

counts instead of the full frequency information has been shown to outperform the standard Multinomial model, and the Bernoulli model, for a variety of tasks (Metsis et al., 2006; Wang and Manning, 2012).

Instead of the commonly used Laplacian (add-1) smoothing, we use a simple heuristic that adjusts the additive smoothing term, depending on the number of observed tokens and the overall vocabulary size, for every dataset individually. Instead of adding 1, we add $\frac{1}{10^k}$, and normalise appropriately afterwards. We defined $k = \left\lfloor \frac{\log |V_{\mathcal{L}\cup\mathcal{U}}|}{\log |T_{\mathcal{L}}|} \right\rfloor$, where $|V_{\mathcal{L}\cup\mathcal{U}}|$ is the total size of the vocabulary and $|T_{\mathcal{L}}|$ is the number of tokens in the labelled data. This approach re-distributes probability mass from observed words to unknown ones less aggressively than add-1 smoothing. We refer to this heuristic as Lidstone-Tokens (LT) smoothing and compare it to add-1 smoothing in a supervised learning scenario.

4.3 Semi-supervised Learning

In these experiments we examine the performance of three semi-supervised learning algorithms — Expectation-Maximization and two more recently proposed algorithms, Semi-supervised Frequency Estimate (Su et al., 2011), and Feature Marginals (Lucas and Downey, 2013).

4.4 Expectation-Maximization

The starting point for the Expectation-Maximization (EM) algorithm is an initial model instance from the labelled data $\mathcal{L}$, which can be obtained in a number of ways. A common approach is to train a Naïve Bayes classifier on the available labelled documents. DUALIST introduced an alternative using the labelled *features*, whose term frequencies are incremented by a pseudo-count, which was found to be more effective for an active learning scenario (Settles, 2011). In order to factor out the effect of active learning and to better study our modifications on datasets without any labelled features, we are using the labelled instances to initialise EM.

The EM algorithm first produces probabilistic class predictions for the unlabelled data $\mathcal{U}$, representing the "E-Step" and subsequently re-estimates the model parameters on all available data $\mathcal{L} \cup \mathcal{U}$ in the "M-Step". These two steps can be repeated until convergence, although for efficiency reasons, DUALIST only performs a single iteration. Furthermore, given the enormous difference in amounts of labelled and unlabelled data, documents in $\mathcal{U}$ are assigned a smaller weight than data in $\mathcal{L}$ in order to not drown out the information learnt from the labelled data. A common approach is to assign every instance in $\mathcal{U}$ a weight of $\alpha = 0.1$, henceforth "EM-CWF"[3] (Nigam et al., 2000; Settles, 2011). In a typical practical application, from which most of our datasets are drawn, we observe only a few hundred labelled documents but several tens or hundreds of thousands of unlabelled instances. In these circumstances, it can be hypothesised that a weight of $\alpha = 0.1$ would be too high, and the unlabelled data would outweigh the labelled data by one to two orders of magnitude. We therefore assign tweets in $\mathcal{U}$ a weight of $\alpha = \frac{|\mathcal{L}|}{|\mathcal{U}|}$, where $|\mathcal{L}|$ represents the number of labelled documents and $|\mathcal{U}|$ represents the number of unlabelled documents. We refer to this weighting scheme as "Proportional Weight Factor" (PWF).

4.5 Semi-supervised Frequency Estimate

The Semi-supervised Frequency Estimate (SFE) algorithm leverages the information $P(w)$ over the combined amount of labelled and unlabelled

[3]CWF means "Constant Weight Factor". For all of our experiments EM-CWF refers to the specific case with $\alpha = 0.1$.

data, to scale the class-conditional probabilities learnt from $\mathcal{L}$. Hence, the probability mass is re-distributed according to a word's overall prevalence in the corpus. Unlike the EM algorithm, SFE only requires a single pass over the data to adjust the model parameters and is thus better able to scale to large amounts of unlabelled data. SFE does not need the adjustment of additional hyper-parameters such as the weighting of probabilistically labelled documents in $\mathcal{U}$.

4.6 Feature Marginals

The Feature Marginals (FM) algorithm also uses the information of $P(w)$ over the labelled and unlabelled data to scale the class-conditional probabilities estimated from the training set. In addition, FM re-distributes the probability mass of $P(w)$ according to the probability of a token in $\mathcal{L}$ occurring in either class. Lucas and Downey (2013) found that their model is especially effective in estimating probabilities for words that have not been seen in the labelled data. In its current form, FM does not generalise to multi-class problems, we therefore perform one-vs-rest classification for datasets with more than two classes.

4.7 Usefulness of Unlabelled Data

Previous work has shown that unlabelled data can be leveraged to create superior models (Chawla and Karakoulas, 2005). The DUALIST framework adopts the assumption that by exploiting semi-supervised learning techniques, a more effective model can be built than by supervised learning alone. We examine whether the benefits of semi-supervised learning hold for the distinctive characteristics in our Twitter datasets.

4.8 Feature Extraction — Unigrams, Bigrams or Trigrams?

We investigate whether classifier performance can be improved by including bigram and trigram features. Wang and Manning (2012) showed that bigram features are especially beneficial for a more complex task such as Sentiment Analysis, but also consistently improve performance on Topic Classification problems for supervised learning settings.

5 Experiments & Discussion

All datasets we use have pre-defined training/testing splits. We tokenise the documents, but do not perform any other pre-processing such as stemming, URL normalisation or stopword removal. All documents are represented as simple bag-of-words vectors. We report micro-averaged F1-Scores for all experiments. When investigating the effect of unlabelled data, we randomly sample 1k, 5k, 10k, 25k, 50k, 100k unlabelled tweets, or use all available unlabelled data. As baseline we use EM-CWF — MNB add-1, which reflects the text classifier and semi-supervised learning algorithm used in DUALIST, with the difference that we use the labelled documents instead of the labelled features for initialising EM. This is to isolate the effects of Naïve Bayes and EM, and to factor out the contributions of active learning. We compare our results in terms of absolute F1-Score gain/loss in comparison to our baseline, or present F1-Score performance trajectories.

5.1 Parameterisation and Selection of the Naïve Bayes Event Model

As Figure 1 shows, Lidstone-Tokens smoothing performs better than add-1 smoothing on 18 out of 26 datasets, and improves F1-Score by 2.5% on average across all datasets, in a supervised learning scenario. We therefore adopt it for all further experiments. We furthermore drop the standard Multinomial Naïve Bayes model and only adopt the binary MNB and the Bernoulli Naïve Bayes (BNB) models for future comparisons, as we found them to be superior to the standard Multinomial model. Our findings are consistent with previously published results of Wang and Manning (2012), and Metsis et al. (2006), who report that binary MNB works better than the standard Multinomial model for a variety of Topic Classification and Sentiment Analysis tasks. Our results also agree with Manning et al. (2008) who found the Bernoulli event model to be a competitive choice for short text classification. For all experiments we use all combinations of binary MNB and BNB together with the three semi-supervised learning algorithms introduced in the previous section — except for BNB + FM, which we found to significantly underperfom the other combinations.

5.2 Semi-supervised Learning Algorithms Comparison

As Figure 2 shows, there are only two datasets (*clacton* and *isis-2*), where the EM-CWF — MNB add-1 baseline outperforms the other semi-supervised learning algorithms. On the other

Name	EM-*M*	EM-*B*	SFE-*M*	SFE-*B*	FM	MNB	EM-C	Name	EM-*M*	EM-*B*	SFE-*M*	SFE-*B*	FM	MNB	EM-C
20news	0.761	0.676	**0.779**	**0.779**	0.743	0.759	0.729	*flood-1*	**0.468**	0.368	0.451	0.456	0.381	0.381	0.382
boo-cheer	0.492	0.516	0.538	**0.539**	0.498	0.496	0.487	*flood-2*	0.669	**0.704**	0.669	0.669	0.683	0.683	0.62
cameron-1	0.781	**0.832**	0.815	0.827	0.814	0.808	0.712	*immigr*	0.956	0.91	0.951	0.948	0.953	**0.962**	0.91
cameron-2	**0.589**	0.529	**0.589**	0.58	**0.589**	0.585	0.451	*isis-1*	0.567	**0.573**	0.533	0.557	0.55	0.563	0.503
cameron-3	0.67	0.683	0.647	0.667	**0.7**	**0.7**	0.62	*isis-2*	0.751	0.755	0.734	0.722	0.758	0.753	**0.808**
clacton	0.52	0.483	0.513	0.513	0.517	0.513	**0.56**	*isis-3*	0.648	**0.667**	0.658	0.648	0.654	0.654	0.533
clegg	0.696	0.724	0.692	0.7	**0.736**	0.724	0.676	*miliband-1*	0.556	0.563	0.544	0.552	0.57	**0.574**	0.533
debate-1	0.627	**0.637**	0.597	0.61	0.63	0.626	0.5	*miliband-2*	0.69	0.69	**0.71**	0.7	0.69	0.7	0.6
debate-2	0.667	0.661	0.567	0.581	0.644	**0.684**	0.396	*misogyny*	**0.953**	**0.953**	0.938	0.949	**0.953**	**0.953**	0.888
duggan-1	0.639	**0.649**	0.634	0.634	0.637	0.634	0.526	*rape*	**0.895**	0.87	0.87	0.88	**0.895**	0.885	0.785
duggan-2	0.585	**0.603**	0.537	0.545	0.575	0.6	0.378	*reviews*	0.826	0.825	**0.831**	**0.831**	0.83	0.83	0.821
duggan-3	0.767	0.75	**0.773**	0.767	0.76	0.75	0.603	*salmond*	**0.69**	**0.69**	0.65	0.68	**0.69**	**0.69**	0.45
farage	0.718	**0.72**	0.698	0.712	0.67	0.716	0.688	*shell*	0.756	**0.798**	0.738	0.755	0.758	0.775	0.715

Table 2: Micro averaged F1-Score for all methods across all datasets. EM-*M*=EM-PWF — binary MNB LT; EM-*B*=EM-PWF — BNB LT; SFE-*M*=SFE — binary MNB LT; SFE-*B*=SFE — BNB LT; FM=FM — binary MNB LT; MNB=supervised binary MNB LT; EM-C=EM-CWF — MNB add-1; Boldfaced numbers mean top performance on the dataset.

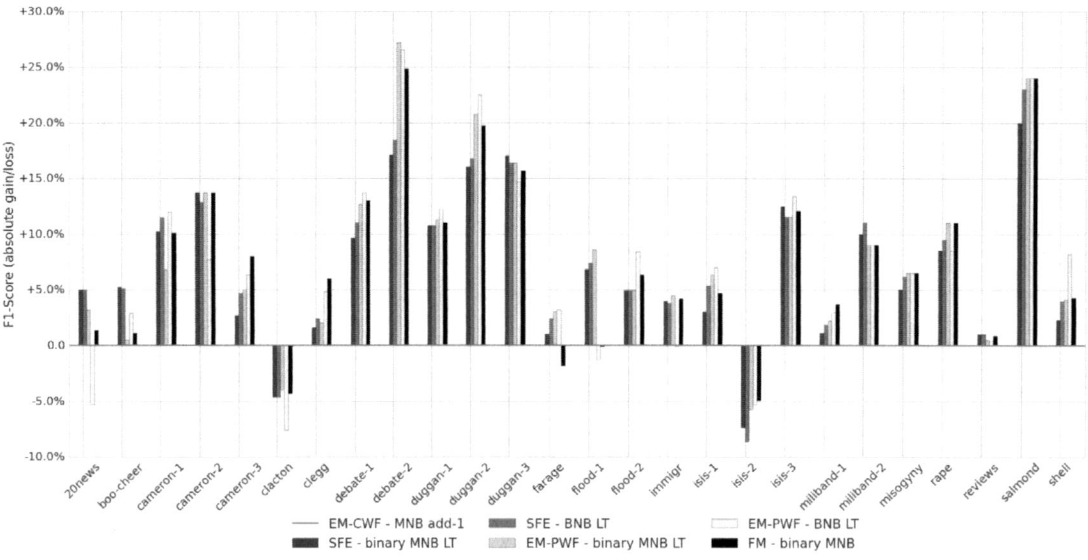

Figure 2: Semi-Supervised Learning algorithm comparison. The baseline is EM-CWF — MNB add-1. PWF refers to our EM weighting scheme. The new algorithms only failed to improve performance on 2 datasets. Our simple enhancements to NB smoothing and EM weighting (see Sections 4.1 and 4.3) improve an NB-EM combination considerably and make it competitive with SFE and FM.

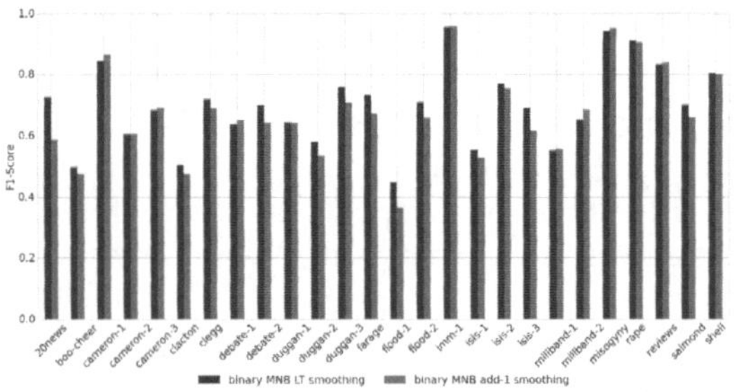

Figure 1: Overall Lidstone-Tokens smoothing achieves an average improvement of 2.5% across all datasets and improves performance on 18 out of 26 datasets. Performance gains are as large as 14% in absolute terms on the *20News* dataset, 8.5% on the *flood-1* dataset and 7.3% on the *isis-2* dataset. Both MNB models use binary counts.

hand, there is no single dominant algorithm that consistently outperforms the others (also see Table 2). Our results confirm that SFE and FM are superior to EM-CWF — MNB add-1 as was shown in the respective publications, and that their improvements can be leveraged for agile social media analysis. Interestingly, our simple modifications to EM improve its performance substantially, making it competitive with SFE and FM on our datasets. Our results furthermore highlight that considerable performance improvements can be gained for the commonly used combination of Naïve Bayes and Expectation-Maximization when their respective hyperparameters are optimised for the given dataset characteristics.

5.3 The Effect of Unlabelled Data

Table 2 shows that adding unlabelled data does not always improve performance. The supervised binary MNB classifier with Lidstone-Tokens smoothing is the top performing method on 6 out of 26 datasets. Only the EM-PWF — BNB LT combination is the top performing method more frequently. Figures 3a and 3b show that EM-CWF — MNB add-1 appears to be very sensitive to the amount of unlabelled data, whereas the other semi-supervised learning algorithms remain relatively stable under a growing amount of unlabelled data. Figure 3a highlights a prototypical case where adding unlabelled data up to a certain threshold improves performance, but *degrades* it when more is added. We observed this behaviour of EM-CWF — MNB add-1 on a number of datasets. Figure 3b shows that EM-PWF — binary MNB LT, FM — binary MNB LT and SFE — binary MNB LT do not make the most effective use of the unlabelled data, hence there is still potential for further improvement in these algorithms. Especially EM-PWF — binary MNB LT is perhaps scaling down the contributions of the unlabelled data too aggressively. This comes at the expense of not leveraging the full potential of the unlabelled documents, but has the advantage of improved stability across varying amounts of unlabelled data as our experiments show.

5.4 The Effect of Adding Bigrams and Trigrams

Contrary to our expectations, adding bigrams or trigrams produced mixed results and did not consistently improve performance on our datasets. An interesting observation is the different behaviour of the various semi-supervised algorithms. For example, adding trigrams improves EM-PWF — binary MNB LT by almost 10% on the *flood-1* dataset, whereas performance goes down by nearly 10% for SFE — binary MNB LT. The reverse effect can be observed on the *shell* dataset. Our findings are in contrast to published results by Wang and Manning (2012) who report that adding bigrams never degraded performance in their experiments. Figures 4a-4c highlight the inconsistent behaviour of adding bigrams or trigrams for three semi-supervised learning algorithms across all datasets[4]. We also ran our experiments with a purely supervised MNB classifier to factor out the effect of semi-supervised learning, which however, resulted in the same inconsistent behaviour (see Figure 4d). A closer investigation of the datasets suggests that the difference might be due to the idiosyncrasy of Twitter where opinions are commonly packaged into multi-word hashtag expressions, which frequently capture the sentiment of a tweet, but are treated as unigrams. For example, expressions such as "#CameronMustGo" and "#CareNotCuts" in the *boo-cheer* dataset, or "#NoSympathy" and "#PoliceMurder" in the *duggan-1* dataset, convey crucial sentiment information. The phenomenon is not exclusive to Sentiment Analysis, hashtag expressions frequently categorise a tweet, e.g. "#ArcticOil" in the *shell* dataset. Such topical information has already been leveraged in a number of previous works, e.g. Weston et al. (2014); Dela Rosa et al. (2011). Therefore, we hypothesise that the potential benefits of bigrams or trigrams cannot be leveraged as effectively for Twitter Sentiment Analysis datasets than for other datasets.

[4]Due to space reasons, we only show figures for the binary MNB variants — the results for the BNB variants are almost identical.

6 Future Work

Our results created a multitude of directions for future research. We plan to investigate the reason behind the inconsistent performance of the semi-supervised learning algorithms across our datasets. We are interested whether it is specific dataset characteristics or particular hyper-parameter configurations that cause e.g. EM-PWF — BNB LT to be the top performing algorithm on the *shell* and *duggan-2* datasets, but the worst performer on the *clacton* and *flood-1* datasets. Moreover, we seek to gain insight why adding bigrams or trigrams *improves* performance on a given dataset for one method, but degrades it for another. We also plan to study whether we can use the unlabelled data more effectively, e.g. by sub-sampling the unlabelled tweets by some criterion. The hypothesis is that there might be a subset of tweets in the unlabelled data which better aligns with the current analysis. We will furthermore examine whether the active learning process, and especially the feature labelling, can be improved in order to create more effective bespoke classifiers with less manual labelling effort. Lastly, we intend to investigate the role of opinionated multi-word hashtag expressions which not only convey topical information, but also express sentiment as we highlighted in the previous section. We therefore intend to assess whether we can leverage the sentiment information of hashtag expressions to improve Sentiment Analysis on our Twitter datasets.

7 Conclusion

In this paper we highlighted the demand for being able to quickly build bespoke classifier pipelines when performing agile social media analysis in practice. We considered different Naïve Bayes event models in conjunction with various semi-supervised learning algorithms on a large range of datasets. We showed that SFE and FM outperform

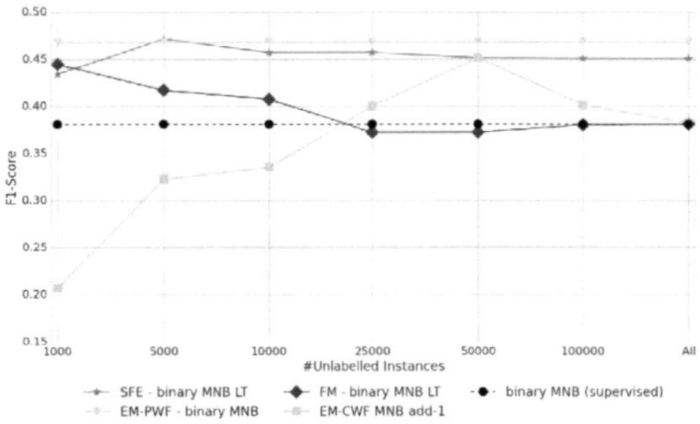

(a) The effect of unlabelled data on the *flood-1* dataset. While EM-PWF — binary MNB LT and SFE — binary MNB LT are relatively stable with increasing amounts of unlabelled data, EM-CWF — MNB add-1 displays its frequently observed "peak-behaviour", where adding unlabelled data would improve performance until a threshold is reached, after which performance degrades again. FM — binary MNB LT shows the opposite effect, where performance decreases in the beginning and then slightly recovers with more unlabelled data.

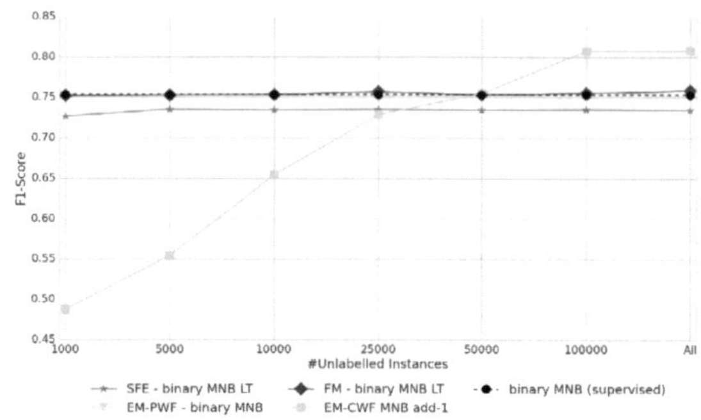

(b) The effect of unlabelled data on the *isis-2* dataset. While the performance of EM-CWF — MNB add-1 increases steadily with more unlabelled data, EM-PWF — binary MNB LT, FM — binary MNB LT and SFE — binary MNB LT remain very stable with increasing amounts of unlabelled data. These results suggest that there is further room for improvement in the latter algorithms to make more effective use of the unlabelled data.

Figure 3: Micro averaged F1-Score over the number of unlabelled instances. The baseline is a supervised binary MNB LT classifier. To reduce clutter, we only present the binary MNB variants of EM-PWF, FM and SFE.

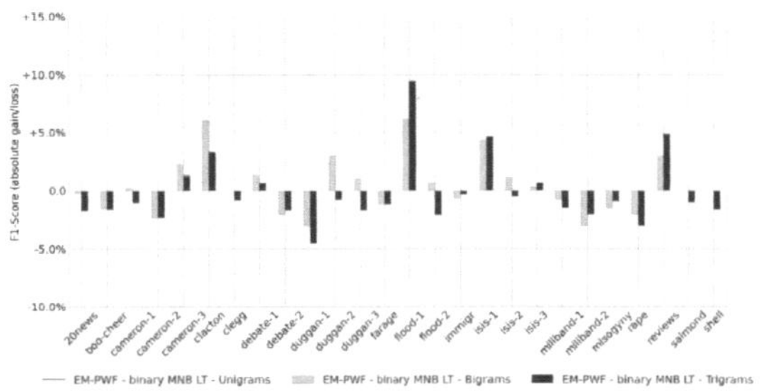

(a) The effect of adding bigrams and trigrams in comparison to a unigram baseline for the EM-PWF — binary MNB LT algorithm.

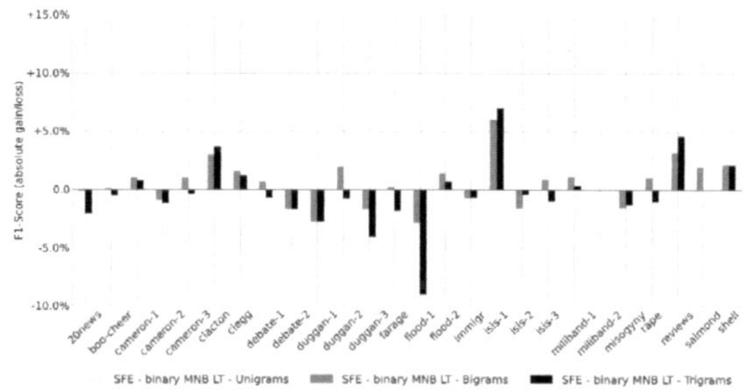

(b) The effect of adding bigrams and trigrams in comparison to a unigram baseline for the SFE — binary MNB LT algorithm.

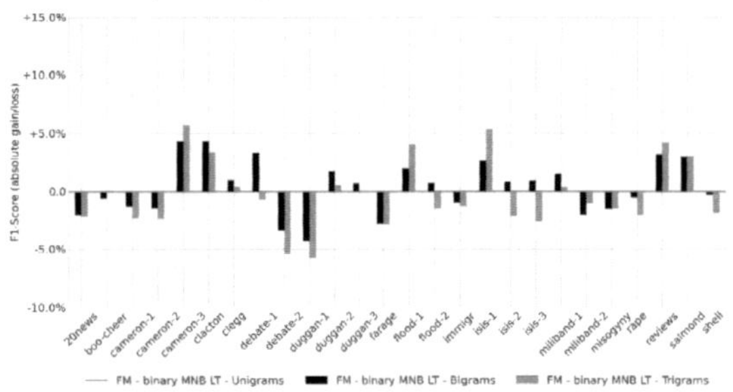

(c) The effect of adding bigrams and trigrams in comparison to a unigram baseline for the FM — binary MNB LT algorithm.

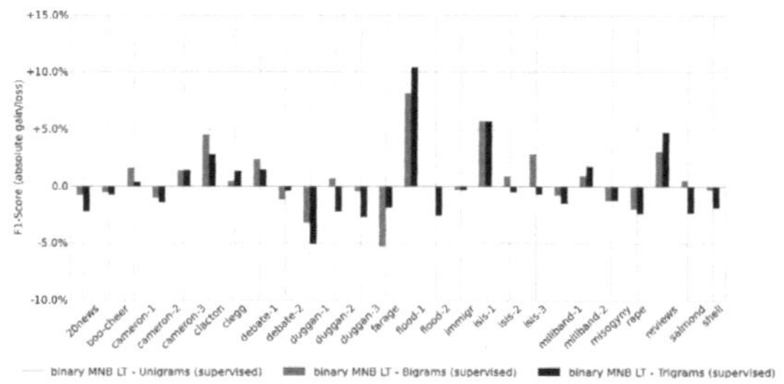

(d) The effect of adding bigrams and trigrams in comparison to a unigram baseline for the supervised binary MNB algorithm.

Figure 4: The effect of adding bigrams and trigrams for various algorithms. No consistent behaviour can be observed across the datasets. This is contrary to the findings of Wang and Manning (2012) who found that adding bigrams always helped for Topic Classification and Sentiment Analysis. Interestingly while we can reproduce the positive effect of bigrams and trigrams on the *reviews* dataset, we find that bigrams or trigrams do not help on the full *20news* dataset (Wang and Manning (2012) used 3 different 2-class subsets of the *20news* dataset). We hypothesise that the disparity between the findings in Wang and Manning (2012) is due to the different characteristics between the Twitter datasets in our study, and the ones used by in their experiments.

EM-CWF — MNB add-1 but also highlighted that the performance of NB-EM combinations can considerably be improved when their hyperparameters are optimised. We showed that with these modifications NB-EM is competitive with SFE and FM on our datasets. Overall we demonstrated that the modifications to Naïve Bayes and EM, and the usage of alternative semi-supervised learning algorithms, outperformed the baseline configuration on almost all datasets. We furthermore pointed out that none of the semi-supervised learning algorithms we evaluated can consistently make effective use of a large amount of unlabelled data. Lastly, we presented the result that adding bigrams or trigrams does not consistently improve performance in an agile scenario on our datasets.

Acknowledgments

We thank Jeremy Reffin, the TAG lab team and our anonymous reviewers for their helpful comments.

References

Sitaram Asur and Bernardo A. Huberman. 2010. Predicting the future with social media. In *Proceedings of the 2010 IEEE/WIC/ACM International Conference on Web Intelligence and Intelligent Agent Technology - Volume 01*, WI-IAT '10, pages 492–499, Washington, DC, USA. IEEE Computer Society.

Jaime Bartlett and Richard Norrie. 2015. Immigration on twitter. http://www.demos.co.uk/publications/immigration-on-twitter.

Jaime Bartlett, Jonathan Birdwell, and Louis Reynolds. 2014a. Like, share, vote. http://www.demos.co.uk/publications/likesharevote.

Jaime Bartlett, Richard Norrie, Sofia Patel, Rebekka Rumpel, and Simon Wibberley. 2014b. Misogyny on twitter. http://www.demos.co.uk/publications/misogyny.

Johan Bollen, Huina Mao, and Xiaojun Zeng. 2011. Twitter mood predicts the stock market. *Journal of Computational Science*, 2(1):1 – 8.

Nitesh V. Chawla and Grigoris I. Karakoulas. 2005. Learning from labeled and unlabeled data: An empirical study across techniques and domains. *J. Artif. Intell. Res. (JAIR)*, 23:331–366.

Pedro Domingos and Michael Pazzani. 1997. On the optimality of the simple bayesian classifier under zero-one loss. *Mach. Learn.*, 29(2-3):103–130, November.

Ken Lang. 1995. Newsweeder: Learning to filter netnews. In *in Proceedings of the 12th International Machine Learning Conference (ML95)*.

Michael Lucas and Doug Downey. 2013. Scaling semi-supervised naive bayes with feature marginals. In *Proceedings of the 51st Annual Meeting of the Association for Computational Linguistics (Volume 1: Long Papers)*, pages 343–351, Sofia, Bulgaria, August. Association for Computational Linguistics.

Andrew L. Maas, Raymond E. Daly, Peter T. Pham, Dan Huang, Andrew Y. Ng, and Christopher Potts. 2011. Learning word vectors for sentiment analysis. In *Proceedings of the 49th Annual Meeting of the Association for Computational Linguistics: Human Language Technologies*, pages 142–150, Portland, Oregon, USA, June. Association for Computational Linguistics.

Christopher D. Manning, Prabhakar Raghavan, and Hinrich Schütze. 2008. *Introduction to Information Retrieval*. Cambridge University Press, New York, NY, USA.

Micol Marchetti-Bowick and Nathanael Chambers. 2012. Learning for microblogs with distant supervision: political forecasting with twitter. In *Proceedings of the 13th Conference of the European Chapter of the Association for Computational Linguistics*, EACL '12, pages 603–612, Stroudsburg, PA, USA. Association for Computational Linguistics.

Andrew McCallum and Kamal Nigam. 1998. A comparison of event models for naive bayes text classification. In *IN AAAI-98 WORKSHOP ON LEARNING FOR TEXT CATEGORIZATION*, pages 41–48. AAAI Press.

Vangelis Metsis, Ion Androutsopoulos, and Paliouras Georgios. 2006. Spam filtering with naive bayes – which naive bayes? In *Third Conference on Email and Anti-Spam (CEAS)*.

Kamal Nigam, Andrew Kachites McCallum, Sebastian Thrun, and Tom Mitchell. 2000. Text classification from labeled and unlabeled documents using em. *Mach. Learn.*, 39(2-3):103–134, May.

Kevin Dela Rosa, Rushin Shah, Bo Lin, Anatole Gershman, and Robert Frederking. 2011. Topical clustering of tweets. In *Proceedings of the ACM SIGIR Special Interest Group on Information Retrieval's 3rd Workshop on Social Web Search and Mining (SIGIR: SWSM 2011)*. ACM.

Burr Settles and Xiaojin Zhu. 2012. Behavioral factors in interactive training of text classifiers. In *Proceedings of the 2012 Conference of the North American Chapter of the Association for Computational Linguistics: Human Language Technologies*, NAACL HLT '12, pages 563–567, Stroudsburg, PA, USA. Association for Computational Linguistics.

Burr Settles. 2009. Active learning literature survey. Computer Sciences Technical Report 1648, University of Wisconsin–Madison.

Burr Settles. 2011. Closing the loop: Fast, interactive semi-supervised annotation with queries on features and instances. In *Proceedings of the 2011 Conference on Empirical Methods in Natural Language Processing*, pages 1467–1478, Edinburgh, Scotland, UK., July. Association for Computational Linguistics.

Jianfeng Si, Arjun Mukherjee, Bing Liu, Qing Li, Huayi Li, and Xiaotie Deng. 2013. Exploiting topic based twitter sentiment for stock prediction. In *Proceedings of the 51st Annual Meeting of the Association for Computational Linguistics (Volume 2: Short Papers)*, pages 24–29, Sofia, Bulgaria, August. Association for Computational Linguistics.

Jiang Su, Jelber S. Shirab, and Stan Matwin. 2011. Large scale text classification using semi-supervised multinomial naive bayes. In Lise Getoor and Tobias Scheffer, editors, *Proceedings of the 28th International Conference on Machine Learning (ICML-11)*, pages 97–104, New York, NY, USA. ACM.

A. Tumasjan, T.O. Sprenger, P.G. Sandner, and I.M. Welpe. 2010. Predicting elections with twitter: What 140 characters reveal about political sentiment. In *Proceedings of the Fourth International AAAI Conference on Weblogs and Social Media*, pages 178–185.

Sida Wang and Christopher Manning. 2012. Baselines and bigrams: Simple, good sentiment and topic classification. In *Proceedings of the 50th Annual Meeting of the Association for Computational Linguistics (Volume 2: Short Papers)*, pages 90–94, Jeju Island, Korea, July. Association for Computational Linguistics.

Jason Weston, Sumit Chopra, and Keith Adams. 2014. #tagspace: Semantic embeddings from hashtags. In *Proceedings of the 2014 Conference on Empirical Methods in Natural Language Processing (EMNLP)*, pages 1822–1827, Doha, Qatar, October. Association for Computational Linguistics.

Simon Wibberley, David Weir, and Jeremy Reffin. 2013. Language technology for agile social media science. In *Proceedings of the 7th Workshop on Language Technology for Cultural Heritage, Social Sciences, and Humanities*, pages 36–42, Sofia, Bulgaria, August. Association for Computational Linguistics.

Simon Wibberley, David Weir, and Jeremy Reffin. 2014. Method51 for mining insight from social media datasets. In *Proceedings of COLING 2014, the 25th International Conference on Computational Linguistics: System Demonstrations*, pages 115–119, Dublin, Ireland, August. Dublin City University and Association for Computational Linguistics.

Utilizing review analysis to suggest product advertisement improvements

Takaaki Tsunoda[†] [*] **Takashi Inui**
Department of Computer Science
University of Tsukuba

Satoshi Sekine
Computer Science Department
New York University

tsunoda@mibel.cs.tsukuba.ac.jp[†]

Abstract

On an e-commerce site, product blurbs (short promotional statements) and user reviews give us a lot of information about products. While a blurb should be appealing to encourage more users to click on a product link, sometimes sellers may miss or misunderstand which aspects of the product are important to their users. We therefore propose a novel task: suggesting aspects of products for an advertisement improvement. As reviews have a lot of information about aspects from the perspective of users, review analysis enables us to suggest aspects that could attract more users. To achieve this, we break this task into the following two subtasks: aspect grouping and aspect group ranking. Aspect grouping enables us to treat product aspects at the semantic level rather than expression level. Aspect group ranking allows us to show users only aspects important for them. On the basis of experimental results using travel domain hotel data, we show that our proposed solution accomplishes NDCG@3 score of 0.739, which shows our solution is effective in achieving our goal.

1 Introduction

What are the most crucial parts of an e-commerce website that provide information to encourage users to buy products? For current websites, they are a product blurb and reviews. Blurbs, which are short promotional statements written by a seller and displayed as a short text advertisement, perform an important role in highlighting

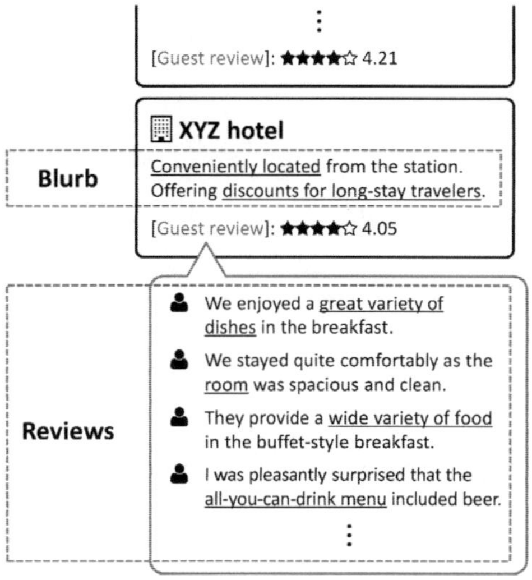

Figure 1: Examples of a blurb and reviews. Aspects of the hotel are underlined.

selling points to users. As it is the among the first things users see, a well written blurb is essential for encouraging users to click on the product link. Reviews, which are opinions or feedbacks on a product written by users who have purchased it, give us direct access to experiences of consumers who have used the product. Unlike blurbs, reviews from a number of users have abundant information about the product from the perspective of users. Figure 1 illustrates examples of a blurb and reviews of a hotel booking website.

Blurbs have to contain descriptions of the most important and appealing aspects of the product because the users will not check the reviews unless they are interested in the product by the blurb. However, due to a blurb writer's misunderstanding, the aspects of the product introduced in the blurb are not always the same as the product aspects that the users consider important or appealing. If these aspects are missing from the blurb, users who are looking for them never discover the

[*] Part of this research was conducted during the first author's internship at Rakuten Institute of Technology New York.

Proceedings of the 6th Workshop on Computational Approaches to Subjectivity, Sentiment and Social Media Analysis (WASSA 2015), pages 41–50, Lisboa, Portugal, 17 September, 2015.

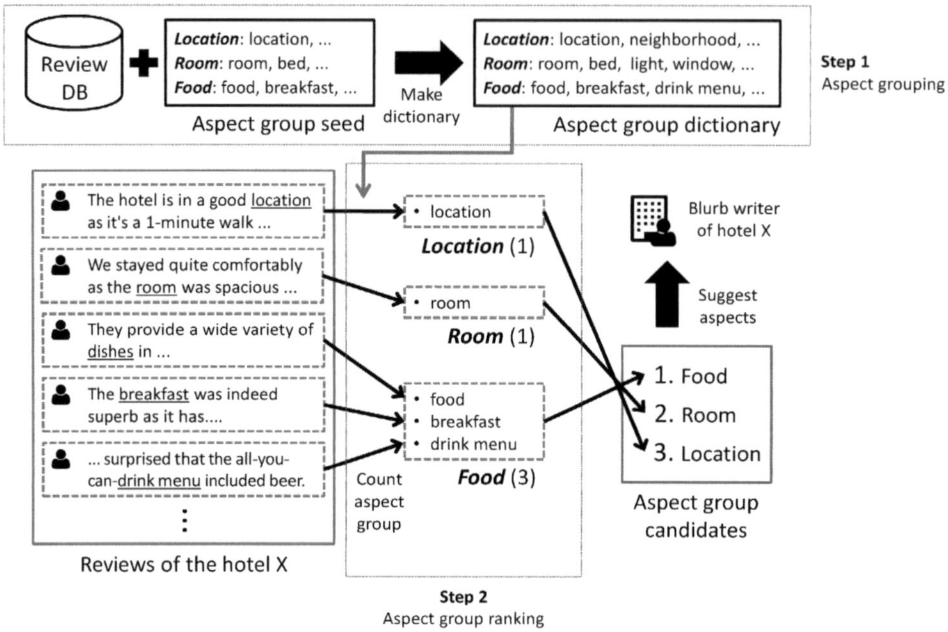

Figure 2: Task overview

existence of this product. For example in Figure 1, if the many users are looking for a hotel that provides great dishes or spacious rooms rather than discounts for long-stay travelers, they might not check the reviews, so the hotel may end up losing many potential customers. According to our observation in the hotel booking website, 81.0% of hotel blurbs lack one or more important aspects in the 3-best setting.

To suggest product blurb improvements, we propose the following novel task: finding aspects of a product that are important to the users and should be included in the blurb. For our initial approach to the task, we concentrate on the user review data. With a sufficient volume of reviews, we are able to determine which aspects of the product are important to users even if these aspects are not present in the blurb.

Figure 2 is an overview of the task. The goal of our task is to show aspect candidates that could be incorporated into the blurb ordered by their importance to users for a given product. To determine which aspects should be incorporated, we divide the task into two steps: aspect grouping and aspect group ranking. First, to treat aspects at the semantic level, we assign aspect expressions to aspect groups. Aspect grouping is essential to show meaningful suggestions, because enumerating aspects that have the same or similar concepts is redundant. Second, to identify important aspects for users, we rank aspect groups on the basis of importance. Aspect group ranking is required to suggest only aspects that improve the blurb, as showing all aspects mentioned in the reviews regardless of their importance would not be helpful for blurb writers.

In this paper, we utilize the following well-known existing techniques for each step to confirm our proposed framework works well. For the aspect grouping, we employ one of the semi-supervised methods described by Zhai et al. (2010). Their technique allows us to make an aspect group dictionary that assigns each aspect expression to aspect group based on a semi-supervised technique with small manual annotation effort. For the aspect group ranking, we adopt an aspect ranking method proposed by Inui et al. (2013). Their ranking method, which is based on log-likelihood ratio (Dunning, 1993), enables us to leverage aspect group scores to extract the aspects that distinguish a product from its competitors.

Our contributions in this paper are as follows:

- We propose a novel task: finding characteristic aspects for blurb improvements.
- To achieve this goal, we break the task into the two subtasks: aspect grouping and aspect group ranking.

- To confirm our two-step framework, we adopt known and suitable methods in each step and investigated the best parameter combinations.

The paper is organized as follows. In the next section, we discuss related work mainly on aspect extraction and aspect ranking. In Section 3, we introduce the proposed method. In Section 4, we evaluate our method with a travel domain data. In Section 5, we conclude the paper and discuss the future directions.

2 Relevant work

Although the task we propose is new, there is a large body of work on sentiment analysis and aspect extraction that we can employ to build the components of our solution. In this section, we concentrate on research most directly relevant or applicable to our task.

First, identifying product aspects as opinion targets has been extensively studied since it is an essential component of opinion mining and sentiment analysis work (Hu and Liu, 2004; Popescu and Etzioni, 2005; Kobayashi et al., 2007; Qiu et al., 2011; Xu et al., 2013; Liu et al., 2014). This direction of research has been changing from merely enumerating aspects to capturing a more structured organization such as aspect meaning, a task that is also attempted as part of this work.

Existing research that focuses on structuring aspect groups is particularly relevant to our task. Although there exist fully unsupervised solutions based on topic modeling (Titov and McDonald, 2008a; Titov and McDonald, 2008b; Guo et al., 2009; Brody and Elhadad, 2010; Chen et al., 2014), the unsupervised approach still faces the challenge of generating coherent aspect groups that can be easily interpreted by humans. On the other hand, approaches using prior knowledge sources or a small amount of annotation data are also studied to maintain high precision while lowering the manual annotation cost (Carenini et al., 2005; Zhai et al., 2010; Chen et al., 2013a; Chen et al., 2013b; Chen et al., 2013c). Particularly, the method proposed by Zhai et al. (2010) can easily incorporate aspect expressions into predefined aspect groups and requires only a small amount of manually annotated data as aspect seeds. Their work utilizes an extension of Naive Bayes classification defined by Nigam et al. (2000), which allows for a semi-supervised approach to assigning words to appropriate aspect groups. Their method serves as a component that enables us to treat aspects at the concept level instead of just the word level.

Lastly, another area applicable to our task is that of ranking aspects on the basis of various indicators, as exemplified by Zhang et al. (2010a), Zhang et al. (2010b), Yu et al. (2011), and Inui et al. (2013). While Zhang et al. (2010a), Zhang et al. (2010b), and Yu et al. (2011) propose aspect ranking methods based on aspect importance in a whole given domain, Inui et al. (2013) aim to find distinguishing aspect expressions of a product from other ones. They use a scoring method to rank aspect expressions and their variants, so theirs is the most appropriate technique for our task of discovering important aspects for users. To employ their approach for our task, we extend their method as described in the section 3.2.

3 Proposed method

To determine which aspects can be included in the blurb of the product, we utilize the following review analysis technique: aspect grouping and aspect group ranking. We begin by assigning aspect expressions to aspect groups to manage aspects at the semantic level. We next score aspect groups to suggest only important aspect groups.

3.1 Aspect grouping

The simplest way to suggest aspects for blurb improvement would be to extract important aspect expressions from product reviews and show them to users. However, according to this approach, phrases like "easy access", "easy to get to", or even "multiple transport options" might be suggested at the same time if the hotel's most characteristic aspect is its location. As they express very similar concept, suggesting all the aspect expressions that are important is not convenient.

To treat the aspects that expresses similar concept the same, we make a dictionary that assigns aspect expressions to higher level semantic groups. For example, in the case of a hotel, the aspect groups are *Location*, *Room*, *Food*, etc. When we treat aspects at the aspect group level, phrases containing words such as transport or access will all belong to a single *Location* group.

To build this dictionary at a minimum cost without much manual annotation effort, we employ one of the semi-supervised methods described by

Zhai et al. (2010). This dictionary allows us to assign each aspect expression in a review text to an appropriate aspect group.

The aspect grouping method of Zhai et al. (2010) we employ is based on a semi-supervised document clustering method proposed by Nigam et al. (2000). Although Nigam et al. (2000)'s method was proposed for document clustering, it can be applied to aspect grouping with Zhai et al. (2010)'s modifications.

The semi-supervised document clustering method of Nigam et al. (2000) is an extension of the Naive Bayes classifier. To use the Naive Bayes classifier in a semi-supervised approach, they applied the Expectation-Maximization (EM) algorithm (Dempster et al., 1977) to estimate labels for unlabeled documents. In this paper, we show only their calculation steps, not the complete derivation. First, learn the simple classifier using only labeled data (Equations (1) and (2)). Next, apply the classifier to unlabeled data to calculate the probabilities of clusters (Equation (3)). Then iterate the learning and application steps using both labeled and unlabeled data until the parameters converge (Equations (1) to (3)). In the iteration step, Equation (3) corresponds to M-step, and Equations (1) and (2) correspond to E-step. The concrete calculation steps are specified below, where w_i is a word, d_i is a document, and c_i is a cluster. $\{w_1, \ldots, w_{|V|}\} = V$, $\{d_1, \ldots, d_{|D|}\} = D$,and $\{c_1, \ldots, c_{|C|}\} = C$ are a vocabulary, a document set, and clusters, respectively. $N_{w,d}$ is the frequency of word w in document d.

$$P(w_t|c_j) = \frac{1 + \sum_{d_i \in D} N_{w_t,d_i} P(c_j|d_i)}{|V| + \sum_{w_m \in V} \sum_{d_i \in D} N_{w_m,d_i} P(c_j|d_i)} \quad (1)$$

$$P(c_j) = \frac{1 + \sum_{d_i \in D} P(c_j|d_i)}{|C| + |D|} \quad (2)$$

$$P(c_j|d_i) = \frac{P(c_j) \prod_{w_k \in d_i} P(w_k|c_j)}{\sum_{c_r \in C} P(c_r) \prod_{w_k \in d_i} P(w_k|c_r)} \quad (3)$$

Zhai et al. (2010) applied to the semi-supervised aspect grouping in the following manner. They construct a bag-of-words, which is pseudo document for clustering, for each aspect expression using its context. The method is as follows: first, for a target aspect expression e, collect all occurrences of e from all reviews. Next, for all occurrences of e, pick words from a context window (t left words, t right words, and the e itself) except for stop-words [1]. We used a window size of $t = 3$, which is the same as that of Zhai et al. (2010). Finally, form bag-of-words d_e for e by summing picked words.

For example, if an aspect expression e is "price" and we find that the following two sentences include this expression, a bag-of-words for e is $d_e = \langle$lowest, price, city, competitive, price, product$\rangle$.

- It was the lowest price in this city.
- A competitive price for this product.

3.2 Aspect group ranking

The next step is ranking aspect groups by their importance to display only those with a higher ranking.

To rank aspect groups, we regard aspect groups that are distinguishing as important ones, and base our approach on an aspect ranking method proposed by Inui et al. (2013). Their ranking method is based on log-likelihood ratio (LLR) (Dunning, 1993), which compares the probabilities of observing the entire data under the hypothesis that a given product and aspect are dependent and a hypothesis that they are independent. In this way, the LLR score takes into account the entire review data including other products' reviews. As it has a higher value for aspects that differentiate a product from the others, it is a great fit for our goal of finding aspects that distinguishes a product from its competitors.

We extend the method proposed by Inui et al. (2013) because their goal differs from ours in two ways. First, as they are interested in ranking aspect expressions regardless of their polarity, expressions that appear many times in negative contexts might obtain high rankings. In contrast, in our task, such aspects are not appropriate for blurb improvements. Second, while they focus on ranking aspect expressions and their variants, we are interested in ranking aspect groups.

For the first point, we select sentences that have positive sentiment before performing the subsequent procedures. More specifically, we make a binary classifier, which classifies a given review sentence into either positive or not positive sentiment. We use the classifier to extract only positive sentiment sentences.

For the second point, we use frequencies of aspect expressions that belong to an aspect group instead of frequencies of a word and its variants to

[1] As we used Japanese reviews for our experiment, we removed particles and auxiliary verbs as stop-words.

calculate LLR. With this approach, the concrete calculation steps of LLR for a product p and aspect group g are as follows. First, we calculate the following four parameters: a, b, c, d.

$$\begin{aligned} a &= \text{Frequency of words in } g \text{ in } S_p \\ b &= \text{Frequency of words in } g \text{ in } S \\ c &= \text{Frequency of words in all aspect groups} \\ &\quad\quad \text{except } g \text{ in } S_p \\ d &= \text{Frequency of words in all aspect groups} \\ &\quad\quad \text{except } g \text{ in } S \end{aligned} \tag{4}$$

where $S_p, S = \bigcup_p S_p$ are a set of positive review sentences in a product p's reviews and in all products' reviews, respectively. Then, when we let $n = a + b + c + d$, the LLR value can be obtained in the following manner.

$$\begin{aligned} \mathrm{LLR}_0 = a \log \frac{an}{(a+b)(a+c)} + b \log \frac{bn}{(a+b)(b+d)} \\ + c \log \frac{cn}{(c+d)(a+c)} + d \log \frac{dn}{(c+d)(b+d)} \end{aligned} \tag{5}$$

Finally, we correct the LLR_0 value as the LLR_0 cannot distinguish between "an aspect group g is characteristic in p" and "an aspect group g is more characteristic in other products than in p". We want to obtain the former one, so we employ the following correction:

$$\mathrm{LLR} = \begin{cases} +\mathrm{LLR}_0 & \text{if } \frac{a}{c} > \frac{b}{d} \\ -\mathrm{LLR}_0 & \text{otherwise} \end{cases} \tag{6}$$

A higher LLR value means the aspect group g is more characteristic for product p.

In addition to this, we also tried using sentence or review frequencies instead of word frequencies to calculate LLR. For example, in the sentence and review levels, parameter a is calculated as follows.

$$\begin{aligned} a_{\mathrm{S-LLR}} &= \text{Frequency of } \underline{\text{sentences}} \\ &\quad\quad \text{that have a word in } g \text{ in } S_p \\ a_{\mathrm{R-LLR}} &= \text{Frequency of } \underline{\text{reviews}} \\ &\quad\quad \text{that have a word in } g \text{ in } S_p \end{aligned}$$

We can calculate b, c, d for the sentence or review level similarly to the above. We did this to attempt to avoid introducing bias from reviews that elaborate on a certain aspect and influence its frequency for a given product. We expect preventing overestimation the occurence of an aspect group from this approach if it is driven by a high frequency within a review from a single user.

4 Experiments

4.1 Experiment conditions

To conduct our experiments, we used hotel blurb and review data from a Japanese website, Rakuten Travel. We chose to focus on this domain as hotels are characterized by numerous aspects, thus presenting a fair challenge for our task. The aggregate review data comes from the publicly available *Rakuten Data Release*[2]. We selected hotels that had between 10 and 1000 user reviews, rendering a total of 13,664 hotels and 2,254,307 user reviews. For data preprocessing, we employed MeCab 0.996 (Kudo et al., 2004) as a word tokenizer and applied a simple rule-based system for sentence segmentation.

To build an aspect dictionary for the travel domain, we predefined the following 12 aspect groups: *Service, Location, View and Landscape, Building, Room, Room facilities, Hotel facilities, Amenities, Bath, Food, Price,* and *Website*. We selected frequent nouns and noun phrases that occurred in at least 1% of all reviews as aspect expressions. For noun phrase, we considered two following types: 1) complex nouns and 2) "A of B", where both of A and B are nouns. After filtering out proper nouns, we obtained 9,844 aspect phrases. For seeds for the semi-supervised learning, we manually labeled the 281 most frequent ones, which are around 3% of the candidates.

To evaluate the dictionary, we examined the performance of sentence labeling. We compared the golden standard and the automated labeling based on the dictionary, which is obtained by regarding aspect groups in which aspect phrases in the dictionary appeared in a sentence as belonging to the sentence's aspect group. Note that we allowed multiple aspect groups in a sentence. For the golden standard dataset, we annotated random sampled 100 reviews, which consist of 450 sentences. We used precision and recall as an evaluation metrics.

To select positive sentiment sentences, we employed a SVM classifier. For training data, we used the TSUKUBA corpus 1.0, which is a sentence level sentiment-tagged corpus included in the Rakuten Data Release. We constructed a bi-

[2]Rakuten Data Release: `http://rit.rakuten.co.jp/opendata.html`. In this paper we use a snapshot of the data released in 2012. Hotel blurbs correspond to the information shown on hotel detail pages.

Table 1: Performance of aspect grouping

Aspect group	Precision	Recall
Service	71.67%	70.49%
Location	64.86%	70.59%
View and Landscape	55.56%	38.46%
Building	85.71%	30.77%
Room	78.18%	64.18%
Room Facilities	52.17%	36.36%
Hotel Facilities	28.57%	8.70%
Amenities	83.33%	31.25%
Bath	88.64%	88.64%
Food	71.62%	79.10%
Price	76.92%	44.44%
Webpage	36.36%	12.90%

Table 2: Performance of aspect group ranking

	NDCG				
Method	@1	@2	@3	@4	@5
R-LLR	0.743	0.736	0.737	0.752	0.770
S-LLR	0.751	0.741	0.739	0.745	0.764
W-LLR	0.777	0.735	0.736	0.737	0.760
R-TScore	0.567	0.597	0.639	0.663	0.693
S-TScore	0.599	0.607	0.647	0.673	0.701
W-TScore	0.589	0.614	0.643	0.657	0.690
R-TF	0.674	0.663	0.676	0.707	0.753
S-TF	0.695	0.678	0.682	0.718	0.760
W-TF	0.648	0.649	0.654	0.705	0.751

nary classifier, which classifies a given review sentence into either positive or non-positive sentiment, from 4,309 review sentences by using scikit-learn 0.15.2 (Pedregosa et al., 2011). By 5-fold cross validation, we confirmed that the classifier achieved 83.08% precision and 79.79% recall for finding positive sentences.

The ranking method we use is based on log-likelihood ratio scoring (**LLR**) as described above. To compare the effectiveness of LLR for aspect group ranking, we compared this method with two baseline methods: aspect group frequency (**TF**), which is the same as parameter a in Equation (4), and T-scores of the relative aspect group frequency in the reviews of each hotel (**TScore**). In addition to this, we examined which level performs better for measuring frequency: word (**W-LLR**), sentence (**S-LLR**), or review (**R-LLR**). Likewise, we compared the effect of the frequency unit on TF and T-scores so that we can also compare between the word (**W-TF**, **W-TScore**), sentence (**S-TF**, **S-TScore**), and review level (**R-TF**, **R-TScore**).

To evaluate the aspect groping methods, we annotated randomly selected 126 hotels for a gold standard dataset. For each hotel, we ranked appropriate aspect groups for a blurb. To judge rank and appropriateness, we referred the following sources: a current blurb, a introduction page of the hotel, and most recent 50 reviews. According to our annotation, the average number of aspect groups that are appropriate for a blurb is 3.09.

We use the Normalized Discounted Cumulative Gain (NDCG) (Järvelin and Kekäläinen, 2002) as evaluation measures. NDCG measures the performance of a ranking system based on the similarity between the system output and the gold standard, defined as:

$$\mathrm{NDCG@}n = \frac{\mathrm{DCG@}n}{\mathrm{IDCG@}n} \quad (7)$$

$$\mathrm{DCG@}n = rel_1 + \sum_{i=2}^{n} \frac{rel_i}{\log_2 i} \quad (8)$$

where n is the rank position to measure, rel_i is the relevance grade for a ith suggested aspect group, IDCG@n is the normalizer to make NDCG@n varying from 0.0 to 1.0. For n, we show $n = 1, \ldots, 5$ (1 to 5-best output) results because the average number of appropriate aspect groups is around 3 according to our annotation, and suggesting a large number of aspects would go against the goal of the task. For rel_i, we used the logarithmic discount $rel_i = 1/\log(1+r)$ where r is the rank of the ith aspect group in the gold standard, which is a feasible discount function for NDCG (Wang et al., 2013).

4.2 Results

4.2.1 Evaluation of aspect grouping

First, we present the performance of aspect grouping. Table 1 shows the dictionary performance for each aspect group.

The result shows the aspect grouping component has reasonable performance except for low recall aspect groups including *Hotel facilities* and *Webpage*. The reason for this is because these aspect groups appear less frequently and difficult to assign aspect expressions to these aspect groups accurately. According to our observation, in the Rakuten Travel, reviewers do not mention about these aspect groups unless they find something special, as these aspect groups are not fundamental aspects of a hotel as opposed to *Room* or *Food*. We examine how this result affects the aspect group ranking in the evaluation of aspect group ranking.

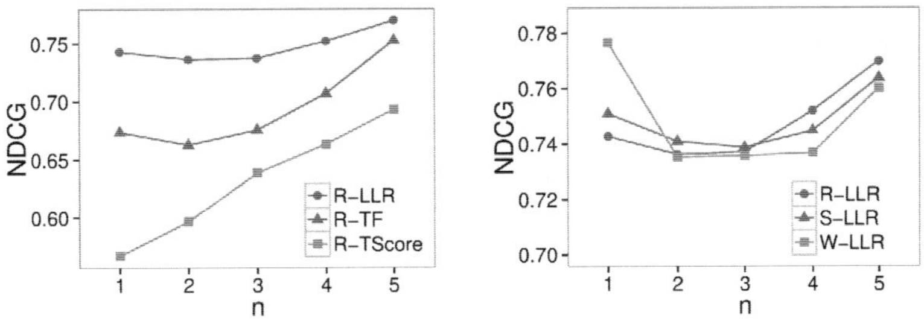

(a) Different ranking methods. (b) Different frequency units.

Figure 3: Performance comparison between ranking methods and frequency units

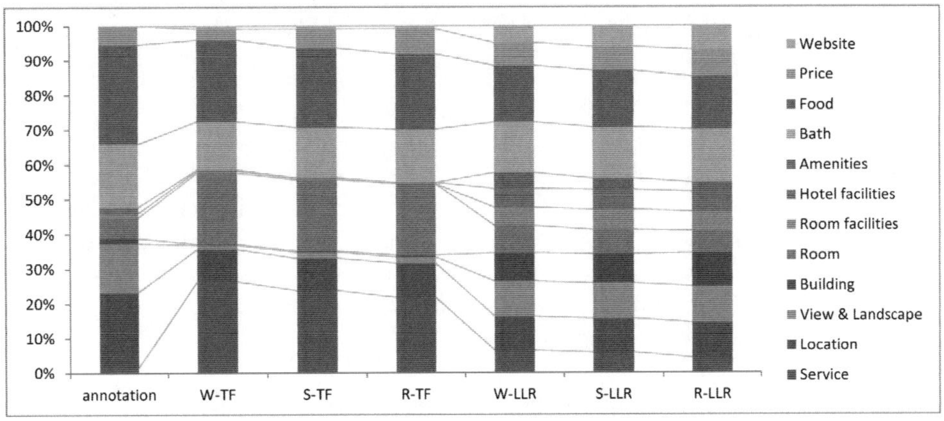

Figure 4: Aspect group distribution at 3-best.

4.2.2 Evaluation of aspect group ranking

Next, we compare the performance between ranking methods (**R-LLR**, **R-TScore**, **R-TF**). Figure 3(a) and top rows of each block of Table 2 show the results obtained by different methods when the aspect group frequency unit is fixed as a single review. According to these results, the log-likelihood ratio score (**R-LLR**) shows a higher NDCG score than the other methods at NDCG@1 to NGCG@5. This establishes that LLR is the most effective method for our task.

Lastly, we compare the performance of the LLR ranking depending on the frequency count unit (**R-LLR**, **S-LLR**, **W-LLR**), as illustrated in Figure 3(b) and the first block of Table 2. The results show that sentence-based **S-LLR** and review-based **R-LLR** have almost the same NDCG score compared to word-based **W-LLR**. Furthermore, we can observe from Table 2 that the same tendency exists for **TF** and **TScore** baselines. This shows that for the purpose of our task, the frequency unit is a less important parameter compared to the ranking method.

For a detailed investigation, we calculated aspect group distribution for the gold standard and outputs for each method at 3-best. Figure 4 illustrates the aspect group distribution. Distribution of TFs, which correspond to how many aspect phrases appeared in reviews, is not very similar to that of the gold standard, especially for aspect groups *Service*, *Room*, *View and Landscape* and *Hotel facilities*. For *Service* and *Room*, we think this is also brought on by the tendency of reviews, that is, many reviewers mentioned them even if reviewers did not find anything special about them as these are fundamental aspects. In contrast to, *View and Landscape* and *Hotel facilities* are not fundamental aspects, so reviewers mention about them only if they find something special. In addition to this, the aspect group dictionary not captures *Hotel facilities* occurrences well as the Recall column of Table 1 shows. On the other hand, distributions of LLR and the gold standard are more similar. The reason for this is the LLR can leverage scores by comparing other

Table 3: Output example. Aspect group column shows system outputs (**S-LLR**) for reviews.

Hotel		Aspect group	Text (for suggestion, an example review sentence)
#1	Blurb	Location	Located in the port town.
	Suggestion	Bath	We enjoyed many kinds of baths including an open air bath, a cascading bath, and a sleeping bath.
		Food	I'm very satisfied with the cuisine that they prepare from the ocean and mountain fare.
		Room	The room was impressively clean like just after refurbishment.
	Annotation	#1:Bath, #2:Food, #3:Room	
#2	Blurb	Building	Reopened on Sep. 10th after complete refurbishment!!
	Suggestion	Bath	There were many private hot-spring bath facilities for families, and the hot-spring water was great!
		Food	I was pleasantly surprised that the all-you-can-drink menu included beer and coffee, and the meals tasted great.
		Amenities	I was impressed with the unlimited towel policy in the hot spring, and skin lotion and other beauty products were provided.
	Annotation	#1:Food, #2:Bath, #3:View and Landscape, #4:Amenities	

hotels' reviews. More specifically, aspect groups mentioned in many hotel reviews like *Service* or *Room* have low scores, and those mentioned in few reviews like *View* or *Hotel facilities* have high scores. Besides, even the dictionary misses mentions of aspect groups like *Hotel facilities*, LLR can mitigate this problem. Meanwhile, the aspect group *Location* is underestimated and *Website* is overestimated. To deal with this problem, employing prior knowledge about which aspects are preferred for blurbs in a given domain might give us better aspect group suggestions.

For the best performing **S-LLR** method at 3-best, NDCG@3 score is 0.739, which allows us to make reasonable suggestions for enhancing some product blurbs. Table 3 shows output examples of our system (**S-LLR**). In the first example, the blurb describes one aspect group: *Location*. This blurb might lose customers who prioritize other aspects of the hotels. To improve this blurb, our system suggests other aspect groups that could be mentioned in the blurb on the basis of reviews of the hotel: *Bath*, *Food*, and *Room* at 3-best. In view of the annotation and the example of review sentences, we can observe that these aspect groups are characteristic and including them in the blurb would improve it. Meanwhile, in the second example, the blurb mentions about *Building*. The suggestions of our system, *Bath*, *Food* and *Amenities* might help blurb improvement as example review sentences show. However, according to the annotation, the aspect group *Amenities* is the fourth while the *View and Landscape* is the third. We think it is from two causes. First, the system suggests without consideration of the aspect group preference in blurbs and results overestimation of *Amenities*. Second, the dictionary captures insufficient reviews which mention about *View and Landscape* as Recall of the aspect grouping is lower as Table 1 shows. We think refining aspect grouping and improving aspect group ranking are both effective to achieve better performance.

5 Conclusions

In this paper, we proposed a novel task of suggesting product blurb improvement and offered a solution to extract important aspect groups from reviews. To achieve our goal, we divided the task into two subtasks, which are aspect grouping and aspect group ranking.

The future directions of our work are as follows. First, instead of using whole given domain reviews to calculate LLR, we could use only real competitors for a target product. For example, in the travel domain, we could use reviews of hotels near to a target hotel to enable the system to suggest the target hotels more unique aspects compared with its competitors. Next, in Table 3, we also showed representative review sentences that illustrate each aspect group. If we could show such sentences along with suggested aspect groups, the system would make writing blurbs much easier. Like in the case of aspect group selection, we could use a scoring method such as LLR to select characteristic sentences.

Acknowledgements

We thank Zofia Stankiewicz for supporting this work as a mentor of the internship program. We would also like to thank to Rakuten, Inc. for releasing the resources of Rakuten Travel.

References

Samuel Brody and Noemie Elhadad. 2010. An unsupervised aspect-sentiment model for online reviews. In *NAACL-HLT-2010*, pages 804–812, June.

Giuseppe Carenini, Raymond T. Ng, and Ed Zwart. 2005. Extracting knowledge from evaluative text. In *K-CAP-2005*, pages 11–18, October.

Zhiyuan Chen, Arjun Mukherjee, Bing Liu, Meichun Hsu, Malu Castellanos, and Riddhiman Ghosh. 2013a. Discovering coherent topics using general knowledge. In *CIKM-2013*, pages 209–218, October.

Zhiyuan Chen, Arjun Mukherjee, Bing Liu, Meichun Hsu, Malu Castellanos, and Riddhiman Ghosh. 2013b. Exploiting Domain Knowledge in Aspect Extraction. In *EMNLP-2013*, pages 1655–1667, October.

Zhiyuan Chen, Arjun Mukherjee, Bing Liu, Meichun Hsu, Malu Castellanos, and Riddhiman Ghosh. 2013c. Leveraging multi-domain prior knowledge in topic models. In *IJCAI-2013*, pages 2071–2077, August.

Zhiyuan Chen, Arjun Mukherjee, and Bing Liu. 2014. Aspect Extraction with Automated Prior Knowledge Learning. In *ACL-2014*, pages 347–358, June.

A. P. Dempster, N. M. Laird, and D. B. Rubin. 1977. Maximum likelihood from incomplete data via the em algorithm. *JOURNAL OF THE ROYAL STATISTICAL SOCIETY*, B 39(1):1–38.

Ted Dunning. 1993. Accurate methods for the statistics of surprise and coincidence. *Computational Linguistics*, 19(1):61–74.

Honglei Guo, Huijia Zhu, Zhili Guo, XiaoXun Zhang, and Zhong Su. 2009. Product feature categorization with multilevel latent semantic association. In *CIKM-2009*, page 1087, November.

Minqing Hu and Bing Liu. 2004. Mining opinion features in customer reviews. In *AAAI-2004*, pages 755–760, July.

Takashi Inui, Yuto Itaya, Mikio Yamamoto, Keiji Shinzato, Yu Hirate, and Kaoru Yamada. 2013. Structuring opinion features by relative characteristics on user-opinion aggregation. *Journal of Natural Language Processing*, 20(1):3–25 (in Japanese).

Kalervo Järvelin and Jaana Kekäläinen. 2002. Cumulated gain-based evaluation of IR techniques. *ACM Transactions on Information Systems (TOIS)*, 20(4):422–446.

Nozomi Kobayashi, Kentaro Inui, and Yuji Matsumoto. 2007. Extracting aspect-evaluation and aspect-of relations in opinion mining. In *EMNLP-CoNLL-2007*, pages 1065–1074, June.

Taku Kudo, Kaoru Yamamoto, and Yuji Matsumoto. 2004. Applying conditional random fields to japanese morphological analysis. In *EMNLP-2004*, pages 230–237, July.

Kang Liu, Liheng Xu, and Jun Zhao. 2014. Extracting Opinion Targets and Opinion Words from Online Reviews with Graph Co-ranking. In *ACL-2014*, pages 314–324, June.

Kamal Nigam, Andrew Kachites McCallum, Sebastian Thrun, and Tom Mitchell. 2000. Text classification from labeled and unlabeled documents using em. *Machine Learning*, 39(2-3):103–134.

F. Pedregosa, G. Varoquaux, A. Gramfort, V. Michel, B. Thirion, O. Grisel, M. Blondel, P. Prettenhofer, R. Weiss, V. Dubourg, J. Vanderplas, A. Passos, D. Cournapeau, M. Brucher, M. Perrot, and E. Duchesnay. 2011. Scikit-learn: Machine learning in Python. *Journal of Machine Learning Research*, 12:2825–2830.

Ana-Maria Popescu and Oren Etzioni. 2005. Extracting product features and opinions from reviews. In *EMNLP-2005*, pages 339–346, October.

Guang Qiu, Bing Liu, Jiajun Bu, and Chun Chen. 2011. Opinion Word Expansion and Target Extraction through Double Propagation. *Computational Linguistics*, 37(1):9–27.

Ivan Titov and Ryan McDonald. 2008a. A Joint Model of Text and Aspect Ratings for Sentiment Summarization. In *ACL-HLT-2008*, pages 308–316, June.

Ivan Titov and Ryan McDonald. 2008b. Modeling online reviews with multi-grain topic models. In *WWW-2008*, page 111, April.

Yining Wang, Liwei Wang, Yuanzhi Li, Di He, and Tie-Yan Liu. 2013. A theoretical analysis of NDCG type ranking measures. In *COLT-2013*, pages 25–54, June.

Liheng Xu, Kang Liu, Siwei Lai, Yubo Chen, and Jun Zhao. 2013. Mining opinion words and opinion targets in a two-stage framework. In *ACL-2013*, pages 1764–1773, August.

Jianxing Yu, Zheng-Jun Zha, Meng Wang, and Tat-Seng Chua. 2011. Aspect ranking: Identifying important product aspects from online consumer reviews. In *ACL-HLT-2011*, pages 1496–1505, June.

Zhongwu Zhai, Bing Liu, Hua Xu, and Peifa Jia. 2010. Grouping product features using semi-supervised learning with soft-constraints. In *COLING-2010*, pages 1272–1280, August.

Kunpeng Zhang, Ramanathan Narayanan, and Alok Choudhary. 2010a. Voice of the customers: mining online customer reviews for product feature-based ranking. In *WOSN-2010*, June.

Lei Zhang, Bing Liu, Suk Hwan Lim, and Eamonn O'Brien-Strain. 2010b. Extracting and ranking product features in opinion documents. In *COLING-2010*, pages 1462–1470, August.

Towards Opinion Mining from Reviews for the Prediction of Product Rankings

Wiltrud Kessler, Roman Klinger, and Jonas Kuhn
Institute for Natural Language Processing
University of Stuttgart
70569 Stuttgart, Germany
{wiltrud.kessler,roman.klinger,jonas.kuhn}@ims.uni-stuttgart.de

Abstract

Opinion mining aims at summarizing the content of reviews for a specific brand, product, or manufacturer. However, the actual desire of a user is often one step further: Produce a ranking corresponding to specific needs such that a selection process is supported. In this work, we aim towards closing this gap. We present the task to rank products based on sentiment information and discuss necessary steps towards addressing this task. This includes, on the one hand, the identification of gold rankings as a fundament for an objective function and evaluation and, on the other hand, methods to rank products based on review information. To demonstrate early results on that task, we employ real world examples of rankings as gold standard that are of interest to potential customers as well as product managers, in our case the sales ranking provided by Amazon.com and the quality ranking by Snapsort.com. As baseline methods, we use the average star ratings and review frequencies. Our best text-based approximation of the sales ranking achieves a Spearman's correlation coefficient of $\rho = 0.23$. On the Snapsort data, a ranking based on extracting comparisons leads to $\rho = 0.51$. In addition, we show that aspect-specific rankings can be used to measure the impact of specific aspects on the ranking.

1 Introduction

Opinion mining (often referred to as sentiment analysis) is the task of identifying opinions about specific entities, products or persons in text. Reviews for products, for instance from Amazon.com, are a typical resource for opinions. Often, opinion mining is approached as a text classification task in which snippets (like sentences, paragraphs, or phrases) are categorized into being objective or subjective and in the latter case positive, negative, or neutral (Liu, 2015; Täckström and McDonald, 2011; Sayeed et al., 2012; Pang and Lee, 2004). More differentiated results can be obtained by methods that additionally identify the target of the opinion, specific mentions of product characteristics usually called aspects (Choi et al., 2010; Johansson and Moschitti, 2011; Yang and Cardie, 2012; Hu and Liu, 2004; Li et al., 2010; Popescu and Etzioni, 2005; Jakob and Gurevych, 2010; Klinger and Cimiano, 2013).

It has been proposed to use the extracted information for summarizing specific information about a product (Hu and Liu, 2004). The main advantage of such result is that a star rating is not only associated to the whole product but separated for specific aspects. This is helpful when a user aims at getting an overview of the content of reviews but it might still be leading to an overwhelming amount of information.

In this work, we propose to aim at generating a ranked list of products and hypothesize that such a ranking would be more helpful for the typical task of a user to select a product based on specific needs than the exact and isolated value. We therefore discuss two main prerequisites to be able to reach that goal: Firstly, we discuss the need for gold ranking information, which is the fundament for evaluation. Such ranking can in addition be used for data-driven optimization of methods to automatically generate such rankings based on structured or textual review (and therefore opinion-mining based) information. In this work, we utilize two external gold standards,

Proceedings of the 6th Workshop on Computational Approaches to Subjectivity, Sentiment and Social Media Analysis (WASSA 2015), pages 51–57,
Lisboa, Portugal, 17 September, 2015.

namely the Amazon.com sales ranking of products of a specific category, and the quality ranking by product aspects available at the website Snapsort.com (a service that collects detailed information about cameras and provides comparisons between them).

Secondly, we discuss different approaches to use (target-oriented) opinion mining methods to produce a ranking of products. We focus on fine-grained methods which associate opinion expressions with different aspects. This enables us to create aspect-specific rankings by using only those expressions that refer to a specific aspect of the product. A ranking from a combination of selected aspects can be used to create specific, personalized rankings. Aspect-specific rankings can also be used to determine the influence of an aspect on the overall ranking.

Previous work in this area is comparatively limited. Ganesan and Zhai (2012) enhance information retrieval models by splitting the query into separate parts for the product's aspects and use a dictionary-based query expansion of opinion words. Tkachenko and Lauw (2014) extract statements comparing products from review texts and generate ranked pairs from these comparisons. They perform two types of evaluations. On the one hand, they compare their system output to the ranking retrieved from a gold standard (annotated by crowdsourcing). On the other hand, they generate a gold standard of product quality for specific predefined characteristics (for instance that smaller is better for cameras). In contrast, our work aims at ranking the products themselves and handles the influence of the aspects as a latent variable without predefining them. Further, we use external sources for evaluation.

We provide the following main contributions:

- We discuss the task of predicting a full ranking of products in addition to isolated prediction of ratings.

- We demonstrate how methods for target-oriented and comparison-based opinion mining can be used to predict product rankings. As real-world examples of such rankings, we use the sales ranking from Amazon.com and the quality ranking from Snapsort.com.

- We show that fine-grained opinion mining methods achieve a substantial performance in predicting these rankings from textual information.

- We present aspect-specific rankings that allow for an understanding of the impact of each aspect on the external ranking.

2 Towards Aspect-based Ranking of Products

Most opinion-mining approaches tackle the task of extracting evaluations of products and aspects (targets of opinion) as the result of the mining process. This leaves the interpretation of the ratings of different aspects to the end user. However, the underlying assumption is that this end user is able to combine the information in a way that it can be utilized for making specific decisions. This utility of the information from opinion mining systems is clearly depending on the use cases and subjective needs. Therefore, important characteristics of a ranking of products are:

- The ranking supports specific needs of an individual or of a downstream task.

- The ranking can be purely subjective or inter-subjective.

- A user can be aware of the factors influencing the preferences leading to a ranking or not.

One instance of a ranking which is directly available from structured meta-data is the *sales ranking* of a category of products from an online shop (in this work, we use the sales ranking of Amazon.com). This ranking addresses for instance the needs of a product manager to maximize the popularity of a product. This ranking is inter-subjective and the user is typically not fully aware of all factors influencing the rank. Such factors are the price of the product, the quality, price-performance ratio, advertisements, etc. Therefore, taking into account information generated by fine-grained opinion-mining methods can shed light on the impact of these aspects on this ranking. If reviews and sales ranking come from the same source, the number of reviews being available for a product can be presumed to correlate (or at least interact) with the number sold. Reviews play an important role for a buying decision, so the interaction will also work in the other direction, when a product has many reviews and most of them are positive, chances go up that people will buy it.

Another instance of an available source of information is an *expert ranking* in which a domain expert compares different products and aspects of them and put them into an order. A common source for such ranking are domain specific magazines or websites with the aim of providing users with a condensed source of information supporting their purchase decision. This ranking is typically purely subjective, however, different factors are taken into account, which might be disclosed or not. In this work, we employ the information made available from Snapsort.com. It is a service that collects detailed information about cameras and provides comparisons between them. Their score incorporates aspects from technical specifications like shutter, viewfinder size, whether image stabilization is available, as well as popularity (how many times the camera has been viewed on the website) or number of lenses available. Such a ranking has been used in recently published previous work by Tkachenko and Lauw (2014) who use a partial expert rating in their gold standard when they specify predefined characteristics for their product (for instance that smaller is better for cameras) and evaluate against these aspect-specific rankings.

Both sales ranking and expert ranking are attempting to combine opinions from or for a set of users. However, a ranking of products might be highly subjective. Therefore, we propose that an actual ranking should be based on crowdsourcing without predefining the aspects taken into account to make a decision. As common in annotation tasks for ranking, requesting a full ranking of a list of products from annotators is a cumbersome challenge. Therefore, we propose that such crowdsourcing task should be set up in a learning-to-rank setting, in which annotators are asked to define a preference to a pair of products. Such annotations can then later be used for compiling an inter-subjective ranking as well as a personalized ranking. This approach is not performed in this paper but constitutes relevant future work. From such rankings, a personalized preference function can be learnt which weights different aspects against each other, even if the user is not aware of these factors.

Related to this proposal is the work by Tkachenko and Lauw (2014) who created a gold standard of textual comparison mentions with crowdsourcing. Ganesan and Zhai (2012) use information from semi-structured reviews in which users provide scores for different aspects.

3 Methods

Our goal is to create a ranked list of products based on sentiment information. To rank products in this work, we compare three methods for textual analysis and two baselines.

Two approaches are based on counting words or phrases with a positive and negative polarity. The first assigns these polarities based on a dictionary in which the respective class is explicitly stated. The polarity score $\text{score}(p)$ for a product p is then calculated as the number of all positive words (pos) in all reviews for this product minus the number of all negative words (neg):

$$\text{score}_{\text{dict}}(p) = \text{pos}(p) - \text{neg}(p)\,. \qquad (1)$$

To account for the impact of longer reviews, we normalize these numbers by the number of tokens in all reviews for the specific product all_p:

$$\overline{\text{score}}_{\text{dict}}(p) = \frac{\text{score(p)}}{\text{all}_p}\,. \qquad (2)$$

The ranked list of products is then created by sorting according to this score. We refer to the two variations of this method as DICT and DICT-NORM.

This first dictionary-based method is easy to implement and to use. However, it might not take into account context specific formulations of polarity expressions. As a second method, we therefore opt for a machine learning-based detection of subjective phrases with their polarities in context, specifically we use JFSA (Joint Fine-Grained Sentiment Analysis Tool, Klinger and Cimiano (2013)[1]). Calculating the product score and ranking is performed analogously to the dictionary-based approach. We refer to the two variations of this method as JFSA and JFSA-NORM.

As our goal is to ultimately generate a ranked list of products, it is a straight-forward idea to exploit textual comparison expressions, as in this example:

$$\underbrace{\text{It}}_{\substack{\text{entity}\\\text{(preferred)}}}\ \text{has a}\ \underbrace{\text{better}}_{\text{predicate}}\ \underbrace{\text{lens}}_{\text{aspect}}\ \text{than}\ \underbrace{\text{the T3i}}_{\substack{\text{entity}\\\text{(not preferred)}}}\,.$$

To extract such comparisons, we employ CSRL (Comparison Semantic Role-Labeler, Kessler and

[1]https://bitbucket.org/rklinger/jfsa

Kuhn (2013)). The system identifies comparative predicates ("better"), the two entities that are involved ("It" and "the T3i"), which one is preferred ("It"), and the compared aspect ("lens"). To identify the products that are referenced, we associate a mentioned entity to the product name (or names) with the minimal cosine similarity on token level. In the example, "the T3i" would be associated with the camera "Canon EOS Rebel T3i". The pronoun "It" is mapped to the reviewed product.

The score for a product is calculated based on the number of times it occurs as a preferred product (pref) minus the number of times it occurs as a non-preferred product (npref):

$$\mathrm{score}_{\mathrm{CSRL}}(p) = \mathrm{pref}(p) - \mathrm{npref}(p)\,. \quad (3)$$

The resulting score for a product is used for sorting analogously to the previous approaches. We refer to this method as CSRL.

We use two baselines that do not take the textual information of a review into account: The first method sorts products by their average star rating (from one to five stars, as assigned by the author of a review) of all reviews for the respective product (STAR). The second method sorts the products by the number of reviews it has received (from none to many, NUMREVIEWS). The intuition is that products which are sold more often gather more reviews.

Two of our methods, JFSA and CSRL recognize aspects of products together with a subjective phrase or comparison, respectively. Besides creating one ranking that is a combined measure of all aspects of the product, we have the option to use only evaluations regarding specific aspects which results in an aspect-specific ranking. As one aspect can be referred to with several expressions, a normalization of the aspect mentions is needed for this filtering. In the experiments in this paper, we use manually compiled lists of textual variations for the most frequent aspects in our dataset[2]. In the target-specific version of a method, subjective phrases or entity mentions are only counted towards the score of a product if there is a token overlap between the recognized aspect and a textual variation of the target aspect.

[2]The lists for aspect mention normalization are available as supplementary material. For instance, *video* contains "video", "videos", "film", "films", "movie", "movies", "record", "records", "recording".

Method	Amazon	Snapsort
STARS	-0.027	**0.436**$*$
NUMREVIEWS	**0.331**$*$	0.095
DICT-NORM (GI)	0.125$*$	-0.148
DICT-NORM (MPQA)	0.142$*$	-0.145
DICT (GI)	0.219$*$	0.426$*$
DICT (MPQA)	0.222$*$	0.441$*$
JFSA-NORM	0.151$*$	-0.230
JFSA	**0.234**$*$	0.404$*$
CSRL	0.183$*$	**0.511**$*$

Table 1: Results (Spearman's ρ) of the target-agnostic methods for predicting the sales ranking of Amazon and the Snapsort quality ranking. Significance over random is marked with $*$ ($p < 0.05$). The best baseline and the best text-based method are marked in bold.

4 Experiments

4.1 Experimental setting

For evaluation, we use camera reviews retrieved from Amazon with the search terms "camera" and "camera" in conjunction with "fuji", "fujifilm", "canon", "panasonic", "olympus", "nikon", "sigma", "hasselblad", "leica", "pentax", "rollei", "samsung", "sony", "olympus". As the first gold ranking, we extract the Amazon sales rank from the product descriptions ("Amazon Best Sellers Rank" in the "Camera & Photo" category) as retrieved between April 14th and 18th, 2015 and include only products for which a rank is provided. The resulting list contains 920 products with a total of 71,409 reviews. Product names are extracted from the title of the page and shortened to the first six tokens to remove additional descriptions.

As a second external gold ranking, we use the quality ranking provided by Snapsort. From the top 150 products in the Amazon sales ranking, 56 are found on Snapsort. We use the rank in the category "best overall" of "all digital cameras announced in the last 48 month" as retrieved on June 12th, 2015.[3]

JFSA is trained on the camera data set by Kessler et al. (2010). CSRL is trained on the camera data by Kessler and Kuhn (2014). For the methods DICT and DICT-NORM, we try two different sources of opinion words, the general

[3]The full list of products with their names and the rankings are available in the supplementary material.

Aspect	#	ρ	σ
performance	637	0.301	0.009
video	600	0.278	0.013
size	513	0.218	0.017
pictures	790	0.213	0.003
battery	541	0.208	0.012
price	625	0.198	0.008
zoom	514	0.196	0.013
shutter	410	0.191	0.016
features	629	0.190	0.009
autofocus	403	0.175	0.013
screen	501	0.136	0.012
lens	457	0.099	0.012
flash	591	0.093	0.011

Table 2: Results (Spearman's ρ and standard deviation σ) of JFSA for predicting the Amazon sales ranking when only the subjective phrases are taken into account which refer to the specified target aspect. The number of products for which at least one evaluation of the target aspect is found is shown in column #.

inquirer dictionary (Stone et al., 1996)[4] and the MPQA subjectivity clues (Wilson et al., 2005)[5].

To measure the correlation of the rankings generated by our different methods with the gold ranking, we calculate Spearman's rank correlation coefficient ρ (Spearman, 1904). We test for significance with the Steiger test (Steiger, 1980).

4.2 Results

As described in Section 2, we take into account two different rankings for evaluation: The Amazon.com sales ranking contains 920 products and is an example for a ranking that may be useful for sales managers or product designers. The second is the expert ranking by Snapsort.com which contains 56 products. These two rankings are conceptually different. There is no correlation between the two rankings ($\rho = -0.04$).

Table 1 shows the results for the baselines and the target-agnostic methods on the gold rankings. There is a pronounced difference between the results for the two gold rankings.

The best result on Amazon (significantly outperforming all other methods) is achieved by counting the reviews ($\rho = 0.33$, NUMREVIEWS).

[4] 3518 entries; 1775 positive, 1743 negative using the categories from Choi and Cardie (2008).

[5] 6456 entries; 2304 positive, 4152 negative.

For Snapsort, however, NUMREVIEWS leads to only $\rho = 0.1$. One factor that explains this difference in performance is the fact that in case of Amazon the reviews and the ranking come from the same source and it is unclear whether the popularity of a product leads to many reviews or a high number of reviews leads to higher sales. Though "popularity" is one aspect that influences the Snapsort rating, it is not as prominent.

The performance of the STARS baseline is not significantly different from random for Amazon. This is partly explained by the fact that among the products with a 5.0 star rating many have only very few reviews (less than 10). This is less of a problem in the Snapsort ranking. Also, we would expect that what is contained in the reviews are quality judgements that are more closely aligned with what Snapsort uses for ranking than what influences sales.

The dictionary-based polarity assignment based ranking (DICT) approximates the sales ranking with $\rho = 0.22$, for both MPQA and GI. Normalization of the polarity scores reduces the correlation. The similarity of the results obtained by the two different dictionaries is reflected in the very high correlation of the resulting rankings (without normalization: $\rho = 0.99$; with normalization: $\rho = 0.8$). However, the non-normalized rankings are not correlated with the normalized rankings of the same dictionary (GI $\rho = -0.16$, MPQA $\rho = -0.14$).

The dictionary-based ranking is slightly outperformed by JFSA with $\rho = 0.23$. Normalization by token number (and therefore implicitly the review count) decreases the performance to $\rho = 0.15$. The difference of JFSA to DICT-NORM (GI) and DICT (MPQA and GI) is significant ($p < 0.05$). For Snapsort, normalization has a strong negative impact.

On Amazon, the ranking achieved with CSRL is mediocre in comparison to the other methods. CSRL suffers more clearly from data sparseness (the highest number of subjective phrases for a product found by JFSA is over 9000, while the highest number of comparisons that mention a given product is 662 for CSRL). On the Snapsort ranking however, CSRL leads to the best result of all experiments with $\rho = 0.51$.

In comparison to using all information extracted from reviews to generate a ranking, the aspect-specific results allow for an understanding of the impact of each aspect on the gold ranking. Aspect-specific rankings for important aspects are highly correlated with the gold ranking, while those for completely irrelevant aspects have a correlation near random. The results for the Amazon sales ranking and JFSA are shown in Table 2. Due to data sparseness, a substantial amount of products receive a score of 0. To eliminate the resulting artificial inflation of ρ while enabling a comparison between methods with different numbers of scored products, we add the zero-scoring products in random order and average over 100 different ranked lists. We omit the results for CSRL and the results on Snapsort which are all close to random.

For the ranking created with JFSA, the aspect *performance* contributes most to approximating the sales ranking ($\rho = 0.30$) followed by *video* ($\rho = 0.28$). Both results outperform the target-agnostic ranking of JFSA ($\rho = 0.23$) (significant for *performance*).

5 Conclusion and Future Work

We have presented the task of predicting a ranking of products and introduced three potential sources for gold rankings: A sales ranking and expert based ranking have been used in the experiments in this paper. In addition, we discussed how to set up a crowdsourcing-based annotation of rankings. We demonstrated early results how to use different opinion mining methods (dictionary-based, machine learning, comparison-based) to predict such rankings. In addition, we have presented experiments on how aspect-specific rankings can be used to measure the impact of that specific information on the ranking.

The methods discussed here show a limited performance, however, these results of approximating a real world ranking are promising and encouraging for further research. Though the correlation scores are comparatively low, they allow for an analysis of the influence of a specific aspect on the ranking as shown for the Amazon sales ranking.

The best result for the Amazon sales ranking is achieved based on the number of reviews (NUMREVIEWS). This might be seen as an instance of the chicken-egg dilemma, and it may be the case that there are many reviews *because* the product has been sold many times. The same effect cannot be observed on Snapsort. It is further worth noting that the average star rating (STARS) is not informative towards Amazon sales ranking, but gives good results on Snapsort.

The methods which take into account the polarity of phrases lead to the second best performance (JFSA and DICT) for Amazon. For Snapsort, the comparison-based CSRL is outperforming all other methods and shows the highest performance of all experiments in this paper ($\rho = 0.51$).

For future work, we plan to formulate the problem in a learning-to-rank setting with data generated in a crowdsourcing paradigm to combine the different measures discussed in this paper and allow for a straight-forward adaptation to different rankings.

Acknowledgments

We thank Christian Scheible for fruitful discussions. Wiltrud Kessler has been supported by a Nuance Foundation grant.

References

Yejin Choi and Claire Cardie. 2008. Learning with compositional semantics as structural inference for subsentential sentiment analysis. In *EMNLP*, pages 793–801. ACL.

Yoonjung Choi, Seongchan Kim, and Sung-Hyon Myaeng. 2010. Detecting Opinions and their Opinion Targets in NTCIR-8. In *NTCIR-8 Workshop Meeting*, pages 249–254.

Kavita Ganesan and ChengXiang Zhai. 2012. Opinion-based entity ranking. *Information Retrieval*, 15(2):116–150.

Minqing Hu and Bing Liu. 2004. Mining and summarizing customer reviews. In *ACM SIGKDD*, pages 168–177.

Niklas Jakob and Iryna Gurevych. 2010. Using anaphora resolution to improve opinion target identification in movie reviews. In *ACL*, pages 263–268.

Richard Johansson and Alessandro Moschitti. 2011. Extracting opinion expressions and their polarities: exploration of pipelines and joint models. In *ACL-HLT*, pages 101–106.

Wiltrud Kessler and Jonas Kuhn. 2013. Detection of product comparisons - How far does an out-of-the-box semantic role labeling system take you? In *EMNLP*, pages 1892–1897. ACL.

Wiltrud Kessler and Jonas Kuhn. 2014. A corpus of comparisons in product reviews. In *LREC*, pages 2242–2248.

Jason S. Kessler, Miriam Eckert, Lyndsie Clark, and Nicolas Nicolov. 2010. The 2010 icwsm jdpa sentment corpus for the automotive domain. In

4th International AAAI Conference on Weblogs and Social Media Data Workshop Challenge (ICWSM-DWC 2010).

Roman Klinger and Philipp Cimiano. 2013. Bi-directional inter-dependencies of subjective expressions and targets and their value for a joint model. In *ACL*, pages 848–854.

Fangtao Li, Minlie Huang, and Xiaoyan Zhu. 2010. Sentiment analysis with global topics and local dependency. In *AAAI*, pages 1371–1376.

Bing Liu. 2015. *Sentiment Analysis*. Cambridge University Press.

Bo Pang and Lillian Lee. 2004. A sentimental education: Sentiment analysis using subjectivity summarization based on minimum cuts. In *ACL*, pages 271–278.

Ana-Maria Popescu and Oren Etzioni. 2005. Extracting product features and opinions from reviews. In *HLT-EMNLP*, pages 339–346. ACL.

Asad Sayeed, Jordan Boyd-Graber, Bryan Rusk, and Amy Weinberg. 2012. Grammatical structures for word-level sentiment detection. In *NAACL-HLT*, pages 667–676. ACL.

Charles Spearman. 1904. The proof and measurement of association between two things. *American Journal of Psychology*, 15:88–103.

James H. Steiger. 1980. Tests for comparing elements of a correlation matrix. *Psychological Bulletin*, 87(2):245–251.

Philip J. Stone, Dexter C. Dunphy, Marshall S. Smith, and Daniel M. Ogilvie. 1996. *General Inquirer: A Computer Approach to Content Analysis*. The MIT Press.

Oscar Täckström and Ryan McDonald. 2011. Semi-supervised latent variable models for sentence-level sentiment analysis. In *ACL-HLT*, pages 569–574.

Maksim Tkachenko and Hady W. Lauw. 2014. Generative modeling of entity comparisons in text. In *CIKM*, pages 859–868.

Theresa Wilson, Janyce Wiebe, and Paul Hoffmann. 2005. Recognizing contextual polarity in phrase-level sentiment analysis. In *HLT*, pages 347–354. ACL.

Bishan Yang and Claire Cardie. 2012. Extracting opinion expressions with semi-markov conditional random fields. In *EMNLP-CoNLL*, pages 1335–1345. ACL.

Classification of deceptive opinions using a low dimensionality representation

Leticia C. Cagnina
LIDIC
Universidad Nacional de San Luis
San Luis, Argentina
lcagnina@unsl.edu.ar

Paolo Rosso
NLE Lab, PRHLT Research Center
Universitat Politècnica de València
Valencia, España
prosso@dsic.upv.es

Abstract

Opinions in social media play such an important role for customers and companies that there is a growing tendency to post fake reviews in order to change purchase decisions and opinions. In this paper we propose the use of different features for a low dimension representation of opinions. We evaluate our proposal incorporating the features to a Support Vector Machines classifier and we use an available corpus with reviews of hotels in Chicago. We perform comparisons with previous works and we conclude that using our proposed features it is possible to obtain competitive results with a small amount of features for representing the data. Finally, we also investigate if the use of emotions can help to discriminate between truthful and deceptive opinions as previous works show to happen for deception detection in text in general.

1 Introduction

Spam is commonly present on the Web through of fake opinions, untrue reviews, malicious comments or unwanted texts posted in electronic commerce sites and blogs. The purpose of those kinds of spam is promote products and services, or simply damage their reputation. A *deceptive* opinion spam can be defined as a fictitious opinion written with the intention to sound authentic in order to mislead the reader. An opinion spam usually is a short text written by an unknown author using a not very well defined style. These characteristics make the problem of automatic detection of opinion spam a very challenging problem.

First attempts for solving this problem considered unsupervised approaches trying to identify duplicate content (Jindal and Liu, 2008), and searching for unusual review patterns (Jindal et al., 2010) or groups of opinion spammers (Mukherjee et al., 2011). Later, supervised methods were presented. Such is the case of (Feng et al., 2012a; Feng et al., 2012b) in which the authors extended the n-gram feature by incorporating syntactic production rules derived from probabilistic context free grammar parse trees. In (Liu et al., 2002) a learning from positive and unlabeled examples (PU-learning) approach was successfully applied to detect deceptive opinion spam, using only few examples of deceptive opinions and a set of unlabeled data. Then, in (Hernández Fusilier et al., 2015a) the authors proposed a PU-learning variant for the same task, concluding the appropriateness of their approach for detecting opinion spam.

In this paper we study the feasibility of the application of different features for representing safely information about clues related to fake reviews. We focus our study in a variant of the stylistic feature character n-grams named character n-grams in tokens. We also study an emotion-based feature and a linguistic processes feature based on LIWC variables. We evaluated the proposed features with a Support Vector Machines (SVM) classifier using a corpus of 1600 reviews of hotels (Ott et al., 2011; Ott et al., 2013). We show an experimental study evaluating the single features and combining them with the intention to obtain better features. After that previous study, we selected the one with we obtained the best results and made direct and indirect comparisons with some other methods. The obtained results show that the proposed features can capture information from the contents of the reviews and the writing style allowing to obtain classification results as good as with traditional character n-grams but with a lower dimensionality of representation.

The rest of the paper is organized as follows. Section 2 describes briefly the proposed features. Section 3 shows the experimental study performed.

Proceedings of the 6th Workshop on Computational Approaches to Subjectivity, Sentiment and Social Media Analysis (WASSA 2015), pages 58–66,
Lisboa, Portugal, 17 September, 2015.

The description of the corpus and the different experiments carried out can also be found in this section. Finally, the main conclusions and future work are in Section 4.

2 Feature Selection for Deception Clues

In this section we describe the three different kinds of features studied in this work and the tools used for their extraction.

2.1 Character n-grams in tokens

The main difference of character n-grams in tokens[1] with respect to the traditional NLP feature character n-grams is the consideration of the tokens for the extraction of the feature. That is, tokens with less than n characters are not considered in the process of extraction neither blank spaces. Character n-grams in tokens preserve the main characteristics of the standard character n-grams (Šilić et al., 2007): *effectiveness* for quantifying the writing style used in a text (Keselj et al., 2003; Stamatatos, 2013), the *independence* of language and domains (Wei et al., 2008), the *robustness* to noise present in the text (Cavnar and Trenkle, 1994), and, *easiness* of extraction in any text. But unlike the traditional character n-grams, the proposed feature obtains a smaller set of attributes, that is, character n-grams in tokens avoids the need of feature dimension reduction. Figure 1 illustrates that difference.

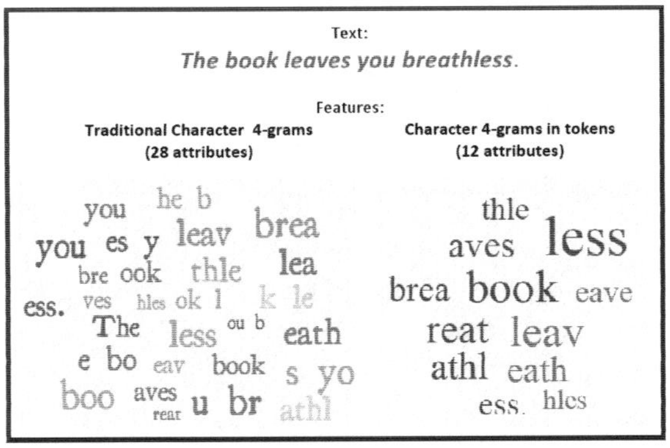

Figure 1: Set of attributes obtained with traditional character n-grams and character n-grams in tokens, considering n=4.

As it can be observed from Figure 1 the amount of attributes obtained with the character n-grams in tokens feature is considerably less, although the effectiveness of this representation still being good, as we will see in Section 3.

For the extraction of character n-grams in tokens we have used Natural Language Toolkit (NLTK) package (Bird et al., 2009) with Python language.

2.2 Emotions-based feature

Previous works have been demonstrated that the use of emotions helps to discriminate truthful from deceptive text (Hancock et al., 2008; Burgoon et al., 2003; Newman et al., 2003). There is some evidence that liars use more negative emotions that truth-tellers. Based on that, we obtained the percentages of positive, negative and neutral emotions contained in the sentences of a document. Then, we have used these values as features in order to represent the polarity of the text.

For the calculation of the percentages of positive, negative and neutral emotions contained in the text we have used the Natural Language Sentiment Analysis API[2] which analyzes the sentiments, labeling a text with its polarity (positive, negative or neutral). We have obtained the polarities of each sentence and then we have obtained the percentages of the polarities associated to the whole document (a review in our case). Finally, we have used those values as features.

2.3 LIWC-based feature: linguistic processes

Several features derived from *Linguistic Inquiry and Word Count* (LIWC) were considered. In particular we have studied those related to functional aspects of the text such as word count, adverbs, pronouns, etc. After performing an early experimental study considering the 26 different variables of the linguistic processes category in LIWC2007 software (Pennebaker et al., 2007), we have concluded that pronouns, articles and verbs (present, past and future tense) would help to distinguish fake from true reviews.

3 Experimental Study

In order to evaluate our proposal, we have performed some experimental study on the first publicly available opinion spam dataset gathered and presented in (Ott et al., 2011; Ott et al., 2013). We first describe the corpus and then we show the different experiments made. Finally we compare our results with those published previously.

[1]Token is considered in this works as any sequence of consecutive characters separated by one or more blank spaces.

[2]http://text-processing.com/demo/sentiment/

3.1 Opinion Spam corpus

The Opinion Spam corpus presented in (Ott et al., 2011; Ott et al., 2013) is composed of 1600 *positive* and *negative* opinions for hotels with the corresponding gold-standard. From the 800 *positive* reviews (Ott et al., 2011), the 400 truthful where mined from TripAdvisor 5-star reviews about the 20 most popular hotels in Chicago area. All reviews were written in English, have at least 150 characters and correspond to users who had posted opinions previously on TripAdvisor (non first-time authors). The 400 deceptive opinions correspond to the same 20 hotels and were gathered using Amazon Mechanical Turk crowdsourcing service. From the 800 *negative* reviews (Ott et al., 2013), the 400 truthful where mined from TripAdvisor, Expedia, Hotels.com, Orbitz, Priceline and Yelp. The reviews are 1 or 2-star category and are about the same 20 hotels in Chicago. The 400 deceptive reviews correspond to the same 20 hotels and were obtained using Amazon Mechanical Turk.

3.2 Truthful from deceptive opinion classification

We have obtained the representations of the opinion reviews considering the features described in Section 2. For all, we have used term frequency-inverse document frequency (tf-idf) weighting scheme. The only text preprocessing made was convert all words to lowercase characters. Naïve Bayes and SVM algorithms in Weka (Hall et al., 2009) were used to perform the classification. We only show the results obtained with SVM because its performance was the best. For all experiments we have performed a 10 fold cross-validation procedure in order to study the effectiveness of the SVM classifier with the different representations. For simplicity, we have used LibSVM[3] which implements a C-SVC version of SVM with a radial basis function. We have run the classifier with the default parameters. The values reported in the tables correspond to the macro average F-measure as it is reported in Weka.
Tables 1, 2 and 3 show the F-measure obtained with each feature proposed for the Opinion Spam corpus.

Table 1 considers only the positive reviews (800 documents). In the first part of the table, we can observe the F-measure obtained with the single features 3 and 4 grams in tokens and, articles, pronouns and verbs extracted from LIWC2007 (referenced as LIWC for simplicity). With the single emotions-based feature (POSNEG in the table) we did not obtain good results; for that reason these are not included in the first part of the table. In the second part of the table, the combination of each single feature was used as representation of the reviews. The best value is in boldface. As we can observe, the best result (F-measure = **0.89**) was obtained with the combination of 4-grams in tokens and the articles, pronouns and verbs (LIWC). With the combination of 3-grams and LIWC feature the F-measure is quite similar.

Feature	F-measure
3-grams in tokens	0.821
4-grams in tokens	0.871
LIWC	0.697
3 + 4-grams in tokens	0.873
3-grams + POSNEG	0.871
4-grams + POSNEG	0.873
3 + 4-grams + POSNEG	0.877
3-grams + LIWC	0.883
4-grams + LIWC	**0.89**

Table 1: Deceptive opinions detection with SVM for positive reviews of Opinion Spam corpus (800 opinions).

Feature	F-measure
3-grams in tokens	0.826
4-grams in tokens	0.851
LIWC	0.69
3 + 4-grams in tokens	0.832
3-grams + POSNEG	0.827
4-grams + POSNEG	0.851
3 + 4-grams + POSNEG	0.827
3-grams + LIWC	0.85
4-grams + LIWC	**0.865**

Table 2: Deceptive opinions detection with SVM for negative reviews of Opinion Spam corpus (800 opinions).

Table 2 shows the results obtained considering only the negative reviews (800 documents). The best result (F-measure = **0.865**) was obtained with the feature 4-grams in tokens plus LIWC variables. It is interesting to note that similar

[3]https://www.csie.ntu.edu.tw/ cjlin/libsvm/

results (although sightly lower) were obtained also with three more features: the single 4-grams in tokens, the combination of the last one with positive and negative emotions percentages, and also with 3-grams combined with LIWC's tokens.

Feature	F-measure
3-grams in tokens	0.766
4-grams in tokens	0.867
LIWC	0.676
3 + 4-grams in tokens	0.854
3-grams + POSNEG	0.858
4-grams + POSNEG	0.87
3 + 4-grams + POSNEG	0.851
3-grams + LIWC	0.866
4-grams + LIWC	**0.879**

Table 3: Deceptive opinions detection with SVM for positive and negative reviews of Opinion Spam corpus (1600 opinions).

Table 3 shows the classification results considering the whole corpus, that is, the combined case of positive plus negative reviews (1600 documents). The best F-measure (**0.879**) was obtained, as the same as the previous cases, with 4-grams in tokens plus LIWC feature. It is worth noting that with the combination of 4-grams in tokens with POSNEG feature seems to be effective when positive and negative polarities are considered together in deception detection, a fact that is not present when just one polarity is considered (see Tables 1 and 2).

As we can observe from Tables 1, 2 and 3, the differences of F-measure values are quite small. In fact, for the almost similar values like, for example, 4-grams in tokens + LIWC compared with 3-grams + LIWC or 3 + 4-grams + POSNEG (see Table 1) the differences are not statistically significant. Consequently we have selected the one with highest F-measure value (4-grams in tokens + LIWC) for simplicity, but some of the other representations can be used instead. In order to analyze the set of attributes corresponding to the feature 4-grams in tokens combined with LIWC, we have calculated the Information Gain ranking.
From this analysis we have observed that the set of attributes with highest information gain are similar for negative and both together polarities corpora. The study shows that 4-grams in tokens are in the top positions of the ranking and those reveal information related to places (*chic, chig, igan* for Chicago and Michigan cities), amenities (*floo, elev, room* for floor, elevator, room) and their characterization (*luxu, smel, tiny* for luxury, smells and tiny). From the 7th position of the ranking we can observe the first LIWC attributes: pronouns (*my, I, we*) and after 15th position we can observe verbs (*is, open, seemed*). Interestingly, the articles can be observed from position 68th in the ranking (*a, the*).
Regarding the corpus considering only the positive reviews, the ranking is similar to the cases analyzed before with exception of the pronouns which appear at 1st position (*my*) and at 16th position (*I, you*). This fact could indicate the presence of many opinions concerned with their own experience (good) making the personal pronouns one of the most discriminative attribute for positive polarity spam opinion detection. With respect to the characterization of the amenities, the adjectives observed in 4-grams in tokens have to do with positive opinions about those (*elax, amaz, good* for relax, amazing and good). Figure 2 illustrates the first positions of the ranking of attributes obtained for positive reviews.

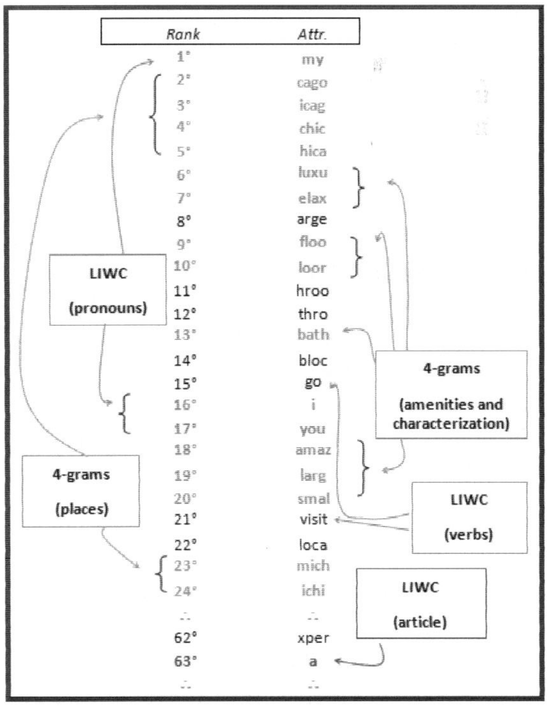

Figure 2: Information gain ranking (partial) for positive reviews.

3.3 Comparison of results

For a comparison of the performance of our proposal, we analyzed the obtained results with respect to the state-of-the-art. We have made a comparison considering the results of five different models. The first four of these were used in an indirect comparison, while just one method was used in a direct comparison of the performance. In (Banerjee and Chua, 2014) the authors presented the results of a logistic regression model using 13 different independent variables: complexity, reading difficulty, adjective, article, noun, preposition, adverb, verb, pronoun, personal pronoun, positive cues, perceptual words and future tense. In (Ren et al., 2014) a semi-supervised model called mixing population and individual property PU learning, is presented. The model is then incorporated to a SVM classifier. In (Ott et al., 2011) the authors used the 80 dimensions of LIWC2007, unigrams and bigrams as set of features with a SVM classifier. In (Feng and Hirst, 2013), profile alignment compatibility features combined with unigrams, bigrams and syntactic production rules were proposed for representing the opinion spam corpus. Then, a multivariate performance measures version of SVM classifier (named SVM^{perf}) was trained. In (Hernández Fusilier et al., 2015b) the authors studied two different representations: character n-grams and word n-grams. In particular, the best results were obtained with a Naïve Bayes classifier using character 4 and 5 grams as features.

As we stated before, two kinds of comparisons are shown: an indirect (we could not obtain the complete set of results reported by the authors) and a direct (the authors kindly made available the results and a statistical comparison can be performed).

In Table 4 we can observe the indirect comparison of our results with those of (Banerjee and Chua, 2014) and (Ren et al., 2014) obtained with a 10 fold cross validation experiment, and then, with a 5 fold cross validation in order to make a fair comparison with the results of (Ott et al., 2011) and (Feng and Hirst, 2013). Note that the results are expressed in terms of the accuracy as those were published by the authors; the results correspond only to positive reviews of the Opinion Spam corpus because the authors experimented in that corpus alone.

From the Table 4 we can observe that the combination of 13 independent variables seems to have the lowest prediction accuracy (accuracy = 70.50%). About the last result, the authors in (Banerjee and Chua, 2014) concluded that only articles and pronouns (over the 13 variables) could significantly distinguish true from false reviews. The accuracy of the semi-supervised model is slightly lower (86.69%) than that of our approach (**89%**), although good enough. The authors concluded that the good performance of the semi-supervised model is due the topic information captured by the model combined with the examples and their similarity (Ren et al., 2014). Then, they could obtain an accurate SVM classifier. Regarding the experiments with the 5 fold cross-validation, we obtained similar results to those of (Ott et al., 2011) and slightly lower than the ones of (Feng and Hirst, 2013). From this last experiment we can observe that using the representation of (Feng and Hirst, 2013) with more than 20138 attributes it is possible to obtain comparable results with those of our approach where we use a smaller representation (1533 attributes).

Model	Accuracy
10 fold cross-validation	
(Banerjee and Chua, 2014)	70.50%
(Ren et al., 2014)	86.69%
Our approach	**89%**
5 fold cross-validation	
(Ott et al., 2011)	89.8%
(Feng and Hirst, 2013)	**91.3%**
Our approach	89.8%

Table 4: Indirect comparison of the performance. Deceptive opinions detection for positive reviews of Opinion Spam corpus (800 opinions).

In Table 5 we can observe the direct comparison of the performance for the positive and negative polarities reviews of the Opinion Spam corpus considering the proposal of (Hernández Fusilier et al., 2015b). First column shows the representation proposed, the second one shows the amount of attributes (Attr.) of the representation, the third column shows the F-measure value (F) obtained after a 10 fold cross-validation process, and the last column shows the p-value obtained in the statistical significance test used to study the differences of performance between (Hernández Fusilier et al., 2015b) approach and ours.

Positive reviews (800 opinions)

Model	Attr.	F	p-value
Character 5-grams*	60797	0.90	0.094
Our approach	1533	0.89	

Negative reviews (800 opinions)

Model	Attr.	F	p-value
Character 4-grams*	32063	0.872	0.748
Our approach	1497	0.865	

* (Hernández Fusilier et al., 2015b).

Table 5: Direct comparison of the performance for deceptive opinions detection.

It is interesting to note that the F-measure values obtained with both approaches are quite similar for positive and negative reviews, as we can observe in Table 5. Regarding the amount of attributes used for each representation of the reviews, it is worth noting that our approach uses 97% and 95% fewer attributes for positive and negative reviews compared with the model of (Hernández Fusilier et al., 2015b). Even using a combination of two simple features as character 4-grams in tokens and LIWC variables as we have proposed, the amount of attributes is considerably lower than the traditional character n-grams without diminishing the quality of the classification. The reason of the lower dimensionality of our representation has to do with the manner in which the n-grams are obtained. The high descriptive power of character n-grams in tokens plus the information added with the LIWC variables seem to be adequate to obtain an accurate classifier (SVM in our case).

In order to determine if the differences of performance of (Hernández Fusilier et al., 2015b) and our approach are statistically significant, we have calculated the Mann-Whitney U-test (Mann and Whitney, 1947). This nonparametric test compares two unpaired groups of values without making the assumption of the normality of the samples. However, the requirements of independence of the samples, the data is continuous and ordinal, there are no ties between the groups and the assumption that the distribution of both groups are similar in shape, are satisfied. The null hypothesis states that the samples come from the same population, that is, the classifiers performs equally well with the proposed models. We have calculated the Mann-Whitney U-test considering a 2-tailed hypothesis and significance level of 0.05. In Table 5 we can observe that the p-value obtained in the comparison of performance of positive reviews corpus is $0.094 > 0.05$ which stands for the difference of results are not statistically significant (the p-value is not ≤ 0.05, then the null hypothesis is not rejected). The same conclusion can be obtained with respect to the results corresponding to the negative reviews corpus, for which the test obtained a p-value of $0.748 > 0.05$. From the last test we concluded that both approaches performs similarly well.
A statistical analysis of variance over the F-measure values obtained in the evaluation of (Hernández Fusilier et al., 2015b) and our approach complements our performance study. This analysis can be obtained from the boxplots[4] with the distribution of F-measure values of each proposal with both polarity reviews corpora. Figures 3 and 4 illustrate this analysis. In both figures we can observe that our approach shows a higher dispersion of values, as well as the best F-measure values (0.94 for positive reviews corpus and 0.915 for negative reviews) and the minimum F-measure values (0.84 and 0.81 for positive and negative polarities respectively) compared to the values obtained with (Hernández Fusilier et al., 2015b) approach. However, the median values obtained with both models are quite similar, reason for what there is not statistical difference of performance as it was demonstrated with the statistical significance test.

4 Conclusions and future work

In this work we have proposed some interesting features for deceptive opinions detection. We have studied how different features contribute to model deception clues. Character n-grams in tokens seems to capture correctly the content and the writing style of the reviews helping this, in some way, to differentiate truthful from deceptive opinions. Many works have demonstrated that emotions-based features can discriminate deceptive text, but in our experimental study this feature seems not to provide too much useful information for detecting deception in reviews. We also have used some variables extracted from LIWC

[4]Boxplots (Tukey, 1977) are descriptive statistical tools for displaying information (dispersion, quartiles, median, etc.) among populations of numerical data, without any assumptions about the underlying statistical distribution of the data.

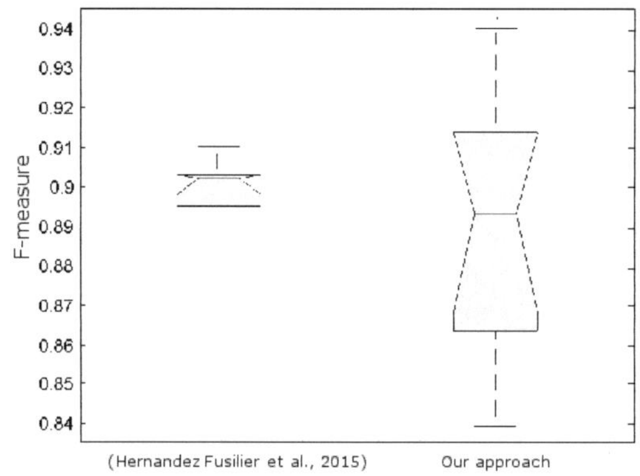

Figure 3: Boxplot for positive reviews corpus in the performance direct comparison.

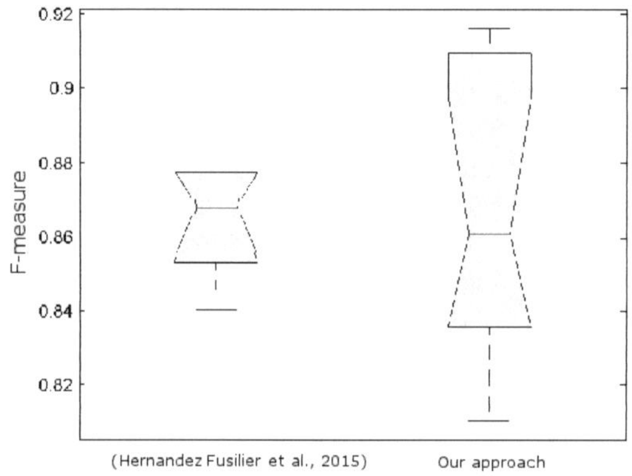

Figure 4: Boxplot for negative reviews corpus in the performance direct comparison.

as pronouns, articles and verbs. That information combined with character 4-grams in tokens was selected for modeling the representation of the reviews. For the experimental study we have used the positive and negative polarities reviews corresponding to the corpora proposed by (Ott et al., 2011; Ott et al., 2013) with 800 reviews each one (400 true and 400 false opinions). We have used both corpora in a separate way but we have performed experiments joining both polarities reviews in a combined corpus of 1600 reviews. From the results obtained with the different features we have concluded that character 4-grams in tokens with LIWC variables performs the best using a SVM classifier. We made also a comparison with the approach of (Hernández Fusilier et al., 2015b) and the results were similar (no statistically significant difference was found), but our low dimensionality representation makes our approach more efficient. For future work we plans to investigate another emotion/sentiment features in order to study the contributions in tasks of deception detection of opinion spam. Also we are interesting to test our model with other corpora related to opinion spam as the one recently proposed in (Fornaciari and Poesio, 2014).

Acknowledgments

The research work of the first author has been partially funded by CONICET (Argentina). The work of the second author was done in the framework of the VLC/CAMPUS Microcluster on Multimodal Interaction in Intelligent Systems, DIANA-APPLICATIONS-Finding Hidden Knowledge in Texts: Applications (TIN2012-38603-C02-01) research project, and the WIQ-EI IRSES project (grant no. 269180) within the FP 7 Marie Curie People Framework on Web Information Quality Evaluation Initiative. The first author would like to thank Donato Hernández Fusilier for kindly providing the results of his method.

References

S. Banerjee and A. Y. K. Chua. 2014. Dissecting genuine and deceptive kudos: The case of online hotel reviews. *International Journal of Advanced Computer Science and Applications (IJACSA)*, Special Issue on Extended Papers from Science and Information Conference 2014:28–35.

S. Bird, E. Klein, and E. Loper. 2009. *Natural Language Processing with Python: Analyzing Text with the Natural Language Toolkit*. O'Reilly, Beijing.

J. K. Burgoon, J. P. Blair, T. Qin, and J. F. Nunamaker Jr. 2003. Detecting deception through linguistic analysis. In H. Chen, R. Miranda, D. D. Zeng, C. Demchak, J. Schroeder, and T. Madhusudan, editors, *Intelligence and Security Informatics*, volume 2665 of *Lecture Notes in Computer Science*, pages 91–101. Springer Berlin Heidelberg.

W. B. Cavnar and J. M. Trenkle. 1994. N-gram-based text categorization. *Ann Arbor MI*, 48113(2):161–175.

V. W. Feng and G. Hirst. 2013. Detecting deceptive opinions with profile compatibility. In *Proceedings of the 6th International Joint Conference on Natural Language Processing, Nagoya, Japan*, pages 338–346.

S. Feng, R. Banerjee, and Y. Choi. 2012a. Syntactic stylometry for deception detection. In *ACL '12, Proceedings of the 50th Annual Meeting of the Association for Computational Linguistics*, pages 171–175. The Association for Computer Linguistics.

S. Feng, L. Xing, A. Gogar, and Y. Choi. 2012b. Distributional footprints of deceptive product reviews. In J. G. Breslin, N. B. Ellison, J. G. Shanahan, and Z. Tufekci, editors, *Proceedings of the Sixth International AAAI Conference on Weblogs and Social Media*, pages 98–105. The AAAI Press.

T. Fornaciari and M. Poesio. 2014. Identifying fake amazon reviews as learning from crowds. In *Proceedings of the 14th Conference of the European Chapter of the Association for Computational Linguistics*, pages 279–287. Association for Computational Linguistics.

M. Hall, E. Frank, G. Holmes, B. Pfahringer, P. Reutemann, and I. H. Witten. 2009. The weka data mining software: an update. *ACM SIGKDD Explorations Newsletter*, 11(1):10–18.

J. T. Hancock, L. E. Curry, S. Goorha, and M. Woodworth. 2008. On lying and being lied to: a linguistic analysis of deception in computer-mediated communication. *Discourse Processes*, 45(1):1–23.

D. Hernández Fusilier, M. Montes-y-Gómez, P. Rosso, and R. Guzmán Cabrera. 2015a. Detecting positive and negative deceptive opinions using pu-learning. *Information Processing & Management*, 51(4):433 – 443.

D. Hernández Fusilier, M. Montes-y-Gómez, P. Rosso, and R. Guzmán Cabrera. 2015b. Detection of opinion spam with character n-grams. In A. Gelbukh, editor, *Computational Linguistics and Intelligent Text Processing*, volume 9042 of *Lecture Notes in Computer Science*, pages 285–294. Springer International Publishing.

N. Jindal and B. Liu. 2008. Opinion spam and analysis. In *Proceedings of the 2008 International Conference on Web Search and Data Mining*, WSDM '08, pages 219–230. ACM.

N. Jindal, B. Liu, and E. Lim. 2010. Finding unusual review patterns using unexpected rules. In J. Huang, N. Koudas, G. J. F. Jones, X. Wu, K. Collins-Thompson, and A. An, editors, *Proceedings of the 19th ACM international conference on Information and knowledge management*, pages 1549–1552. ACM.

V. Keselj, F. Peng, N. Cercone, and C. Thomas. 2003. N-gram-based author profiles for authorship attribution. In *Proceedings of the Conference Pacific Association for Computational Linguistics, PACLING'03*, pages 255–264, Dalhousie University, Halifax, Nova Scotia, Canada.

B. Liu, W. S. Lee, P. S. Yu, and X. Li. 2002. Partially supervised classification of text documents. In *Proceedings of the Nineteenth International Conference on Machine Learning*, ICML '02, pages 387–394. Morgan Kaufmann Publishers Inc.

H. B. Mann and D. R. Whitney. 1947. On a test of whether one of two random variables is stochastically larger than the other. *The Annals of Mathematical Statistics*, 18(1):50–60.

A. Mukherjee, B. Liu, J. Wang, N. Glance, and N. Jindal. 2011. Detecting group review spam. In *Proceedings of the 20th International Conference Companion on World Wide Web*, WWW '11, pages 93–94. ACM.

M. L. Newman, J. W. Pennebaker, D. S. Berry, and J. M. Richards. 2003. Lying words: predicting deception from linguistic styles. *Personality and Social Psychology Bulletin*, 29(5):665–675.

M. Ott, Y. Choi, C. Cardie, and J. T. Hancock. 2011. Finding deceptive opinion spam by any stretch of the imagination. *Proceedings of the 49th Annual Meeting of the Association for Computational Linguistics: Human Language Technologies*, 1:309–319.

M. Ott, C. Cardie, and J. T. Hancock. 2013. Negative deceptive opinion spam. In *NAACL-HLT 2013, Proceedings of the 2013 Conference of the North American Chapter of the Association for Computational Linguistics: Human Language Technologies*, pages 497–501. The Association for Computational Linguistics.

J. W. Pennebaker, C. K. Chung, M. Ireland, A. Gonzales, and R. J. Booth. 2007. The development and psychometric properties of LIWC2007. In *LIWC webpage. http://www.liwc.net/LIWC2007LanguageManual.pdf*, pages 1–22, Austin, Texas, USA. LIWC.net.

Y. Ren, D. Ji, and H. Zhang. 2014. Positive unlabeled learning for deceptive reviews detection. In A. Moschitti, B. Pang, and W. Daelemans, editors, *Proceedings of the 2014 Conference on Empirical Methods in Natural Language Processing, EMNLP 2014, October 25-29, 2014, Doha, Qatar, A meeting of SIGDAT, a Special Interest Group of the ACL*, pages 488–498. ACL.

E. Stamatatos. 2013. On the Robustness of Authorship Attribution Based on Character n-gram Features. *Journal of Law and Policy*, 21(2):421–439.

J. W. Tukey. 1977. *Exploratory data analysis*. Pearson Education, Inc., Massachussets, USA.

A. Šilić, J. Chauchat, B. Dalbelo Bašić, and A. Morin. 2007. N-grams and morphological normalization in text classification: A comparison on a croatian-english parallel corpus. In J. Neves, M. F. Santos, and J. M. Machado, editors, *Progress in Artificial Intelligence*, volume 4874 of *Lecture Notes in Computer Science*, pages 671–682. Springer Berlin Heidelberg.

Z. Wei, D. Miao, J. Chauchat, and C. Zhong. 2008. Feature selection on chinese text classification using character n-grams. In *3rd International Conference on Rough Sets and Knowledge Technology (RSKT 08), Chengdu, China*, Lecture Notes in Computer Science, pages 500–507. Springer, Heidelberg, Germany.

Extending effect annotation with lexical decomposition

Josef Ruppenhofer and Jasper Brandes
Department of Information Science and Natural Language Processing
Hildesheim University
D-31141 Hildesheim
{ruppenho|brandesj}@uni-hildesheim.de

Abstract

In this contribution, we report on an effort to annotate German data with information relevant to opinion inference. Such information has previously been referred to as *effect* or couched in terms of event-evaluation functors. We extend the theory and present an extensive scheme that combines both approaches and thus extends the set of inference-relevant predicates. Using these guidelines to annotate 726 German synsets, we achieve good inter-annotator agreement.

1 Introduction

In recent years, there has been increasing interest in inferring implicit opinions in addition to capturing explicit expressions of opinion. A series of papers by Reschke and Anand as well as Wiebe and her collaborators (Anand and Reschke, 2010; Reschke and Anand, 2011; Deng et al., 2013; Wiebe and Deng, 2014) has shown the great potential of opinion inference: speakers and authors leave many implicit opinions for hearers to infer. While these additional inferred opinions involve sentences or clauses that bear no explicit sentiment at all, they very often interact with sentences or clauses that do bear explicit sentiment, as in example (1).

(1) She is disappointed that Peter is **happy** because the Colts LOST.

In (1), we can infer, for instance, that Peter, the (nested) source of the explicit sentiment (in boldface) towards the event as a whole, is also negative towards the Colts football team given that the event affected them negatively (in small caps). As laid out in great detail by Wiebe and Deng (2014), given partial knowledge about explicit subjective expressions, sources' attitudes about participants and knowledge about the effects of events on their participants, people can generate contextually defeasible inferences about the missing pieces. And inferences can build on prior inferences: in the above example, we can further defeasibly infer that 'she' potentially holds the opposite opinion towards the Colts from Peter, given that she is disappointed at his attitude.

Although opinion inference is a pragmatic process, it relies on rich lexical knowledge of subjective expressions and of predicates, which entail some kind of effect.[1] While a great deal of effort has been devoted to the acquisition of explicit sentiment expressions, the acquisition of information that is relevant for opinion inference is in its infancy, by comparison.

In this paper, we report on an effort to manually annotate effect-relevant predicates in GermaNet (Hamp and Feldweg, 1997), a WordNet-like (Fellbaum, 1998) electronic lexical resource for German. The purpose of annotating the word senses of lemmas that have at least some effect-entailing senses is to construct a gold standard for evaluating automatic systems that provide a complete automatic annotation of the senses in the resource via label propagation along the lines of Choi and Wiebe (2014). Here we focus on the following contributions of our work:

- We extend the range of predicates covered, relative to Choi and Wiebe (2014).
- We provide a typology of effect-relevant predicates in terms of lexical decomposition.
- We explicitly take account of the syntax-semantics interface and mark the argument that is affected.
- We report inter-annotator agreement results for labeling lexical entries with argument-

[1] Work on connotation detection by Feng et al. (2011) can be seen as addressing the issue of determining sources' attitudes in those cases when they are aligned with their stereotypical attitudes within particular (discourse) communities or cultures.

Proceedings of the 6th Workshop on Computational Approaches to Subjectivity, Sentiment and Social Media Analysis (WASSA 2015), pages 67–76,
Lisboa, Portugal, 17 September, 2015.

specific effect information, whereas so far only agreement on annotations of corpus instances has been studied.

This paper proceeds as follows. In §2, we present related work. In §3, we describe the way we chose the lexical entries we annotated. §4 lays out our own annotation scheme and its differences to prior work. We report on the inter-annotator agreement that we were able to achieve applying our scheme in §5. We offer our conclusions in §6.

2 Related work

The relevance of predicates to the inference of attitudes towards the events they are used to refer to was explored by Reschke and Anand (2011) who treat predicates and their arguments as functors that map tuples of argument and verb properties to evaluations. An example is given in Table 1. The first line of the table applies to the situation where there is a possessor (x) who is valued positively by some nested source and a possession (y) that is also valued positively. If the relation between them is *have* (third column), that relation is valued positively from the external point-of-view. If the relation is *lack*, that relation is valued negatively. The table shows that the reasoning for *lack* also applies to events of withholding and depriving which result in lack.[2]

x	y	have	lack	withhold	deprive
+	+	+	-	-	-
+	-	-	+	+	undef.
-	+	-	+	+	+
-	-	+	-	-	undef

Table 1: Functors for verbs embedding a state of possession

It is important to keep in mind that the goal of the inference procedure is to assess the attitude of an external observer on the event. Thus, while an external viewer may feel positively towards a situation where a person he or she dislikes, *x*, lacks something desirable, *y*, the relevant possessor, *x*, will most likely feel negatively about this lack. Reschke and Anand's functor are intended only to capture the former attitude, of the observer, but not the latter, of the participant.[3]

Reschke and Anand (2011) focus on classes of verbs assuming that verb classes such as verbs of creation behave consistently due to lexical entailments about their arguments. They focus on three prominent kinds of entailments: ones related to possession, existence and affectedness. Reschke and Anand (2011) test the correctness of the predictions generated by their theory by annotating actual corpus instances. They do not evaluate the agreement on the presence of the lexical entailments for predicates themselves. Instead, they simply identified the verbs having particular lexical entailments by inspecting FrameNet's frames (Baker et al., 1998; Ruppenhofer et al., 2010) and its hierarchy.

While acquisition or validation of a large lexicon was not the aim of Reschke and Anand (2011), it is the focus of later work by Choi and Wiebe (2014) who seek to generate EffectWordNet, a large lexical resource based on WordNet, in which information relevant for opinion inferences is recorded. The notion to which the annotation of the WordNet word senses appeals is that of effect rather than the more specific entailments used by Reschke and Anand (2011). The idea is that in order to determine a nested source's view on an event, one first needs to look at the positive or negative effect that the event has on its object.[4] In combination with the attitude towards the object this yields the evaluation of the state that results from the event. That evaluation can then be transferred onto the agent or cause responsible for bringing about the effect, and onto the overall action brought about by the agent or cause. Consider this example taken from Choi and Wiebe (2014):

(2) The bill would curb skyrocketing health care costs.

The reasoning applied to this example is that since *skyrocketing* conveys negative sentiment towards *curb*'s object *health care costs*, which is negativey affected by the event of curbing, we understand that the writer feels positively towards the curbing event and the *bill* that brings it about.

The idea of looking specifically at the positive or negative effect on a particular affected entity (=object) features only in Choi and Wiebe's

[2]The possessor x of *withhold* and *deprive* is the grammatical object of these verbs in active-form sentences rather than the subject as in the case of *have* and *lack*. However, this difference is unimportant to the logic that applies.

[3]In cases where the participant and the reporter/observer coincide, as when somebodys says "I don't have any money", the two judgements also coincide. But this is just contingently and not necessarily the case.

[4]Note that as in the case of Reschke and Anand (2011), the goal is to infer the attitude of an external viewer toward the event, rather than that of a participant.

(2014) theory. In the work of Reschke and Anand (2011), it is left implicit. Consider again Table 1: the plus and minus signs encode attitudes of an external viewer towards participants and events but they do not capture the nature of how (some) participants are affected. Further, as indicated by the variable names for the participants (*x*,*y*), no affected entity is identified.

In the work of Choi and Wiebe (2014), all WordNet word senses of 1143 lemmas were manually annotated as +/-effect. This data was then used as seed and test data for a label propagation algorithm that spread effect information throughout WordNet. In a prior study by Deng et al. (2013), textual instances of effect-predicates were annotated as triples consisting of <agent, +/-effect event,object>.[5] In addition, the writer's attitude toward the agents and objects of those events was captured.

3 Data

As noted in the introduction, our ultimate goal is to create a WordNet-like resource for German with information relevant to opinion inference that is similar to the English EffectWordNet. Following the approach of Choi and Wiebe (2014), we want to annotate word senses in GermaNet V9.0 (Hamp and Feldweg, 1997), the sister resource to WordNet for German, that can serve both as training / seed data for automatic methods for graph-based label propagation, and also as a gold standard for evaluating automatic methods.

In picking German synsets to annotate, we made use of the work done by the EffectWordNet group. We extracted all 745 synsets from the EffectWordNet gold standard that were annotated as either +effect or -effect. We omitted all synsets annotated as Null in the source synsets. We then retrieved 273 corresponding German synsets from BabelNet (Navigli and Ponzetto, 2010) on the basis of the WordNet synset IDs. Using the German lemma information and the POS information in BabelNet, we next extracted 998 unique synsets from GermaNet that contained any word senses for the lemmas found in the 273 BabelNet synsets. After expanding the set again based on lemmas found in GermaNet but not in BabelNet, we obtained 1492 GermaNet synsets.

As we will show in §4.2, our annotation scheme does not only focus on the *effect* on an entity caused by an agent but also allows for the annotation of uncaused states an entity may find itself in. We therefore must include inchoative and resultative verbs as well as resultative adjectives in our data set. Thus, we manually culled inchoative verbs such as *aufblühen* 'blossom', resultative verbs like *verblühen* 'wither' and adjectives (e.g. *hoch*, 'high') from various German lexicons. We extracted all corresponding GermaNet synsets by their lemma and POS information, resulting in 163 verbal and 52 adjectival synsets. After removing duplicate synsets that were found a second time as part of the search for uncaused states, our final data set consists of 1667 GermaNet synsets.

Figure 1 displays an instance of a GermaNet synset, along with its annotations. The key parts for our purposes are

a the initial pair of square brackets containing our effect annotations (bold-face);

b the orth forms set, which lists the lemmas of the synset (underlined);

c the paraphrases, which help us understand the intended senses of the lemmas (italics);

d and the example sentences (lines beginning with "# GermaNet").

Unlike in (Effect)WordNet, each example sentence is accompanied by a syntactic subcategorization frame which lists the set of arguments and adjuncts occurring with the lemma being exemplified. Thus, in the first sentence, *gefallen* is realized with a noun phrase in nominative case (NN) and another in dative case (DN). We refer to these morphosyntactic phrase labels in our effect annotations, as illustrated by the arrows in Figure 1. For instance, the initial block in the example says that for the verb *mögen* 'like' the participant coded as an accusative noun phrase (AN) is positively affected, whereas for the verb *gefallen* 'please' the participant coded as a nominative case noun phrase (NN) is positively affected.

As suggested by the synset in Figure 1, taking valence information into account is important: without it, we are unable to reliably identify which argument is affected in which way. Ideally, we could make use of either a German counterpart to PropBank or FrameNet. However, there is no German PropBank and the Salsa lexicon (Burchardt et al., 2006), which uses the FrameNet formalism, has too low a coverage. It thus makes most sense

[5] We follow Choi and Wiebe (2014) and apply the more recent term *+/-effect* instead of the earlier *goodFor/badFor*.

```
35:[+Effect:AN:mögen;+Effect:NN:gefallen] id: 52110, orth forms: [gefallen, mögen],
paraphrases: jemand findet etwas gut; jemandem angenehm sein; jemanden
oder etwas gern haben, lieben (etwas schwächere Form)
verben        Allgemein        [annotation-uncertain|meaning-uncertain]
# GermaNet:  Ihm gefällt Klassische Musik. NN.DN
# GermaNet:  Er mag diese Musik. NN.AN
```

Figure 1: Annotation of a synset

to use GermaNet which is large, structured on the sense-level and has example sentences with associated subcategorization patterns that allow us to access at least syntactic, if not semantic valence.[6] We supply our annotation labels with the understanding that they cover only the syntactic frames exemplified by GermaNet. While these may not include all possible frames, they seem to cover the major syntactic frames for the predicates.

4 Scheme

Our overall approach is a mixture of the functor approach to event evaluation of Reschke and Anand (2011) and of the object-focused approach of Choi and Wiebe (2014). Like Choi and Wiebe (2014) we annotate synsets in a WordNet-like resource but inspired by Reschke and Anand (2011) we annotate a wider variety of predicates and also cover cases where the focus on an affected object alone is not enough to allow a judgment about how the event as a whole should be evaluated.

For practical reasons, our annotations are done with reference to syntactic subcategorization frames that come with example sentences for the GermaNet synsets. Conceptually, we find it useful to reason about the annotation task in terms of lexical decompositions and semantic roles along the lines of e.g. Rappaport Hovav and Levin (1998) and Tenny (1994), *inter alia*.

We present our basic approach in §4.1 and discuss extensions to it and further considerations in the following subsections §4.2-§4.4.

4.1 Underlying linguistic model of effects

Let us consider the prototypical case of predicates relevant for opinion inference, namely ones that involve a causal event (*Cause*) that brings about a resulting event, the (*Effect*). A clear example of such a predicate is *produce* in (3).

[6]Further example sentences are available through the WebCage corpus (Henrich et al., 2012) which, however, lack explicit syntactic frame information. We only use these additional sentences to ascertain the relevant meaning.

(3) [The explosion `Cause`] PRODUCED [a loud "bang" `Effect`].

Example (3) would be a simple +effect-verb in terms of Choi and Wiebe (2014). So it is for us: we mark its German counterpart *produzieren* as *+Effect:AN* to capture the positive effect on its accusative object.

However, in many cases, the effect does not appear directly as a single argument of the predicate but is expressed in two semantically interconnected phrases, one expressing an affected participant and another expressing the relevant situation that affects that participant. The *Patient* is typically realized as an object for verbal predicates. The situation-referring constituent, which we call *Eventuality*, can be of various forms: it can be a verb phrase (4), an adjectival phrase (5), a prepositional phrase, or some other type of unit that can function as a predicate. Semantically, the Patient is the 'subject' of the Eventuality predicate: e.g. (5) could be paraphrased as 'My mortal fear and faintness brings it about that I am deadly pale.'

(4) [The explosion `Cause`] MADE [me `Patient`] [fear for my life `Eventuality`].

(5) [My mortal fear and faintness `Cause`] must have MADE [me `Patient`] [deadly pale `Eventuality`].

In our annotation scheme, rather than leave these cases out of consideration, we explicitly record that, in order to assess the effect on the Patient in object position, we need to consider the Eventuality expressed in the secondary predicate. We mark this dependence between the two phrases with the symbol $\sim$. For instance, for the German equivalent of *make* in (5), *machen*, we would mark *Effect:AN$\sim$BM* not specifying + or -, where AN represents the accusative object and BM (adverbial of manner) covers the adjectival secondary predicate. This information can be used to, for instance, compose the polarity of the sentence in (4) as follows. First, we compute if 'me/I fear for my life' is a positive or negative event, for which we can use information in our resource about the verb *fear*. Second, we input the result of that first computation to the basic cause-event reasoning used for the simple case in (3).

While verbs like *cause* and *make* are very generic and require the nature of the Eventuality to be specified explicitly, other verbs can be thought of as incorporating the Eventuality. For instance, we can think of the event structure of *carve* as "Agent causes Patient to exist by carving it" (cf. example (6)). In the syntax, the Eventuality "to exist" is not expressed because it is already contained in the meaning of *carve*.

(6) As well as painting, [he `Agent`] CARVED [images `Patient`] from sandalwood.

For the verb *carve*, we record that its active-form object is its Patient, which we take to be positively affected by coming into existence, in line with Reschke and Anand (2011)'s Existence entailment or the guidance of Deng & Wiebe's annotation manual that "To Exist is Good". The annotation for German *schnitzen* would be *+Effect:AN*. In a parallel way, verbs of destruction can be thought of as including a negation of the existence-eventuality: *destroy* is "Agent causes Patient to no longer exist". Accordingly, we would mark the Patients of *destroy* and *kill* as negatively affected; the German counterparts *zerstören* and *töten* would receive the annotation *-Effect:AN* for their accusative objects.

If we allow that the Eventuality can be implicit in the verb's meaning, we can also analyze verbs related to transfer in a similar way. The meaning of *give* is "Agent causes Recipient to have Theme" but in the syntax there is no separate expression of the notion of having: it is incorporated by *give*. As in the case of *make* in (4–5) the positive or negative quality of the Effect cannot be assessed based on either the Recipient or the Theme alone.

(7) [Bill `Agent`] GAVE [my mom `Recipient`] [a valuable painting `Theme`].

It is clear that we first need to figure out the Effect's polarity on the basis of "Recipient have Theme", for which we reason along the lines of Reschke and Anand's functor in Table 1. From there, we can proceed to the general level of "Cause causes Effect". Accordingly, the annotation for German *geben* would be *Effect:DN*$\sim$*AN*, which captures the dependence between the dative Recipient phrase (DN) and the accusative Theme phrase (AN). Note that the order matters: the (animate) Recipient's state changes more saliently by coming into possession of the (inanimate) Theme than the other way around. For (7), we reason with Reschke and Anand (2011) that it's good if a person we like has something good. Assuming we like our mothers, the possession of the valuable painting is good. Since agents and causes get credit and blame for the good and bad things they bring about, Bill is evaluated positively.

The idea of decomposing verb meanings can be applied to yet more verb groups. For instance, verbs that refer to an item attaining a lower or higher position on a scale can be decomposed as "Cause causes Item to be higher/lower (on some scale)", with the Eventuality "to be higher/lower" being implicit.

(8) [Water privatization `Cause`] RAISED [prices `Item`].

While Deng & Wiebe treat increases as a metaphorical case of existence, the evaluative logic behind these cases could also be couched as a functor in the style of Reschke and Anand (2011). Basically, "Increase is good, decrease is bad". For the German equivalent of *raise*, *erhöhen* we would annotate *+Effect:AN* to capture the positive effect on its accusative object. For the antonym *senken*, we would annotate *-Effect:AN*.

4.2 Evaluation of pure states / post-states

The last examples of the previous section suggest that there is no particular reason to focus solely on verbs that contain causation as part of their meaning. Just as we treat both *good* and *improve* (or: *bad* and *deteriorate*) as equally relevant explicit sentiment predicates, so we can treat the non-subjective adjective *high* (or: *low*), the intransitive verb *rise* (or: *decline, fall*) and the transitive verb *raise* (or: *decrease, lower*) as relevant to opinion inference.

As argued by Reschke and Anand (2011), "The evaluation of a change of state is equivalent to the evaluation of the end state.". This can be readily seen by taking into account sets of lexical decompositions such as those for the verbs *raise* and *rise* and the adjective *high* in (9–11), which alert us to series of related predicates and make explicit what the relevant (end) states are.

(9) causative *raise.v*: [x CAUSE [BECOME [y <high>]]]

(10) inchoative *rise.v*: [BECOME [y <high>]]

(11) stative *high.a*: [y <high>]

Regarding the scalar predicates *high* and *low*, we reason "more is good, less is bad". Analogously to the object of the transitive *raise* or the subject of the intransitive *rise*, we thus mark the head noun that is modified by the adjective *high* as being in a positive state. Similarly, we annotate the head of *low* as being in a negative state. Recall that "in a positive state" for *high* is meant to metaphorically take the perspective of the entity referred to by the head, for example *rents* in (12). The overall evaluation of the situation described by (12) also depends on the evaluation of the external viewer's attitude towards high rents: if he or she is a landlord, it will tend to be positive; if he or she is a renter, it is most likely negative.

(12) She said [rents `Item`] are HIGH in Paris.

The states that are relevant to opinion inference are not necessarily ones with a single participant. There are also cases of relational states that we need to take into account. The verbs of possession covered by the functor in Table 1 are one important subclass. But we can also consider predicates like *similar*, *like*, and *resemble*, which talk about states of similarity ([y <similar> z]).

(13) Charles Krauthammer said ..."[Putin `Item1`] is LIKE [Hitler `Item2`] but he's more subtle and he's also weaker, ..."

Basically, if there is sentiment towards Item2, then it is imputed to Item1 as well by dint of the comparison (cf. Table 2). By paying attention to lexical decompositions, we know that we can reason in a parallel way about inchoative verbs and causative verbs that denote events with an end state of (dis)similarity. Accordingly, for the causative predicate like *angleichen* 'make sth equal to sth else', we would mark *Effect:AN∼DN* to capture the fact that the Effect on the changed accusative object depends on the nature of the dative object. Note that in this case, unlike with *geben* in (7) the accusative phrase refers to the affected participant. The ordering of the arguments around the "∼"-symbol thus captures information that is lost in Anand and Reschke's notation, where affected participants are not identified.

A second prominent class of relational states are, interestingly enough, inherent sentiment predicates.

(14) My best friend Martha just told me that [she `Experiencer`] LOVES [Sarah Palin `Stimulus`].

Item1	Item2	*similar*	*differ*
+	+	+	-
+	-	-	+
-	+	+	-
-	-	-	+

Table 2: Functor for predicates of similarity

While the Experiencer's inherent positive sentiment specified by *love* toward the Stimulus-object is clear, the state itself is also open to support opinion inferences. The basic reasoning could be couched as "positive/negative sentiment is useful/harmful for the Stimulus". Accordingly, for the verb *lieben* 'love', we mark the object as being in a positive effect state (*+Effect:AN*).

Example (14) is underspecified. Assuming that the speaker approves of Sarah Palin herself, she will feel positive that her friend shares the sentiment. Assuming that the speaker has so far not liked Sarah Palin, he or she may now have a conflicted attitude towards her friend Martha. Martha's positive sentiment benefits Sarah Palin, and since the speaker does not like Palin, he or she should therefore also disapprove of the source of that (emotional) support for Palin.

A third large class of relational states concerns locative prepositions and causative predicates such as *put, throw, remove* etc. If the (post-)state is valued in some way, then so is the event (and potentially its author). For concrete physical locations, it is, however, often not obvious what value to attach to the Figure and Ground arguments a priori. Even Grounds that come heavily connotated with one polarity, can carry a different polarity, when we take into account the specifics of Figure and Ground (cf. (15) vs. (16)). For metaphorical locations, it seems that the 'Ground' expressions that metaphorically evoke a state are often readily interpretable as to polarity, as in (17). The operative logic for these cases is that "good/bad entities should be in good/bad states" (cf. Table 3).

(15) [The laundry `Figure`] LAY [in the mud `Ground`].

(16) [The rhinoceros `Figure`] LAY [in the mud `Ground`].

(17) ...they DROVE [the company `Figure`] [into the ditch `Ground`].

The German verb *liegen* 'lie' would be marked as *Effect:NN∼BL* to capture the fact that the effect on the Figure, coded as a nominative noun

Figure	Ground	in	out of
+	+	+	-
+	-	-	+
-	+	-	+
-	-	+	-

Table 3: Functor for predicates of location

phrase (NN), depends on the nature of the Ground, coded as a kind of locative adverbial phrase (BL).

With some locative verbs, we face a certain difficulty because they incorporate their Theme argument. E.g. *asphaltieren* 'to asphalt, tarmac' refers to a transfer of some material onto a surface. The evaluation of tarmacking depends on whether we think the 'Theme' (=asphalt) is appropriately put on the location in question. We can mark the location as affected but the polarity depends on the theme. Since it is not realized explicitly as a phrase, we hint at its relevance by annotating *Effect:AN~Context*.

4.3 Logical operators

While we can often identify states (and specifically, post-states) as the most relevant concept for opinion-inference, it is clear that we need to deal with certain logical operators that can occur inside complex semantic decompositions. Consider *enable* and *possible*.

(18) This workshop ENABLED delegates to learn more about practical intervention strategies.

(19) This workshop made it POSSIBLE for delegates to learn more about practical intervention strategies.

(20) It is POSSIBLE for delegates to learn more about practical intervention strategies.

The causative verb *enable* allows for paraphrases as in (19). If we focus solely on the effect of (19), we get sentence (20). Although possibility is certainly different from existence, the logic is the same: to be possible is good, to be impossible is bad. Accordingly, if we approve of the delegates' learning about practical intervention strategies, we will approve of the workshop. Since permission and requirement can be couched in terms of possibility, the aforementioned logic also applies to predicates such as *obligatory*, *permit* etc.

(21) It was OBLIGATORY to eat fish on certain fast days laid down by the church.

In (21), we can paraphrase *obligatory* as "not possible not to do X". Assuming eating fish is viewed negatively, not eating it is positive. The possibility of not eating it is positive, too, but once that possibility is negated, we are left with a negatively evaluated situation. Similarly, if in (18) we replaced *enable* by *prevent* (and adjusted other syntax accordingly), we would come to the opposite conclusion because *prevent* can be decomposed as "cause it not to be possible for X to do Y".

4.4 Pragmatic inference vs. lexical sentiment

It is desirable to keep the positive/negative state characterization of a predicate separate from any additional sentiment that the predicate may carry. To modify an example of Reschke and Anand (2011), consider the following pair of sentences:

(22) Tom injured the burglar.

(23) Tom abused the burglar.

Both sentences imply a negative effect on the burglar. Given that the burglar is likely evaluated negatively, we could infer that the injuring event and its agent are evaluated positively or at least neutrally in (22). In (23), this is not possible since *abuse* lexically specifies negative evaluation on the abusing event and its author, however deserving of injury the abusee may be. In our annotation, the negative effect on the victim of abuse is preserved. We prefer to let the lexical sentiment information conflict with, and override, the effect-based inference. This makes sense as the negative evaluation of the victim may (at least for some people) constitute an attenuating circumstance. If we ignored the effect altogether, this nuance would be lost.

For some words, the choice between a treatment in terms of lexically inherent sentiment and a treatment as pragmatic inference is difficult to make. As an example, consider the verb *fawn*. On the lexical analysis, the negative characterization of another person's speech as fawning is inherent in the meaning of *fawn*. On the inference account, it just happens that speakers often describe other people's behavior as fawning when they themselves dislike the person that the other people have positive sentiment for. The inference that the speaker disapproves of the fawning and of the fawners would then simply follow from the logic applied to sentiment states (cf. §4.2).

(24) The critics at Cannes FAWNED all over these like they'd never seen kung fu before . . .

5 Inter-annotator agreement

We assess the inter-annotator agreement for the annotation task by two measures: percent agreement and κ (Cohen, 1960). Percent agreement is the ratio of all identically annotated synsets against all annotated synsets. For each annotated synset, we compare the annotations from both annotators. If they are identical, the synset receives a credit of 1, while the synset receives no credit in case they are different. Finally, for all annotated synsets we add up the credit and divide the sum by the number of annotated synsets. Note that for synsets with multiple annotations, we do not consider the order of the individual annotations.

For κ, we proceed as follows. For each GermaNet synset, we extract the phrase labels from the valence frames that come with the example sentences. In order not to artificially inflate or deflate the inter-annotator agreement, we discard any duplicate valence frames that may arise from syntactically identical examples. From the extracted phrase labels, we construct three types of units: (i) phrase labels-only (**PHL**), (ii) phrase label relations (**REL**) and (iii) context-dependent phrase labels (**CON**). **PHL** relates to annotations like *+Effect:AN* where there is positive/negative effect on one phrase label. Units of type **REL** correspond to all pairwise combinations of phrase labels of a given valence frame. An annotation example is *Effect:NN∼AN* where the effect on NN is dependent on the evaluation of AN. Context-dependent effect on an entity, annotated as e.g. *Effect:AN∼Context*, corresponds to **CON**. For this unit, we construct a combination between a given phrase label and the term "Context", connected by the $\sim$ symbol. Finally, for each annotation of a synset, we project the annotation onto these units. For cases, where there is no match, we ascribe "Default" for no annotation. We then compute Cohen's κ separately for each of the three units.

In total, two annotators, both authors of this paper, independently annotated 726 GermaNet synsets over two annotation phases. In the exploratory phase I, we annotated 226 GermaNet synsets following the annotation guidelines for EffectWordNet by Choi and Wiebe (2014). In phase II, we annotated 500 synsets using the scheme presented in §4. In both phases, for each annotation round, we randomly selected the synsets to be annotated and discussed differences after the annotation and accordingly adjusted the guidelines.

The agreement results are presented in Table 4. Due to different annotation formats, we only report κ values for the annotations from phase II. For phase II, the agreement after the first 100 instances is very good with percent agreement values around 0.8 and κ values between 0.75 and 0.94. The first round (1-100) had low results because it was the first attempt to apply our own more extensive scheme. After each annotation round, we adjudicated the annotations, resolving almost all differences between the annotators. The bottom row in Table 4 shows the agreement results for all annotations *after* adjudication. Note that we manually reannotated the adjudicated synsets from phase I according to the final guidelines, in order to be able to include them in the overall computation of the inter-annotator agreement and for use as additional seed data in future work on label propagation.

It is not possible to directly compare our results to the annotation for EffectWordNet. Though that annotation effort was bigger in that all 1030 WordNet senses of 1143 lemmas were covered, the annotation was only done by a single annotator (Choi and Wiebe, 2014). Thus, no agreement information is available for those annotations. However, the relevant annotator had taken part in a prior annotation study (Choi et al., 2014), where two annotators achieved a κ of 0.75 on 151 senses that were to be labeled as either +effect; -effect; or neutral.

By contrast, we performed double annotation on 726 GermaNet synsets. However, our annotation scheme is more extensive in several respects. It allows for the annotation of more opinion inference-relevant predicates and it takes into account syntactic valence information about the entity affected. Despite this added complexity, we have achieved good agreement results for all of the GermaNet senses that we have annotated so far.

Among the synset members of the 726 annotated synsets, there are 148 unique lemmas with more than one GermaNet synset whose different senses have all been annotated. Following Choi and Wiebe (2014), we conduct an analysis of the effect ambiguity for these lemmas across their different senses. We find 110 of the 148 lemmas (74.3%) to have an inconsistent effect on an affected entity (polarity / affected entity, or both) across their different senses. 26 of these 110 lemmas show effects with different polarities on an affected entity. Consider e.g. *ausstoßen* which entails a positive effect on its object in its 'to emit

	Synsets	Percent agreement	Cohen's Kappa PHL	REL	CON
Phase I	1-59	0.75	n/a	n/a	n/a
	60-133	0.68	n/a	n/a	n/a
	134-226	0.76	n/a	n/a	n/a
Phase II	1-100	0.46	0.16	0.17	0.18
	101-150	0.76	0.87	0.92	0.93
	151-200	0.68	0.78	0.85	0.78
	201-250	0.76	0.81	0.86	0.91
	251-300	0.80	0.80	0.75	0.84
	301-401	0.80	0.84	0.81	0.85
	402-500	0.82	0.91	0.90	0.95
Adjud.	1-726	0.97	0.98	0.98	0.99

Table 4: Inter-annotator agreement for phase I (EffectWordNet scheme) and phase II (our scheme). Bottom row: agreement after adjudication.

sth' sense[7] but negative effect on its object in the sense of 'to expel so'. This indicates that effect ambiguity is also prevalent in German and confirms the need for a sense-level lexical resource.

6 Conclusion and Future Work

We have presented an annotation scheme for effect-related information in a lexical resource that significantly extends prior work. We have broadened the coverage, and made more systematic the understanding of effect-related predicates by framing them in terms of lexical decomposition. First, in addition to effects resulting from causing events, we also take into account resulting states of events that need not involve a specific cause (e.g. *fall*) and even simple states and properties (e.g. *high*). Second, the states or relations that occur in effect-related predicates are not limited to ones referring to existence, possession or affectedness. Verbs of location, similarity, and sentiment are relevant, too. Third, our annotation scheme deals explicitly with predicates where the evaluation of an event requires considering a relation between two semantic roles (e.g. *give [me] [a cookie]*, *make [Kim] [happy]*).

We have achieved good levels of agreement given the complexity of the task. In successfully working on German data, we have provided further evidence that opinion inference and the relevance of lexical knowledge to support it are independent of specific languages.

A significant benefit of relating our annotations to example sentences and their syntactic valence descriptions is that we thereby generated sense-disambiguated data that can be used in evaluating an opinion-inference system for German. The GermaNet data that we have annotated so far will be made available to the research community.[8] In ongoing work, we are finishing the double annotation of the second half of our data set, which we will then also publish. In addition, we are beginning to experiment with ways to propagate the effect information on our seed data throughout GermaNet's verbal and adjectival synsets.

With regard to the annotation scheme, one issue that we have not dealt with so far is that for a given predicate multiple end states could be relevant, depending on the context. As an example consider the synset containing verbs of resource extraction such as *gewinnen* and *fördern*, which can co-occur with arguments realizing the agent, the theme and the source location. On the one hand, the agent's possession that results from oil/gas/mineral extraction may be relevant in some contexts such as thinking about the wealth of nations. On the other hand, the theme's (dis)location can be relevant, for instance, when arguing about whether to extract fossil fuels or leave them in the ground to mitigate climate change. Predicates with multiple relevant post-states may account for some of our annotation differences. Studying this issue more calls for performing annotation of actual corpus instances along the lines of Deng et al. (2013).

Another issue that we are pursuing is the inventory of different functors that are needed to reason about the post-states. Compare the functors for possession in Table 1, for similarity in Table 2, and for location in Table 3. All of them involve two arguments. Ignoring the role names, we see that the functors for possession and location are isomorphic, while that for similarity is different. Given a small number of arguments for a (post-)state and the possible assignments of +/- values to these arguments and to the state, only a relatively small number of functor types is at all possible. The question is which of the possible functors actually occur, and with what frequency.

Acknowledgments

The authors were partially supported by the German Research Foundation (DFG) under grant RU 1873/2-1.

[7]For instance, emitting smoke causes the smoke to exist.

[8]`http://www.uni-hildesheim.de/ruppenhofer/pages/datasets.html`

References

Pranav Anand and Kevin Reschke. 2010. Verb classes as evaluativity functor classes. *Proceedings of Verb 2010*, pages 98–103.

Collin F. Baker, Charles J. Fillmore, and John B. Lowe. 1998. The berkeley framenet project. In *Proceedings of the 36th Annual Meeting of the Association for Computational Linguistics and 17th International Conference on Computational Linguistics - Volume 1*, ACL '98, pages 86–90, Stroudsburg, PA, USA. Association for Computational Linguistics.

Aljoscha Burchardt, Katrin Erk, Anette Frank, Andrea Kowalski, Sebastian Padó, and Manfred Pinkal. 2006. The salsa corpus: a german corpus resource for lexical semantics. In *Proceedings of the 5th International Conference on Language Resources and Evaluation (LREC-2006)*, pages 969–974.

Yoonjung Choi and Janyce Wiebe. 2014. +/-effectwordnet: Sense-level lexicon acquisition for opinion inference. In Alessandro Moschitti, Bo Pang, and Walter Daelemans, editors, *Proceedings of the 2014 Conference on Empirical Methods in Natural Language Processing, EMNLP 2014, October 25-29, 2014, Doha, Qatar, A meeting of SIGDAT, a Special Interest Group of the ACL*, pages 1181–1191. ACL.

Yoonjung Choi, Lingjia Deng, and Janyce Wiebe. 2014. Lexical acquisition for opinion inference: A sense-level lexicon of benefactive and malefactive events. In *Proceedings of the 5th Workshop on Computational Approaches to Subjectivity, Sentiment and Social Media Analysis*, pages 107–112, Baltimore, Maryland, June. Association for Computational Linguistics.

Jacob Cohen. 1960. A coefficient of agreement for nominal scales. *Educational and psychological measurement*, 20(1):37–46.

Lingjia Deng, Yoonjung Choi, and Janyce Wiebe. 2013. Benefactive/malefactive event and writer attitude annotation. In *Proceedings of the 51st Annual Meeting of the Association for Computational Linguistics (Volume 2: Short Papers)*, pages 120–125, Sofia, Bulgaria, August. Association for Computational Linguistics.

Christiane Fellbaum. 1998. *WordNet*. Wiley Online Library.

Song Feng, Ritwik Bose, and Yejin Choi. 2011. Learning general connotation of words using graph-based algorithms. In *Proceedings of the Conference on Empirical Methods in Natural Language Processing*, pages 1092–1103. Association for Computational Linguistics.

Birgit Hamp and Helmut Feldweg. 1997. GermaNet - a Lexical-Semantic Net for German. In *Proceedings of ACL workshop Automatic Information Extraction and Building of Lexical Semantic Resources for NLP Applications*, pages 9–15, Madrid, Spain.

Verena Henrich, Erhard Hinrichs, and Tatiana Vodolazova. 2012. Webcage: a web-harvested corpus annotated with germanet senses. In *Proceedings of the 13th Conference of the European Chapter of the Association for Computational Linguistics*, pages 387–396. Association for Computational Linguistics.

Roberto Navigli and Simone Paolo Ponzetto. 2010. Babelnet: Building a very large multilingual semantic network. In *Proceedings of the 48th annual meeting of the association for computational linguistics*, pages 216–225. Association for Computational Linguistics.

Malka Rappaport Hovav and Beth Levin. 1998. Building verb meanings. *The projection of arguments: Lexical and compositional factors*, pages 97–134.

Kevin Reschke and Pranav Anand. 2011. Extracting contextual evaluativity. In *Proceedings of the Ninth International Conference on Computational Semantics*, pages 370–374, Oxford, UK.

Josef Ruppenhofer, Michael Ellsworth, Miriam R.L. Petruck, Christopher R. Johnson, and Jan Scheffczyk. 2010. *FrameNet II: Extended Theory and Practice*. International Computer Science Institute, Berkeley, California. Distributed with the FrameNet data.

Carol L Tenny. 1994. *Aspectual roles and the syntax-semantics interface*. Springer.

Janyce Wiebe and Lingjia Deng. 2014. An account of opinion implicatures. *CoRR*, abs/1404.6491.

Analysing domain suitability of a sentiment lexicon by identifying distributionally bipolar words

Lucie Flekova[1]*, Eugen Ruppert[2] and **Daniel Preoţiuc-Pietro[3]**

[1]Ubiquitous Knowledge Processing Lab, Technische Universität Darmstadt
[2] FG Language Technology, Technische Universität Darmstadt
[3] Computer & Information Science, University of Pennsylvania
flekova@ukp.informatik.tu-darmstadt.de, ruppert@lt.tu-darmstadt.de, danielpr@sas.upenn.edu

Abstract

Contemporary sentiment analysis approaches rely heavily on lexicon based methods. This is mainly due to their simplicity, although the best empirical results can be achieved by more complex techniques. We introduce a method to assess suitability of generic sentiment lexicons for a given domain, namely to identify frequent bigrams where a polar word switches polarity. Our bigrams are scored using Lexicographers Mutual Information and leveraging large automatically obtained corpora. Our score matches human perception of polarity and demonstrates improvements in classification results using our enhanced context-aware method. Our method enhances the assessment of lexicon based sentiment detection algorithms and can be further used to quantify ambiguous words.

1 Introduction

Sentiment prediction from microblogging posts is of the utmost interest for researchers as well as commercial organizations. State-of-the-art sentiment research often focuses on in-depth semantic understanding of emotional constructs (Trivedi and Eisenstein, 2013; Cambria et al., 2013; De Marneffe et al., 2010) or neural network models (Socher et al., 2013; Severyn and Moschitti, 2015). However, recent sentiment prediction challenges show that the vast majority of currently used systems is still based on supervised learning techniques with the most important features derived from pre-existing sentiment lexica (Rosenthal et al., 2014; Rosenthal et al., 2015).

Sentiment lexicons were initially developed as general-purpose resources (Pennebaker et al., 2001; Strapparava et al., 2004; Hu and Liu, 2004; Wilson et al., 2005). Recently, there has been an increasing amount of work on platform-specific lexicons such as Twitter (Mohammad, 2012; Mohammad et al., 2013). However, even customized platform- and domain-specific lexica still suffer from ambiguities at a contextual level, e.g. *cold* beer (+) or *cold* food (-), *dark* chocolate (+) or *dark* soul (-).

In this paper, we propose a method to assess the suitability of an established lexicon for a new platform or domain by leveraging automatically collected data approximating sentiment labels (silver standard). We present a method for creating switched polarity bigram lists to explicitly reveal and address the issues of a lexicon in question (e.g. the positivity of ***cold** beer, **dark** chocolate* or ***limited** edition*). Note that the contextual polarity switch does not necessarily happen on sense level, but within one word sense. We demonstrate that the explicit usage of such inverse polarity bigrams and replacement of the words with high ambiguity improves the performance of the classifier on unseen test data and that this improvement exceeds the performance of simply using all in-domain bigrams. Further, our bigram ranking method is evaluated by human raters, showing high face validity.

2 Related Work

Sentiment research has tremendously expanded in the past decade. Overall, sentiment lexicons are the most popular inputs to polarity classification (Rosenthal et al., 2015; Rosenthal et al., 2014), although the lexicons alone are far from sufficient. Initial studies relied heavily on explicit, manually crafted sentiment lexicons (Kim and Hovy, 2004; Pang and Lee, 2004; Hu and Liu, 2004). There have been efforts to infer the polarity lexicons automatically. Turney and Littman (2003) determined the semantic orientation of a target word t by comparing its association with two seed sets of manually crafted target words. Others derived the polar-

* Project carried out during a research stay at the University of Pennsylvania

Proceedings of the 6th Workshop on Computational Approaches to Subjectivity, Sentiment and Social Media Analysis (WASSA 2015), pages 77–84,
Lisboa, Portugal, 17 September, 2015.

ity from other lexicons (Baccianella et al., 2010; Mohammad et al., 2009), and adapted lexicons to specific domains, for example using integer linear programming (Choi and Cardie, 2009).

Lexicons are not stable across time and domain. Cook and Stevenson (2010) proposed a method to compare dictionaries for amelioration and pejoration of words over time. Mitra et al. (2014) analyzed changes in senses over time. Dragut et al. (2012) examined inconsistency across lexicons.

Negation and its scope has been studied extensively (Moilanen and Pulman, 2008; Pang and Lee, 2004; Choi and Cardie, 2009). Polar words can even carry an opposite sentiment in a new domain (Blitzer et al., 2007; Andreevskaia and Bergler, 2006; Schwartz et al., 2013; Wilson et al., 2005). Wilson et al. (2005) identified polarity shifter words to adjust the sentiment on phrase level. Choi and Cardie (2009) validated that topic-specific features would enhance existing sentiment classifiers. Ikeda et al. (2008) first proposed a machine learning approach to detect polarity shifting for sentence-level sentiment classification. Taboada et al. (2011) presented a polarity lexicon with negation words and intensifiers, which they refer to as contextual valence shifters (Polanyi and Zaenen, 2006). Research by Kennedy and Inkpen (2006) dealt with negation and intensity by creating a discrete modifier scale, namely, the occurrence of *good* might be either *good*, *not good*, *intensified good*, or *diminished good*. A similar approach was taken by Steinberger et al. (2012). Polarity modifiers, however, do not distinguish cases such as *cannot be bad* from *cannot be worse*.

Further experiments revealed that some nouns can carry sentiment per se (e.g. *chocolate*, *injury*). Recently, several noun connotation lexicons have been built (Feng et al., 2013; Klenner et al., 2014) based on a set of seed adjectives. One of the biggest disadvantages of polarity lexicons, however, is that they rely on either positive or negative score of a word, while in reality it can be used in both contexts even within the same domain (Volkova et al., 2013).

3 Method

This section describes our methodology for identifying ambiguous sentiment bearing lexicon words based on the contexts they appear in. We demonstrate our approach on two polarity lexicons consisting of single words, namely the lexicon of Hu and Liu (Hu and Liu, 2004), further denoted **HL**, and the **MPQA** lexicon (Wilson et al., 2005). First we use a corpus of automatically collected Twitter sentiment data set of over one million tweets (detailed in section 3.2) to compute bigram polarities for the lexicon words and determine contexts which alter the polarity of the original lexicon word. Using the JoBimText framework (Biemann and Riedl, 2013), we build a large Twitter bigram thesaurus which serves as a background frequency distribution which aids in ranking the bigrams (see section 3.1). For each lexicon word, we then replace the most ambiguous words with bigrams. We compare this on sentiment prediction with a straightforward usage of all bigrams.

3.1 Twitter Bigram Thesaurus

Methods based on word co-occurrence have a long tradition in NLP research, being used in tasks such as collocation extraction or sentiment analysis. Turney and Littman (2003) used polarity seeds to measure words which co-occur with positive/negative contexts. However, the PMI is known to be sensitive to low count words and bigrams, overemphasising them over high frequency words. To account for this, we express the mutual information of a word bigram by means of Lexicographer's Mutual Information (LMI).[1] The LMI, introduced by Kilgarriff et al. (2004), offers an advantage to Pointwise Mutual Information (PMI), as the scores are multiplied by the bigram frequency, boosting more frequent combinations of word (w) and context (c).

$$\text{PMI}(w,c) = \log_2\left(\frac{f(w,c)}{f(w)\cdot f(c)}\right)$$

$$\text{LMI}(w,c) = \text{PMI}(w,c)\cdot f(w,c)$$

3.2 Bigram Sentiment Scores

We compute the LMI over a corpus of positive, respectively negative tweets, in order to obtain positive (LMI_{pos}) and negative (LMI_{neg}) bigram scores. We combine the following freely available data, leading to a large corpus of positive and negative tweets:

- 1.6 million automatically labeled tweets from the Sentiment140 data set (Go et al., 2009), collected by searching for positive and negative emoticons;

[1]An online demo illustrating the score values and distributional term similarities in this Twitter space can be found at the LT website `http://maggie.lt.informatik.tu-darmstadt.de/jobimviz/`

- 7,000 manually labeled tweets from University of Michigan;[2]
- 5,500 manually labeled tweets from Niek J. Sanders;[3]
- 2,000 manually labeled tweets from the STS-Gold data set (Saif et al., 2013).

We filtered out fully duplicate messages, as these appear to bring more noise than realistic frequency information. The resulting corpus contains 794,000 positive and 791,000 negative tweets. In pursuance of comparability between the positive and negative LMI scores, we weight the bigrams by their relative frequency in the respective data set, thus discounting rare or evenly distributed bigrams, as illustrated for negative score in:

$$\text{LMI}_{neg_{REL}}(w,c) = \text{LMI}_{neg}(w,c) \cdot \frac{f_{neg}(w,c)}{f_{neg}(w,c) + f_{pos}(w,c)}$$

Since the LMI scores from a limited sized data set are not the most reliable, we further boost them by incorporating scores from a background corpus (LMI_{GLOB}) – described below. This approach emphasizes significant bigrams, even when their score in one polarity data set is low:

$$\text{LMI}_{neg_{GLOB}}(w,c) = \text{LMI}_{neg_{REL}}(w,c) \cdot \text{LMI}_{GLOB}(w,c)$$

As background data we use a Twitter corpus of 1 % of all tweets from the year 2013, obtained through the Twitter Spritzer API. We filtered this corpus with a language filter,[4] resulting in 460 million English tweets.

For each bigram, we then compute its semantic orientation:

$$\text{LMI}_{SO} = \text{LMI}_{pos_{GLOB}} - \text{LMI}_{neg_{GLOB}}$$

These two large bigram lists, which at this point still contain all bigrams from the Twitter sentiment corpus, are then filtered by sentiment lexica, as we are only interested in bigrams with at least one word from the original sentiment lexicon (containing sigle words). We chose two sentiment polarity lexica for our experiments:

- the **HL** lexicon (Hu and Liu, 2004) having 4,782 negative and 2,004 positive words (e.g. *happy, good, bad*);
- the **MPQA** sentiment lexicon (Wilson et al., 2005), with 1,751 positive and 2,693 negative words.[5]

The most interesting candidates for a novel bigram sentiment lexicon are:

- bigrams containing a word from a **negative** lexicon, which has a **positive semantic orientation** LMI_{SO}, i.e. having higher global LMI in the positive data set than in the negative;
- bigrams containing a word from a **positive** lexicon with **negative semantic orientation** LMI_{SO}

The top ranked bigrams, where local contextualization reverts the original lexicon score, are listed for both lexicons in Table 1. We can observe that the polarity shifting occurs in a broad range of situations, e.g. by using polar word as an intensity expression (***super*** *tired*), by using polar word in names (***desperate*** *housewives,* frank *iero*), by using multiword expressions, idioms and collocations (***cloud*** *computing,* ***sincere*** *condolences,* ***light*** *bulbs*), but also by adding a polar nominal context to the adjective (***cold*** *beer/person,* ***dark*** *chocolate/thoughts,* ***stress*** *reliever/management,* ***guilty*** *pleasure/feeling*).

3.3 Quantifying Polarity

We have shown how to identify words which switch to the opposite polarity based on their word context. Our next goal is to identify words which occur in many contexts with both the original and the switched polarity and therefore are, without further disambiguation, harmful in either of the lexicons. With this aim we calculate a polarity score POL_{word} for each word (w) in the polarity lexicon, using the number of its positive and negative contexts determined by their semantic orientation LMI_{SO} as previously computed:

$$\text{POL}(w) = p_{pos}(w) - p_{neg}(w)$$

where we define $p_{pos}(w)$ and $p_{neg}(w)$, as the count of positive and negative bigrams respectively, of a

[2] http://inclass.kaggle.com/c/si650winter11/data

[3] http://www.sananalytics.com/lab/twitter-sentiment/

[4] https://github.com/shuyo/language-detection

[5] This lexicon also contains neutral words, which might be interesting for some applications. Since the **HL** lexicon does not feature neutral words, we chose to omit those entries for comparable results. The words in **MPQA** are further distinguished as 'strong' or 'weak' by POS tag. Since we do not maintain POS information in our distributional LMI lists, we chose to utilize all indicators equally.

Negative to Positive			
HL		MPQA	
Word	Context	Word	Context
limit	why-	vice	-versa
sneak	-peek	stress	-reliever
impossible	mission-	down	calmed-
lazy	-sunday	deep	-breath
desperate	-housewives	long	-awaited
cold	-beer	cloud	-computing
guilty	-pleasure	dark	-haired
belated	-birthday	bloody	-mary
Positive to Negative			
HL		**MPQA**	
Word	Context	Word	Context
luck	good-	super	-duper
wisdom	-tooth	happy	-camper
well	oh-	just	-puked
work	gotta-	heart	-breaker
hot	-outside	gold	-digger
better	feels-	light	-bulbs
super	-tired	sincere	-condolences
enough	-money	frank	-iero

Table 1: Bigrams with opposite LMI sentiment orientation than the original lexicon word. Note that the polarity rarely changes on sense level i.e., same sense can have different polar contexts.

lexicon word, divided by the count of all bigrams of that word:

$$p_{neg}(w) = \frac{\sum(w,c)_{\forall(w,c):\text{LMI}_{SO}<0}}{\sum(w,c)}$$

Lexicon words with the lowest absolute polarity score and the highest number of different contexts (w,c) are listed in Table 2.

4 Experiments

To evaluate the quality of our bigrams, we perform two studies. First, we rate our inverted polarity bigrams intrinsically using crowdsourced annotations. Second, we assess the performance of the original and adjusted lexicons on a distinct expert-constructed data set of 1,600 Facebook messages annotated for sentiment. The disambiguated bigram lexicons are available on author's website.

4.1 Intrinsic Evaluation

We crowdsource ratings for the inverted polarity bigrams found using both the **HL** and **MPQA** lexicon. The raters were presented a list of 100 bigrams of each lexicon, with 25% having the same positive polarity as in the original lexicon, 25% the same negative polarity, 25% switching polarity from positive unigram to negative bigram and the remaining

HL				
Word	POL(w)	$\#(w,c)_{pos}$	$\#(w,c)_{neg}$	orig
hot	.022	1151	1101	+
support	.022	517	494	+
important	-.023	204	214	+
super	-.043	734	801	+
crazy	-.045	809	886	-
right	-.065	3061	3491	+
proper	-.093	242	292	+
worked	-.111	275	344	+
top	.113	516	411	+
enough	-.114	927	1167	+
hell	.115	616	488	-
MPQA				
Word	POL(w)	$\#(w,c)_{pos}$	$\#(w,c)_{neg}$	orig
just	-.002	742	738	+
less	.009	51	50	-
sound	-.011	43	44	+
real	.027	35	37	+
little	.032	354	332	-
help	-.037	42	39	+
back	-.046	191	174	+
mean	.090	24	20	-
down	-.216	154	239	-
too	-.239	252	411	-

Table 2: Most ambiguous sentiment lexicon words. Table displays the proportion of their positive and negative contexts and the original lexicon polarity.

quarter vice versa. They had to answer the question 'Which polarity does this word pair have?', given *positive*, *negative* and also *neutral* as options. Each bigram is rated by three annotators and the majority vote is selected. The inter-annotator agreement is measured using weighted Cohen's κ (Cohen, 1968), which is especially useful for ordered annotations, as it accounts not only for chance, but also for the seriousness of a disagreement between annotators. κ can range from -1 to 1, where the value of 0 represents an agreement equal to chance while 1 equals to a perfect agreement, i.e. identical annotation values. We obtained an agreement of weighted Cohen's $\kappa = 0.55$, which represents a "moderate agreement" (Landis and Koch, 1977). The confusion matrix of average human judgement compared to our computed bigram polarity is shown in Table 3. Some of the bigrams, especially for the MPQA lexicon, were assessed as objective, which our LMI method unfortunately does not reflect beyond the score value (neutral words are less polar). However, the confusion between negatively and positively labeled bigrams was very low.

	HL			MPQA		
	Pos.	Neu.	Neg.	Pos.	Neu.	Neg.
Pos.	30	10	9	21	24	3
Neg.	11	10	30	5	18	25

Table 3: Confusion matrix for the majority vote of word polarity by three annotators.

4.2 Extrinsic Evaluation

We evaluate our method on a data set of Facebook posts annotated for positive and negative sentiment by two psychologists. The posts are annotated on a scale from 1 to 9, with 1 indicating strong negative sentiment and 9 strong positive sentiment. An average rating between annotators is considered to be the final message score. Ratings follow a normal distribution, i.e. with more messages having less polar score. An inter-annotator agreement of weighted Cohen's $\kappa = 0.61$ on exact score was reached, representing a "substantial agreeement"(Landis and Koch, 1977). Given our task, in which we attempt to improve on misleading bipolar words, we removed the posts annotated as neutral (rating 5.0). This left us with 2,087 posts, of which we use only those containing at least one word from the polarity lexicons of our interest, i.e., 1,601 posts for **MPQA** and 1,526 posts for **HL**. We then compute a sentiment score of a post as a difference of positive and negative word counts present in the post. If a bigram containing the lexicon word is found, its LMI_{SO} score is used instead of the lexicon word polarity score. For the two lexicons and their modifications, we employ two evaluation measures - Pearson correlation of the sentiment score of a post with the affect score, and classification accuracy on binary label, i.e., distinguishing if the affect is negative (1–4) or positive (6–9). Table 4 presents our results of four experiments using the following features:

- using the original unigram lexicon only (1);
- using original lexicon corrected by polarity score of lexicon bigrams when they appear (2–4);
- using pruned unigram lexicon, removing words that exceed entropy threshold of 0.99 or appear in more contexts of the opposite polarity than of the assumed one (5);
- using pruned unigram lexicon corrected by polarity score of (unpruned) lexicon bigrams when they appear (6–8);
- all bigrams (9).

		HL		MPQA	
Id	Features	Acc.	Corr.	Acc.	Corr.
1	Unigrams	.7070	.5828	.6608	.4473
2	Unigrams + Bigrams	.7215	.5959	.6633	.4478
3	Unigrams + Bigrams_+	.7123	.5928	.6621	.4468
4	Unigrams + Bigrams_-	.7163	.5973	.6621	.4472
5	Pruned	.7228	.6131	.6627	.4817
6	Pruned + Bigrams	**.7333**	.5943	**.6646**	.4917
7	Pruned + Bigrams_+	.7150	.6264	.6633	.4907
8	Pruned + Bigrams_-	.7287	.6330	.6640	.4929
9	All in-domain Bigrams	.6907	.1837	**.7008**	.1812

Table 4: Predictive performance using lexicon based methods, displaying the classification accuracy and linear correlation of the affect score to LMI. Using McNemar's two-tailed test, there is a significant difference on $p<0.05$ level between the runs 1 and 2, 5 and 6 and 1 and 5 for BL, and between the runs 1 and 6 for MPQA.

Table 4 shows that adding contextual bigrams brings a consistent improvement (1 vs. 2, 5 vs. 6). Especially the negative part of the bigram lexica, including bigrams of negative words which have positive orientation, consistently improves results (1 vs. 4, 5 vs. 8). Likewise, pruning of the lexicon with the polar entropy score (1 vs. 5) enhances the sentiment prediction performance. For both polarity lexicons the best performance is achieved by combining the two effects (8).

In case of the first lexicon, the performance is even higher than in case of applying for the same data a fully in-domain bigram lexicon, generated from the same large public Twitter corpus (Mohammad et al., 2013).

The correction of negative unigrams to positive bigrams does not improve the prediction as much as its counterpart. The main cause appears to be the fact that those expressions with shifted polarity shall be rather neutral - as discussed in section 4.1 and by some recent research (Zhu et al., 2014).

4.3 Discussion

Usage of bigrams does not always bring improvement, but sometimes also introduces new errors. One of the frequent sources of errors appears to be the remaining ambiguity of the bigrams due to more complex phrase structure. While the bigrams are tremendously helpful in message chunks such as '*holy shit, tech support...*', where the *holy* (+1) and *support* (+1) is replaced by its appropriately polar contexts (-0.35, -0.85), the same replacement is harmful in a post '*holy shit monday night was amazing*'. Same applies for bigrams such as *work ahead* (-0.89) in '*new house....yeah!! lots of work ahead of us!!!*' or *nice outside* (-0.65) in '*it's nice outside today!*'.

Additionally, the performance suffers when a longer negation window is applied, such as *feeling sick* in the post '*Isn't feeling sick woohoo!*'. In our setup we did not employ explicit polarity switchers commonly used with word lexicons (Wilson et al., 2005; Pang and Lee, 2008; Steinberger et al., 2012) since the context captured by the bigrams often incorporated subtle negation hints per se, including their misspelled variations. This would make the combination of bigrams with more sophisticated syntactic features challenging.

Another very interesting issue are the bigrams which are explicitly positive but have learnt their negative connotation from a broader context, such as *happy camper* or *looking good*, which are more often used jointly with negations. Posts that use these bigrams without negation ('*someone is a happy camper!*') then lead to errors, and similarly a manual human assessment without a longer context fails. This issue concerns distributional approaches in general.

Lastly, several errors arise from the non-standard, slang and misspelled words which are not present often enough in our silver standard corpus. For example, while *love you* is clearly positive, *love ya* has a negative score. On corpora such as Twitter, further optimization of word frequency thresholds in lexical methods requires special attention.

5 Conclusion

Lexicon based methods currently remain, due to their simplicity, the most prevalent sentiment analysis approaches. While it is taken for granted that using more in-domain training data is always helpful, a little attention has been given to determining how much and why a given general-purpose lexicon can help in a specific target domain or platform. We introduced a method to identify frequent bigrams where a word switches polarity, and to find out which words are bipolar to the extent that it is better to have them removed from the polarity lexica. We demonstrated that our scores match human perception of polarity and bring improvement in the classification results using our enhanced context-aware method. Our method enhances the assessment of lexicon based sentiment detection algorithms and can be further used to quantify ambiguous words.

Acknowledgements

LF and DP-P acknowledge the support from Templeton Religion Trust, grant TRT-0048. The work of ER has been supported by the German Federal Ministry of Education and Research (BMBF) within the context of the Software Campus project LiCoRes under grant No. 01IS12054

References

Alina Andreevskaia and Sabine Bergler. 2006. Mining WordNet for a fuzzy sentiment: Sentiment tag extraction from WordNet glosses. In *Proceedings of the 11th Conference of the European Chapter of the Association for Computational Linguistics*, EACL, pages 209–216.

Stefano Baccianella, Andrea Esuli, and Fabrizio Sebastiani. 2010. SentiWordNet 3.0: An enhanced lexical resource for sentiment analysis and opinion mining. In *Proceedings of the Seventh International Conference on Language Resources and Evaluation*, LREC, pages 2200–2204.

Chris Biemann and Martin Riedl. 2013. Text: Now in 2D! a framework for lexical expansion with contextual similarity. *Journal of Language Modelling*, 1(1):55–95.

John Blitzer, Mark Dredze, and Fernando Pereira. 2007. Biographies, Bollywood, boom-boxes and blenders: Domain adaptation for sentiment classification. In *Proceedings of the 45th Annual Meeting of the Association for Computational Linguistics*, ACL, pages 440–447.

Erik Cambria, Bjorn Schuller, Yunqing Xia, and Catherine Havasi. 2013. New avenues in opinion mining and sentiment analysis. *IEEE Intelligent Systems*, (2):15–21.

Yejin Choi and Claire Cardie. 2009. Adapting a polarity lexicon using integer linear programming for domain-specific sentiment classification. In *Proceedings of the 2009 Conference on Empirical Methods in Natural Language Processing*, EMNLP, pages 590–598.

Jacob Cohen. 1968. Weighted kappa: Nominal scale agreement provision for scaled disagreement or partial credit. *Psychological bulletin*, 70(4).

Paul Cook and Suzanne Stevenson. 2010. Automatically identifying changes in the semantic Ooientation of words. In *Proceedings of the Seventh International Conference on Language Resources and Evaluation*, LREC, pages 129–149.

Marie-Catherine De Marneffe, Christopher D Manning, and Christopher Potts. 2010. Was it good? It was provocative. Learning the meaning of scalar adjectives. In *Proceedings of the 48th Annual Meeting of the Association for Computational Linguistics*, ACL, pages 167–176.

Eduard Dragut, Hong Wang, Clement Yu, Prasad Sistla, and Weiyi Meng. 2012. Polarity consistency checking for sentiment dictionaries. In *Proceedings of the 50th Annual Meeting of the Association for Computational Linguistics*, ACL, pages 997–1005.

Song Feng, Jun Seok Kang, Polina Kuznetsova, and Yejin Choi. 2013. Connotation lexicon: A dash of sentiment beneath the surface meaning. In *Proceedings of the 51st Annual Meeting of the Association for Computational Linguistics*, ACL, pages 1774–1784.

Alec Go, Richa Bhayani, and Lei Huang. 2009. Twitter sentiment classification using distant supervision. *CS224N Project Report, Stanford*, 1.

Minqing Hu and Bing Liu. 2004. Mining and summarizing customer reviews. In *Proceedings of the tenth ACM SIGKDD International conference on Knowledge Discovery and Data Mining*, KDD, pages 168–177.

Daisuke Ikeda, Hiroya Takamura, Lev-Arie Ratinov, and Manabu Okumura. 2008. Learning to shift the polarity of words for sentiment classification. In *Proceedings of the International Joint Conference on Natural Language Processing*, IJCNLP, pages 296–303.

Alistair Kennedy and Diana Inkpen. 2006. Sentiment classification of movie reviews using contextual valence shifters. *Computational Intelligence*, 22(2):110–125.

Adam Kilgarriff, Pavel Rychly, Pavel Smrz, and David Tugwell. 2004. Itri-04-08 the sketch engine. *Information Technology*, 105.

Soo-Min Kim and Eduard Hovy. 2004. Determining the sentiment of opinions. In *Proceedings of the 20th international conference on Computational Linguistics*, COLING, pages 1367–1378.

Manfred Klenner, Michael Amsler, and Nora Hollenstein. 2014. Inducing domain-specific noun polarity guided by domain-independent polarity preferences of adjectives. In *Proceedings of the 52nd Annual Meeting of the Association for Computational Linguistics*, ACL, pages 18–23.

J Richard Landis and Gary G Koch. 1977. The measurement of observer agreement for categorical data. *biometrics*, pages 159–174.

Sunny Mitra, Ritwik Mitra, Martin Riedl, Chris Biemann, Animesh Mukherjee, and Pawan Goyal. 2014. That's sick dude!: Automatic identification of word sense change across different timescales. In *Proceedings of the 52nd Annual Meeting of the Association for Computational Linguistics*, ACL, pages 1020–1029.

Saif Mohammad, Cody Dunne, and Bonnie Dorr. 2009. Generating high-coverage semantic orientation lexicons from overtly marked words and a thesaurus. In *Proceedings of the 2009 Conference on Empirical Methods in Natural Language Processing*, EMNLP, pages 599–608.

Saif Mohammad, Svetlana Kiritchenko, and Xiaodan Zhu. 2013. NRC-Canada: Building the state-of-the-art in sentiment analysis of tweets. In *Second Joint Conference on Lexical and Computational Semantics*, volume 2 of **SeM*, pages 321–327.

Saif Mohammad. 2012. #emotional tweets. In *Proceedings of the First Joint Conference on Lexical and Computational Semantics*, *SEM, pages 246–255.

Karo Moilanen and Stephen Pulman. 2008. The good, the bad, and the unknown: Morphosyllabic sentiment tagging of unseen words. In *Proceedings of the 46th Annual Meeting of the Association for Computational Linguistics on Human Language Technologies*, ACL, pages 109–112.

Bo Pang and Lillian Lee. 2004. A sentimental education: Sentiment analysis using subjectivity summarization based on minimum cuts. In *Proceedings of the 42nd annual meeting on Association for Computational Linguistics*, ACL, pages 271–278.

Bo Pang and Lillian Lee. 2008. Opinion mining and sentiment analysis. *Foundations and Trends in Information Retrieval*, 2:1–135.

James W. Pennebaker, Martha E. Francis, and Roger J. Booth. 2001. *Linguistic Inquiry and Word Count.*

Livia Polanyi and Annie Zaenen. 2006. Contextual valence shifters. In *Computing attitude and affect in text: Theory and applications*, pages 1–10. Springer.

Sara Rosenthal, Preslav Nakov, Alan Ritter, and Veselin Stoyanov. 2014. Semeval-2014 task 9: Sentiment analysis in Twitter.

Sara Rosenthal, Preslav Nakov, Svetlana Kiritchenko, Saif Mohammad, Alan Ritter, and Veselin Stoyanov. 2015. Semeval-2015 task 10: Sentiment analysis in Twitter. In *Proceedings of the 9th International Workshop on Semantic Evaluation, SemEval.*

Hassan Saif, Miriam Fernandez, Yulan He, and Harith Alani. 2013. Evaluation datasets for Twitter sentiment analysis: A survey and a new dataset, the STS-gold. In *Proceedings of the 1st International Workshop on Emotion and Sentiment in Social and Expressive Media: Approaches and Perspectives from AI*, ESSEM.

H Andrew Schwartz, Johannes C Eichstaedt, Lukasz Dziurzynski, Margaret L Kern, Eduardo Blanco, Stephanie Ramones, Martin E P Seligman, and Lyle H Ungar. 2013. Choosing the right words: Characterizing and reducing error of the word count approach. In *Proceedings of the Second Joint Conference on Lexical and Computational Semantics*, *SEM, pages 296–305.

Aliaksei Severyn and Alessandro Moschitti. 2015. Twitter sentiment analysis with deep convolutional neural networks. In *Proceedings of the 38th International ACM SIGIR Conference on Research and Development in Information Retrieval*, pages 959–962.

Richard Socher, Alex Perelygin, Jean Y Wu, Jason Chuang, Christopher D Manning, Andrew Y Ng, and Christopher Potts. 2013. Recursive deep models for semantic compositionality over a sentiment treebank. In *Proceedings of the 2012 Joint Conference on Empirical Methods in Natural Language Processing and Computational Natural Language Learning*, EMNLP, pages 1642–1649.

Josef Steinberger, Mohamed Ebrahim, Maud Ehrmann, Ali Hurriyetoglu, Mijail Kabadjov, Polina Lenkova, Ralf Steinberger, Hristo Tanev, Silvia Vazquez, and Vanni Zavarella. 2012. Creating sentiment dictionaries via triangulation. *Decision Support Systems*, 53(4).

Carlo Strapparava, Alessandro Valitutti, et al. 2004. WordNet Affect: An affective extension of WordNet. In *Proceedings of the Fourth International Conference on Language Resources and Evaluation*, LREC, pages 1083–1086.

Maite Taboada, Julian Brooke, Milan Tofiloski, Kimberly Voll, and Manfred Stede. 2011. Lexicon-based methods for sentiment analysis. *Computational Linguistics*, 37(2):267–307.

Rakshit S Trivedi and Jacob Eisenstein. 2013. Discourse connectors for latent subjectivity in sentiment analysis. In *HLT-NAACL*, pages 808–813.

Peter D Turney and Michael L Littman. 2003. Measuring praise and criticism: Inference of semantic orientation from association. *ACM Transactions on Information Systems*, 21(4):315–346.

Svitlana Volkova, Theresa Wilson, and David Yarowsky. 2013. Exploring sentiment in social media: Bootstrapping subjectivity clues from multilingual twitter streams. In *Proceedings of the 51st Annual Meeting of the Association for Computational Linguistics on Human Language Technologies*, ACL, pages 505–510.

Theresa Wilson, Janyce Wiebe, and Paul Hoffmann. 2005. Recognizing contextual polarity in phrase-level sentiment analysis. In *Proceedings of the 2005 Joint Conference on Empirical Methods in Natural Language Processing and Computational Natural Language Learning*, EMNLP, pages 347–354.

Xiaodan Zhu, Hongyu Guo, Saif Mohammad, and Svetlana Kiritchenko. 2014. An empirical study on the effect of negation words on sentiment. In *Proceedings of the 52rd Annual Meeting of the Association for Computational Linguistics*, ACL, pages 304–313.

Imagisaurus: An Interactive Visualizer of Valence and Emotion in the Roget's Thesaurus

Saif M. Mohammad
National Research Council Canada
saif.mohammad@nrc-cnrc.gc.ca

Abstract

The form of a thesaurus often restricts its use to word look ups and finding related words. We present *Imagisaurus*, an online interactive visualizer for the *Roget's Thesaurus*, which not only provides a way for word lookups but also helps users quickly grasp the nature and size of the thesaurus taxonomy. Imagisaurus connects thesaurus entries with a large valence and emotion association lexicon. Easy-to-use sliders give the user fine control over depicting only those categories with the desired strength of association with positive or negative sentiment, as well as eight basic emotions. A second interactive visualization is used to explore the emotion lexicon. Both the *Roget's Thesaurus* and the emotion lexicon have tens of thousands of entries. Our visualizers help users better understand these lexical resources in terms of their make up as a whole.

1 Introduction

The *Roget's Thesaurus* (Roget, 1852) was created by Peter Roget in 1852 and originally included about 15,000 English words. Since then a number of newer versions of the thesaurus have been published, and each has included more terms than the previous version. *Roget's* taxonomic structure, which is inspired by philosophical work of Leibniz on symbolic thought (Leibniz and Parkinson, 1995; Leibniz, 1923), groups words into six *classes*: words expressing abstract relations, words relating to space, words relating to matter, words relating to the intellectual faculties, words relating to the voluntary powers, and words relating to the sentient and moral powers. These six classes are further partitioned into thirty nine *sections*, which are in-turn divided into one thousand *categories*. Each category lists about 20 to 200 related words and expressions. These categories can be thought of as coarse concepts.

Widely used by writers, lexicographers, students, and the lay person, the thesaurus is most commonly accessed to identify a word or phrase that best captures what one wants to communicate. Researchers in many fields find use for the thesaurus, for example those exploring literary, social science, psychological, and cognitive theories involving word usage. Not surprisingly, there is a vast and growing body of work in Computational Linguistics that makes use of the *Roget's Thesaurus*, including Masterman (1957), Morris and Hirst (1991), Yarowsky (1992), Mohammad and Hirst (2006), Mohammad (2008), and Grefenstette (2012). However, despite its substantial range and scope of use, manual access to information in the thesaurus is often restricted to looking up a word and finding its neighbors. Existing online portals for the *Roget's Thesaurus* present a very traditional, non-interactive, text-only interface.[1]

We present an online interactive visualizer for the *Roget's Thesaurus*, which we call *Imagisaurus*.[2] Imagisaurus allows users to access information about words, classes, sections, and categories through four separate sub-visualizations that are linked to each other. Clicking on a unit selects it and filters information in all other sub-visualizations, showing information that is relevant only to the selection. The hierarchical structure of the thesaurus is shown in proportion to the size of its components—where size is defined to be the number of words included in the thesaurus unit (category, section, etc.). This allows users to determine which thesaurus units are more populous. Additionally, Imagisaurus links the *Roget's*

[1] http://www.roget.org
http://machaut.uchicago.edu/rogets

[2] Imagisaurus: http://www.purl.com/net/imagisaurus
Imagisaurus currently uses the copyright-free Project Gutenberg version of the thesaurus (Roget, 1911).

Proceedings of the 6th Workshop on Computational Approaches to Subjectivity, Sentiment and Social Media Analysis (WASSA 2015), pages 85–91,
Lisboa, Portugal, 17 September, 2015.

Thesaurus with a large emotion lexicon and lets users interactively discover categories strongly associated with various affect categories: positive and negative valence (sentiment), as well as emotions of joy, sadness, fear, trust, disgust, anticipation, anger, and surprise. Easy-to-use sliders give the user fine control over depicting only those categories with the desired strength of association with an affect category.

Word–Affect association lexicons, such as the NRC Emotion Lexicon, are themselves large semantic resources used not only by computational linguists, but also by researchers in psychology, marketing, advertising, and public health. Thus we developed a second online interactive visualization for the NRC Emotion Lexicon.

Both the *Roget's Thesaurus* and the emotion lexicon have tens of thousands of entries. Thus obtaining a feel for them by manually reading every entry is prohibitive. Our visualizers, created using the visualization tool Tableau, help users better understand these lexical resources in terms of their make up as a whole.[3] Both visualizers are made available online and are free to use.[4]

2 Affect Associations

Many words such as *good* and *delighted* express affectual states such as positive sentiment, negative sentiment, joy, anger, and so on. Apart from literal, denotative, meaning, words also have *associations* with sentimental, emotional, cultural, and social overtones. For example, *skinny* and *slender* primarily convey information about girth, but additionally *skinny* is associated with a slight negative sentiment, whereas *slender* is associated with positive sentiment. Similarly, *party* is associated with joy whereas *test results* is associated with anticipation.[5] The *Roget's Thesaurus* groups related terms within the same category, and this means that a category can include terms associated with many affect categories.

The thesaurus itself makes no claims on the affect associations of its constituent words (denotative or connotative). However, recently large resources have been created that capture the affect associations of thousands of words: The General Inquirer (GI) has sentiment labels for about 3,600 terms (Stone et al., 1966). Hu and Liu (2004) manually labeled about 6,800 words and used them for detecting sentiment of customer reviews. Affective Norms for English Words (ANEW) has pleasure (happy–unhappy), arousal (excited–calm), and dominance (controlled–in control) ratings for 1034 words.[6] The WordNet Affect Lexicon (WAL) (Strapparava and Valitutti, 2004,) has a few hundred words annotated with associations to the six Ekman emotions. The NRC Emotion Lexicon has association labels for over 14,000 words with positive and negative sentiment, as well as the set of eight Plutchik emotions (Mohammad and Turney, 2010; Mohammad and Turney, 2013).[7] These labels were compiled through crowdsourcing. Lexicons for word–affect associations are used in automatic classification systems as well as systems that track affectual words in text (for example in literary analysis and for assessing well-being in social media posts).

We use the NRC Emotion Lexicon in Imagisaurus because of its large coverage and associations with both sentiment and emotions. However, other affect lexicons can also be plugged into the same visualization design.

3 Imagisaurus

Figure 1 shows a screenshot of Imagisaurus. (The tooltip info box, which shows information about the taxonomic unit over which the mouse pointer is hovering, can be ignored for now.) Observe that there are four sub-visualizations: Index, Classes, Sections, and Categories. On the top right corner is a legend showing the colors in which the six thesaurus classes are shown. (The colors were chosen somewhat at random, the only requirement being that they be easily distinguishable.) Below the legend are ten sliders corresponding to affect densities of ten affect categories (two sentiments and eight emotions).

The Index shows the index of the thesaurus, that is, it lists all the words in the thesaurus in alphabetical order along with the categories they are included in. The hierarchical structure of the thesaurus, in terms of its classes, sections, and categories, is shown through the three treemap visualizations—one for each level of the hierar-

[3] http://www.tableau.com

[4] Imagisaurus: http://www.purl.com/net/imagisaurus
Emotion Lexicon Viz.: http://www.purl.com/net/EmoLexViz

[5] Some of these connotations may be cultural, for example, dating may be seen unfavorably in some cultures, however, many connotations add to the denotative meanings of words and are commonly known.

[6] http://csea.phhp.ufl.edu/media/anewmessage.html

[7] www.purl.com/net/NRCemotionlexicon

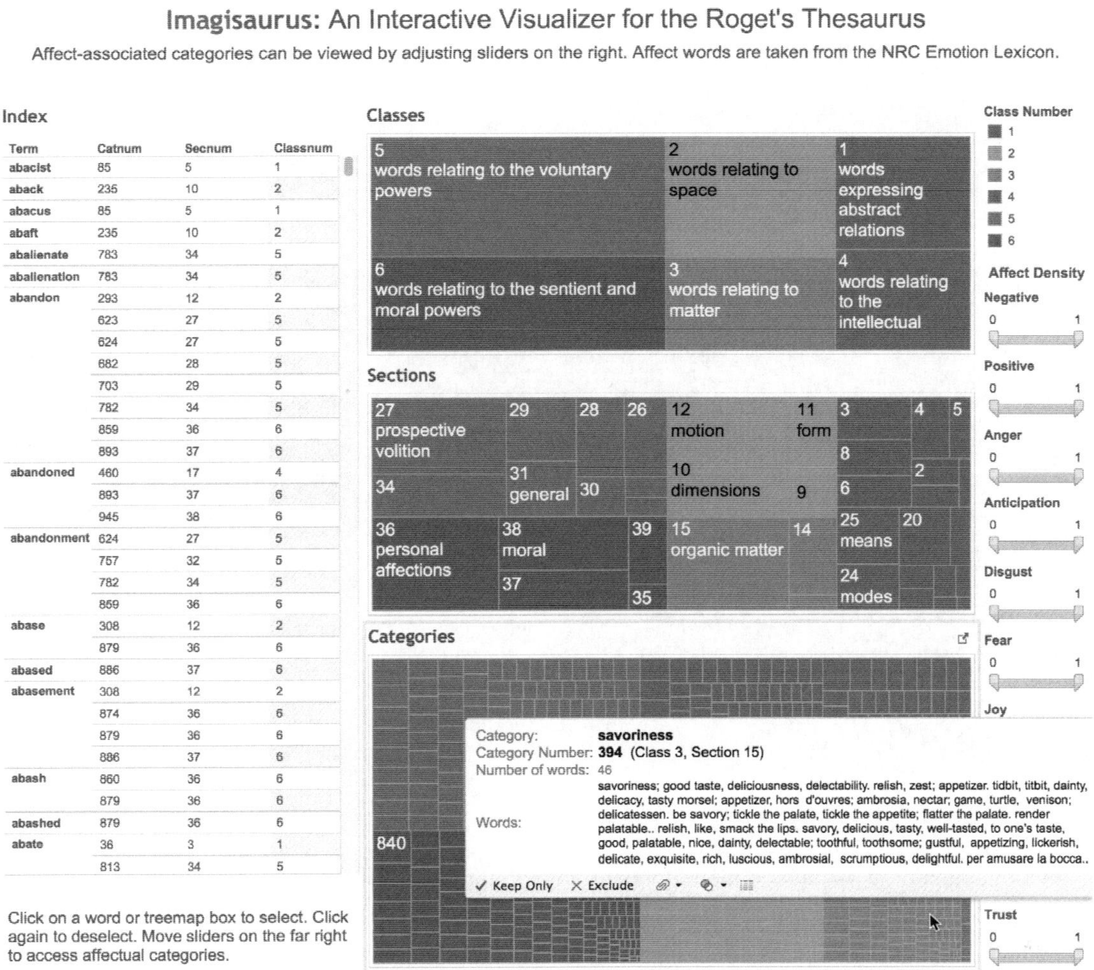

Figure 1: Screenshot of Imagisaurus when one moves the mouse pointer over one of the boxes in the Categories treemap. The tooltip info box pops up showing information pertaining to what is being hovered on—in this case category number 394 (savoriness).

chy. A treemap is a kind of visualization that partitions a large box representing one level into many smaller boxes pertaining to the descendant nodes.

If the box size permits, the name and number of the taxonomic unit is printed in it. For example, the name–number information for all classes and some sections is printed in the default view. This information is not shown for most of the categories in the default view, but as described ahead, when certain selections are made to reduce the number of categories, then this information appears even for the categories. Hovering over any box will always give the corresponding name-number information through a tooltip info box.

We describe each of the four sub-visualizations in the subsections below.

3.1 Index

The Index lists the words in alphabetical order. Users can scroll down the list to quickly locate the word they are interested in. They can then see which thesaurus categories the word is listed in (second column, Catnum), and also the corresponding section number (Secnum), and Class number (Classnum). Clicking on the word filters out information in all four sub-visualizations, leaving information pertaining only to the chosen word. For example, Figure 2 shows a screenshot of the treemaps for when the user clicks on the Index entry *abandon*. Observe that the three treemaps now show a blowup of information relevant only the chosen word: specifically, the classes, sections, and categories *abandon* is listed in.

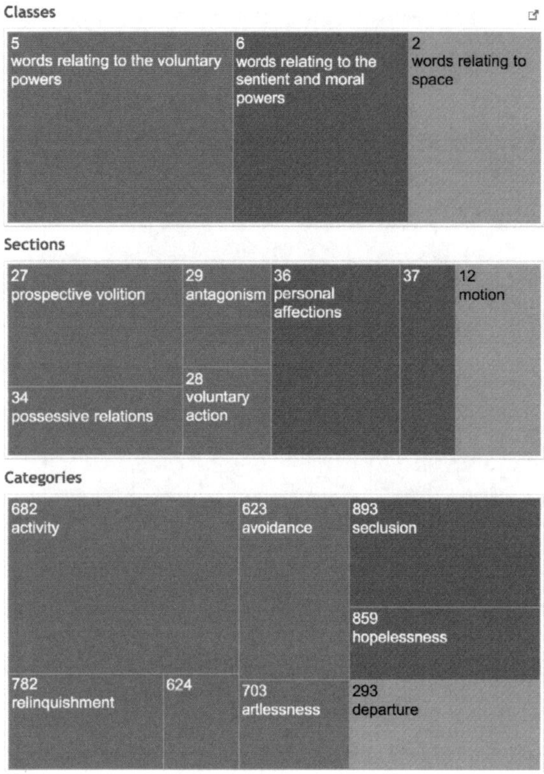

Figure 2: Filtered view in Imagisaurus when one clicks on the word *abandon* in the index.

3.2 Classes

The Classes treemap shows the six thesaurus classes as boxes. The size of each box is proportional to the number of words in the class. The treemap places the biggest boxes on the top left and the smallest boxes on the bottom right. This allows users to instantly gain a rough estimate of how large each class is. One can see for example that Section 5 has the most words and Section 4 the least. When selections are made in one of the other sub-visualizations and the Classes treemap filters to show relevant information (as in Figure 2 for example), one can then examine the sizes of the now-relevant classes. (For example, in Figure 2, one can now see the relative sizes of the three classes that list *abandon*.)

3.3 Sections

The Sections treemap shows all (or a selection) of sections in the *Roget's Thesaurus*. (Clicking on a particular class filters the Sections treemap to show only the relevant sections.) The sections are first grouped by class, and then within each

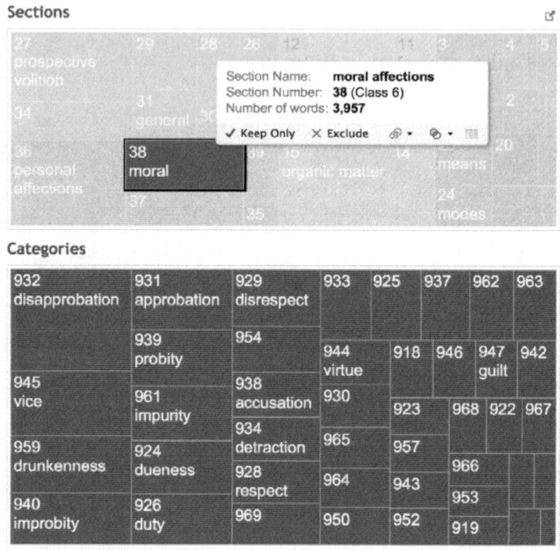

Figure 3: The Sections and categories Treemaps when one clicks on the Section 38 (moral).

of these groups they are ordered as per number of words in the sections. This allows users to quickly determine which sections are more dominant within a class. Clicking on a section filters information as one would expect. Figure 3 shows how the Sections treemap and the Categories treemap appear when one clicks on section 38 (moral). Observe that the Categories treemap now shows only those categories that are within section 38. The Index also filters to show rows for only those words that are listed in section 38.

3.4 Categories

The Categories treemap shows all (or a selection) of categories in the thesaurus. (Clicking on a class or section filters the categories treemap.) The categories are first grouped by class, and then within each of these groups they are ordered as per number of words in the categories. This allows users to determine which categories are more populous. Hovering on top of a category reveals a tooltip info box that shows not only the category name and number, but also the number of words in the category and a list of all these words. Recall that Figure 1 shows an example of this tooltip info box. Clicking on a category filters information in the Index to show only the rows for the words in the chosen category. The Class and Section treemaps show the class and section of the category.

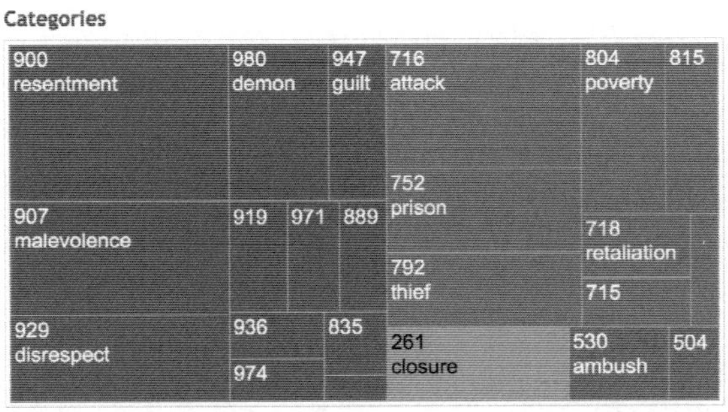

Figure 4: Categories treemap with the **anger** density slider set to range 0.7–1.

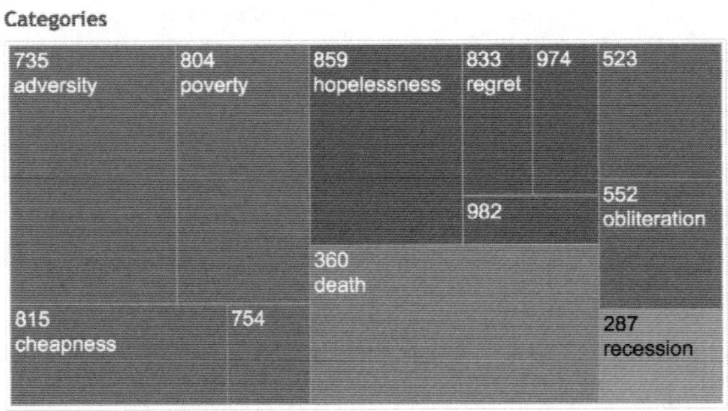

Figure 5: Categories treemap with the **sadness** density slider set to range 0.7–1.

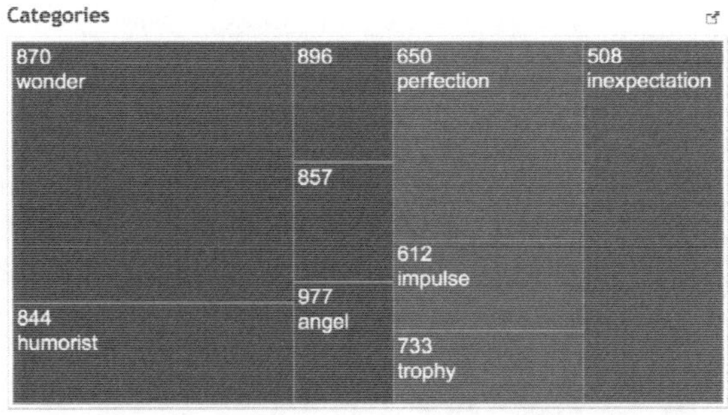

Figure 6: Categories treemap with **surprise** density and **positive** density sliders both set to > 0.4.

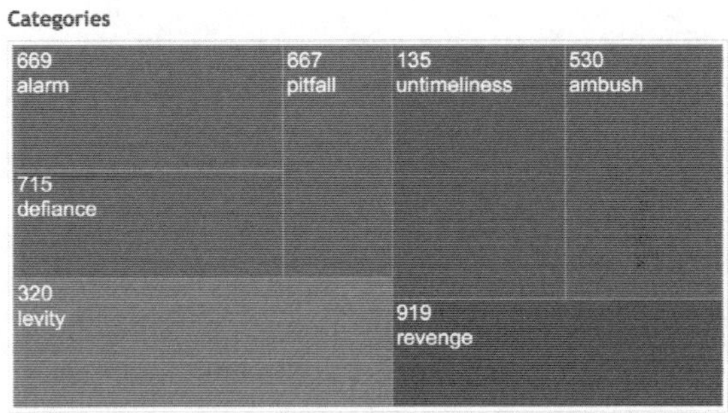

Figure 7: Categories treemap with **surprise** density and **negative** density sliders both set to > 0.4.

3.4.1 Identifying Affectual Categories

We now discuss how the *Roget's Thesaurus* is linked with the NRC Emotion Lexicon to display categories that have strong associations with various sentiments and emotions.

For each category *cat*, we calculate affect density for affect *aff* using the formula shown below:

$$\textit{Affect Density (cat,aff)} = \frac{\textit{NumAssociated}}{\textit{NumTotal}} \qquad (1)$$

where *NumAssociated* if the number of words in *cat* associated with *aff* and *NumTotal* is the number of words in *cat* that are listed in the NRC Emotion Lexicon. Thus, for example, if a category has 50 words, 40 of which are listed in the NRC Emotion Lexicon, and 30 of these are associated with positive sentiment, then the category has a positive affect density of 30/40 = 0.75.

We calculated affect densities for both sentiments and all eight emotions covered in the NRC Emotion Lexicon. For each of these affects, Imagisaurus shows density sliders on the far right. Both the lower end (to the left) and the upper end (to the right) of the slider can be moved with the mouse pointer. Adjusting a slider filters the Categories treemap to show only those categories with affect densities within the range of the slider. For example, Figure 4 shows the Categories treemap as it appears when the lower end of the anger density slider is moved to 0.7 and the upper end is left at 1. One can compare it to Figure 5 which shows the categories with sadness density between 0.7 and 1. Observe that the former shows categories such as resentment, attack, and ambush, whereas the latter shows categories such as adversity, hopelessness, and death. One can even manipulate multiple sliders to create multiple filters that apply at the same time. For example, Figure 6 shows categories with surprise and positive densities each greater than 0.4. We see categories such as wonder, humorist, and perfection. On the other hand, Figure 7 shows categories with surprise and negative densities each greater than 0.4. We see categories such as alarm, untimeliness, and ambush.

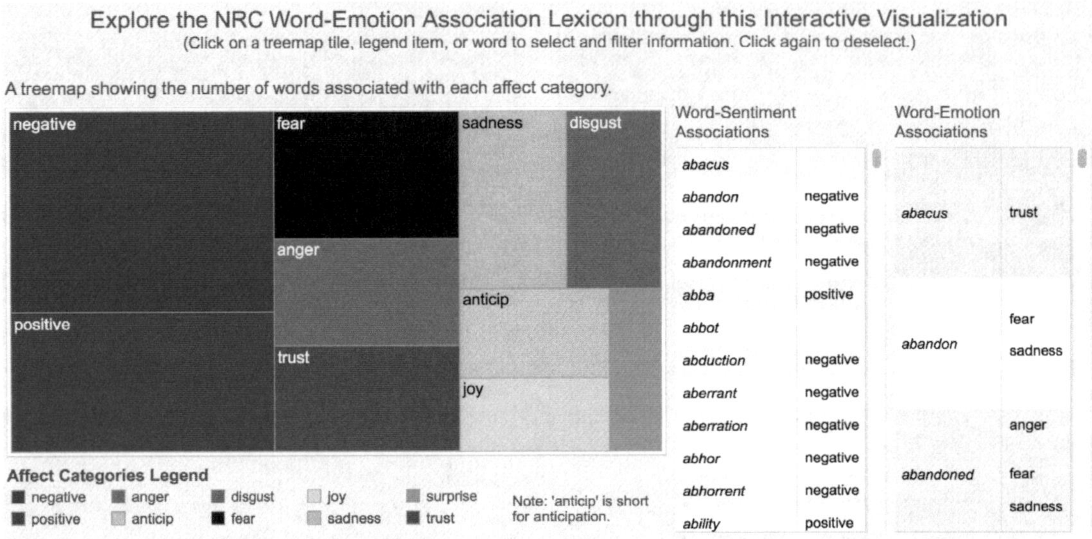

Figure 8: An interactive visualizer for the NRC Emotion Lexicon.

4 Visualizing words–affect associations

We developed a second online interactive visualization to explore word–emotion and word–sentiment associations directly in the NRC Emotion Lexicon. Figure 8 shows a screenshot of this visualization. The treemap on the left shows the various affect categories. The sizes of the boxes in the treemap are proportional to the number of words associated with the corresponding affect. Observe that, word associations with negative sentiment are more frequent than associations with positive. The associations with fear, anger and trust are much more frequent compared to associations with joy and surprise. On the right are two index views for word–sentiment and word–emotion associations respectively. Clicking on a word in one of the index views, filters information in all of the other sub-visualizations to show information relevant to that word. Clicking on a box in the treemap, filters information in all other sub-visualizations to show information relevant only to the chosen affect category.

5 Summary and Future Work

We developed an online interactive visualizer for the *Roget's Thesaurus* called Imagisaurus. Imagisaurus allows users to access information about thesaurus words, classes, sections, and categories through four separate sub-visualizations that are linked to each other. The structure of the thesaurus is shown in proportion to the size of its components—where size is defined to be the number of words included in the thesaurus unit (category, section, etc.). Clicking on a unit selects it and filters information in all other sub-visualizations. We also link the thesaurus with an emotion lexicon such that manipulating simple sliders allows users to view categories associated with affect categories. With its intuitive and easy-to-use interface that allows interactive exploration of the *Roget's Thesaurus*, we believe Imagisaurus will benefit researchers, practitioners, and the lay persons alike. We also developed a second visualization to explore the NRC Emotion Lexicon. Both visualizers are made freely available online.

This work explores the *Roget's Thesaurus* and the NRC Emotion Lexicon, but the same framework can be used to explore other lexical resources too: for example, other thesauri in English and other languages; semantic networks such as WordNet and VerbNet; versions of the NRC Emotion Lexicon in other languages; and sentiment lexicons such as the NRC Hashtag Sentiment lexicon and Sentiment 140 Lexicon (Mohammad et al., 2013; Kiritchenko et al., 2014).[8] Our future work will extend previous work on visualizing literature (Mohammad and Yang, 2011; Mohammad, 2012) by incorporating interactivity among sub-visualizations and by capturing affectual information associated with characters and plot structure.

[8]http://www.purl.com/net/lexicons

References

Gregory Grefenstette. 2012. *Explorations in automatic thesaurus discovery*, volume 278. Springer Science & Business Media.

Minqing Hu and Bing Liu. 2004. Mining and summarizing customer reviews. In *Proceedings of the 10th ACM SIGKDD International Conference on Knowledge Discovery and Data Mining*, KDD '04, pages 168–177, New York, NY, USA. ACM.

Svetlana Kiritchenko, Xiaodan Zhu, and Saif M. Mohammad. 2014. Sentiment analysis of short informal texts. *Journal of Artificial Intelligence Research (in press)*.

Gottfried Wilhelm Leibniz and George Henry Radcliffe Parkinson. 1995. *Philosophical writings*. Everyman.

GW Leibniz. 1923. Calculus ratiocinator. *Samtliche Schriften und Briefe. Reichel, Darmstadt*.

Margaret Masterman. 1957. The thesaurus in syntax and semantics. *Mechanical Translation*, 4(1-2):35–43.

Saif Mohammad and Graeme Hirst. 2006. Distributional measures of concept-distance: A task-oriented evaluation. In *Proceedings of the 2006 Conference on Empirical Methods in Natural Language Processing*, pages 35–43. Association for Computational Linguistics.

Saif M. Mohammad and Peter D. Turney. 2010. Emotions evoked by common words and phrases: Using mechanical turk to create an emotion lexicon. In *Proceedings of the NAACL-HLT 2010 Workshop on Computational Approaches to Analysis and Generation of Emotion in Text*, LA, California.

Saif M. Mohammad and Peter D. Turney. 2013. Crowdsourcing a word–emotion association lexicon. *Computational Intelligence*.

Saif Mohammad and Tony Yang. 2011. Tracking Sentiment in Mail: How Genders Differ on Emotional Axes. In *Proceedings of the 2nd Workshop on Computational Approaches to Subjectivity and Sentiment Analysis (WASSA 2.011)*, pages 70–79, Portland, Oregon. Association for Computational Linguistics.

Saif Mohammad, Svetlana Kiritchenko, and Xiaodan Zhu. 2013. NRC-Canada: Building the state-of-the-art in sentiment analysis of tweets. In *Proceedings of the International Workshop on Semantic Evaluation*, SemEval '13, Atlanta, Georgia, USA, June.

Saif Mohammad. 2008. *Measuring semantic distance using distributional profiles of concepts*. Ph.D. thesis, University of Toronto.

Saif M. Mohammad. 2012. From once upon a time to happily ever after: Tracking emotions in mail and books. *Decision Support Systems*, 53(4):730–741.

Jane Morris and Graeme Hirst. 1991. Lexical cohesion computed by thesaural relations as an indicator of the structure of text. *Computational linguistics*, 17(1):21–48.

Peter Mark Roget. 1852. *Roget's Thesaurus of English Words and Phrases*. Longman Group Ltd., Harlow, Essex, England.

Peter Mark Roget. 1911. *Roget's Thesaurus of English Words and Phrases*. TY Crowell Company.

Philip Stone, Dexter C. Dunphy, Marshall S. Smith, Daniel M. Ogilvie, and associates. 1966. *The General Inquirer: A Computer Approach to Content Analysis*. The MIT Press.

Carlo Strapparava and Alessandro Valitutti. 2004. Wordnet-Affect: An affective extension of WordNet. In *Proceedings of the 4th International Conference on Language Resources and Evaluation (LREC-2004)*, pages 1083–1086, Lisbon, Portugal.

David Yarowsky. 1992. Word-sense disambiguation using statistical models of Roget's categories trained on large corpora. In *Proceedings of the 14th International Conference on Computational Linguistics (COLING-92)*, pages 454–460, Nantes, France.

Personality Traits on Twitter
—or—
How to Get 1,500 Personality Tests in a Week

Barbara Plank
Center for Language Technology
University of Copenhagen, Denmark
Njalsgade 140, DK-2300 Copenhagen S
bplank@cst.dk

Dirk Hovy
Center for Language Technology
University of Copenhagen, Denmark
Njalsgade 140, DK-2300 Copenhagen S
dirk.hovy@hum.ku.dk

Abstract

Psychology research suggests that certain personality traits correlate with linguistic behavior. This correlation can be effectively modeled with statistical natural language processing techniques. Prediction accuracy generally improves with larger data samples, which also allows for more lexical features. Most existing work on personality prediction, however, focuses on small samples and closed-vocabulary investigations. Both factors limit the generality and statistical power of the results. In this paper, we explore the use of social media as a resource for large-scale, open-vocabulary personality detection. We analyze which features are predictive of which personality traits, and present a novel corpus of 1.2M English tweets annotated with Myers-Briggs personality type and gender. Our experiments show that social media data can provide sufficient linguistic evidence to reliably predict two of four personality dimensions.

1 Introduction

Individual author attributes play an important role in customer modeling, as well as in business intelligence. In either task, Natural Language Processing (NLP) is increasingly used to analyze and classify extra-linguistic features based on textual input. Extra-linguistic and linguistic features are assumed to be sufficiently correlated to be predictive of each other, which in practice allows for mutual inference (Pennebaker et al., 2003; Johannsen et al., 2015). A whole body of work in NLP is concerned with attribute prediction from linguistic features (Rosenthal and McKeown, 2011; Nguyen et al., 2011; Eisenstein et al., 2011; Volkova et al., 2013; Alowibdi et al., 2013; Ciot et al., 2013; Volkova et al., 2015). Apart from demographic features, such as age or gender, there is also a growing interest in personality types.

Predicting personality is not only of interest for commercial applications and psychology, but also for health care. Recent work by Preoţiuc-Pietro et al. (2015) investigated the link between personality types, social media behavior, and psychological disorders, such as depression and post-traumatic stress disorder. They found that certain personality traits are predictive of mental illness. Similarly, Mitchell et al. (2015) show that linguistic traits are predictive of schizophrenia.

However, as pointed out by Nowson and Gill (2014), computational personality recognition is limited by the availability of labeled data, which is expensive to annotate and often hard to obtain. Given the wide array of possible personality types, limited data size is a problem, since low-probability types and combinations will not occur in statistically significant numbers. In addition, many existing data sets are comprised of written essays, which usually contain highly canonical language, often of a specific topic. Such controlled settings inhibit the expression of individual traits much more than spontaneous language.

In this work, we take a data-driven approach to personality identification, to avoid both the limitation of small data samples and a limited vocabulary. We use the large amounts of personalized data voluntarily produced on social media (e.g., Twitter) to collect sufficient amounts of data. Twitter is highly non-canonical, and famous for an almost unlimited vocabulary size (Eisenstein, 2013; Fromreide et al., 2014). In order to enable data-driven personality research, we combine this data source with self-assessed Myers-Briggs Type Indicators (Briggs Myers and Myers, 2010), denoted MBTIs. Myers-Briggs uses four binary dimensions to classify users (INTROVERT–EXTROVERT,

Proceedings of the 6th Workshop on Computational Approaches to Subjectivity, Sentiment and Social Media Analysis (WASSA 2015), pages 92–98,
Lisboa, Portugal, 17 September, 2015.

INTUITIVE–SENSING, THINKING–FEELING, JUDGING–PERCEIVING), e.g., INTJ, ENTJ, etc., amounting to 16 different types. MBTIs have the distinct advantage of being readily available in large quantities on social media.

We are aware of the ongoing discussion in the psychological literature about the limited expressiveness of MBTI, and a preference for Big Five (Goldberg, 1990; Bayne, 1994; Furnham, 1996; Barbuto Jr, 1997). We are, however, to some extent agnostic to the theoretical differences. MBTI does presumably still capture aspects of the users' personality. In fact, several dimensions are correlated to the Big Five (Furnham, 1996).

Over a time frame of one week, we collect a corpus of 1.2M tweets from 1,500 users that self-identify with an MBTI. We provide an analysis of the type distribution and compare it to existing statistics for the general population. We train predictive models and report performance for the individual dimensions. In addition, we select the most relevant features via stability selection (Meinshausen and Bühlmann, 2010) and find that—apart from linguistic features—gender and count statistics of the user are some of the most predictive features for several dimensions, even when controlling for gender.

Our results indicate that certain personality distinctions, namely INTROVERT–EXTROVERT (I–E) and THINKING–FEELING (T–F), can be predicted from social media data with high reliability, while others are very hard to model with our features. Our open-vocabulary approach improves considerably as the amount of available data increases.

Contributions In this paper we i) demonstrate how large amounts of social media data can be used for large-scale open-vocabulary personality detection; ii) analyze which features are predictive of which personality dimension; and iii) present a novel corpus of 1.2M English tweets (1,500 authors) annotated for gender and MBTI. The code is available at: `https://bitbucket.org/bplank/wassa2015`

2 Data

Our question is simple: given limited amounts of time (one week, including corpus creation and statistical analysis), how much personality type information can we gather from social media—and is it informative? Using MBTI types and the sheer amounts of user-generated data, we show that social media can be a valuable resource.

I	ISTJ 75	ISFJ 77	**INFJ 257**	INTJ 193
	ISTP 22	ISFP 51	INFP 175	INTP 111
E	**ESTP 15**	ESFP 26	ENFP 148	ENTP 70
	ESTJ 36	ESFJ 36	ENFJ 106	ENTJ 102

Table 1: The 16 MBTI (total users: 1,500) and their raw count. Most frequent/rarest type in bold.

E–I	539 (36%)	961 (64%)
N–S	1162 (77%)	338 (23%)
T–F	624 (42%)	876 (58%)
J–P	882 (59%)	618 (41%)
female–male	939 (63%)	561 (37%)

Table 2: Distribution over dimensions and gender.

Identifying users In order to collect our data, we first search for users that self-identify with one of the 16 MBTIs. We search for mentions of any of the 16 types, plus "Briggs", which we found to be less often misspelled than "Myers". We then manually check all files and remove all tweets that contain more than one type. This typically relates to people describing a switch, referring to another person, or bot posts; this step removes around 30% of the tweets. We additionally label each user as male or female, if discernible. We remove all users whose gender could not be discerned.

In the end, our collection contains 1,500 distinct users with type and gender information. Table 1 shows the distribution over types, Table 2 shows the distribution over each dimension and gender. Figure 1 compares the MBTI type distribution of our Twitter corpus to general population estimates[1] (cf. §3).

We observe that the distribution in our corpus is shifted towards introverts and females (Figure 1 and Table 2). It has been observed before (Goby, 2006) that there is a significant correlation between online–offline choices and the MBTI dimension of EXTRAVERT–INTROVERT. Extroverts are more likely to opt for offline modes of communication, while online communication is presumably easier and more accessible for introverts. Our corpus reflects this observation.

[1] `http://www.capt.org/mbti-assessment/`

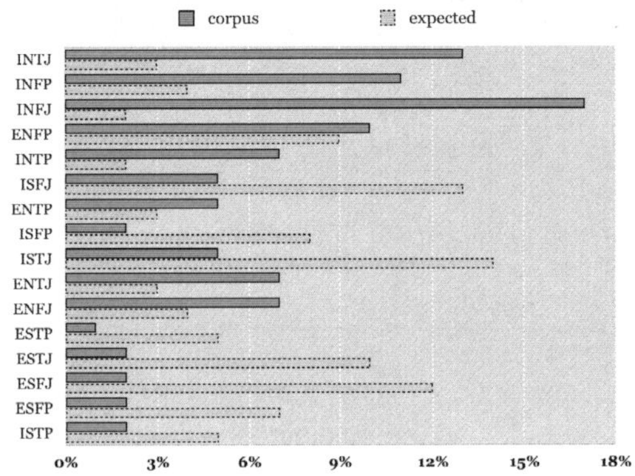

Figure 1: Comparison of MBTI distribution in Twitter corpus and general US population.

Corpus collection For each user, we download their most recent tweets. We require them to have at least 100 tweets, and collect a maximum of 2000 tweets. The final corpus contains 1.2 million tweets (19M tokens, average tweet: 16.1 tokens).

3 Statistical Analysis and Comparison

Using Twitter data naturally introduces a selection bias. We only have access to users who use Twitter and self-report their MBTI, while in previous studies participants were recruited to fill out a questionnaire and write texts specifically for the experiment.[2]

In order to quantify the differences to the general population, we compare the obtained MBTI distribution to general population estimates. Figure 1 shows that our Twitter distribution differs significantly from the general population (Spearman, $p < 0.05$) and exhibits different biases. There are many more introverts, and the data is shifted towards females (63%). While self-expression is easier for introverts online (Goby, 2006), our corpus also shows advertising/sensationalism bias. People like to tweet about rare events, e.g.,

> "Took a Myers-Briggs Personality Test. Received INFJ. Turns out only 1-2% of the population are that type #Interesting".

Interestingly, infrequent MBTIs in the general population (the first three bars in Figure 1, i.e., INFJ, INFP, INTJ) are amongst the most frequent types in our Twitter sample. Upon manual inspection of the data, we found that of the users reporting infrequent types, more than 60% belong to the three most frequent types in our corpus.

Despite the different biases, collecting linguistic data in this way has the advantage that it reflects actual language use, allows large-scale analysis and is less affected by interviewer biases.

4 Experiments

Model In order to predict each of the four dimensions from data, we train a logistic regression classifier.[3] As features, we use binary word n-grams ($n \in \{1, 2, 3\}$), gender, and several discretized count-based meta-features, i.e., counts of tweets, followers, statuses (total of tweets and retweets), favorites (number of favorited tweets) and listed counts (number of lists on which the Twitter user appears). Preliminary experiments showed that removing stopwords (and thus, removing personal pronouns) harms performance. The data is pre-processed, i.e., tokenized,[4] hashtags, URLs and usernames are replaced with unique tokens. We also remove any tweets containing a mention of one of the 16 MBTIs.

Feature selection In addition to type prediction, we perform feature selection to obtain insights into the classes. We use *stability selection* (Meinshausen and Bühlmann, 2010) to select the most discriminative features. We do *not* use the results of this selection in the predictive models.

We want to find the features that carry a high weight, irrespective of the conditions, in the entire data set. The conditions in this case are the *data composition* and *regularization*. In order to simulate different data compositions, we sample 100 times from the data. We use a sample size of 75% with replacement. For each sample, we fit a logistic regression model with a randomly set L_1 regularization constant, which encourages sparse feature weights. We average the weight vectors of all 100 induced models and select the features with the highest positive weight, representing the probability of being selected in each sample.

[2]Most of these questionnaires are administered in Psychology introduction classes, which introduces its own bias, though. See Henrich et al. (2010).

[3]Using the `sklearn` toolkit.

[4]Tokenizer from: `http://wwbp.org/`

5 Results

Table 3 shows the prediction accuracy for a majority-class baseline and our models on the full data set (10-fold cross-validation). While the model clearly improves on the I–E and F–T distinctions, we see no improvements over the baseline for S–N, and even a slight drop for P–J. This indicates that for the latter two dimensions, we either do not have the right features, or there is not linguistic evidence for them, given that they are more related to perception. The results from Luyckx and Daelemans (2008) on Dutch essays also suggest that P–J is difficult to learn.

Given the heavy gender-skew of our data, we run additional experiments in which we control for gender. The gender-controlled dataset contains 1070 authors. The results in Table 4 show the same tendency as in the previous setup.

	I–E	S–N	T–F	P–J
Majority	64.1	77.5	58.4	58.8
System	**72.5**	77.4	**61.2**	55.4

Table 3: Accuracy for four discrimination tasks with 2000 tweets/user.

	I–E	S–N	T–F	P–J
Majority	64.9	79.6	51.8	59.4
System	**72.1**	79.5	**54.0**	58.2

Table 4: Prediction performance for four discrimination tasks with 2000 tweets/user controlled for gender.

Figure 2 shows the effect of increased data size on prediction accuracy for the two best dimensions. Already from as little as 100 tweets, our model outperforms the baseline and is comparable to other studies. More data leads to better prediction accuracy. For I–E, there seems to be more headroom, while the accuracy of T–F plateaus after 500 tweets in the original dataset and slightly decreases in the gender-controlled setup. The trend on I–E also holds when controlling for gender as a confounding factor, while for T–F the highest performance is obtained with 500 tweets/user. In general, though, the results emphasize the benefits of large-scale analysis, especially for distinguishing the I–E dimension.

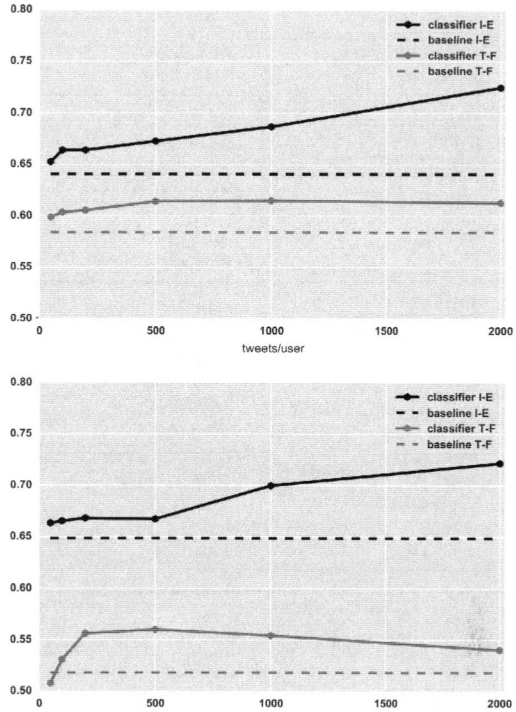

Figure 2: Learning curves and majority baselines for I–E and T–F on whole data set (top) and gender-balanced (bottom). x-axis = #tweets/user, y-axis = classification accuracy.

5.1 Predictive features

Table 5 shows the top 10 features for I–E and F–T found by stability selection. Our results show that linguistic features are by far the most predictive features for personality.

However, meta-features of the user account can also provide strong cues. More followers seem to indicate extroverts: a follower count of 100-500 users is a moderately strong indicator for extroverts (0.37). Interestingly, a status count of 1000–5000 tweets is a strong feature for introvert prediction (0.77), while less than 500 statuses correlate with extroverts (0.43). Similarly, if a user is member of 5-50 lists, it is indicative of introverts (0.64), while being in less than 5 lists is predictive of extroverts (0.55). These results support the finding that introverts prefer online media for communication (Goby, 2006).

Gender is another non-linguistic cue. In the gender-controlled experiment for the I–E dimension, gender is no longer a predictive feature, in contrast to the original dataset. For the F–T dis-

INTROVERT	EXTROVERT
someone 0.91	**pull** 0.96
probably 0.89	**mom** 0.81
favorite 0.83	**travel** 0.78
stars 0.81	**don't get** 0.78
b 0.81	**when you're** 0.77
writing 0.78	posted 0.77
, the 0.77	#HASHTAG is 0.76
status count $<$ 5000 0.77	comes to 0.72
lol 0.74	**tonight !** 0.71
but i 0.74	join 0.69
THINKING	FEELING
must be 0.95	out to 0.88
drink 0.95	difficult 0.87
red 0.91	the most 0.85
from the 0.89	couldn't 0.85
all the 0.88	me and 0.8
business 0.85	in @USER 0.8
to get a 0.81	**wonderful** 0.79
hope 0.81	what it 0.79
june 0.78	trying to 0.79
their 0.77	! so 0.78

Table 5: Stability selection: most predictive features and their probabilities in the original dataset. Features in bold are predictive in both gender-balanced and original dataset (top 10 in both).

tinction, however, gender is actually fairly well-correlated with the respective classes for both types of experiments, albeit somewhat weaker for the gender-controlled setup (for T, GENDER=MEN is 0.57 in the original vs. 0.27 in the controlled experiment; for F, GENDER=FEMALE is 0.78 vs. 0.54). This indicates that gender is still an effective feature in predicting the F–T dimension when controlling for its distributional effect, while it is less important for distinguishing I–E.

6 Related work

Personality information can be valuable for a number of applications. Mitchell et al. (2015) studied self-identified schizophrenia patients on Twitter and found that linguistic signals may aid in identifying and getting help to people suffering from it.

Luyckx and Daelemans (2008) present a corpus for computational stylometry, including authorship attribution and MBTIs for Dutch. The corpus consists of 145 student (BA level) essays. They controlled for topic by asking participants to write about a documentary on artificial life. In a follow-up study, they extended the corpus to include reviews and both Big Five and MBTI information (Verhoeven and Daelemans, 2014). Instead, we focus on English and social media, a more spontaneous sample of language use.

Even when using social media, most prior work on personality detection can be considered small-scale. The 2014 Workshop on Computational Personality Recognition hosted a shared task of personality detection on 442 YouTube video logs (Celli et al., 2014). Celli et al. (2013) also examined Facebook messages of 250 users for personality. In contrast, our study uses 1.2M tweets from 1,500 different users.

The only prior large-scale open-vocabulary work on social media studies Facebook messages (Schwartz et al., 2013a; Schwartz et al., 2013b; Park et al., 2015). To date, their study represents the largest study of language and personality. Through a Facebook app, they collected personality types and messages from 75,000 Facebook users. They found striking variations in language use with personality, gender and age. Our approach is simpler, requires no tailored app, and can be used to collect large amounts of data quickly.

7 Conclusions

We use the self-reported Myers-Briggs type of Twitter users to collect a large corpus of tweets and train predictive models for each dimension.

Our results show that we can model the I–E (INTROVERT–EXTROVERT) and F–T (FEELING–THINKING) distinction fairly well. Learning the other two dimensions turns out to be hard. We find that linguistic features account for most of the predictive power of our models, but that meta-information, such as gender, number of followers, statuses, or list membership, add valuable information.

The distribution of Myers-Briggs personality types observed in our Twitter corpus differs from the general population, however, the data reflects real language use and sample sizes with sufficient statistical power. Our results suggest that while theoretically less well-founded than traditional approaches, large-scale, open-vocabulary analysis of user attributes can help improve classification accuracy and create insights into personality profiles.

Acknowledgements

We would like to thank the reviewers for their constructive feedback, as well as Lyle Ungar and Ben Verhoeven for suggestions.

References

Jalal S Alowibdi, Ugo A Buy, and Philip Yu. 2013. Empirical evaluation of profile characteristics for gender classification on twitter. In *Machine Learning and Applications (ICMLA), 2013 12th International Conference on*, volume 1, pages 365–369. IEEE.

John E Barbuto Jr. 1997. A critique of the myers-briggs type indicator and its operationalization of carl jung's psychological types. *Psychological Reports*, 80(2):611–625.

Rowan Bayne. 1994. The" big five" versus the myers-briggs. *PSYCHOLOGIST-LEICESTER-*, 7:14–14.

Isabel Briggs Myers and Peter Myers. 2010. *Gifts differing: Understanding personality type*. Nicholas Brealey Publishing.

Fabio Celli, Fabio Pianesi, David Stillwell, and Michal Kosinski. 2013. Workshop on computational personality recognition (shared task). In *Proceedings of the Workshop on Computational Personality Recognition*.

Fabio Celli, Bruno Lepri, Joan-Isaac Biel, Daniel Gatica-Perez, Giuseppe Riccardi, and Fabio Pianesi. 2014. The workshop on computational personality recognition 2014. In *Proceedings of the ACM International Conference on Multimedia*, pages 1245–1246. ACM.

Morgane Ciot, Morgan Sonderegger, and Derek Ruths. 2013. Gender inference of twitter users in non-english contexts. In *Proceedings of the 2013 Conference on Empirical Methods in Natural Language Processing, Seattle, Wash*, pages 18–21.

Jacob Eisenstein, Noah Smith, and Eric Xing. 2011. Discovering sociolinguistic associations with structured sparsity. In *Proceedings of ACL*.

Jacob Eisenstein. 2013. What to do about bad language on the internet. In *Proceedings of NAACL*.

Hege Fromreide, Dirk Hovy, and Anders Søgaard. 2014. Crowdsourcing and annotating NER for Twitter #drift. In *LREC*.

Adrian Furnham. 1996. The big five versus the big four: the relationship between the myers-briggs type indicator (mbti) and neo-pi five factor model of personality. *Personality and Individual Differences*, 21(2):303 - 307.

Valerie Priscilla Goby. 2006. Personality and online/offline choices: Mbti profiles and favored communication modes in a singapore study. *CyberPsychology & Behavior*, 9(1):5–13.

Lewis R Goldberg. 1990. An alternative" description of personality": the big-five factor structure. *Journal of personality and social psychology*, 59(6):1216.

Joseph Henrich, Steven J Heine, and Ara Norenzayan. 2010. The weirdest people in the world? *Behavioral and brain sciences*, 33(2-3):61–83.

Anders Johannsen, Dirk Hovy, and Anders Søgaard. 2015. Cross-lingual syntactic variation over age and gender. In *Proceedings of CoNLL*.

Kim Luyckx and Walter Daelemans. 2008. Personae: a corpus for author and personality prediction from text. In *LREC*.

Nicolai Meinshausen and Peter Bühlmann. 2010. Stability selection. *Journal of the Royal Statistical Society: Series B (Statistical Methodology)*, 72(4):417–473.

Margaret Mitchell, Kristy Hollingshead, and Glen Coppersmith. 2015. Quantifying the language of schizophrenia in social media. In *Proceedings of the 2nd Workshop on Computational Linguistics and Clinical Psychology: From Linguistic Signal to Clinical Reality*.

Dong Nguyen, Noah A Smith, and Carolyn P Rosé. 2011. Author age prediction from text using linear regression. In *Proceedings of the 5th ACL-HLT Workshop on Language Technology for Cultural Heritage, Social Sciences, and Humanities*.

Scott Nowson and Alastair J Gill. 2014. Look! who's talking?: Projection of extraversion across different social contexts. In *Proceedings of the 2014 ACM Multi Media on Workshop on Computational Personality Recognition*, pages 23–26. ACM.

Greg Park, H Andrew Schwartz, Johannes C Eichstaedt, Margaret L Kern, David J Stillwell, Michal Kosinski, Lyle H Ungar, and Martin EP Seligman. 2015. Automatic personality assessment through social media language. *Journal of Personality and Social Psychology*.

James W Pennebaker, Matthias R Mehl, and Kate G Niederhoffer. 2003. Psychological aspects of natural language use: Our words, our selves. *Annual review of psychology*, 54(1):547–577.

Daniel Preoţiuc-Pietro, Johannes Eichstaedt, Gregory Park, Maarten Sap, Laura Smith, Victoria Tobolsky, Hansen Andrew Schwartz, and Lyle H Ungar. 2015. The role of personality, age and gender in tweeting about mental illnesses. In *Proceedings of the Workshop on Computational Linguistics and Clinical Psychology: From Linguistic Signal to Clinical Reality*, NAACL.

Sara Rosenthal and Kathleen McKeown. 2011. Age prediction in blogs: A study of style, content, and online behavior in pre-and post-social media generations. In *Proceedings of the 49th Annual Meeting of the Association for Computational Linguistics: Human Language Technologies-Volume 1*, pages 763–772. Association for Computational Linguistics.

Hansen Andrew Schwartz, Johannes C Eichstaedt, Lukasz Dziurzynski, Margaret L Kern, Eduardo Blanco, Michal Kosinski, David Stillwell, Martin EP Seligman, and Lyle H Ungar. 2013a. Toward personality insights from language exploration in social media. In *AAAI Spring Symposium: Analyzing Microtext*.

Hansen Andrew Schwartz, Johannes C Eichstaedt, Margaret L Kern, Lukasz Dziurzynski, Stephanie M Ramones, Megha Agrawal, Achal Shah, Michal Kosinski, David Stillwell, Martin EP Seligman, et al. 2013b. Personality, gender, and age in the language of social media: The open-vocabulary approach. *PloS one*, 8(9).

Ben Verhoeven and Walter Daelemans. 2014. CLiPS Stylometry Investigation (CSI) corpus: A Dutch corpus for the detection of age, gender, personality, sentiment and deception in text. In *LREC*.

Svitlana Volkova, Theresa Wilson, and David Yarowsky. 2013. Exploring demographic language variations to improve multilingual sentiment analysis in social media. In *Proceedings of EMNLP*.

Svitlana Volkova, Yoram Bachrach, Michael Armstrong, and Vijay Sharma. 2015. Inferring latent user properties from texts published in social media (demo). In *Proceedings of the Twenty-Ninth Conference on Artificial Intelligence (AAAI)*, Austin, TX, January.

Negation Scope Detection for Twitter Sentiment Analysis

Johan Reitan **Jørgen Faret** **Björn Gambäck** **Lars Bungum**
{johan.reitan,jorgenfar}@gmail.com {gamback,larsbun}@idi.ntnu.no
Department of Computer and Information Science
Norwegian University of Science and Technology
Sem Sælands vei 7–9, NO–7491 Trondheim, Norway

Abstract

The paper describes the first sophisticated negation scope detection system for Twitter sentiment analysis. The system has been evaluated both on existing corpora from other domains and on a corpus of English Twitter data (*tweets*) annotated for negation. It produces better results than what has been reported in other domains and improves the performance on tweets containing negation when incorporated into a state-of-the-art Twitter sentiment analyser.

1 Introduction

Exploring public opinion on various subjects has always been an important part of humans' information gathering behaviour. Where one in the past needed to conduct surveys to learn about opinion trends, the availability of online data expressing sentiment has allowed for non-intrusive data mining to extract this information. Over the last decade, there has been a substantial increase in the amount of work done in the field of sentiment analysis, which has largely followed the available data, in recent years shifting the field towards Twitter data, i.e., towards Twitter sentiment analysis.

Twitter[1] is a micro-blogging site that allows users to write textual entries ('*tweets*') of up to 140 characters. The tweets are available through Twitter's API and represent a real-time information stream of opinionated data. Performing language processing on tweets presents new challenges because of their informal nature. Tweets often contain misspellings, slang and abbreviations, and unconventional linguistic means, such as capitalization or elongation of words to show emphasis. Additionally, tweets contain special features like *emoticons* and *hashtags* that may have analytical value.

The ability to handle linguistic negation of terms is an important aspect of sentiment classification. The *valence* of a segment of text (its communicated positive or negative attitude) can be equated to its sentimental orientation, and valence shifters are terms that change the sentimental orientation of other terms. In sentiment analysis, negators often act as valence shifters, since flipping a proposition's truth value significantly shifts, or reverses, the valence it conveys. Givón (1993) defines two forms of grammatical negation: *morphological*, where individual words are negated with an affix, and *syntactic*, where a set of words is negated by a word or phrase; the topic of the present paper. Negators in syntactical negation, known as *negation cues* or *negation signals*, function as operators, with an associated affected scope of words (Morante and Sporleder, 2012). The most common negation cue in English is *not*, along with its contractions, such as *couldn't* or *isn't* (Tottie, 1991).

Negation classifiers have been developed for other domains with dramatic performance improvements (Section 2). However, almost all state-of-the-art Twitter sentiment analysis systems use a simple approach of marking as negated all terms from a negation cue to the next punctuation (Section 3). We present this simple model as a baseline, but improve on it by introducing sophisticated negation scope detection for Twitter sentiment analysis.

Several negation-annotated corpora are available, but none for the Twitter domain. To be able to evaluate Twitter negation detection and to train supervised machine learning classifiers, a corpus of tweets was annotated with negation meta-data. The new and existing corpora are detailed in Section 4.

Sections 5 and 6 describe the construction of two classification systems: a Twitter negation scope detector and a state-of-the-art sentiment analyser incorporating the negation classifier, as well as experiments conducted on the two systems. Section 7 summarizes the results and suggests future work.

[1] https://www.twitter.com

Proceedings of the 6th Workshop on Computational Approaches to Subjectivity, Sentiment and Social Media Analysis (WASSA 2015), pages 99–108,
Lisboa, Portugal, 17 September, 2015.

2 Negation Scope Detection, NSD

The main application area of identifying the scope of negation, or negation scope detection (NSD), was originally biomedical texts, such as clinical reports and discharge summaries, but has in recent times shifted towards sentiment analysis (SA). Early solutions were typically rule-based, such as the NegFinder (Mutalik et al., 2001) and NegEx (Chapman et al., 2001) systems, that both heavily incorporated the use of regular expressions. NSD was the focus of a shared task at *SEM 2012 (Morante and Blanco, 2012), and in 2010 CoNLL included a similar sub-task on detecting speculation cues and their affected scope (Farkas et al., 2010). Most well-performing submissions to both tasks used supervised machine learning approaches.

Morante and Daelemans (2009) developed an NSD system that uses meta-learning for classification. They applied this approach to the CoNLL'10 shared task and achieved the best F_1-score of all participating teams. The tokens were first tagged and split into chunks, and the main algorithm then consisted of two steps: signal identification (negation cue detection) and scope identification. For the first phase, Morante and Daelemans (2009) used a decision tree to classify if a token is at the beginning, inside or outside a negation signal. In the second phase, a Conditional Random Fields (CRF)-based meta-learner predicted scope classes based on the output from three classifiers, a Support Vector Machine (SVM), a k-nearest neighbour classifier and a CRF classifier. Zhu et al. (2010) also worked on biomedical texts and proposed a rule-based shallow semantic parsing solution: they set the negation signal as the predicate, and then use an SVM-based binary classifier to find the negated scope by identifying the correct argument(s).

Wiegand et al. (2010) surveyed the effects of NSD on SA, concluding it to be "highly relevant". Moilanen and Pulman (2007) built an SA system with a sophisticated NSD mechanism focused on syntactic composition. Potts (2011) achieved $\sim 12\,\%$ better accuracy with a simple model marking as negated all terms from a detected negation cue to the next punctuation. Councill et al. (2010) utilized the MaltParser (Nivre et al., 2007) for tokenization, part-of-speech-tagging, and creation of a dependency tree to generate a feature vector for training a CRF classifier. Tested on consumer reviews, the classifier improved F_1 scores by $29.5\,\%$ and $11.4\,\%$ on positive resp. negative sentiments.

3 Twitter Sentiment Analysis, TSA

The typical approach to Twitter sentiment analysis (TSA) is a supervised machine learning system with three main steps: preprocessing, feature extraction, and classification. Preprocessing aims to reduce noise and consists of a variety of filters, e.g., to normalize user mentions by substituting them with the tag `||T||` and URLs with `||U||` (Agarwal et al., 2011), prefix *retweets* (reposts of previous content) with "RT", and substitute letters that occur many times sequentially in elongated words (e.g., *happyyyyyy*) with one or two occurrences of the letter. It was previously common to filter out hashtags (Selmer et al., 2013, e.g), since those when used as intended (to categorize posts by topic) offer little sentiment information; however, Mohammad (2012) shows that they add sentiment by indicating the tone of the message or the writer's emotions.

Much recent progress in the field has been in connection to the International Workshop on Semantic Evaluation (SemEval), which since 2013 (Nakov et al., 2013) has included shared tasks on Sentiment Analysis in Twitter, with expression-level subtasks, to correctly classify the overall polarity of whole tweets. Many later systems have based their feature matrix on the SemEval'13 top submission (Mohammad et al., 2013). Tang et al. (2014) define it as the state-of-the-art feature set ('STATE'). This set will be further discussed in Section 6.1, but includes most typically used features such as word and character n-grams, different types of token frequencies, and a set of prior polarity sentiment lexica.

Most well-performing systems for TSA use a supervised machine learning-based classifier. An analysis of the classification algorithms used by the ten top ranking submissions to SemEval'14 (Rosenthal et al., 2014) shows that SVM and Logistic Regression were the most popular choices.

Few state-of-the-art TSA systems address negation systematically, but rather use the simple model described by Potts (2011), to assign a negation cue scope over all terms to the next punctuation. So do the top-3 SemEval'14 systems (Miura et al., 2014; Tang et al., 2014; Günther et al., 2014) and almost all SemEval'15 systems treating negation, including two of the top-3 (Hagen et al., 2015; Hamdan et al., 2015), although Rosenthal et al. (2015) mention negation as one area the systems focused on.

If the model includes prior polarity lexica, just inverting the sentiment polarity of negated terms is incorrect (Kiritchenko et al., 2014): positive terms when negated tend to shift polarity and decrease their intensity, while negative terms mostly stay negative with reduced intensity. Kiritchenko et al. (2014) thus created tweet-specific sentiment lexica containing scores for terms in affirmative and negated contexts: *NRC Hashtag Sentiment Lexicon* and *Sentiment140 Lexicon*. The lexica added clear performance improvements (5.83 % average F_1 increase over the five SemEval'14 data sets), even though the negated contexts were simply assumed to be from a negation cue to the next punctuation.

Plotnikova et al. (2015) created one of the better SemEval'15 systems by using the heuristic of assigning a negation cue scope over the 4 next tokens, which compares well with the 3.8 average tokens in the negation scope for our Twitter Negation Corpus (Table 1). Only one SemEval'15 system utilized an alternative treatment: Cerezo-Costas and Celix-Salgado (2015) trained a CRF-based classifier to detect the scope of what they call "denier particles" (i.e., negation) and "reversal verbs" (e.g., 'avoid', 'prevent'), that reverse the polarity of the terms in their scope. The system did not perform well over all, but ranked #1 on the 2014 tweet sarcasm data.

4 Data Sets

There are negation scope corpora available for other domains and sentiment-annotated data available from the SemEval TSA tasks. However, performing NSD using supervised machine learning requires a set of tweets annotated for negation cues and scopes, so such a corpus was also developed. The new and existing data sets are described below.

BioScope Corpus is a collection of bio-medical texts annotated for speculation and negation (Vincze et al., 2008). It consists of three subcorpora: medical free texts (6,383 sentences), biological full papers (2,670), and biological scientific abstracts (11,871). The free text part differs significantly from the others in that it contains mainly short and concise sentences. The rate of negation, though, is even across the entire corpus: 13.6 % of the sentences in the free texts, 12.7 % in the full papers, and 13.5 % in the abstracts contain negation.

SFU Review Corpus contains 400 reviews (50 each from 8 domains such as movies and consumer products) annotated at the token level for negation and speculation by Simon Fraser University (Konstantinova et al., 2012). In total, it consists of 17,263 sentences, with 18.1 % containing negation.

Number of tweets	4,000
Total number of tokens	61,172
Average tokens per tweet	15.3
Average tokens per sentence	10.2
Tweets containing negation	539
Total number of scopes	615
Average cues per negated tweet	1.14
Average tokens in scope	3.8

Table 1: Twitter Negation Corpus

SemEval Twitter sentiment analysis data have been annotated using Mechanical Turk, and include training, development and test sets, as well as out-of-domain test sets. Due to Twitter's privacy policy, the data cannot be distributed directly, but is downloaded with a script that uses tweet IDs to match tweets with their sentiment labels. Tweets that have been deleted since the data sets' creation are unavailable, and the sets grow smaller over time. The total size of the SemEval'14 data when downloaded by us, in November 2014, was 12,754 tweets.

Twitter Negation Corpus contains 4,000 tweets downloaded through Twitter's API and annotated by two of the authors using a web application developed for this purpose. The application retrieves a tokenized tweet from the database and displays it as a container of HTML buttons, where each button represents a token. The user clicks a token to mark it as a negation cue and on corresponding tokens to mark the scope. Inter-annotator agreement was calculated at token and full scope level. The token level score is the number of tokens annotators agree on divided by the total number of tokens. It is an unbalanced measure as tokens in affirmative contexts greatly outnumber those in negated. Full scope agreement entails that annotator scopes match completely. Token level agreement was 98.9 % and full scope agreement 73.8 %. All scope conflicts were reviewed and resolved after discussion.

Statistics for the corpus are shown in Table 1, with figures relating to negation in the lower half. Tottie (1991) states that the frequency of negation in written English is 12.8 %, and the fraction of tweets containing negation, 13.5 % (539/4000) is quite close to that. The average number of tokens per sentence is 10.2 and the average scope size is 3.8. For comparison, the equivalent numbers of the full paper BioScope sub-corpus are 26.2 and 8.8 (Morante and Daelemans, 2009), which indicates that simpler language is used in the Twitter corpus.

aint	*cannot*	cant	*darent*	didnt
doesnt	*dont*	hadnt	*hardly*	hasnt
havent	*havnt*	isnt	*lack*	*lacking*
lacks	neither	never	no	*nobody*
none	*nor*	not	nothing	nowhere
mightnt	*mustnt*	*neednt*	*oughtnt*	*shant*
shouldnt	*wasnt*	*without*	wouldnt	*n't

Table 2: Lexicon of negation cues

5 Negation Scope Detection Experiments

Two classifiers were created: one to detect the scope of negation and one to assign sentiment. The negation classifier was used in the feature extraction process for the sentiment classifier (Section 6).

Negation scope detection (NSD) is a binary classification problem, where each token is determined to be either in an affirmative or a negated context. For NSD experiments, we report precision (P), recall (R), F_1 score, and the *percentage of correctly classified scopes* (PCS): For classification tasks where the output is a sequence, metrics that only consider individual units regardless of their order are often insufficient. PCS measures the accuracy of a scope classifier: a scope is considered correctly classified if, for a given negation cue, every token in its associated scope has been correctly marked.

5.1 Negation Classifier Architecture

The classification algorithm consists of two steps: negation cue detection and scope identification. Cue detection is performed by a pattern-matching approach with a lexicon of explicit cues adopted from Councill et al. (2010), as shown in Table 2, where **n't* matches all strings with the suffix *n't*. Note that this list is more extensive than the one of Potts (2011), used in many SemEval systems. Four cues on Potts' list are not in Table 2 (*noone, couldnt, wont, arent*), while the 17 cues in italics are not listed by Potts. An inspection of the 37 cues appearing in the Twitter Negation Corpus revealed seven more cues / spelling variants included on neither list (*idk, dnt, cudnt, ain, eint, neva, neeeever*).

Tweets are preprocessed with the TweeboParser dependency parser (Kong et al., 2014), that performs tokenisation, part-of-speech tagging and parsing, labeling each token with its dependency head. A dependency-based binary CRF classifier then for each token determines whether it is in a negated or affirmative context. The CRF implementation by Okazaki (2007) is used, with a Python binding created by Peng and Korobov (2014).

Feature	Description
Word	lower-case token string
POS	part-of-speech tag of the token
DRight	distance to nearest negation cue to the right
DLeft	distance to nearest negation cue to the left
DepD	number of edges to nearest negation cue
Dep1POS	POS tag of the 1st order dependency head
Dep1D	number of edges to nearest negation cue from the 1st order dependency head
Dep2POS	POS tag of the 2nd order dependency head
Dep2D	number of edges to nearest negation cue from the 2nd order dependency head

Table 3: Negation classifier feature set

The classifier is a Twitter-tailored version of the system described by Councill et al. (2010) with one change: the dependency distance from each token to the closest negation cue has been added to the feature set, which is shown in Table 3. The distances (DRight and DLeft) are the minimun linear token-wise distances, i.e., the number of tokens from one token to another. Dependency distance (DepD) is calculated as the minimum number of edges that must be traversed in a dependency tree to move from one token, to another. The classifier takes a parameter, *max distance*, that specifies the maximum distance to be considered (all longer distances are treated as being equivalent). This applies to both linear distance and dependency distance.

5.2 Negation Cue Detection

The created Conditional Random Fields negation classifier was evaluated on the Twitter Negation Corpus. The data set was split into two subsets: a development set and an evaluation set. The development set consists of 3,000 tweets and the evaluation set of 1,000 tweets. To ensure more reliable training and testing, given the heavy label imbalance of the corpus, the split was stratified, with the same ratio of tweets containing negation in both subsets.

The actual negation cues in the annotated training data are used when training the classifier, but a lexicon-based cue detection approach is taken during classification. When applied to the Twitter Negation Corpus, the cue detector achieved a precision of 0.873 with a recall of 0.976, and hence an F_1 score of 0.922. In comparison, Morante and Daelemans (2009) use a list of negation cues extracted from their training data and thus have perfect cue detection precision, but recall varying from 0.957 (full papers) to 0.987 (abstracts) on the three BioScope sub-corpora.

Data	NSD model	P	R	F_1	PCS
Test	Sophisticated	0.972	0.923	0.853	64.5
	Gold standard	0.841	0.956	0.895	66.3
	Simple	0.591	0.962	0.733	43.1
Train	Sophisticated	0.849	0.891	0.868	66.3

Table 4: Negation classifier performance

Inspection of the cue detection output reveals that the classifier mainly struggles with the separation of words used both as negators and exclamations. By far the most significant of these is *no*, with 35 of its 90 occurrences in the corpus being as a non-cue; often it occurs as a determiner functioning as a negator (e.g., "there were no letters this morning"), but it may occur as an exclamation (e.g., "No, I'm not ready yet" and "No! Don't touch it").

Despite the high recall, cue outliers such as *dnt neva*, or *cudnt* could potentially be detected by using word-clusters. We expanded the lexicon of negation cues to contain the whole set of Tweet NLP word clusters created by Owoputi et al. (2013) for each lexical item. Recall was slightly increased, to 0.992, but precision suffered a dramatic decrease to 0.535, since the clusters are too inclusive. More finely-grained word clusters could possibly increase recall without hurting precision.

5.3 NSD Classifier Performance

To determine the optimal parameter values, a 7-fold stratified cross validation grid search was performed on the development set over the L1 and L2 CRF penalty coefficients, $C1$ and $C2$ with a parameter space of $\{10^{-4}, 10^{-3}, 10^{-2}, 0.1, 1, 10\}$, in addition to *max distance* (see Section 5.1) with a $[5, 10]$ parameter space. The identified optimal setting was $C1 = 0.1, C2 = 1,$ *max distance* $= 7$.

The performance of the *sophisticated* negation scope classifier with the parameter set selected through grid search was evaluated on the held-out test data. The classifier was also tested on the same evaluation set with *gold standard* cue detection (i.e., with perfect negation signal identification).

To establish a baseline for negation scope detection on the Twitter Negation Corpus, we also implemented the simple model described in Section 2 and used by almost all SemEval TSA systems handling negation: When a negation cue is detected, all terms from the cue to the next punctuation are considered negated. Note though, that by using an extended cue dictionary, our *simple* baseline potentially slightly improves on state-of-the-art models.

Data	Classifier	P	R	F_1	PCS
SFU	Sophisticated	0.668	0.874	0.757	43.5
BioScope full	CRF	0.808	0.708	0.755	53.7
	MetaLearn	0.722	0.697	0.709	41.0
	Sophisticated	0.660	0.610	0.634	42.6
	Simple	0.583	0.688	0.631	43.7
	SSP	0.582	0.563	0.572	64.0

Table 5: Out-of-domain NSD performance

Results from the test run on the evaluation data, and the test on the evaluation set with gold standard cue detection are shown in Table 4, together with the simple baseline, as well as a 7-fold cross validation on the development set.

The classifier achieves very good results. The run on the evaluation set produces an F_1 score of 0.853, which is considerably higher than the baseline. It also outperforms Councill et al. (2010) who achieved an F_1 score of 0.800 when applying a similar system to their customer review corpus.

5.4 Out-of-Domain Performance

Although the negation classifier is a Twitter-tailored implementation of the system described by Councill et al. (2010) with minor modifications the use of a different CRF implementation, POS-tagger and dependency parser may lead to considerable performance differences. To explore the out-of-domain capacity of the classifier, it was evaluated on the SFU Review corpus and the biological full paper part of BioScope, as that sub-corpus has proved to be difficult for negation identification.

Table 5 shows the 5-fold cross-validated performance of the sophisticated negation scope identifier on both corpora, as well as the simple baseline on Bioscope together with the results reported on the same data for the approaches described in Section 2. 'CRF' denotes the CRF-based system from Councill et al. (2010), 'MetaLearn' the meta-learner of Morante and Daelemans (2009), and 'SSP' the shallow semantic parsing solution by Zhu et al. (2010).

As can be seen, the twitter-trained sophisticated negation classifier performs reasonably well on the SFU Review Corpus, but struggles when applied to BioScope, as expected. It is outperformed in terms of F_1 score by Councill et al. (2010) and Morante and Daelemans (2009), but reaches a slightly better PCS than the latter system. The modest F_1 score is likely caused by the use of upstream preprocessing tools tailored towards Twitter language, which differs significantly from that of biomedical texts.

Notably, the simple model is a strong baseline, which actually outperforms the shallow parser on F_1 score and the meta-learner on percentage of correctly classified scopes (PCS).

6 An NSD-enhanced Sentiment Classifier

The Twitter sentiment analysis includes three steps: preprocessing, feature extraction, and either training the classifier or classifying samples. A Support Vector Machine classifier is used as it is a state-of-the-art learning algorithm proven effective on text categorization tasks, and robust on large feature spaces. We employ the SVM implementation `SVC` from `Scikit-learn` (Pedregosa et al., 2011), which is based on libsvm (Chang and Lin, 2011).

6.1 Sentiment Classifier Architecture

The preprocessing step substitutes newline and tab characters with spaces, user mentions with the string "*@someuser*", and URLs with "http://someurl" using a slightly modified regular expression by *@stephenhay*,[2] matching URLs starting with protocol specifiers or only "www".

The feature extraction step elicitates characteristics based on the STATE set, as shown in Table 6; the top four features are affected by linguistic negation, the rest are not. There are two term frequency-inverse document frequency (TF-IDF) vectorizers, for *word n-grams* ($1 \leq n \leq 4$) and for *character n-grams* ($3 \leq n \leq 5$). Both ignore common English stop words, convert all characters to lower case, and select the 1,000 features with highest TF-IDF scores. Tokens in a negation scope are appended the string `_NEG`. The *negated tokens* feature is simply a count of the tokens in a negated context.

The *NRC Hashtag Sentiment Lexicon* and *Sentiment140 Lexicon* (Kiritchenko et al., 2014) contain sentiment scores for words in negated contexts. For lookups, the first negated word in a negation scope is appended with `_NEGFIRST`, and the rest with `_NEG`. The sentiment lexica feature vectors are adopted from Kiritchenko et al. (2014) and contain the number of tokens with $score(w) \neq 0$, the total score, the maximal score, and the score of the last token in the tweet. We also use *The MPQA Subjectivity Lexicon* (Wilson et al., 2005), *Bing Liu's Opinion Lexicon* (Ding et al., 2008), and the *NRC Emotion Lexicon* (Mohammad and Turney, 2010), assigning scores of $+/-2$ for strong and $+/-1$ for weak degrees of sentiment. The resulting four

Feature	Description
Word n-grams	contiguous token sequences
Char n-grams	contiguous character sequences
Negated tokens	number of negated tokens
Sentiment lexica	feature set for each lexicon
Clusters	tokens from '1000 word clusters'
POS	part-of-speech tag frequency
All caps	upper-case tokens
Elongated	tokens with repeated characters
Emoticons	positive and negative emoticons
Punctuation	punctuation mark sequences
Hashtags	number of hashtags

Table 6: Sentiment classifier STATE feature set

feature vectors contain the sum of positive and negative scores for tokens in affirmative and negated contexts, equivalently to Kiritchenko et al. (2014).

Instead of adding only the presence of words from each of the 1000 clusters from CMU's Tweet NLP tool[3] in the *clusters* feature, as Kiritchenko et al. (2014) did, we count occurrences for each cluster and represent them with a feature. Input to the *POS* feature is obtained from the Twitter part-of-speech tagger (Owoputi et al., 2013). The *emoticons* feature is the number of happy and sad emoticons, and whether a tweet's last token is happy or a sad. The *all-caps*, *elongated* (tokens with characters repeated more than two times), *punctuation* (exclamation or question marks), and *hashtag* features are straight-forward counts of the number of tokens of each type. All the matrices from the different parts of the feature extraction are concatenated column-wise into the final feature matrix, and scaled in order to be suitable as input to a classifier.

The classifier step declares which classifier to use, along with its default parameters. It is passed the resulting feature matrix from the feature extraction, with which it creates the decision space if training, or classifies samples if predicting. Using the negation scope classifier with the parameters identified in Section 5.3, a grid search was performed over the entire Twitter2013-train data set using stratified 10-fold cross validation to find the C and γ parameters for the SVM classifier. A preliminary coarse search showed the radial basis function (RBF) kernel to yield the best results, although most state-of-the-art sentiment classification systems use a linear kernel.

A finer parameter space was then examined. The surface plots in Figure 1 display the effects of the C

[2] `mathiasbynens.be/demo/url-regex`

[3] `http://www.ark.cs.cmu.edu/TweetNLP/`

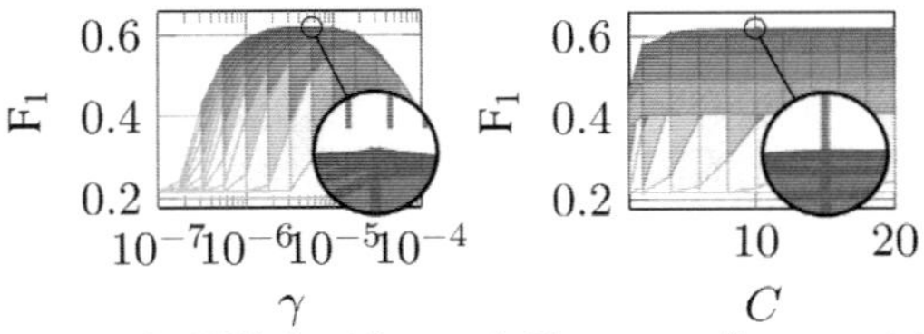

Figure 1: SVM grid search F_1 scores for γ and C

and γ parameters on the classifier's F_1 score. The combination of parameters that scored best was $C = 10$ and $\gamma \approx 5.6 * 10^{-6}$, marked by circles. Increasing C beyond 10 gives no notable change in F_1 score. The combination of a small γ and higher values of C means that the classifier is quite generalized, and that increasing C (regularizing further) makes no difference. It also suggests that the data is noisy, requiring a great deal of generalization.

In order to allow a user to query Twitter for a search phrase on live data, the classifier is wrapped in a web application using the Django web framework.[4] The resulting tweet hits are classified using a pre-trained classifier, and presented to the user indicating their sentiment polarities. The total distribution of polarity is also displayed as a graph to give the user an impression of the overall opinion.

6.2 Sentiment Classifier Performance

The SVM was trained on the Twitter2013-train set using the parameters identified through grid search, and tested on the Twitter2014-test and Twitter2013-test sets, scoring as in Table 7. Sentiment classification is here treated as a three-class task, with the labels positive, negative, and objective/neutral. In addition to precision, recall, and F_1 for each class, we report the *macro-average* of each metric across all classes. Macro-averaging disregards class imbalance and is calculated by taking the average of the classification metric outputs for each label, equally weighting each label, regardless of its number of samples. The last column of the table shows the *support*: the number of samples for each label in the test set.

As can be seen in the table, the classifier performed worst on negative samples. Figure 2 displays the confusion matrices for the Twitter2013-test set (the Twitter2014 matrices look similar). If there were perfect correlation between true and predicted labels, the diagonals would be completely red. However, the confusion matrices show (clearer in the normalized version) that the classifier is quite biased towards the neutral label (illustrated with 😐),

[4] https://djangoproject.com

Label	P	R	F_1	Support
		Twitter2014-test		
positive	0.863	0.589	0.700	805
neutral	0.568	0.872	0.688	572
negative	0.717	0.487	0.580	156
avg / total	0.738	0.684	0.684	1533
		Twitter2013-test		
positive	0.851	0.581	0.691	1273
neutral	0.627	0.898	0.739	1369
negative	0.711	0.426	0.533	467
avg / total	0.731	0.697	0.688	3109

Table 7: Sentiment classifier performance

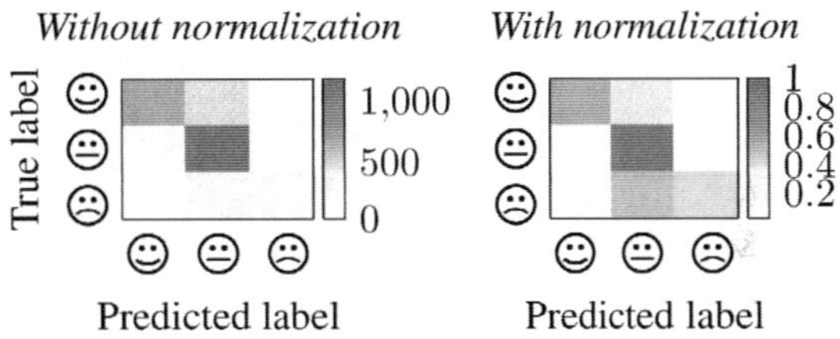

Figure 2: Sentiment classifier confusion matrices

as can be seen from the warm colours in the ☺ and ☹ true label cells of the 😐 predicted label column, in particular misclassifying negative samples. This is likely an effect of the imbalanced training set, where neutral samples greatly outnumber negative.

6.3 TSA Feature Ablation Study

The results of an ablation study of the TSA classifier are shown in Table 8, where the *all* rows (n-grams/counts) refer to removing all features in that group. Most apparently, the *sentiment lexica* feature has the greatest impact on classifier performance, especially on the Twitter2013-test set. This may be since the most important lexica (Sentiment140 and NRC Hashtag Sentiment) were created at the same time as the Twitter2013 data, and could be more accurate on the language used then.

The *character n-gram* feature slightly damages performance on the Twitter2014-test set, although making a positive contribution on the Twitter2013 data. This is most likely caused by noise in the data, but the feature could be sensitive to certain details that appeared after the Twitter2013 data collection.

The majority of the count features do not impose considerable changes in performance, although the *all-caps* feature decreases performance on both test data sets, most likely only introducing noise.

	Features	Twitter test 2014	Twitter test 2013
	All	0.684	0.688
n-grams	– word n-grams	0.672	0.674
	– char n-grams	0.688	0.676
	– *all n-grams*	0.664	0.667
	– sentiment lexica	0.665	0.657
frequency count features	– clusters	0.666	0.677
	– POS	0.684	0.685
	– all caps	0.685	0.689
	– elongated	0.682	0.687
	– emoticons	0.681	0.688
	– punctuation	0.682	0.688
	– hashtag	0.684	0.688
	– negation	0.684	0.688
	– *all counts*	0.665	0.671

Table 8: Sentiment classifier ablation (F_1 scores)

However, the Tweet NLP *clusters* feature has a large impact, as anticipated. Tweets contain many misspellings and unusual abbreviations and expressions, and the purpose of this feature is to make generalizations by counting the occurrences of clusters that include similar words.

6.4 Effect of Negation Scope Detection

Table 9 shows the effects of performing negation scope detection on several variations of the sentiment classification system and data sets. The first six rows give results from experiments using the Twitter2013-training and Twitter2014-test sets, and the remaining rows results when using only a subset of the data: tweets that contain negation, as determined by our NSD system. The rows are grouped into four segments, where each segment shows scores for a classifier using either no, simple or sophisticated negation scope detection. The segments represent different feature sets, either using *all* features or only the features that are directly affected by *negation*: word and character n-grams, sentiment lexica, and negation counts.

In every case, taking negation into account using either the simple or the sophisticated method improves the F_1 score considerably. Using all the data, the sophisticated solution scores marginally better than the simple one, but it improves more clearly upon the simple method on the negated part of the data, with F_1 improvements ranging from $4.5\,\%$ to $6.1\,\%$ (i.e., from 0.029 to 0.039 F_1 score).

Features	NSD method	P	R	F_1
All tweets (training and test sets)				
all	No	0.730	0.659	0.653
	Simple	0.738	0.676	0.675
	Sophisticated	0.738	0.684	0.684
negation	No	0.705	0.618	0.601
	Simple	0.728	0.663	0.662
	Sophisticated	0.729	0.667	0.665
Only tweets containing negation				
all	No	0.598	0.599	0.585
	Simple	0.653	0.654	0.644
	Sophisticated	0.675	0.682	0.673
negation	No	0.609	0.604	0.586
	Simple	0.648	0.654	0.633
	Sophisticated	0.681	0.696	0.672

Table 9: Sentiment classification results

7 Conclusion and Future Work

The paper has introduced a sophisticated approach to negation scope detection (NSD) for Twitter sentiment analysis. The system consists of two parts: a negation cue detector and a negation scope classifier. The cue detector uses a lexicon lookup that yields high recall, but modest precision. However, the negation scope classifier still produces better results than observed in other domains: an F_1 score of 0.853 with $64.5\,\%$ correctly classified scopes, indicating that the Conditional Random Fields-based scope classifier is able to identify the trend of certain dictionary cues being misclassified.

A sentiment classifier for Twitter data was also developed, incorporating several features that benefit from negation scope detection. The results confirm that taking negation into account in general improves sentiment classification performance significantly, and that using a sophisticated NSD system slightly improves the performance further.

The negation cue variation in the Twitter data was quite low, but due to part-of-speech ambiguity it was for some tokens unclear whether or not they functioned as a negation signal. A more intricate cue detector could in the future aim to resolve this.

The study builds on current state-of-the-art Twitter sentiment analysis features, but other features could tentatively make better use of well-performing negation scope detection. The negated contexts underlying the utilized sentiment lexica are, for example, based on a simple NSD model, so might be improved by more elaborate solutions.

References

Apoorv Agarwal, Boyi Xie, Ilia Vovsha, Owen Rambow, and Rebecca Passonneau. 2011. Sentiment analysis of Twitter data. In *Proceedings of the 49th Annual Meeting of the Association for Computational Linguistics: Human Language Technologies*, pages 30–38, Portland, Oregon, June. ACL. Workshop on Languages in Social Media.

Héctor Cerezo-Costas and Diego Celix-Salgado. 2015. Gradiant-analytics: Training polarity shifters with CRFs for message level polarity detection. In *Proceedings of the 9th International Workshop on Semantic Evaluation*, pages 539–544, Denver, Colorado, June. ACL.

Chih-Chung Chang and Chih-Jen Lin. 2011. LIBSVM: A library for support vector machines. *ACM Transactions on Intelligent Systems and Technology*, 2(3):27:1–27:27, April.

Wendy W. Chapman, Will Bridewell, Paul Hanbury, Gregory F. Cooper, and Bruce G. Buchanan. 2001. A simple algorithm for identifying negated findings and diseases in discharge summaries. *Journal of Biomedical Informatics*, 34(5):301–310, October.

Isaac G. Councill, Ryan McDonald, and Leonid Velikovich. 2010. What's great and what's not: learning to classify the scope of negation for improved sentiment analysis. In *Proceedings of the 48th Annual Meeting of the Association for Computational Linguistics*, pages 51–59, Uppsala, Sweden, July. ACL. Workshop on Negation and Speculation in Natural Language Processing.

Xiaowen Ding, Bing Liu, and Philip S. Yu. 2008. A holistic lexicon-based approach to opinion mining. In *Proceedings of the 2008 International Conference on Web Search and Data Mining*, pages 231–240, Stanford, California, February. ACM.

Richárd Farkas, Veronika Vincze, György Móra, János Csirik, and György Szarvas. 2010. The CoNLL-2010 shared task: Learning to detect hedges and their scope in natural language text. In *Proceedings of the 14th Conference on Computational Natural Language Learning*, pages 1–12, Uppsala, Sweden, July. ACL.

Talmy Givón. 1993. *English grammar: A function-based introduction*. John Benjamins, Amsterdam, The Netherlands.

Tobias Günther, Jean Vancoppenolle, and Richard Johansson. 2014. RTRGO: Enhancing the GU-MLT-LT system for sentiment analysis of short messages. In *Proceedings of the 8th International Workshop on Semantic Evaluation*, pages 497–502, Dublin, Ireland, August. ACL.

Matthias Hagen, Martin Potthast, Michael Büchner, and Benno Stein. 2015. Webis: An ensemble for Twitter sentiment detection. In *Proceedings of the 9th International Workshop on Semantic Evaluation*, pages 582–589, Denver, Colorado, June. ACL.

Hussam Hamdan, Patrice Bellot, and Frederic Bechet. 2015. Lsislif: Feature extraction and label weighting for sentiment analysis in Twitter. In *Proceedings of the 9th International Workshop on Semantic Evaluation*, pages 568–573, Denver, Colorado, June. ACL.

Svetlana Kiritchenko, Xiaodan Zhu, and Saif M. Mohammad. 2014. Sentiment analysis of short informal texts. *Journal of Artificial Intelligence Research*, 50:723–762, August.

Lingpeng Kong, Nathan Schneider, Swabha Swayamdipta, Archna Bhatia, Chris Dyer, and Noah A. Smith. 2014. A dependency parser for tweets. In *Proceedings of the 2014 Conference on Empirical Methods in Natural Language Processing*, pages 1001–1012, Doha, Qatar, October. ACL.

Natalia Konstantinova, Sheila C.M. de Sousa, Noa P. Cruz, Manuel J. Maña, Maite Taboada, and Ruslan Mitkov. 2012. A review corpus annotated for negation, speculation and their scope. In *Proceedings of the 8th International Conference on Language Resources and Evaluation*, pages 3190–3195, Istanbul, Turkey, May. ELRA.

Yasuhide Miura, Shigeyuki Sakaki, Keigo Hattori, and Tomoko Ohkuma. 2014. TeamX: A sentiment analyzer with enhanced lexicon mapping and weighting scheme for unbalanced data. In *Proceedings of the 8th International Workshop on Semantic Evaluation*, pages 628–632, Dublin, Ireland, August. ACL.

Saif Mohammad and Peter Turney. 2010. Emotions evoked by common words and phrases: Using Mechanical Turk to create an emotion lexicon. In *Proceedings of the 2010 Human Language Technology Conference of the North American Chapter of the Association for Computational Linguistics*, pages 26–34, Los Angeles, California, June. ACL. Workshop on Computational Approaches to Analysis and Generation of Emotion in Text.

Saif Mohammad, Svetlana Kiritchenko, and Xiaodan Zhu. 2013. NRC-Canada: Building the state-of-the-art in sentiment analysis of tweets. In *Second Joint Conference on Lexical and Computational Semantics (*SEM), Volume 2: Proceedings of the 7th International Workshop on Semantic Evaluation*, SemEval '13, pages 321–327, Atlanta, Georgia, June. ACL.

Saif Mohammad. 2012. #Emotional tweets. In *First Joint Conference on Lexical and Computational Semantics (*SEM), Volume 2: Proceedings of the 6th International Workshop on Semantic Evaluation*, pages 246–255, Montréal, Canada, June. ACL.

Karo Moilanen and Stephen Pulman. 2007. Sentiment composition. In *Proceedings of the 6th International Conference on Recent Advances in Natural Language Processing*, pages 378–382, Borovets, Bulgaria, September.

Roser Morante and Eduardo Blanco. 2012. * SEM 2012 shared task: Resolving the scope and focus of negation. In *First Joint Conference on Lexical and Computational Semantics (*SEM), Volume 2: Proceedings of the 6th International Workshop on Semantic Evaluation*, pages 265–274, Montréal, Canada, June. ACL.

Roser Morante and Walter Daelemans. 2009. A metalearning approach to processing the scope of negation. In *Proceedings of the 13th Conference on Computational Natural Language Learning*, pages 21–29, Boulder, Colorado, June. ACL.

Roser Morante and Caroline Sporleder. 2012. Modality and negation: An introduction to the special issue. *Computational Linguistics*, 38(2):223–260.

Pradeep G. Mutalik, Aniruddha Deshpande, and Prakash M. Nadkarni. 2001. Use of general-purpose negation detection to augment concept indexing of medical documents: A quantitative study using the UMLS. *Journal of the American Medical Informatics Association*, 8(6):598–609, November.

Preslav Nakov, Zornitsa Kozareva, Sara Rosenthal, Veselin Stoyanov, Alan Ritter, and Theresa Wilson. 2013. SemEval-2013 Task 2: Sentiment analysis in Twitter. In *Second Joint Conference on Lexical and Computational Semantics (*SEM), Volume 2: Proceedings of the 7th International Workshop on Semantic Evaluation*, SemEval '13, pages 312–320, Atlanta, Georgia, June. ACL.

Joakim Nivre, Johan Hall, Jens Nilsson, Atanas Chanev, Gülşen Eryiğit, Sandra Kübler, Svetoslav Marinov, and Erwin Marsi. 2007. MaltParser: A language-independent system for data-driven dependency parsing. *Natural Language Engineering*, 13(2):95–135, January.

Naoaki Okazaki. 2007. CRFsuite: a fast implementation of conditional random fields (CRFs). `www.chokkan.org/software/crfsuite/`.

Olutobi Owoputi, Brendan O'Connor, Chris Dyer, Kevin Gimpel, Nathan Schneider, and Noah A. Smith. 2013. Improved part-of-speech tagging for online conversational text with word clusters. In *Proceedings of the 2013 Conference of the North American Chapter of the Association for Computational Linguistics: Human Language Technologies*, pages 380–390, Atlanta, Georgia, June. ACL.

Fabian Pedregosa, Gaël Varoquaux, Alexandre Gramfort, Vincent Michel, Bertrand Thirion, Olivier Grisel, Mathieu Blondel, Peter Prettenhofer, Ron Weiss, Vincent Dubourg, Jake Vanderplas, Alexandre Passos, David Cournapeau, Matthieu Brucher, Matthieu Perrot, and Édouard Duchesnay. 2011. Scikit-learn: Machine learning in Python. *Journal of Machine Learning Research*, 12(1):2825–2830.

Terry Peng and Mikhail Korobov. 2014. python-crfsuite. `github.com/tpeng/python-crfsuite`.

Nataliia Plotnikova, Micha Kohl, Kevin Volkert, Stefan Evert, Andreas Lerner, Natalie Dykes, and Heiko Ermer. 2015. KLUEless: Polarity classification and association. In *Proceedings of the 9th International Workshop on Semantic Evaluation*, pages 619–625, Denver, Colorado, June. ACL.

Christopher Potts. 2011. Sentiment symposium tutorial. In *Sentiment Analysis Symposium*, San Francisco, California, November. Alta Plana Corporation. `http://sentiment.christopherpotts.net/`.

Sara Rosenthal, Alan Ritter, Preslav Nakov, and Veselin Stoyanov. 2014. SemEval-2014 Task 9: Sentiment analysis in Twitter. In *Proceedings of the 8th International Workshop on Semantic Evaluation*, pages 73–80, Dublin, Ireland, August. ACL.

Sara Rosenthal, Preslav Nakov, Svetlana Kiritchenko, Saif Mohammad, Alan Ritter, and Veselin Stoyanov. 2015. SemEval-2015 Task 10: Sentiment analysis in Twitter. In *Proceedings of the 9th International Workshop on Semantic Evaluation*, pages 451–463, Denver, Colorado, June. ACL.

Øyvind Selmer, Mikael Brevik, Björn Gambäck, and Lars Bungum. 2013. NTNU: Domain semi-independent short message sentiment classification. In *Second Joint Conference on Lexical and Computational Semantics (*SEM), Volume 2: Proceedings of the 7th International Workshop on Semantic Evaluation*, SemEval '13, pages 430–437, Atlanta, Georgia, June. ACL.

Duyu Tang, Furu Wei, Bing Qin, Ting Liu, and Ming Zhou. 2014. Coooolll: A deep learning system for Twitter sentiment classification. In *Proceedings of the 8th International Workshop on Semantic Evaluation*, pages 208–212, Dublin, Ireland, August. ACL.

Gunnel Tottie. 1991. *Negation in English Speech and Writing: A Study in Variation.* Academic Press, San Diego, California.

Veronika Vincze, György Szarvas, Richárd Farkas, György Móra, and János Csirik. 2008. The BioScope corpus: biomedical texts annotated for uncertainty, negation and their scopes. *BMC Bioinformatics*, 9(Suppl 11):S9, November.

Michael Wiegand, Alexandra Balahur, Benjamin Roth, Dietrich Klakow, and Andrés Montoyo. 2010. A survey on the role of negation in sentiment analysis. In *Proceedings of the 48th Annual Meeting of the Association for Computational Linguistics*, pages 60–68, Uppsala, Sweden, July. ACL. Workshop on Negation and Speculation in Natural Language Processing.

Theresa Wilson, Paul Hoffmann, Swapna Somasundaran, Jason Kessler, Janyce Wiebe, Yejin Choi, Claire Cardie, Ellen Riloff, and Siddharth Patwardhan. 2005. OpinionFinder: A system for subjectivity analysis. In *Proceedings of the 2005 Human Language Technology Conference and Conference on Empirical Methods in Natural Language Processing*, pages 34–35, Vancouver, British Columbia, Canada, October. ACL. Demonstration Abstracts.

Qiaoming Zhu, Junhui Li, Hongling Wang, and Guodong Zhou. 2010. A unified framework for scope learning via simplified shallow semantic parsing. In *Proceedings of the 2010 Conference on Empirical Methods in Natural Language Processing*, pages 714–724, Cambridge, Massachusetts, October. ACL.

A Linguistically Informed Convolutional Neural Network

Sebastian Ebert and **Ngoc Thang Vu** and **Hinrich Schütze**
Center for Information and Language Processing
University of Munich, Germany
{ebert|thangvu}@cis.lmu.de, inquiries@cislmu.org

Abstract

Sentiment lexicons and other linguistic knowledge proved to be beneficial in polarity classification. This paper introduces a linguistically informed Convolutional Neural Network (lingCNN), which incorporates this valuable kind of information into the model. We present two intuitive and simple methods: The first one integrates word-level features, the second sentence-level features. By combining both types of features our model achieves results that are comparable to state-of-the-art systems.

1 Introduction

This paper explores the use of Convolutional Neural Networks (CNN) for sentiment analysis. CNNs reach state-of-the-art results in several polarity classification tasks (Mohammad et al., 2013; Tang et al., 2014a; Kim, 2014; Severyn and Moschitti, 2015; Kalchbrenner et al., 2014). Reasons are their ability to deal with arbitrary input sentence lengths and to preserve word order. Moreover, they learn to find the most important polarity indicators and ignore the rest of the sentence. That is beneficial, since most of the words in a text do not convey sentiment information. Finally, CNNs can make use of powerful pretrained word representations (e.g., Mikolov et al. (2013)).

However, training such a model requires a large amount of labeled training data. One approach to address this issue is to enlarge training data in a semi-supervised fashion (Severyn and Moschitti, 2015). Instead, we propose to make use of already available linguistically motivated resources. Especially sentiment lexicons are important cues for polarity classification (cf. Mohammad et al. (2013)).

We introduce two intuitive and simple methods of incorporating linguistic features into a CNN.

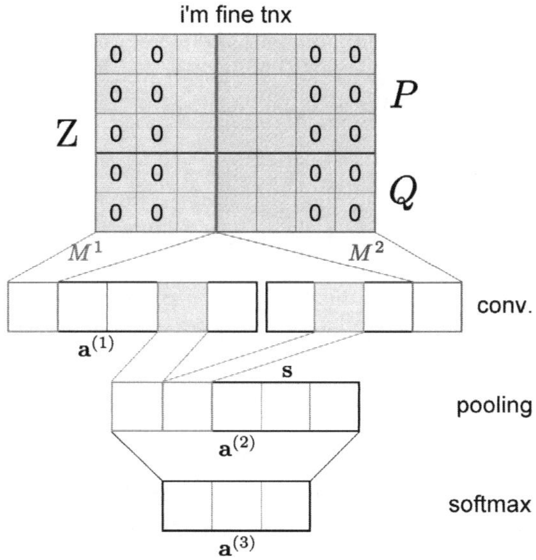

Figure 1: LingCNN architecture

The resulting architecture is called *linguistically informed CNN (lingCNN)*. The first method is to add features to every word in a sentence. That enables the model to learn interactions between words and between individual word embeddings and linguistic features. The second method is to add feature vectors that are computed based on the entire sentence. The results show that word-level features can improve the classification and are more beneficial than sentence-level features. However, the combination of both methods reaches the best performance and yields results that are comparable to state-of-the-art on the SemEval Twitter polarity data set.

2 LingCNN Architecture

Figure 1 depicts the lingCNN architecture. We use the following terminology. $LT \in \mathbb{R}^{d \times |V|}$ denotes a lookup table that assigns each word in the vocabulary V a d-dimensional vector. Given a sequence of n tokens t_1 to t_n the model concatenates all n

Proceedings of the 6th Workshop on Computational Approaches to Subjectivity, Sentiment and Social Media Analysis (WASSA 2015), pages 109–114,
Lisboa, Portugal, 17 September, 2015.

word representations to the input of the lingCNN:

$$Z = \begin{bmatrix} | & | & & | \\ LT_{\cdot,t_1} & & \cdots & LT_{\cdot,t_n} \\ | & & | & | \end{bmatrix}$$

The lingCNN consists of three types of layers (in the following indicated by a superscript index): a convolution layer, a max pooling layer, and a fully connected softmax layer.

2D Convolution Using a convolution matrix $M \in \mathbb{R}^{d \times m}$ (also called filter matrix) the lingCNN performs a 2d convolution:

$$\mathbf{a}_o^{(1)} = \sum_{i=1}^{d} \sum_{j=1}^{m} M_{i,j} Z_{i,o+j}$$

, where $\mathbf{a}^{(1)}$ is the layer's activation and $o \in [0, n-m]$ is the current position of the convolution.

The width of the filter m specifies how many words the filter spans ($m \in \{3, 4\}$ in Figure 1). The model uses multiple filter sizes at this level and several filters per filter size. Furthermore, we make use of *wide convolution* (Kalchbrenner et al., 2014), which pads the input Z with $m-1$ zero columns at the left and right side (i.e., the sentence length becomes $n + 2 * (m-1)$). This makes sure that every column of the filter reaches every column of the input. The model uses 2d convolution, because a filter that span all d dimensions in height has the advantage that it can find features that interact with multiple dimensions.

Max Pooling To keep only the most salient features, the lingCNN selects the largest value of each convolution output. This way we hope to find the most important polarity indicators, independently of their position. To the remaining values we add a bias $b^{(2)}$ and apply a rectified linear unit nonlinearity: $\mathbf{a}^{(2)} = \max(0, \mathbf{a}^{(1)} + b^{(2)})$ (Nair and Hinton, 2010).

Softmax Next, the output values of the pooling layer are concatenated with a sentence-level feature vector $\mathbf{s}$: $\mathbf{a}^{(2)'} = [\mathbf{a}^{(2)}\ \mathbf{s}]$, which is the input to a fully connected layer: $\mathbf{z} = W\mathbf{a}^{(2)'} + b^{(3)}$. This layer converts its input into a probability distribution over the sentiment labels using the softmax function: $\mathbf{a}_i^{(3)} = \frac{\exp(\mathbf{z}_i)}{\sum_j \exp(\mathbf{z}_j)}$.

3 Word-level Features

To incorporate linguistic features at word-level into the learning process we create the lookup table by concatenating two matrices: $LT = \begin{bmatrix} P \\ Q \end{bmatrix}$. $P \in \mathbb{R}^{d_P \times |V|}$ denotes a matrix of low-dimensional word representations, so called *word embeddings*. d_P, the size of the embeddings, is usually set to 50 – 300, depending on the task. We train skip-gram word embeddings (Mikolov et al., 2013) with the word2vec toolkit[1] on a large amount of Twitter text data. Previous work showed that pretrained word embeddings are helpful in various tasks (e.g., Kim (2014)). We first downloaded about 60 million tweets from the unlabeled Twitter Events data set (McMinn et al., 2013). The vocabulary is built out of all the words of the SemEval training data and the 50k most frequent words of the Twitter Events data set. Additionally, an *unknown* word is added to the vocabulary to learn a word embedding for out-of-vocabulary words. Finally, a skip-gram model with 60-dimensional vectors is trained on the unlabeled data and used to initialize the word embeddings matrix P. The matrix P is further fine-tuned during model training.

In addition to P, we introduce another matrix $Q \in \mathbb{R}^{d_Q \times |V|}$, which contains external word features. In this case d_Q is the number of features for a word. The features in Q are precomputed and not embedded into any embeddings space, i.e., Q is fixed during training. We use the following feature types:

Binary Sentiment Indicators Binary features that indicate a word's prior polarity. We create two such features per word per lexicon. The first feature indicates positive and the second negative polarity of that word in the lexicon. The lexicons for this feature type are MPQA (Wilson et al., 2005), Opinion lexicon (Hu and Liu, 2004), and NRCC Emotion lexicon (Mohammad and Turney, 2013).

Sentiment Scores The Sentiment140 lexicon and the Hashtag lexicon (Mohammad et al., 2013) both provide a score for each word instead of just a label. We directly incorporate these scores into the feature matrix. Both lexicons also contain scores for bigrams and skip ngrams. In such a case all words of the ngram receive the same ngram score.

[1]https://code.google.com/p/word2vec/

Binary Negation Following Christopher Potts,[2] we mark each word between a negation word and the next punctuation as negated.

In total each word receives 13 additional features ($3 * 2$ binary, $2 * 3$ scores, 1 negation). Since lingCNN performs a 2d convolution, it allows the detection of features that interact with word embeddings and linguistic features.

4 Sentence-level Features

An alternative to adding word-level features into the training process is to add sentence-level features. These features are concatenated with the pooling layer's output to serve as additional input for the softmax layer as described above. We use the following feature types:

Counts We use the following counts: number of terms that are all upper case; number of elongated words such as 'coooool'; number of emoticons;[3] number of contiguous sequences of punctuation; number of negated words.

Sentiment Scores The computed lexicon features are the number of sentiment words in a sentence, the sum of sentiment scores of these words as provided by the lexicons, the maximum sentiment score, and the sentiment score of the last word. These four numbers are calculated for all 5 previously mentioned sentiment lexicons. Moreover, they are computed separately for the entire tweet, for each POS tag, for all hashtag tokens in the tweet, and for all capitalized words in the tweet (Mohammad et al., 2013).

5 Experiments and Results

5.1 Data

To evaluate the lingCNN, we use the SemEval 2015 data set (Rosenthal et al., 2015). We train the model on the SemEval 2013 training and development set and use the SemEval 2013 test set as development set (Nakov et al., 2013; Rosenthal et al., 2015). The final evaluation is done on the SemEval 2015 test set. Table 1 lists all data set sizes in detail.

To test the generality of our findings we additionally report results on the manually labeled test set of the Sentiment140 corpus (Sent140) (Go et al., 2009). It contains about 500 tweets (cf. Table 1), which were collected by searching Twitter for specific categories, e.g., movies.

	total	pos	neg	neu
training set	9845	3636	1535	4674
development set	3813	1572	601	1640
SemEval test set	2390	1038	365	987
Sent140 test set	498	182	177	139

Table 1: Data set sizes.

The examples in all data sets are labeled with one of the three classes: *positive*, *negative*, or *neutral*.[4] Similar to the SemEval shared task we report the macro F_1 score of the positive and negative classes, i.e., $F_{1,macro} = (F_{1,positive} + F_{1,negative})/2$.

Prepocessing The SemEval and Sentiment140 data as well as the unlabeled Twitter Events data set, which is used for pretraining word embeddings, are preprocessed in the following way: Tweets are first tokenized with the CMU tokenizer (Owoputi et al., 2013). Afterwards, all user mentions are replaced by '<user>' and all urls by '<web>'. We keep hashtags, because they often contain valuable information such as topics or even sentiment.

Punctuation sequences like '!?!?' can act as exaggeration or other polarity modifiers. However, the sheer amount of possible sequences increases the out-of-vocabulary rate dramatically. Therefore, all sequences of punctuations are replaced by a list of distinct punctuations in this sequence (e.g., '!?!?' is replaced by '[!?]').

5.2 Model Settings

Baseline Systems We use the SemEval 2013 and SemEval 2014 winning system (Mohammad et al., 2013) as baseline. This system uses a Support Vector Machine (SVM) for classification. According to their analysis, bag-of-word features ($\{1, 2, 3\}$-grams for words and $\{3, 4, 5\}$-grams for characters) and linguistic features are the most important ones. Therefore, we implement both of them. There are three feature settings: (i) only bag-of-words features (for both, word and characters), (ii) only linguistic features, and (iii) the combination of bag-of-words and linguistic features. We use LIBLINEAR (Fan et al., 2008) to train the model and optimized the C parameter on the development set.

[2]http://sentiment.christopherpotts.net/lingstruc.html

[3]The list of emoticons was taken from SentiStrengh: http://sentistrength.wlv.ac.uk/

[4]objective instances were considered to be neutral

For reference we add the first and second best systems of the SemEval 2015 tweet level polarity task: Webis (Hagen et al., 2015) and UNITN (Severyn and Moschitti, 2015). Webis is an ensemble based on four systems, which participated in the same task of SemEval 2014. The UNITN system trains a CNN similar to ours. They rely on pretraining the entire model on a large distant supervised training corpus (10M labeled tweets). This approach is orthogonal to ours and can easily be combined with our idea if linguistic feature integration. This combination is likely to increase the performance further.

LingCNN To analyze the effect of the linguistic features and our extensions we train different CNN models with different combinations of features: (i) only pretrained word embeddings, (ii) integration of word-level features, and (iii) integration of sentence-level features. The model updates all parameters during training $\theta = \{P, M^*, W, b^{(*)}\}$. We set the embeddings size to $d_P = 60$. Our model uses filters of width $2 - 5$ with 100 filters each. We train the models for a maximum of 30 epochs with mini-batch stochastic gradient descent (batch size: 100). The training was stopped when three consecutive epochs lead to worse results on the development set (early stopping). We use AdaGrad (Duchi et al., 2011) for dynamic learning rate adjustment with an initial learning rate of 0.01 and ℓ_2 regularization ($\lambda = 5e^{-5}$).

5.3 Results

Baselines Table 2 lists the SVM results. Similar to Mohammad et al. (2013)'s findings, the combination of ngram and linguistic features gives the best performance. Both SemEval participating systems beat the baseline by a large margin.

LingCNN The lower part of Table 2 shows the lingCNN results. With only word-level features the model yields similar performance to the SVM with only linguistic features. Adding sentence-level features improves the performance to the level of the SVM baseline system with bag-of-words and linguistic features. We see that using pretrained word embeddings to initialize the model yields large improvements. Sentence features on top of that can not improve the performance further. However, word-level features together with pretrained word embeddings yield higher performance. The best result is reached by the combination of word embeddings and both types of linguistic features. This performance is comparable with both state-of-the-art SemEval winner systems.

model	features			SemEval	Sent140
SVM	bow			50.51	67.34
	ling.			57.28	66.90
	bow + ling.			59.28	70.21
Webis				64.84	-
UNITN				64.59	-
	emb.	word	sent.		
lingCNN		+		57.83	72.58
		+	+	59.24	74.36
	+			62.72	77.59
	+		+	62.61	79.14
	+	+		63.43	80.21
	+	+	+	**64.46**	**80.75**

Table 2: Results of baselines (upper half) and lingCNN (lower half).

5.4 Analysis

Examples Here, we analyze examples on why the linguistic features help. Consider the example "saturday night in with toast , hot choc & <user> on e news #happydays". Only the hashtag '#happydays' indicates polarity. The hashtag exists in the sentiment lexicon, but does not exist in the training vocabulary. Therefore, there is no embedding for it. Here is another example: "shiiiiit my sats is on saturday . i'm going to fail". 'Fail' is strongly negative in all lexicons. However, it occurs only 10 times in the training set. That is likely not enough to learn a good sentiment-bearing embedding. As a result, the CNN without linguistic knowledge classifies the tweet as neutral. Having linguistic features enables the model to implicitly incorporate sentiment information into the word embeddings, helping to classify this example correctly.

Corpus Size In this section we analyze the benefit of linguistic features with respect to the size of the training corpus. Table 3 shows the performance of the CNN with and without linguistic features, where we only use the first 1000 and 3000 training samples. We clearly see that linguistic features are helpful in all cases. Especially, where only limited training data is available, the performance difference is large. Even with only 1000 training samples, the CNN with linguistic features yields a reasonable result of 60.89. The CNN that does not have access to this source of information reaches only 49.89. Although, the performance

	1000	3000	all
emb.	49.89	58.10	62.72
emb. + word + sent.	60.89	62.51	64.46

Table 3: Different training set sizes.

of the CNN without linguistic features increases much for 3000 training examples, this model is still more than 4 points behind the linguistically informed model.

6 Related Work

Collobert et al. (2011) published the first CNN architecture for a range of natural language processing tasks. We adopt their idea of using look-up tables to incorporate linguistic features at the word-level into the CNN.

Since then CNNs have been used for a variety of sentence classification tasks (e.g., Zeng et al. (2014)), including polarity classification (e.g., Kim (2014)). Kalchbrenner et al. (2014) showed that their DCNN for modeling sentences can achieve competitive results in this field. Our CNN architecture is simpler than theirs.

There are alternative approaches of integrating linguistic features into model training. By adding more labeled data, implicit knowledge is given to the model. This approach usually requires manual labeling effort. A different approach is to incorporate linguistic knowledge into the objective function to guide the model training. For instance Tang et al. (2014b) incorporate the polarity of an ngram into a hinge loss function.

Tang et al. (2014a) used a CNN to compute representations of input sentences. These representation together with linguistic features on sentence-level form the input to an SVM. In contrast, we use linguistic features at the word-level, which allows interaction between linguistic features and word embeddings. Furthermore, we use similar sentence-features and directly incorporate them into the CNN.

In addition to CNNs, researchers have been using different neural network architectures. However, each of these has its own disadvantages. A deep feed forward network cannot model easily that inserting many types of words into a string (e.g., "happy to drive my new car" vs "happy to drive my *red* new car") does not change sentiment. Recurrent Neural Networks (RNN) (Elman, 1990) and Long Short Term Memory networks (LSTM) (Hochreiter and Schmidhuber, 1997) are powerful for unbounded dependencies, but tweets are short; the sentiment of a tweet is usually determined by one part of it and unlike RNN/LSTM, convolution plus max pooling can learn to focus on that. Recursive architectures like the Recursive Neural Tensor Network (Socher et al., 2013). assume some kind of hierarchical sentence structure. This structure does not exist or is hard to recognize for many noisy tweets.

As mentioned before, we use the SemEval 2013 and SemEval 2014 winning system (Mohammad et al., 2013) as baseline. Moreover, we include several features of their system to improve the CNN.

7 Conclusion

In this paper we introduced an intuitive and simple way of incorporating linguistic word-level and sentence-level features into a CNN architecture. Using such features yields significant improvements on two polarity classification Twitter data sets. Using both feature types, our lingCNN performs comparable to state-of-the-art systems.

References

Ronan Collobert, Jason Weston, Léon Bottou, Michael Karlen, Koray Kavukcuoglu, and Pavel Kuksa. 2011. Natural Language Processing (almost) from Scratch. *JMLR*, 12.

John C. Duchi, Elad Hazan, and Yoram Singer. 2011. Adaptive Subgradient Methods for Online Learning and Stochastic Optimization. *JMLR*, 12.

Jeffrey L. Elman. 1990. Finding Structure in Time. *Cognitive Science*, 14(2).

Rong-En Fan, Kai-Wei Chang, Cho-Jui Hsieh, Xiang-Rui Wang, and Chih-Jen Lin. 2008. LIBLINEAR: A Library for Large Linear Classification. *JMLR*, 9.

Alec Go, Richa Bhayani, and Lei Huang. 2009. Twitter Sentiment Classification using Distant Supervision.

Matthias Hagen, Martin Potthast, Michel Büchner, and Benno Stein. 2015. Webis: An Ensemble for Twitter Sentiment Detection. In *SemEval*.

Sepp Hochreiter and H. Jürgen Schmidhuber. 1997. Long Short-Term Memory. *Neural Computation*, 9(8).

Minqing Hu and Bing Liu. 2004. Mining and Summarizing Customer Reviews. In *KDD*.

Nal Kalchbrenner, Edward Grefenstette, and Phil Blunsom. 2014. A Convolutional Neural Network for Modelling Sentences. In *ACL*.

Yoon Kim. 2014. Convolutional Neural Networks for Sentence Classification. In *EMNLP*.

Andrew J. McMinn, Yashar Moshfeghi, and Joemon M. Jose. 2013. Building a large-scale corpus for evaluating event detection on twitter. In *CIKM*.

Tomas Mikolov, Kai Chen, Gregory S. Corrado, and Jeffrey Dean. 2013. Efficient Estimation of Word Representations in Vector Space. In *ICLR*.

Saif M. Mohammad and Peter D. Turney. 2013. Crowdsourcing a Word-Emotion Association Lexicon. *Computational Intelligence*, 29(3).

Saif M. Mohammad, Svetlana Kiritchenko, and Xiaodan Zhu. 2013. NRC-Canada: Building the State-of-the-Art in Sentiment Analysis of Tweets. In *SemEval*.

Vinod Nair and Geoffrey E. Hinton. 2010. Rectified Linear Units Improve Restricted Boltzmann Machines. In *ICML*.

Preslav Nakov, Sara Rosenthal, Zornitsa Kozareva, Veselin Stoyanov, Alan Ritter, and Theresa Wilson. 2013. SemEval-2013 Task 2: Sentiment Analysis in Twitter. In *SemEval*.

Olutobi Owoputi, Brendan O'Connor, Chris Dyer, Kevin Gimpel, Nathan Schneider, and Noah A. Smith. 2013. Improved Part-of-Speech Tagging for Online Conversational Text with Word Clusters. In *NAACL HLT*.

Sara Rosenthal, Preslav Nakov, Svetlana Kiritchenko, Saif M. Mohammad, Alan Ritter, and Veselin Stoyanov. 2015. SemEval-2015 Task 10: Sentiment Analysis in Twitter. In *SemEval*.

Aliaksei Severyn and Alessandro Moschitti. 2015. UNITN: Training Deep Convolutional Neural Network for Twitter Sentiment Classification. In *SemEval*.

Richard Socher, Alex Perelygin, Jean Wu, Jason Chuang, Christopher D. Manning, Andrew Y. Ng, and Christopher Potts. 2013. Recursive Deep Models for Semantic Compositionality Over a Sentiment Treebank. In *EMNLP*.

Duyu Tang, Furu Wei, Bing Qin, Ting Liu, and Ming Zhou. 2014a. Coooolll: A Deep Learning System for Twitter Sentiment Classification. In *SemEval*.

Duyu Tang, Furu Wei, Nan Yang, Ming Zhou, Ting Liu, and Bing Qin. 2014b. Learning Sentiment-Specific Word Embedding for Twitter Sentiment Classification. In *ACL*.

Theresa Ann Wilson, Janyce Wiebe, and Paul Hoffmann. 2005. Recognizing Contextual Polarity in Phrase-Level Sentiment Analysis. In *HLT/EMNLP*.

Daojian Zeng, Kang Liu, Siwei Lai, Guangyou Zhou, and Jun Zhao. 2014. Relation Classification via Convolutional Deep Neural Network. In *COLING*.

How much does word sense disambiguation help in sentiment analysis of micropost data?

Chiraag Sumanth
PES Institute of Technology
Bangalore, India
chiraagsumanth@gmail.com

Diana Inkpen
University of Ottawa
Ottawa, Canada
diana.inkpen@uottawa.ca

Abstract

This short paper describes a sentiment analysis system for micro-post data that includes analysis of tweets from Twitter and Short Messaging Service (SMS) text messages. We discuss our system that makes use of Word Sense Disambiguation techniques in sentiment analysis at the message level, where the entire tweet or SMS text was analysed to determine its dominant sentiment. Previous work done in the area of Word Sense Disambiguation does not throw light on its influence on the analysis of social-media text and micropost data, which is what our work aims to achieve. Our experiments show that the use of Word Sense Disambiguation alone has resulted in an improved sentiment analysis system that outperforms systems built without incorporating Word Sense Disambiguation.

1 Introduction

Twitter is an online social networking and microblogging service that enables users to send and read short 140-character messages called "tweets". As of the first quarter of 2015, the microblogging service averaged at 236 million monthly active users. Worldwide over 350 billion SMS text messages are exchanged across the world's mobile networks every month, with over 15 percent of these messages being classified as commercial or marketing messages. The process of sentiment analysis involves text analytics, linguistics and accepted language processing to determine and dig subjective information from source materials. Sentiment analysis finds applications in various domains such as marketing, business and commerce (Jansen et al., 2009), healthcare (Chew and Eysenbach, 2010; Salathe and Khandelwal, 2011; Greaves et al., 2013), tourism and travel (Gonzalez-Rodriguez et al., 2014), and disaster management (Verma et al., 2011; Gao et al., 2011; Mandel et al., 2012).

One of the first problems that is encountered by any natural language processing system is that of lexical ambiguity, be it syntactic or semantic (Jurafsky and Martin, 2008). The resolution of a word's syntactic ambiguity has largely been solved in language processing by part-of-speech taggers which predict the syntactic category of words in text with high levels of accuracy. The problem is that words often have more than one meaning, sometimes fairly similar and sometimes completely different. The meaning of a word in a particular usage can only be determined by examining its context. **Word Sense Disambiguation (WSD)** is the process of identifying the sense of a polysemic word[1]. Different approaches to WSD (Mihalcea, 2010) include knowledge-based systems such as Lesk algorithm and adapted Lesk algorithm (Banerjee and Pederson, 2002), unsupervised corpus-based systems (Schutze, 1998; Ng, Wang, and Chan, 2003), and supervised corpus-based systems (Chklovski and Mihalcea, 2002).

Subjectivity Word Sense Disambiguation (SWSD) was shown to improve contextual opinion analysis by Akkaya et al. (2009). The authors state that SWSD is midway between pure dictionary classification and pure contextual interpretation. For SWSD, the context of the word is considered in order to perform the task, but the subjectivity is determined solely by the dictionary. A supervised learning approach was used, in which a different classifier was trained for each lexicon entry for which training data was present. Thus, they described their work as similar to targeted WSD, with two labels *Subjective* (S) and *Objective* (O). By applying SWSD to contextual polarity classification (positive/negative/neutral),

[1] As described in http://aclweb.org

Proceedings of the 6th Workshop on Computational Approaches to Subjectivity, Sentiment and Social Media Analysis (WASSA 2015), pages 115–121,
Lisboa, Portugal, 17 September, 2015.

they observed an accuracy improvement of 3 percentage points over the original classifier (Wilson et al., 2005a) calculated on the SenMPQA dataset. Additionally, Rentoumi et al. (2009) showed that WSD is valuable in polarity classification of sentences containing figurative expressions.

It should be noted that the above work did not focus on using WSD for social-media or micropost data, which is the primary focus area of our work.

Babelfy (Moro et al., 2014)[2] is a unified, multilingual, graph-based approach to Entity Linking and Word Sense Disambiguation based on a loose identification of candidate meanings coupled with a densest sub-graph heuristic which selects high-coherence semantic interpretations. We have used Babelfy for WSD in our work. Babelfy is based on the BabelNet 3.0 multilingual semantic network (Navigli and Ponzetto, 2012), and jointly performs WSD and entity linking in three steps:

- It associates with each vertex of the BabelNet semantic network, i.e., either concept or named entity, a semantic signature, that is, a set of related vertices. This is a preliminary step which needs to be performed only once, independently of the input text.
- Given an input text, it extracts all the linkable fragments from this text and, for each of them, lists the possible meanings according to the semantic network.
- It creates a graph-based semantic interpretation of the whole text by linking the candidate meanings of the extracted fragments using the previously-computed semantic signatures. It then extracts a dense sub-graph of this representation and selects the best candidate meaning for each fragment.

BabelNet 3.0, on which Babelfy is based, is obtained from the automatic integration of WordNet 3.0, Open Multilingual WordNet, Wikipedia, OmegaWiki, Wiktionary and Wikidata. We chose to use Babelfy for WSD as experiments on six gold-standard datasets show the state-of-the-art performance of Babelfy, as well as its robustness across languages. Its evaluation also demonstrates that Babelfy fares well both on long texts, such as those of the WSD tasks, and short and highly-ambiguous sentences, such as the ones in KORE50.[3]

[2]http://babelfy.org/about

[3]http://www.yovisto.com/labs/ner-benchmarks/

2 Dataset

We used the Dataset from Conference on Semantic Evaluation Exercises (SemEval-2013) (Wilson et al., 2013)[4] for *Task 2: Sentiment Analysis in Twitter* and focused on sub-task B where the sentiment for the entire tweet/SMS was supposed to be determined. The organizers created and shared sentiment-labelled tweets for training, development, and testing. The task organizers also provided a second test dataset, composed of Short Message Service (SMS) messages. However, no SMS specific training data was provided or used. The datasets we used are described in Table 1.

Dataset	Positive	Negative	Neutral
Tweets			
Train	3,045 (37%)	1,209 (15%)	4,004 (48%)
Test	1,527 (41%)	601 (16%)	1,640 (43%)
SMS			
Test	492 (23%)	394 (19%)	1,208 (58%)

Table 1: Dataset Class Distribution.

The total number of annotated tweets in the training data is 8,258 tweets and in the testing data is 3,813 tweets. The total number of messages in the SMS testing data is 2,094 messages.

3 System Description

We will describe the system we have developed in the following sections.

3.1 Lexicons

Our system made use of a single lexical resource described below:

- SentiWordNet (Baccianella et al., 2010) is a lexical resource for opinion mining. SentiWordNet assigns to each synset of WordNet three sentiment scores: positivity, negativity, objectivity; that is, SentiWordNet contains positivity, negativity, and objectivity scores for each sense of a word, totally adding up to 1.0 for every sense of the word.

[4]http://www.cs.york.ac.uk/semeval-2013/task2

3.2 Features

We used the tokenizer of the Carnegie Mellon University (CMU) Twitter NLP tool (Gimpel et al., 2011) to tokenize the training and testing data. We also performed more pre-processing such as stop-word removal and word stemming using the tools provided by the NLTK: the Natural Language Toolkit (Loper and Bird, 2002). Additionally, we used word segmentation for hashtags (starting with #) and user-ids (starting with @) re-inserted them after segmentation.

Each tweet or SMS text was represented as a vector made up of three features:

- For each term in the pre-processed text, retrieve the SentiWordNet scores for that sense matching the same sense of that term word, determined from Babelfy. This is not performed for terms that do not appear in SentiWordNet. These are the three features:
  - The total positive score for the entire text, determined by aggregating the SentiWordnet Positive (P) scores of the each sentiment for every term and normalized by dividing this by the total length of the text.
  - The total negative score for the entire text, determined by aggregating the SentiWordnet Negative (N) scores of the each sentiment for every term and normalized by dividing this by the total length of the text.
  - The total Neutral/Objective[5] score for the entire text, determined by aggregating the SentiWordnet Objective (O) scores of the each sentiment for every term and normalized by dividing this by the total length of the text.

4 Results

The initial phase of the system is unsupervised, where the unlabelled tweets and SMS text messages in the test dataset are pre-processed as described in the previous section and then subject to the following:

- Word Sense Disambiguation, of all possible terms in the text, using Babelfy.
- Matching the disambiguated word senses for each term with the Positive (P), Negative (N) and Objective/Neutral (O) scores from the matching sense of that term, using SentiWordNet. The total P, N and O scores for the text are calculated as described in the previous section.

The output of the above phase is the three-featured vector representation of each tweet or SMS text message.

We subsequently use supervision to make the system learn how to combine these three numeric features, representing each text, and reach a decision on the sentiment of that text. Thus, we repeat the above process and construct a three-featured vector (P, N and O scores) representation for each tweet present in the training dataset to be used by a supervised classifier for training.

This combined approach has the following advantages:

- Large amounts of unlabelled data can be processed and the three-featured vector representation for that dataset can be constructed without any supervision or training required.
- We use only three features (P, N and O scores) in the supervised training, and also do not use dataset-specific features such as bag of words, and therefore, the system should be easily adaptable to process other microposts datasets as well even if the topic words change in time (the so-called concept drift phenomenon).

We used supervised learning classifiers from Weka (Witten and Frank, 2005). As for the exact classifier, we used the Random Forest Decision Tree with their default settings. Random forests correct for decision trees' habit of over-fitting to their training set.

We decided to use the Random Forest over a Support Vector Machine (SVM), called SMO in Weka as the Random Forest outperformed the SMO model (default configuration in Weka) in both 10-fold cross validation of the training data, and also when used with the testing data. Random Forest has been previously shown to have outperformed SVM (Caruana and Niculescu-Mizil, 2006).

Table 2 below shows the overall accuracy for the baseline and our system, evaluated based on

[5]The SemEval organizers considered Neutral and Objective as equivalent in the dataset, which is why we have chosen to use them interchangeably here.

10-fold cross validation on the provided training data (contained only tweets but no SMS texts), using the Random Forest classifier. The baseline in Table 6 is the accuracy of a trivial classifier that puts everything in the most frequent class, which is Neutral/Objective for the training data (the ZeroR classifier in Weka).

System	Accuracy
Baseline	45.26
Our System	58.55

Table 2: Accuracies reported for 10-fold cross validation of training data.

The Precision, Recall and F-score metrics for the Twitter test data are shown in Table 3.

Class	Precision	Recall	F-Score
Positive	69.40	54.30	60.90
Negative	57.50	31.50	40.60
Neutral	60.00	81.30	69.10

Table 3: Results for Twitter test data, for each class.

The Precision, Recall and F-score metrics for the SMS test data are shown in Table 4.

Class	Precision	Recall	F-Score
Positive	52.60	62.80	57.30
Negative	67.50	30.40	41.90
Neutral	73.30	81.30	77.10

Table 4: Results for SMS test data, for each class.

Our main focus is to show whether Word Sense Disambiguation helps improve sentiment analysis of micropost data. Therefore, we have evaluated our system using only unigram lexicons and compared our results with that of the all-unigram-features results of the system developed by NRC-Canada (Mohammad et al., 2013), that was ranked first in the same task in the SemEval 2013 competition[6]. These unigram features included punctuation, upper-case words, POS tags, hashtags, unigram-only emotion and sentiment lexicons, emoticon detection, elongated words, and negation detection.

It may be noted that the NRC-Canada system did use several other bigram and n-gram features in their final, best-scoring submission such as word-ngrams, character-ngrams, token-clusters and multiple lexicons containing unigram, bigram, unigram-bigram pairs and bigram-bigram pairs, none of which we are using. It did not however feature the use of WSD.

In this work, we are not trying to show that our system is the best-scoring system in this task. Instead, we choose to only use unigram lexicons, and compared our results to that of the NRC-Canada system's reported score for all-unigram-features, and show the improvement observed over that score only, by using WSD for sentiment analysis.

Table 5 summarizes the results obtained by NRC-Canada for their system using all-unigram-features, and the results obtained with our system. The official metric used for evaluating system performance by the task organizers is average F-score for the positive and negative class.

Dataset	Tweets	SMS
Baseline 1 (Majority classifier)	29.19	19.03
Baseline 2 (First sense of correct POS)	34.65	29.75
NRC-Canada (All unigram features)	39.61	39.29
Our System	**50.75**	**49.60**

Table 5: Comparison of Average F-scores for positive/negative classes. All scores reported are for the test datasets

Table 5 also shows baseline results (Baseline 1) obtained by a majority classifier that always predicts the most frequent class as output. Since the final Average F-score is based only on the F-scores of positive and negative classes and not on neutral, the majority baseline shown, chose the most frequent class among positive and negative, which in this case was the positive class. The results shown in Baseline 2 are obtained for an similar system as ours, but in this case, we do not disambiguate word senses, and instead the reported SentiWordNet scores of first sense of the word for the right part-of-speech are chosen.

[6]We chose SemEval 2013 data and not data from the more recent editions of SemEval, because unigram-features-only score of the best scoring system (NRC-Canada) was reported in their SemEval 2013 submission. There has been no reported changes or improvements for the all-unigram-features only model in the recent editions. Additionally, the training data remained the same as SemEval 2013 for the recent editions as well.

It should be noted that we have only used three numeric-feature vectors to represent the data for training our system and no additional features such as unigram or n-grams, punctuation, token-clusters, upper-case words, elongated words, negation detection, emoticons or n-gram lexicons have been used. Using so few features has also helped determine that the considerable improvement in performance reported below can be primarily attributed only to WSD and the P, N and O scores that are determined from the SentiWordNet lexicon as a result of disambiguating the text, which then form the only three features in the vector used to represent the message. There are no other features used in our system that can claim to have contributed to the improved performance.

Therefore, we report an improvement of **11.14** percentage points for tweets and **10.31** percentage points for SMS text messages, over the all-unigram-features score of the NRC-Canada best-scoring system, when evaluated for the test dataset provided, despite our system not utilizing several other unigram features that were discussed above, but focussing only on the three WSD features instead.

5 Error Analysis

The results obtained reveal that the worst performing class as the Negative class. In both the cases of tweets and SMS text messages, the Precision and Recall for the Negative class is relatively lower than the same for the Positive and Neutral classes.

Error Analysis of the supervised classifier output revealed that the following may be the reasons:

1. Considerably lesser samples of negative tweets in training data (comprises only 15% of the training dataset). Therefore, the trained model maybe biased towards the more frequent classes, that is Positive and Neutral classes.

2. We have used SentiWordNet as the only lexical resource and no polarity or sentiment lexicons were used. Removal of such lexicons was reported to have the highest negative pact on performance (a loss in F-score of above 8.5 points for both tweets and SMS text) according to Mohammad et al. (2013)

3. We have not used word n-grams or character n-grams in our system as features and this was also reported to have a detrimental impact on performance (a loss in F-score of 7.25 points for tweets and 1.2 points for SMS text) according to (Mohammad et al., 2013)

4. Our system does not feature any negation-detection or encoding-detection, such as emoticons, punctuations, or upper-case letters which may characterize the sentiment of the entire text.

5. Accuracy of SentiWordNet sentiments and WSD of Babelfy[7] may have resulted in wrong sentiment scores being given and affected system performance.

It is important to note that these features have not been included into our current system as the objective of this work is to establish the primary contribution and influence of Word Sense disambiguation, without being aided by other features, in the improvement of sentiment analysis on social-media and micropost data. However, our future work will explore the addition of several other features to the current system, in addition to the existing WSD-aided features to further improve system performance.

6 Conclusion

We have presented our system that throws light on the positive influence that WSD can have when it comes to analyzing social-media and micropost data. We observe significant and considerable improvements obtained in sentiment analysis of micropost data such as tweets and SMS text messages, that can be primarily attributed only to WSD, when compared to systems developed without using WSD. Our approach, a combination of unsupervised and supervised phases, does not make use of any dataset-dependent features, it can be easily adapted to analyze other micropost datasets as well. It can also work well for future data. Since we are not using bag of words features, our system is not prone to performance degradation due to concept drift.

Acknowledgements

The authors would like to thank the Mitacs Globalink program for facilitating this collaborative work.

[7]Babelfy reported an F1-score of 84.6 on the SemEval 2007 WSD dataset. However this is not a micropost or social-media text dataset.

References

Cem Akkaya, Janyce Wiebe, and Rada Mihalcea. 2009. Subjectivity word sense disambiguation. In *Proceedings of the 2009 Conference on Empirical Methods in Natural Language Processing: Volume 1-Volume 1*, pages 190–199. Association for Computational Linguistics.

Stefano Baccianella, Andrea Esuli, and Fabrizio Sebastiani. 2010. Sentiwordnet 3.0: An enhanced lexical resource for sentiment analysis and opinion mining. In *LREC*, volume 10, pages 2200–2204.

Satanjeev Banerjee and Ted Pedersen. 2002. An adapted lesk algorithm for word sense disambiguation using wordnet. In *Computational linguistics and intelligent text processing*, pages 136–145. Springer.

Rich Caruana and Alexandru Niculescu-Mizil. 2006. An empirical comparison of supervised learning algorithms. In *Proceedings of the 23rd international conference on Machine learning*, pages 161–168. ACM.

Cynthia Chew and Gunther Eysenbach. 2010. Pandemics in the age of twitter: content analysis of tweets during the 2009 h1n1 outbreak. *PloS one*, 5(11):e14118.

Timothy Chklovski and Rada Mihalcea. 2002. Building a sense tagged corpus with open mind word expert. In *Proceedings of the ACL-02 workshop on Word sense disambiguation: recent successes and future directions-Volume 8*, pages 116–122. Association for Computational Linguistics.

Huiji Gao, Geoffrey Barbier, and Rebecca Goolsby. 2011. Harnessing the crowdsourcing power of social media for disaster relief. *IEEE Intelligent Systems*, (3):10–14.

Kevin Gimpel, Nathan Schneider, Brendan O'Connor, Dipanjan Das, Daniel Mills, Jacob Eisenstein, Michael Heilman, Dani Yogatama, Jeffrey Flanigan, and Noah A Smith. 2011. Part-of-speech tagging for twitter: Annotation, features, and experiments. In *Proceedings of the 49th Annual Meeting of the Association for Computational Linguistics: Human Language Technologies: short papers-Volume 2*, pages 42–47. Association for Computational Linguistics.

MR Gonzalez-Rodriguez, MR Martinez-Torres, and SL Toral. 2014. Monitoring travel-related information on social media through sentiment analysis. In *Proceedings of the 2014 IEEE/ACM 7th International Conference on Utility and Cloud Computing*, pages 636–641. IEEE Computer Society.

Felix Greaves, Daniel Ramirez-Cano, Christopher Millett, Ara Darzi, and Liam Donaldson. 2013. Harnessing the cloud of patient experience: using social media to detect poor quality healthcare. *BMJ quality & safety*, 22(3):251–255.

Bernard J Jansen, Mimi Zhang, Kate Sobel, and Abdur Chowdury. 2009. Twitter power: Tweets as electronic word of mouth. *Journal of the American society for information science and technology*, 60(11):2169–2188.

Daniel Jurafsky and James Martin. 2008. Speech and language processing: An introduction to speech recognition. *Computational Linguistics and Natural Language Processing. Prentice Hall.*

Edward Loper and Steven Bird. 2002. Nltk: The natural language toolkit. In *Proceedings of the ACL-02 Workshop on Effective tools and methodologies for teaching natural language processing and computational linguistics-Volume 1*, pages 63–70. Association for Computational Linguistics.

Benjamin Mandel, Aron Culotta, John Boulahanis, Danielle Stark, Bonnie Lewis, and Jeremy Rodrigue. 2012. A demographic analysis of online sentiment during hurricane irene. In *Proceedings of the Second Workshop on Language in Social Media*, pages 27–36. Association for Computational Linguistics.

Rada Mihalcea. 2010. Word sense disambiguation. In *Encyclopedia of Machine Learning*, pages 1027–1030. Springer.

Saif M Mohammad, Svetlana Kiritchenko, and Xiaodan Zhu. 2013. Nrc-canada: Building the state-of-the-art in sentiment analysis of tweets. In *Second Joint Conference on Lexical and Computational Semantics (* SEM)*, volume 2, pages 321–327.

Andrea Moro, Alessandro Raganato, and Roberto Navigli. 2014. Entity linking meets word sense disambiguation: a unified approach. *Transactions of the Association for Computational Linguistics*, 2:231–244.

Roberto Navigli and Simone Paolo Ponzetto. 2010. Babelnet: Building a very large multilingual semantic network. In *Proceedings of the 48th annual meeting of the association for computational linguistics*, pages 216–225. Association for Computational Linguistics.

Hwee Tou Ng, Bin Wang, and Yee Seng Chan. 2003. Exploiting parallel texts for word sense disambiguation: An empirical study. In *Proceedings of the 41st Annual Meeting on Association for Computational Linguistics-Volume 1*, pages 455–462. Association for Computational Linguistics.

Vassiliki Rentoumi, George Giannakopoulos, Vangelis Karkaletsis, and George A Vouros. 2009. Sentiment analysis of figurative language using a word sense disambiguation approach. In *RANLP*, pages 370–375.

Marcel Salathé and Shashank Khandelwal. 2011. Assessing vaccination sentiments with online social media: implications for infectious disease dynamics and control. *PLoS Comput Biol*, 7(10):e1002199.

Hinrich Schütze. 1998. Automatic word sense discrimination. *Computational linguistics*, 24(1):97–123.

Sudha Verma, Sarah Vieweg, William J Corvey, Leysia Palen, James H Martin, Martha Palmer, Aaron Schram, and Kenneth Mark Anderson. 2011. Natural language processing to the rescue? extracting" situational awareness" tweets during mass emergency. In *ICWSM*. Citeseer.

Theresa Wilson, Janyce Wiebe, and Paul Hoffmann. 2005. Recognizing contextual polarity in phrase-level sentiment analysis. In *Proceedings of the conference on human language technology and empirical methods in natural language processing*, pages 347–354. Association for Computational Linguistics.

Ian H Witten and Eibe Frank. 2005. *Data Mining: Practical machine learning tools and techniques*. Morgan Kaufmann.

Predicting Ratings for New Movie Releases from Twitter Content

Wernard Schmit
Tilburg University
Postbus 90153
5000 LE Tilburg
w.h.w.schmit@uvt.nl

Sander Wubben
Tilburg University
Postbus 90153
5000 LE Tilburg
s.wubben@uvt.nl

Abstract

With microblogging platforms such as Twitter generating huge amounts of textual data every day, the possibilities of knowledge discovery through Twitter data becomes increasingly relevant. Similar to the public voting mechanism on websites such as the Internet Movie Database (IMDb) that aggregates movies ratings, Twitter content contains reflections of public opinion about movies. This study aims to explore the use of Twitter content as textual data for predictive text mining. In this study, a corpus of tweets was compiled to predict the rating scores of newly released movies on IMDb. Predictions were done with several different machine learning algorithms, exploring both regression and classification methods. In addition, this study explores the use of several different kinds of textual features in the machine learning tasks. Results show that prediction performance based on textual features derived from our corpus of tweets improved on the baseline for both regression and classification tasks.

1 Introduction

Textual data from Twitter can be seen as an extensive source of information regarding an extremely broad variety of subjects. With millions of users actively expressing themselves online, a huge amount of data is generated every day. Since this data for a large part consists of human expressions, Twitter data can be seen as a valuable collection of human opinion or sentiment, which can be automatically extracted with relatively high accuracy (Pak & Paroubek, 2010).

Automatic sentiment analysis has been applied to many different fields, showing both scientific and commercial value. Sentiment analysis is a powerful way of discovering public attitude towards a variety of entities, including businesses and governments (Pang & Lee, 2008). Although brief of nature, tweets can serve as source of information regarding the overall appreciation of these entities. This has been demonstrated in a study that focused on brand management and the power of tweets as electronic word of mouth (Jansen, Zhang, Sobel, & Chowdury, 2009). Sentiment analysis is often treated as a classification task, by automatically predicting classes corresponding to sentiment values (Agarwal, Xie, Vovsha, Rambow, & Passonneau, 2011).

Besides extracting sentiment through classification, textual data has proven to be useful in machine learning tasks aimed at predicting numerical values. This type of predictive text mining has been applied in a useful way to economics, by making predictions of stock prices based on press releases (Mittermayer, 2004). Similarly, text mining has also been used to predict box office revenues of films, using a corpus of tweets (Asur & Huberman, 2010).

This study aims to continue the exploration of the predictive capabilities of Twitter data by using a corpus of tweets to predict rating scores of newly released movies on IMDb. The prediction of IMDb scores through data from social media has been explored before (Oghina, Breuss, Tsagkias, & De Rijke, 2012). However, this study differs from previous work by focusing solely on textual data from Twitter as opposed to non-textual data from other social media.

Proceedings of the 6th Workshop on Computational Approaches to Subjectivity, Sentiment and Social Media Analysis (WASSA 2015), pages 122–126,
Lisboa, Portugal, 17 September, 2015. ©2015 Association for Computational Linguistics.

In order to explore the predictive capabilities of tweets, several machine learning experiments were conducted for this study. This includes regression experiments in order to predict the IMDB rating of the movie. Alternatively, this study also explores the prediction of classes corresponding to a range of numerical values: a classifcation approach. Both regression and classification methods have proven useful in the field of text mining, specifically concerning user sentiment (Pang & Lee, 2005).

2 Methodology

Several machine learning experiments were conducted for this study. These experiments required the collection and preprocessing of the Twitter corpus, which will be briefly discussed in the following sections, as well as the experimental setup.

2.1 Data collection and processing

Tweets were collected using Twitter's API. Between March 30th 2015 and April 28th 2015, Tweets were collected that mentioned one of 68 recently released movies. The IMDB scores of these movies ranged from 5.0 to 8.9 out of 10.

In order to eliminate uninformative tweets, all retweets and tweets containing hyperlinks were excluded from the dataset. Similarly, all Twitter usernames were removed from the tweets. All movie titles were replaced with the string: '<TITLE>' and the tweets were saved in tuples with their corresponding IMDb rating score. After preprocessing the data, the corpus consisted of 118,521 tweets usable for experimentation. This anonymized, preprocessed corpus has been made available online.[1] Examples of tuples with tweets and scores include: (*'just watched <TITLE> for the first time. absolutely fantastic film.'*, 8.5) and (*'<TITLE> would be a good movie if it didn't suck so much'*, 5.4).

The IMDb rating scores served as the target valuables in the regression experiments. For the classification experiments, classes were constructed as target valuables. The following classes corresponding to the IMDb scores were created for classification tasks:

- *'Very High'*: 8.0 and above (ca. 29K tweets)
- *'High'*: between 7.0 and 8.0 (ca. 42K tweets)
- *'Average*: between 6.0 and 7.0 (ca. 31K tweets)
- *'Low'*: between 5.0 and 6.0 (ca. 16k tweets)

We used a held out development set of 3400 tweets to optimize parameters for the machine learning experiments.

2.2 Experimental setup

The Python module Sci-Kit Learn was chosen as the tool for the machine learning experiments.[2] Sci-Kit Learn provides options for various machine learning algorithms usable for both regression and classification tasks. This module makes a convenient tool for our machine learning tasks.

For the machine learning experiments we used textual features from the tweets as input, and performance scores after 10-fold cross validation as output, similar to previous experiments in this field (Oghina, Breuss, Tsagkias, & De Rijke, 2012). For regression tasks, the mean-squared error (MSE) was used as the performance metric, as this metric takes the severity of the prediction errors into account. For this metric, lower scores mean better results (Witten, Frank, & Hall, 2011). Classification tasks used F1-scores to measure performance (Witten, Frank, & Hall, 2011).

Since our data is not evenly distributed among classes (popular movies generate more tweets), our experiments used baselines for comparison that take into account the distribution of the dataset. Regression performances were compared to a baseline performance of predictions based on the mean of the target valuables. Classification performances were compared to baseline performance of stratified predictions: a classifier that makes predictions based on the data distribution over classes.

2.3 Features

Features were constructed from the textual content of the tweets. *N*-grams in tweets were transformed into numeric TF-IDF vectors, similar to the predictive text mining experiment of Mittermayer (2004). TF-IDF vectors were incorporated in order to appropriately apply weights to the terms in our corpus.

Experiments were run with several ranges of *n*-grams as basis for the TF-IDF vectors. The use of unigrams, bigrams, trigrams and combinations of these *n*-grams was explored in experimentation on

[1]https://dl.dropboxusercontent.com/u/20984922/Dataset%20Tweets%20%2B%20IMDb%20Rating%20Scores.csv

[2] http://www.scikit-learn.org

a held out development set. Additionally, the use of *stemming* was explored by applying a Porter Stemmer from Python module NLTK.[3] This was done in order to reduce model complexity (Meyer, Hornik, & Feinerer, 2008). The constructed TF-IDF vectors for the (stemmed) *n*-grams were used as training input for the machine learning algorithms.

2.4 Machine learning algorithms

For both regression and classification tasks, several different algorithms were used for experimentation. For regression tasks, we used the Linear Regression (LR) and Support Vector Regression (SVR) implementations from Sci-Kit Learn. Both algorithms have been used successfully in previous experiments. LR was used in a previous experiment regarding the prediction of IMDb rating scores (Oghina, Breuss, Tsagkias, & De Rijke, 2012). SVR has been used similarly for predicting ordinal sentiment scores (Pang & Lee, 2005).

For classification tasks, Support Vector Classification (SVC) and Stochastic Gradient Descent Classification (SGD) were used. SGD is considered a useful algorithm for experiments with large amounts of training data (Bespalov, Bai, Qi, & Shokoufandeh, 2011). Similar to SVR, the use of support vector machines can lead to accurate decision boundaries for classification tasks (Gunn, 1998). The SGD implementation used a hinged loss function, similar to the loss function used in SVC.

For both SVR and SVC an automatic grid search was performed on the development set to determine the optimal parameters. This grid search showed that for both SVR and SVC a linear kernel and a C value of 1.0 led to the best performance results.

3 Results

While both regression and classification experiments used the same features, performances were different between regression and classification tasks. This section shows the results for the best performing configurations for both regression and classification tasks.

3.1 Regression results

N-grams	Stems	Algorithm	Baseline	MSE
Unigrams, Bigrams, Trigrams	YES	SVR	.998	**.529**
Unigrams, Bigrams	YES	SVR	.998	.536
Unigrams, Bigrams, Trigrams	YES	LR	.998	.569

Table 1: Best regression results

The best performing regression configurations show a relatively large improvement on the baseline, as can be witnessed in Table 1. Results show that the best regression result is achieved by using the SVR algorithm on stemmed combinations of unigrams, bigrams and trigrams. For the three best configurations, combinations of *n*-grams yielded the best results, when combined with stemming.

Experimentation with different amounts of training data show that results improved with larger amounts of data. Figure 1 shows the learning curve for the best performing regression configuration, performing 10-fold cross validation for each experiment. This curve shows that it is likely that performance will improve with more data than was used in these experiments.

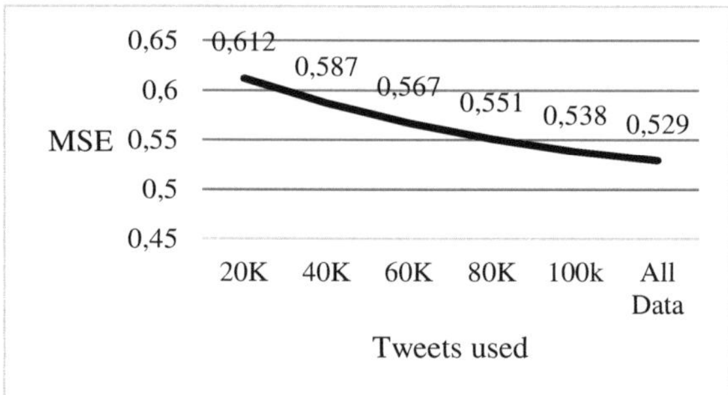

Figure 1: Learning curve regression

[3] http://www.nltk.org.

3.2 Classification results

N-grams	Stems	Algorithm	Baseline	F1
Unigrams, Bigrams, Trigrams	YES	SVC	.274	**.534**
Unigrams, Bigrams, Trigrams	NO	SVC	.274	.529
Unigrams, Bigrams, Trigrams	YES	SGD	.274	.529

Table 2: Best classification results

Table 2 shows that the best performing classification configurations also managed to improve over the baseline. The best performing configuration used stemmed combinations of unigrams, bigrams and trigrams and the SVC algorithm. The three best performing configurations all show that the combination of these *n*-grams leads to the best results. However, the use of stemming is not always required to achieve a relatively high performance, as is shown by the second best performing configuration.

Experiments with different amounts of training data for the best performing classification configuration again show that more data led to better results. These experiments again used 10-fold cross validation for each experiment. The learning curve for the best performing classification configuration shows that it is likely that the optimal amount of training data has not yet been reached.

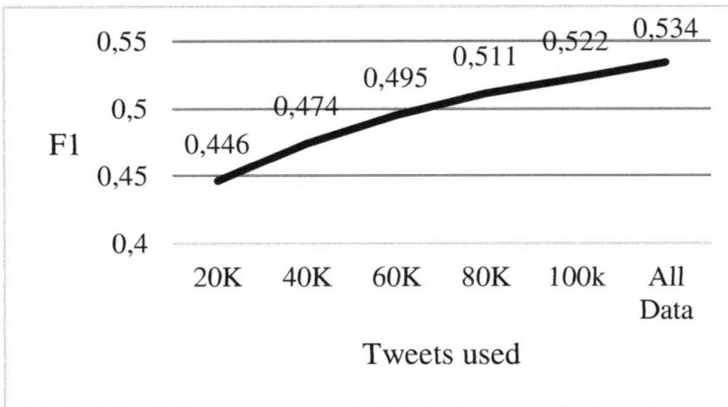

Figure 2: Learning curve for classification

4 Conclusion

As the results of the experiments show, IMDb rating scores can be predicted to a certain extent using a supervised machine learning approach. Both the prediction of exact numerical rating scores and the prediction of classes corresponding to a range of numerical scores, achieved a certain degree of success compared to their respective baselines.

The best performing regression configuration achieved an MSE of .529. This was achieved by using stemmed combinations of unigrams, bigrams and trigrams. While this configuration led to an improvement on the baseline of mean predictions, which achieved an MSE of .998, there is still room for improvement. The best performing configuration of Oghina, Breuss, Tsagkias, & De Rijke (2012) achieved a RMSE of .523 for the prediction of IMDb rating scores, which translates to an MSE of .273. This model clearly outperforms our best performing configuration. However, our experiments focus solely on textual features derived from Twitter, as opposed to also including numerical features from other social media. Furthermore, in their model, more than 1,6 milion tweets were used, whereas this study used a dataset consisting of roughly 118K tweets. It can be concluded that our best performing model is not the optimal prediction model for IMDb scores, but it does show that textual features can be useful for prediction of this kind.

Classification results also showed that predicting IMDb rating scores using tweets as training data can have a certain degree of success. The best performing configuration had an F1- score of .534, while the stratified baseline achieved an F1-score of .274, based on predictions according to the class distribution of the training data.

Our classification results can be compared to other studies that performed classification tasks. The study of Agarwal, Xie, Vovsha, Rambow, & Passonneau (2011) explored 3-way classification for sentiment analysis. Their best performing model attained an F1-score of .605. This is higher than our best performing score, but note that our experiments dealt with one more target variable. It should also be noted that this study deals with more general sentiment analysis, while our study is specifically aimed at predicting classes corresponding to IMDb scores. Our results show that a classification approach can be useful in predicting these classes.

5 Discussion

While this study has shown some interesting results regarding the predictive capabilities of tweets, there remains plenty of room for future research. There are more possibilities to explore regarding the dataset, the algorithms and the features. Learning curves show that it is likely that the optimal amount of data was not used in these experiments, which is something to be explored. Additionally, this study shows that the use of stemming and combinations of n-grams should always be explored.

This study shows that using merely textual features is not the optimal method of predicting scores on IMDb, as the model of Oghina, Breuss, Tsagkias, & De Rijke (2012) clearly outperforms our configurations, which expanded on merely using textual features. For future research, if the goal is to optimize these predictions, it is clear that expanding on textual features is wise, for example by including metadata from the tweets. A well functioning system that uses data from social media could serve as a barometer that forecasts appreciation of newly released films. Such a system would also provide insight into the opinions of a different population of the internet rather than merely IMDb voters.

When focusing specifically on the predictive capabilites of textual data from Twitter, there are other options to consider for future research. Features used in our experiments can prove valuable, but different options should also be explored. For example, the use of character n-grams may prove useful. Similarly, the ratio of positive to negative tweets as a feature may lead to better predictions. This would require first performing sentiment classification on the tweets, before attempting to predict the IMDb scores.

Besides further possibilities regarding the size of the dataset and feature engineering, other machine learning algorithms can also be explored. Different algorithms are better suited for datasets of different sizes, it is worth researching which algorithms lead to the best performance for different sizes of training data. By continuing research in this field, predictive possibilities of tweets can be further explored, discovered and applied, not merely for IMDb scores, but for many different fields.

References

Agarwal, A., Xie, B., Vovsha, I., Rambow, O., & Passonneau, R. (2011). Sentiment analysis of Twitter data. *LSM '11 Proceedings of the Workshop on Languages in Social Media*, Pages 30-38.

Asur, S., & Huberman, B. A. (2010). *Predicting the Future With Social Media.* Palo Alto: HP Labs.

Bespalov, D., Bai, B., Qi, Y., & Shokoufandeh, A. (2011). *Sentiment Classification Based on Supervised Latent.* Princeton, NJ: NEC Labs America.

Gunn, S. (1998). *Support Vector Machines for Classification and Regression.* Southampton: University of Southampton.

Jansen, B., Zhang, M., Sobel, K., & Chowdury, A. (2009). Twitter Power: Tweets as Electroninc Word of Mouth. *JOURNAL OF THE AMERICAN SOCIETY FOR INFORMATION SCIENCE AND TECHNOLOGY*, 2169-2188.

Meyer, D., Hornik, K., & Feinerer, I. (2008). Text mining infrastructure in R. *Journal of Statistical Software*, 1-54.

Mittermayer, M. (2004). Forecasting Intraday Stock Price Trends with Text Mining Techniques. *Proceedings 37th Annual Hawaii Int, Conference on System Sciences (HICSS)*, (p. 64). Big Island.

Oghina, A., Breuss, M., Tsagkias, M., & De Rijke, M. (2012). *Predicting IMDB Movie Ratings Using Social Media.* Amsterdam: ISLA.

Pak, A., & Paroubek, P. (2010). *Twitter as a Corpus for Sentiment Analysis and Opinion Mining.* Orsay Cedex, France: Laboratoire LIMSI-CNRS.

Pang, B., & Lee, L. (2005). Seeing stars: Exploiting class relationships for sentiment categorization with respect to rating scales. *Proceedings of ACL 2005.*

Pang, B., & Lee, L. (2008). *Opinion Mining and Sentiment Analysis.* Sunnyvale, CA: Yahoo! Research.

Witten, I., Frank, E., & Hall, M. (2011). *Data Mining: Practical Machine Learning Tools and Techniques.* Amsterdam: Morgan Kaufman.

Beyond Sentiment: Social Psychological Analysis of Political Facebook Comments in Hungary

Márton Miháltz, Tamás Váradi
Research Institute for Linguistics, Hungarian Academy of Sciences
Benczúr utca 33, Budapest
H-1068 Hungary
mmihaltz@gmail.com
varadi.tamas@nytud.mta.hu

István Csertő, Éva Fülöp, Tibor Pólya
Institute of Cognitive Neuroscience And Psychology, Hungarian Academy of Sciences
Magyar tudósok körútja 2.
Budapest, H-1117 Hungary
{cserto.istvan, fulop.eva, polya.tibor}@ttk.mta.hu

Pál Kővágó
Institute of Psychology, University of Pécs
Ifjúság útja 6, Pécs
H-7624 Hungary
kovago.pal@ttk.mta.hu

Abstract

This paper presents the methodology and results of a project for the large-scale analysis of public messages in political discourse on Facebook, the dominant social media site in Hungary. We propose several novel social psychology-motivated dimensions for natural language processing-based text analysis that go beyond the standard sentiment-based analysis approaches. Communion describes the moral and emotional aspects of an individual's relations to others, while agency describes individuals in terms of the efficiency of their goal-orientated behavior. We treat these by custom lexicons that identify positive and negative cues in text. We measure the level of optimism in messages by examining the ratio of events talked about in the past, present and future by looking at verb tenses and temporal expressions. For assessing the level of individualism, we build on research that correlates it to pronoun dropping. We also present results that demonstrate the viability of our measures on 1.9 million downloaded public Facebook comments by examining correlation to party preferences in public opinion poll data.

1 Introduction

Social media (SM) is becoming an increasingly important channel for communications in politics. In Hungary, Facebook is the dominant SM platform, with 4.27M registered Hungarian users (59.2% penetration of 7.2M people with internet access, which represents 43% of the total population)[1]. No political party or politician can afford to miss the opportunity of extending their influence by regularly publishing status update messages (posts) on their Facebook pages that are potentially accessible by all Facebook users (i.e., marked as "public"). Most political actors enable discussions (commenting) on their pages, which means other users are able to publicly respond to (post comments about) the original posts or to each other's responses. This constitutes a vast and vivid source of political or politics-inspired discussions, debates, expressions of sentiment, support or dissent. Most importantly, the participating social media users also happen to be real-life voters.

In this paper, we present a set of tools and resources that enable the collection and analysis of Hungarian public Facebook comments written in response to public posts published on the pages of Hungarian politicians and political organizations. Besides the identification of relevant entities and sentiment polarity in these messages, our investigations focused on methods for detecting and quantifying psychological and sociopsy-

[1] Source: http://www.internetworldstats.com/europa.htm

Proceedings of the 6th Workshop on Computational Approaches to Subjectivity, Sentiment and Social Media Analysis (WASSA 2015), pages 127–133,
Lisboa, Portugal, 17 September, 2015.

chological phenomena including *agency and communion, optimism/pessimism and individualism/collectivism*. These indicators are based on previous results in the area of social psychology research. The main contribution of this paper is the proposal of these new, social psychology-motivated dimensions for the analysis of attitudes expressed in social media that go beyond the standard sentiment (emotional polarity) analysis approaches. With these we hope to get better answers to questions like: what are the trends in the reactions to SM messages of political actors, and how do these correlate to real-life political actions and events, such as elections and votes? How do political communication and discussions shape the psychological states and social values of various SM user groups, such as supporters of political powers?

The rest of this paper is organized as follows: the next section presents our data sources and the methods of our analysis with respect to social psychology and the challenges presented by processing social media language. We then present preliminary empirical results that demonstrate the viability of our proposed approach by examining correlation with a real-life political event, general elections in Hungary in 2014.

2 Methods

There were three major election events in Hungary in 2014: general elections for seats in the National Assembly (Hungarian Parliament) in April, elections for seats in the European Parliament in May, and municipal elections in October. In order to focus on the debates surrounding these events, we collected the names of nominated and elected representatives and their political organizations involved in these campaigns (sources used: valasztas.hu (official election data) and Hungarian Wikipedia.) Using these names, we identified 1341 different Facebook pages that belong to Hungarian political organizations (parties, their regional and associated branches etc.) and politicians (candidates and elected representatives etc.) of years 2013 and 2014. We used both official pages (administered by the agents of the political actors the pages are about) and fan pages (administered by independent communities).

We used the Facebook Graph API to collect public posts and the associated public comments from these sources dated between October 2013 and September 2014 once a week. One week after each harvest, another script was used to check for new comments that arrived to already downloaded posts. In total, our corpus contains 141K Facebook posts and 1.9 million comments from 226K users, constituting over 46 million running words.

In order to be able to analyze sentiment and the other sociopsychological measures we had to first process the comment messages using the following pipeline: segmentation and tokenization, morphological analysis, part-of-speech tagging and lemmatization. This was followed by the extraction of relevant entities and the identification of their party affiliations using custom lexicons compiled into finite state automatons using the open source *NooJ*[2] tool (Silberztein 2005), which uses finite state automata compiled from custom grammars to annotate text. We also used NooJ to annotate expressions of sentiment and other sociopsychological phenomena using custom lexicons and grammars. The following sections give details about the background and development of these components.

2.1 Social Psychological Analysis

Scientific Narrative Psychology (SNP) is a complex approach to text-based theory building and longitudinal, quantitative assessment of psychological phenomena in the analysis of self and group narratives in the field of social, personality and clinical psychology (László 2008). Our methods for the sociopsychological content analysis of Facebook comments in this project builds on earlier work extending it to the domain of SM discourse in politics.

Current approaches to analyzing attitudes in social media messages mainly focus on one psychological viewpoint, emotional polarity (sentiment analysis), as in (Ceron et al. 2014; Chen et al. 2010; Costa et al. 2015; Hammer et al. 2014; O'Connor et al. 2010; Sobkowicz, Kaschesky and Bouchard 2012; Tumasjan et al. 2010). In addition to also measuring sentiment, we extend this framework by proposing several new aspects that offer insights into further psychological and social phenomena which might be important indicators in the assessment or prediction of the attitudes and behavior of online communities. In addition, while the majority of previous work on analyzing social media focuses on Twitter, such as (Asur et al. 2010; Balahur 2013; Costa et al. 2015; Habernal et al. 2013; Kouloumpis et al. 2011; Lietz et al. 2014; Sidorenko et al. 2013; Tumasjan et al. 2010), we use public comments

[2] http://nooj4nlp.net/

from Facebook, which is the dominant SM channel in Hungary.

According to social psychology theory social value judgments can be described along two lines (Abele and Wojciszke 2007; Abele et al. 2008). *Agency* describes an individual in terms of the efficiency of their behavior oriented to their personal goals (motivation, competence and control). *Communion* describes the moral and emotional aspects of an individual's relations to other group members, individuals or groups (cooperation, social benefit, honesty, self-sacrifice, affection, friendship, respect, love etc.). Both types have positive and negative dimensions, and can be used to describe social behavior, for example when relating to a political organization one supports or opposes. Our *agency and communion* NooJ component annotates comments using lexicons that contain 650 different expressions.

Individuals differ in the way past, present or future events dominate their thinking. When a person's thinking is dominated by the past, they are likely to view the world unchangeable. Thinking dominated by the present indicates the importance of realistically attainable goals, while future-dominated thinking usually sees open possibilities. We assume that optimistic people tend to talk more about the future and less about the past, while pessimists talk more about the past and less about the present, which is supported by previous studies (Habermas et al. 2008; Kunda 1999). This bears significance in situations when a person may choose to focus on any of the three temporal aspects. As an example, when making political decisions one might focus on either prior events leading up to the decision, on carrying out the decision itself or on the implied future consequences. Our NooJ grammar for *optimism/pessimism* annotates expressions of time using morphological information (verb tenses) and by recognizing some temporal expressions. Based on these, we calculated an optimism indicator (higher value, higher degree of optimism) using the ratio of present and future expressions to all expressions (past, present, future).

Individualism represents the importance of the category of the self when thinking about the world: individualistic societies keep the actions of the individual in focus, while collectivist societies focus on the actions of groups. Studies have shown a correlation between the usage/omission of personal pronouns (pronoun drop) and the levels of individualism in societies (Kashima and Kashima 1999). We extend this idea by assuming that pronoun drop can be used to compare the level of individualism between groups within a society as well. Our *individualism/collectivism* NooJ grammar relies on only part-of-speech and morphological information to annotate personal pronouns and verbs or nouns with personal inflections. By calculating the ratio between the former and the latter we estimated the rate of actually versus potentially appearing pronouns which yielded a measure of individualism (higher score indicating higher degree of individualism).

We also measured *sentiment* in the comments by means of a NooJ automaton we created for the annotation of positive and negative emotions using a lexicon of 500 positive and 420 negative nouns, verbs, adjectives, adverbs, emoticons and multi-word expressions. It also uses a number of rules to treat elements of context that might affect polarity (e.g. negation).

To facilitate the creation of the custom lexicons for the NooJ grammars above, we created a sample corpus that contains 176K comments from 569 different Hungarian politics-related Facebook pages, totaling 5.45M words. The corpus was analyzed using our standard NLP tools. The lexicons for sentiment, agency and communion were constructed by 6 independent human annotators who coded words in the sample corpus that occurred with a frequency of 100 or more (about 3500 total) for each category. In the cases where at least 4 annotators agreed, a seventh annotator made the final decision.

2.2 Adapting NLP Tools to Social Media

All of the NLP tools that were used for preprocessing the comments were developed for a linguistic domain (using standard language texts, mostly newswire) that is different from the language used in Facebook comments. The latter has a high tendency for phenomena like typos and spelling errors, non-standard punctuation use, use of slang expressions, emoticons and other creative uses of characters, substitution of Hungarian accented characters by their unaccented variants etc. For this reason, our readily available tools suffered from degradation in performance. To overcome this problem, we employed a two-fold approach: we applied normalizations to the input and also extended our tools to adapt them to the SM language domain.

To properly investigate the problems arising from processing SM language, we created a corpus of 1.2 million Facebook comments (29M running words total), which was analyzed by the vanilla NLP tools. Unknown types with a frequency of 15 or higher (about 14,000 types) were manually inspected (with reference to their contexts) to yield an overview of common problems that showed regularity and lists of unknown, frequent and important words and expressions.

Based on these findings, our tokenizer was augmented by pre- and post-processing routines that resolved some of the issues arising from non-standard use of spaces and punctuation. We also used lists to normalize commonly misspelled words and slang expressions. Unknown but frequent and important words were added to the morphological analyzer's lexicon using analogous known words in the same morphological paradigms, which enabled the analysis of arbitrary inflected forms of these words.

For the identification of relevant named entities (names of persons (politicians) and organizations (parties)) we tested a maximum entropy classifier tool trained to resolve Hungarian named entities (Varga and Simon 2007). However, because of its low performance on Facebook comments, we made a decision to use custom, domain-specific, lexicon-based NE recognition, which relies on names, name variants, nicknames and party affiliations of relevant political actors collected from the development corpus described above.

2.3 Evaluation

In order to evaluate the reliability of our named entity, sentiment and social psychological annotations, we constructed two gold standard sets of 336 and 672 Facebook comments. Each set contained messages from all political parties' Facebook pages in the same distribution as in the complete 1.9M comment corpus (FIDESZ-KDNP 25.2%, EGYÜTT-2014 19.3%, JOBBIK 19.2%, MSZP 16.6%, DK 12.5%, PM 4.2%, LMP 2.9%). In the smaller set, three human annotators annotated each comment for the political affiliations of named entities (persons and organizations), while in the larger set they identified expressions of sentiment, agency, communion and the linguistic markers used by our optimism and individualism measures. *Table 1* shows the results of evaluating the annotations produced by our system against these gold standards.

Annotation Type	**Precision**	**Recall**	**F1**
Party affiliations	98.36	57.14	72.29
Pos. sentiment	82.56	74.50	77.38
Neg. sentiment	67.03	53.68	59.62
Pos. agency	70.59	69.43	52.83
Neg. agency	65.79	25.51	36.76
Pos. communion	65.75	38.40	48.48
Neg. communion	96.39	41.45	57.97
Individualism: pers. pronouns	35.20	65.63	45.82
Individualism: inflections	77.27	94.74	85.12
Optimism: past	78.90	93.97	85.78
Optimism: present	31.40	92.54	46.88
Optimism: future	32.80	67.03	44.04

Table 1: Evaluation of annotations against the gold standards

The results show that while the performance of the annotations of party affiliations and sentiment, agency and communion expression are generally acceptable, there are serious issues with the annotations of linguistic markers for individualism and optimism. Preliminary investigations revealed problems with the manual coding of some markers in the gold standard sets, we are currently working on identifying these issues in order to be able to re-annotate the gold standard and repeat evaluation measurements for our optimism and individualism indicators.

We also evaluated the performance of sentiment analysis based on our sentiment annotations. We assigned a sentiment score to each sentence in each comment by subtracting the number of negative sentiment expressions from the number of positive sentiment expressions, and normalized by the number of words in the sentence. We then mapped this score to a 3-value sentiment polarity indicator: -1 if the sentiment score was negative, 0 if it was 0 (neutral), or 1 if it was positive. We also calculated sentiment polarity for each sentence in each comment in the gold standard set to compare against our automatically obtained polarity indicators (Table 2). Our system performed well above the baseline method, which worked by assigning the most frequent polarity value (neutral) observed in the gold standard.

	#Sent.	Acc.
All sentences in GS	1295	-
Neutral polarity (baseline)	920	71.04
Correctly identified polarity	1096	84.63

Table 2: Accuracy of sentiment polarity recognition

3 Experiments

We conducted several experiments to test the viability of our proposed agency, communion, optimism and individualism measures. We examined how well these could indicate changes in public attitude towards major political powers in the context of the April 2014 parliamentary elections in Hungary. We processed our corpus of 1.9 million Facebook comments using the above tools to calculate scores and indicators for each comment. We grouped comments for each political party's Facebook pages, aggregated results for each month and compared them to the results of a traditional public opinion survey[3]. We used monthly party popularity (support) data available from confident voters. Since we did not have any information available about the party preferences of our Facebook comment authors, we operated under the simple assumption that the majority of commenters communicating on a given party's Facebook page are the supporters of that party. This means that indicators measured from the comments posted at the Facebook page of a given political party were assumed to characterize the attitudes of the supporters of that party.

To assess our optimism and individualism indicators, we first correlated their values to party popularities. We expected that higher degrees of individualism would indicate higher responsibility for party choices, which would imply higher party popularity rates. We found nearly significant positive correlation for individualism (r=.22, p=.052). However, for our optimism indicator we measured negative correlation (r=-.22, p=.055) with party popularity, which did not support our hypothesis that a higher rate of optimism would indicate a higher ability to make party choices. This might be explained by the assumption that past events also play an important role in political preferences.

We also examined how values of our optimism and individualism measures behaved before and after the parliamentary elections in April 2014. Both indicators showed notable changes in the time period immediately following the elections. Individualism levels increased, which might be explained by the decline of the significance of cooperation and unity after elections within politically organized groups. The levels of optimism also showed a change after the elections, but only increased on pages related to the winning party (FIDESZ-KDNP), and decreased on the pages of all other parties. This might be explained by the different experiences of success and failure: success leads to higher optimism, while defeat leads to decrease in optimism.

Our hypotheses about the relationship between party popularities and agency/communion were based on two observations in social psychology. First, the phenomenon of intergroup bias refers to a pattern when members of a group tend to overrate their own group while devaluing outside groups in situations of intergroup competence or conflict. Second, while people judge members of outside groups primarily through the aspect of communion, they tend to evaluate themselves and other members of their own groups via the aspect of agency. Based on these, we expected to find significant negative correlation between both positive agency and negative communion on the one hand and party popularity on the other: low or decreasing support represents a threatening situation to group identity that leads to compensation manifesting in the overrating of one's in-group and the devaluation of out-groups.

In the 6-month period preceding the parliamentary elections, we found negative correlation between positive agency (number of identified positive agency expressions normalized by total number of tokens in the comments in the time period) and party popularity (r=-.429, p=.05). We also found strong negative correlation (r=-.677, p=.05) between party popularity and agency polarity score (difference of positive and negative agency normalized by sum of positive and negative agency) in the same period. After the elections, while there was no correlation between party popularity and agency, there was a high rate of negative correlation with negative communion (r=-.574, p=.01) and communion polarity score (r=-454, p=.05). This also supported our initial hypothesis: the lower the popularity of a given party the stronger the devaluation of other parties through negative communion linguistic content. This might serve to protect

[3] http://www.tarki.hu/hu/research/elect/gppref_table_03.html

threatened identity and build group cohesion in parties with less than expected success.

We also found that average positive agency was higher than average negative agency in the whole time period, the difference being significant (p=.001, using Student's t-test). Average negative communion was also significantly (p=.001) higher than average positive communion. Looking at the changes between before and after elections the rate of average positive agency showed significant decrease (p=.01). This might be linked to the fact that acquiring and keeping power is a more crucial issue in the tense competition before elections than in the subsequent period.

4 Conclusion

We presented our experiments to collect and analyze Facebook comments in Hungarian politics using novel sociopsychological measures that extend the possibilities for the assessment of attitudes expressed in text beyond sentiment analysis. We found that our proposed indicators for agency and communion are valid tools from a psychological perspective and can be useful for detecting changes in opinion on social media sites of political groups. While our individualism and optimism measures showed mixed results, they also show potential to bring new sides to SM text analysis in politics.

All the resources (complete corpus of 1.9M comments with full annotation, ontology of relevant political actors) and the source codes of our tools to process them are available for download[4].

5 Acknowledgements

We wish to thank the thorough work of the conference reviewers. Special thanks to Anikó Hannák for her helpful suggestions. Work described in this paper was supported by the TrendMiner project, which was co-funded by the FP7-ICT programme of the European Commission (project reference nr. 287863).

References

Abele, A. E. and Wojciszke, B. 2007. Agency And Communion From The Perspective of Self Versus Others. *Journal of Personality and Social Psychology* 93:751-763.

Abele, A. E.; Cuddy, A. J. C.; Judd, C. M.; and Yzerbyt, V. Y. 2008. Fundamental Dimensions of Social Judgment. European *Journal of Social Psychology* 38:1063-1065.

Asur, S.; Huberman, B.A. 2010. Predicting the Future with Social Media. *Web Intelligence and Intelligent Agent Technology* 492-499.

Balahur, A. 2013. Sentiment Analysis in Social Media Texts. *Proceedings of the 4th Workshop on Computational Approaches to Subjectivity, Sentiment and Social Media Analysis*, 120-128.

Ceron, Andrea; Curini, Luigi and M Iacus, Stefano. 2014. Every tweet counts? How sentiment analysis of social media can improve our knowledge of citizens' political preferences with an application to Italy and France. *New Media & Society* 16:340-358.

Chen , Bi, Leilei Zhu, Daniel Kifer, and Dongwon Lee. 2010. What Is an Opinion About? Exploring Political Standpoints Using Opinion Scoring Model. *Proceedings of the Twenty-Fourth AAAI Conference on Artificial Intelligence* 1007–1012.

Costa, Jean M. R., Rahmtin Rotabi, Elizabeth L. Murnane and Tanzeem Choudhury. 2015. It is not only about Grievances - Emotional Dynamics in Social Media during the Brazilian Protests. *Proceedings of the Ninth International AAAI Conference on Web and Social Media* 594-597.

Csertő, I., and László, J. 2013. Intergroup evaluation as an indicator of emotional elaboration of collective traumas in national historical narratives. *Sociology Study* 3: 207-224.

Habermas, T.; Ott, L. M.; Schubert, M.; Schneider, B.; and Pate, A. 2008. Stuck in the Past: Negative Bias, Explanatory Style, Temporal Order, and Evaluative Perspective in Life Narratives of Clinically Depressed Individuals. *Depression and Anxiety* 25: 1091-4269.

Habernal, I.; Ptáček, T and Steinberger, J. 2013. Sentiment Analysis in Czech Social Media Using Supervised Machine Learning. *Proceedings of the 4th Workshop on Computational Approaches to Subjectivity, Sentiment and Social Media Analysis*, 65-74.

Hammer, Hugo Lewi, Per Erik Solberg and Lilja Øvrelid. 2014. Sentiment classification of online political discussions: a comparison of a word-based and dependency-based method. *Proceedings of the 5th Workshop on Computational Approaches to Subjectivity, Sentiment and Social Media Analysis* 90–96.

Kashima, E. S., and Kashima, Y. 1998. Culture and language: The case of cultural dimensions and personal pronoun use. *Journal of Cross-Cultural Psychology* 29:461-486.

[4] http://corpus.nytud.hu/trendminer

Kouloumpis, E; Wilson, T.; and Moore, J. 2011. Twitter sentiment analysis: The good the bad and the omg!. *ICWSM* 11:538-541.

Kunda, Z. 1999. *Social Cognition. Making Sense of People*. Cambridge, Mass.: MIT Press.

László, J. 2008. *The Science of Stories: An introduction to Narrative Psychology*. London, New York: Routledge.

László, J.; Csertő, I.; Fülöp, É.; Ferenczhalmy, R.; Hargitai, R.; Lendvai, P.; Péley, B.; Pólya, T.; Szalai, K.; Vincze, O.; and Ehmann, B. 2013. Narrative Language as an Expression of Individual and Group Identity: The Narrative Categorical Content Analysis. *SAGE Open* 3:1-12.

Lietz, H.; Wagner, C.; Bleier, A. and Strohmaier, M. When Politicians Talk. 2014. Assessing Online Conversational Practices of Political Parties on Twitter. *International AAAI Conference on Weblogs and Social Media* 285-294.

O'Connor, B.; Balasubramanyan, R.; Routledge, B. R.; and Smith, N. A. 2010. From Tweets to Polls: Linking Text Sentiment to Public Opinion Time Series. *ICWSM* 11:122-129.

Sidorenko, W.; Sonntag, J.; Krüger, N.; Stieglitz, S. & Stede, M. 2013. From newspaper to microblogging: What does it take to find opinions? *Proceedings of the 4th Workshop on Computational Approaches to Subjectivity, Sentiment and Social Media Analysis* 81-86.

Silberztein M. 2005. NooJ: a Linguistic Annotation System for Corpus Processing. *HLT/EMNLP* 2005 10-11.

Sobkowicz, P.; Kaschesky, M.; and Bouchard, G. 2012. Opinion Mining in Social Media: Modeling, Simulating, and Forecasting Political Opinions in The Web. *Government Information Quarterly* 29: 470-479.

Tumasjan, A.; Sprenger, T. O.; Sandner, P. G.; and Welpe, I. M. 2010. Predicting Elections with Twitter: What 140 Characters Reveal about Political Sentiment. *ICWSM* 10:178-185.

Varga, D.; E. Simon. 2007. Hungarian named entity recognition with a maximum entropy approach. *Acta Cybernetica* 18(2):293-301.

Verb-centered Sentiment Inference with Description Logics

Manfred Klenner
Computational Linguistics
University of Zurich
Switzerland
klenner@cl.uzh.ch

Abstract

We introduce description logics as a means to carry out sentiment inferences triggered by some verbs on their semantic roles. Verbs might impose polar effects on some roles, but also have polar expectations on other roles. For instance, an entity inherits a positive polarity just by being actor of some verb ("she succeeds"). More complicated scenarios arise if we take subclause embeddings, negation and polarity conflicts into consideration. Polarity propagation and effect inversion need to be coped with, then. We have implemented a prototype in OWL covering a substantial subset of our verb lexicon covering about 140 German verbs.

1 Introduction

Verbs and their role in sentiment analysis have raised some interest only recently, cf. Neviarouskaya et al. (2009), Reschke and Anand (2011), Maks and Vossen (2012), Hollenstein et al. (2014), Deng and Wiebe (2014). More or less common to these approaches is the notion of sentiment inferences triggered by verbs. For instance, given the sentence "Greece blames EU and IMF for 'obstacles' in talks", we expect that the PP ("for") must be something negative and we understand that the direct object ("EU") receives a negative effect and that the subject ("Greece") is the source of this. The aforementioned approaches differ much in the details, but they all strive to cope with this kind of implicit information.

More complicated cases such as "U.N. Refugee Chief criticizes Europe for not rescueing migrants" raise the need to cope with subclause embedding and negation. Even polarity conflicts might arise as in "Palestinian students admire terrorist Dalal Mughrabi" where a negative direct object seems to produce an odd scenario. However, what about "I hugely admire refugees" where we have a negative direct object as well ("refugee" is negative in the way "ill" is), but where no polarity clash seems to be arising. We argue that fine-grained distinctions are needed to distinguish these cases, namely to distinguish factual from emotional and moral polarities. In this article, we simplify matters and introduce a concept called *sympathy entity* which covers factual negative entities such as refugee etc.

In order to draw sentiment inferences, rules are needed and their application must not interfere with each other nor should the set of rules be inconsistent (which is a problem for complex rule-based systems). We believe description logics (Baader, 2009) is well suited as a framework to model such an inference task. The big advantage is that we do not need to care about the order in which rules are applied; also consistency checks are part of the machinery. Our model is a competence model that - at least in principle - should be able to properly cope with arbitrarily complex embeddings and negation.

2 Related Work

We only discuss the most prominent approaches. A rule-based approach based on semantic verb classes was introduced by Neviarouskaya et al. (2009). Also fine-grained polarity labels are used there, namely the one from Appraisal Theory (Martin and White, 2005); positive or negative polarities are either related to appreciation (object inherent properties like "beautiful"), affect or judgement (the moral side, say "cheating"). Each verb instantiation is described from an internal and an external perspective. For example, "to admire a mafia leader" is classified as affective positive (the subjects attitude) given the internal perspective while it is judgement negative externally. The authors do not give any details about how they carry out rule application. Also, compared to our frame-

Proceedings of the 6th Workshop on Computational Approaches to Subjectivity, Sentiment and Social Media Analysis (WASSA 2015), pages 134–139,
Lisboa, Portugal, 17 September, 2015.

work, they are not able to tell "admire refugees" from "admire a mafia leader" as discussed above.

Reschke and Anand (2011) capture the polarity of a verb frame instantiation as a function of the polarity of the verb's roles. For instance, if a terrorist loses something positive, then this is positive as a whole. No rules are specified, just evaluativity classes are defined. It is hard to see how less drastic cases are to be treated (e.g. "the thief who loses all his friends" - is this positive?).

Recently, Deng and Wiebe (2014) have introduced an ambitious conceptual framework for inferring (sentiment) implications. Here, the private state of the author of a sentence is in question, what his attitudes towards various targets in the sentence are (and also what he believes the private states of the agents of the sentence would be). Rules within a graph-based model are used, propagation continues until no rules can be applied anymore. The model builds (in part) on the ideas described in Reschke and Anand (2011) (to commit a crime is good for the crime since it comes into existence), in contrast to Neviarouskaya et al. (2009) no external perspective is envisaged. "to admire" is a good-for situation, it is unclear how this influences the critical cases: "admire refugees" compared to "admire a mafia leader. Does the last example produces a polarity conflict? We would say that it should and that the subject receives a negative effect as a consequence.

3 Verb Polarity Frames

Some verbs do impose polar restrictions and cast polar perspectives on their complements, see Klenner et al. (2014a) and Klenner et al. (2014b). Take "to blame someone for something". As a consequence of the instantiation of "to blame" the direct object receives a negative effect and we expect the PP to realize something negative (or something neutral that contextually is perceived as being negative). We distinguish *verb role expectations* from *verb role effects*. *Effects* are propagated as the result of the verb frame instantiation (given a concrete sentence), while *expectations* are a kind of presuppositional aspects of the meaning of a verb - they are constant under negation: "not to blame for X" and "to blame for X", both presuppose that X is negative.

Verb polarity frames are used to capture this kind of information: "to blame" is a "direct object negative effect verb" and it also is a "PP complement negative expectation verb". Our German verb model comprises about 140 verbs (about 300 verb polarity frames) and their effects and expectations. Although there are cases, where a particular syntactic frame of a verb allows for more than one verb sense, this is not the rule. Often sortal restrictions might help in these cases ("sorgen für" in German might denote "care for", if a person is involved and "to organize", if e.g. a non-animate object takes the role: "sorgen für Verpflegung", "to organize food"). Word sense disambiguation (of verbs) is thus not so much a problem and we ignore the rare cases, where we would need it.

We are not interested in the private state of the author of a text, but in the polar conceptualization the text imposes on potential targets. Our goal is a target-specific sentiment analysis, which means that we focus on positive and negative contexts the target is in. Verb polarity frames capture the unmarked condition of verb usage. That is, deviations (e.g. expectation violations) are possible, but they lead to sanctions. For instance, if someone criticizes something positive or if someone supports something negative then he receives a negative effect (stemming from - what we call - a polarity clash between verb polarity frame and the polarity of the actual filler object). A *polarity clash* or violation arises, if a polar expectation or a polar effect casted from the verb meets an inverse entity polarity that comes either from the polarity lexicon or from noun phrase composition ("sick colleague").

Our polarity lexicon comprises about 6,700 nouns and adjectives (see Clematide and Klenner (2010)). Nouns that denote factual negative concepts form a new class of objects, namely those that deserve (or have) our sympathy (refugee, victim, hostage, depressed and poor people etc.). This helps to overcome problems with sentiment composition: "to admire something negative" is negative, except if we talk about negative entities that have our sympathy: "to admire a sick colleague" (no polarity clash) compared to "to admire a cheating colleague" (polarity clash).

The distinction between verb effects and verb expectations is crucial - we need both. Effects might result in positive or negative polarity attributions to entities, which is not true for expectations. Both are needed in order to identify unexpected and in a sense deviating situations as in "to blame for success".

4 A Case Study

In order to clarify the kind of sentiment inferences we envisage, we work through the sentence: "Die ganze Welt kritisiert Europa dafür, dass es den Flüchtlingen nicht hilft." A translation which preserves the German subclause construction is given in example 1. Examples 2-4 are variants of it regarding negation, i.e. "not" or "refuse to" (POS = positive):

1) criticize that NOT POS: The whole world criticizes Europe for the fact that it does not help the migrants.

→ In our verb model, "to criticize" imposes a negative effect on both, the direct object and the subclause. "to help" has a positive effect on the indirect object, which gives a positive situation, while the "criticize" frame is negative. Here, no (positive) effect is propagated to "migrants" since the subclause is negated, an "ordinary" negative effect is given to "Europe" (stemming from "criticize"). Moreover, "not to help someone who needs our help" is an odd situation (we call it a *Neg_Clash_Situation)* and the subject of such a situation (Europe) is penalized (it is per definitionem a *Neg_Clash_Entity*).

2) criticize that POS: Russia has criticized Europe for the fact that it helps the Ukraine.

→ "Ukraine" receives a positive effect; since a violation ("to criticize": a negative effect meets a positive sentence) is encountered, "Russia", as the actor of such a situation clash, is a Neg_Clash_Entity, while "Europe" receives a negative effect from being criticized (but since "criticize" is here a Neg_Clash_Situation, this might be regarded as irrelevant or neutralized - not yet implemented).

3) NOT (refuse to) criticize that NOT POS: China has refused to criticize Europe for the fact that it does not help the migrants.

→ "Europe" and "China" are of class Neg_Clash_Entity

4) NOT (refuse to) criticize that POS: USA has refused to criticize Europe for the fact that it helps the Ukraine. → "Ukraine" gets a positive effect

Deeper embeddings are possible, e.g.: "The USA forces the UN not to criticize Europe for the fact that it helps the Ukraine." Eventually, our model should be able to handle this (and all permutations of "not" among the clauses) as well.

5 A Prototype Implementation

We use the description logic OWL (Horrocks and Patel-Schneider, 2011) to represent the verb model, the effect propagation, the polarity clash classes, and we let the reasoner carry out all inferences coupled with sentiment propagation. Our model is meant to be a competence mode: we model cases even if they hardly are to be found in real texts. We are interested in the underlying principles (the correct predictions), not so much in the empirical impact (in terms of recall) given a sentiment analysis application.

Description logics (DL) were first introduced in the 1980s – so called KL-ONE languages. The big advantage of this (subset of predicate) logic is that the consistency of a knowledge base and also decidability are guaranteed. The reasoner can be used to relate instances from the so-called A-Box (assertions) to the concept hierachy, the terminological part (the T-Box). The system cares for the proper (truth) maintenance of derived facts, ie. if an assertion is ceased, any inferences made on the basis of it are ceased as well. We use the Protégé[1] editor for engineering and HermiT (Glimm et al., 2014) as an inference machinery. The following OWL specifications are given in Manchester Syntax (Horridge et al., 2006).

5.1 A-Box Representation

In order to carry out inferences, individuals (class instantiations) need to be specified (then reasoning or realization, the DL term, might be triggered). Verbs are referred to by a constant representing a verb event instantiation. Technically, their base form followed by a digit is used (e.g. blame-1 is an instance of a blame event). Binary relations link the participants to their event. We stick with grammatical functions (subject, etc.) for readability, but they are meant to represent arguments (AO, A1, etc.). The labels subj, obja (direct object), objd (indirect object) and objc (complement clause) are modelled as OWL properties, we also define a property class "participant" that covers subj, obja and objd and we define inverse properties, e.g. subj-of.

So "Russland kritisiert, dass Europa der Ukraine hilft" (take the translation given in section 4, example 2) would be represented as given in Fig. 1. The class "asserted" is used to indicate

[1]available from http://protege.stanford.edu/

that the verb instance is not negated (non_asserted, otherwise).

Figure 1: Instance Representation

5.2 Concepts for Sentiment Inference

Verbs have effects and expectations (see section 3 for their definition). Effects are directly applied if a verb polarity frame instantiation is feasible without any violation (e.g. of expectations). A target then is classified as a Pos_Eff_Entity or Neg_Eff_Entity depending on the polarity frame. If everything is as expected, the instantiation as a whole is classified as a Pos_Situation or a Neg_Situation according to the verb class. A violation occurs if a polar effect or polar expectation is not met. Then a Neg_Clash_Situation is found. Effects might get inverted or canceled and the subject of the situation is classified as a Neg_Clash_Entity. A situation that embeds a Neg_Clash_Situation is also a Neg_Clash_Situation and its subject then becomes a Neg_Clash_Entity and so on.

5.3 T-Box Representation

Fig. 2 shows a simplified version of the taxonomy. We distinguish attributes (Attribute, polar and non-polar adjectives) from entities (Entity) and situations (Situation). Entities comprise non-polar entities (e.g. nations) and polar entities, which divide into Neg_Entity and Pos_Entity (the polarity lexicon entries) and Eff_Polar_Entity (meant to capture the inferred verb effects), Neg_Clash_Entity (expectation violation entities) and Composed_Polar_Entity – the class that realizes noun phrase composition (e.g. that "cheating colleague" is negative). Sympathy_Entity is meant to capture entities that have our sympathy (e.g. "refugee").

Situations are divided into polar situations (Polar_Situation) which capture positive and negative clause level denotations and Neg_Clash_Situations

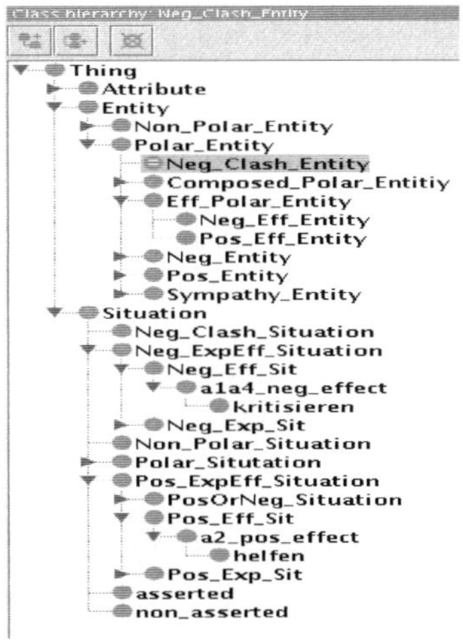

Figure 2: OWL Classes (partial)

(violation of subclause expectations or effects, e.g. "criticizes something positive") and the various verb classes.

Verb classes are represented as primitive (undefined) concepts, their class name indicates effect and expectation patterns. For instance, "helfen" ("to help") is, among others, a a2_pos_effect verb, since the indirect object receives a positive effect. We use the following shortcuts: a0, a1, a2, a3, a4 for subj, direct object, indirect object, PP complement, clausal complement, respectively. A primitive definition prevents the reasoner from automatically determining class membership. There is no need to let the reasoner classify verbs, since the parse tree provides all information needed in order to identify the verb class (the verb lemma, its grammatical roles).

The class a2_pos_effect is a subclass of Pos_Eff_Situation. In order to assign the effect that comes with the verb classes, the concept Pos_Eff_Entity is defined as a non-primitive subclass (equivalence class in Protégé) of Eff_Polar_Entity[2]:

objd-of some (a2_pos_effect and asserted)

That is, the indirect object (objd) of a a2_pos_effect verb that is not negated (i.e. asserted) is automatically classified as a Pos_Eff_Entity (i.e. it gets a positive effect). The equivalent in terms of predicate logic is:

$$\forall x : (\exists y : \text{objd–of}(x, y) \wedge \text{a2\_pos\_effect}(y) \wedge \text{asserted}(y)) \rightarrow \text{Pos\_Eff\_Entity}(x)$$

A situation (denoted by the verb and its instan-

[2] All definitions given here are simplified.

tiated roles) is positive situation (a subclass of Polar_Situation from Fig. 2), if (among others):

a2_pos_effect and asserted and (objd some (Sympathy_Entity or Comp_Neut_Entity or Comp_Pos_Entity))

That is: the verb is a a2_pos_effect and asserted (not negated) and the indirect object of that verb is an entity that has our sympathy or is a composed positive or neutral entity (nouns without further modification like "Ukraine" are treated as simply composed, neutral entities).

The verb "to criticize" is a a1a4_neg_effect verb, the direct object as well as the subclause inherit a negative effect. For our example ("Russia has criticized Europe for the fact that it helps the Ukraine") we get (see Fig. 3): "helfen-5" is a positive situation[3], thus, a polarity clash occurs ("criticize something positive").

Figure 3: Sentiment Inferences

The class Neg_Clash_Situation captures this (cf. Fig. 4). The first line states that a situation with a participant (a property class that subsumes subj, obja and objd) that is a M_Neg_Comp_Entity and is at the same time a Pos_Effect_Entity, is a Neg_Clash_Situation. That is, any situation, where a (morally) negative entity has received a positive effect, is a situation clash.

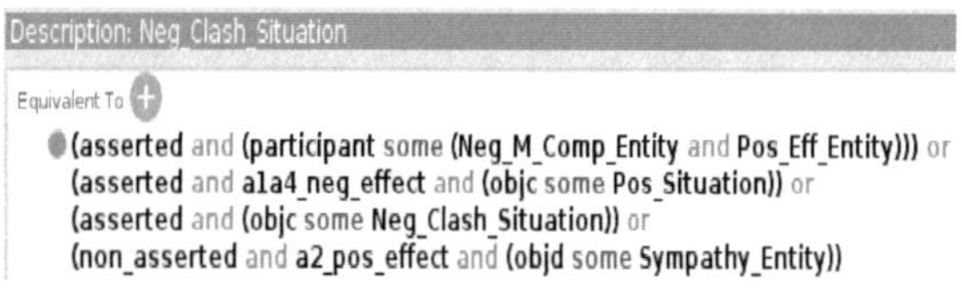

Figure 4: Neg_Clash_Situation

According to line 2 (and 3), a non-negated a1a4_neg_effect verb that embeds a Pos_Situation (or, to capture recursive cases, a Neg_Clash_Situation) is classified as a Neg_Clash_Situation. "kritisieren-5" is classified accordingly (see Fig. 3) and the next step is to propagate this situation polarity clash to the subject. We define a Neg_Clash_Entity to be the subject of a Neg_Clash_Situation: (subj-of some Neg_Clash_Situation). In our case, this holds for "Russland-5". Russia thus is penalized for criticizing a positive situation.

[3]Lines marked in yellow are inferred by the reasoner.

5.4 The Current State of the Model

A dependency parse of a sentence is easily converted into the input format of our model. One just has to take the verb from the tree, take the lemma as its class, create a verb instance, find its grammatical roles and create constants in order to provide individual referents. If the verb is negated, its OWL instance is set to non_asserted.

We have created an interface to a dependency parser (Sennrich et al., 2009), but just worked with hand-crafted sample sentences (that are inspired by real sentences, anyway). We expect that an empirical evaluation will reveal gaps in the model and parts that need to be refined. It is already clear that we need to deal more explicitly with implication signatures of verbs in the sense of Nairn et al. (2006). For instance, German "zwingen" turns out to be a one-way implicative (which is in line with its English translation "to force"). Thus, negated "zwingen" does not entail anything regarding the factuality (truth) of its complement clause.

Currently, we have 12 verb classes in the model, covering about 80 different verbs.

6 Conclusions

This paper introduces description logics as a framework for verb-centered sentiment inferences. We have sketched a model and implemented a prototype of it in order to demonstrate the power of such an approach. Subclause embedding, negation and polarity conflicts can be handled in such a framework in a very concise way. We have not yet fully explored the various model variants that appear to be interesting. Further experiments and an empirical evaluation are needed.

Acknowlegements: I am indebted to my colleague Michael Amsler for the specification of the German verb model, which I used as a basis for my explorations. I would like to thank Simon Clematide for his suggestions. This work has been partially supported by the Swiss Commission for Technology and Innovation (CTI) under the grant 17384.1 PFES-ES.

References

Franz Baader. 2009. Description logics. In Franconi-E. Eiter Th. Gutierrez C. Handschuh S. Rousset M.-C. Schmidt R. Tessaris, S., editor, *Reasoning Web: Semantic Technologies for Information Systems*, pages 1–39. Springer.

Simon Clematide and Manfred Klenner. 2010. Evaluation and extension of a polarity lexicon for German. In *Proceedings of the First Workshop on Computational Approaches to Subjectivity and Sentiment Analysis (WASSA)*, pages 7–13.

Lingjia Deng and Janyce Wiebe. 2014. Sentiment propagation via implicature constraints. *Meeting of the European Chapter of the Association for Computational Linguistics (EACL-2014)*.

Birte Glimm, Ian Horrocks, Boris Motik, Giorgos Stoilos, and Zhe Wang. 2014. HermiT: An OWL 2 reasoner. *Journal of Automated Reasoning*, 53(3):245–269.

Nora Hollenstein, Michael Amsler, Martina Bachmann, and Manfred Klenner. 2014. Sa-uzh: Verb-based sentiment analysis. In *Proceed. of the 8th Intern. Workshop on Semantic Evaluation (SemEval 2014)*, pages 503–507.

Matthew Horridge, Nick Drummond, John Goodwin, Alan Rector, Robert Stevens, and Hai H Wang. 2006. The Manchester OWL syntax. In *OWL: Experiences and Directions (OWLED)*.

Ian Horrocks and Peter F. Patel-Schneider. 2011. KR and reasoning on the Semantic Web: OWL. In John Domingue, Dieter Fensel, and James A. Hendler, editors, *Handbook of Semantic Web Technologies*, chapter 9, pages 365–398. Springer.

Manfred Klenner, Michael Amsler, and Nora Hollenstein. 2014a. Verb polarity frames: a new resource and its application in target-specific polarity classification. In *Proceedings of KONVENS 2014*, pages 106–115.

Manfred Klenner, Susanna Tron, Michael Amsler, and Nora Hollenstein. 2014b. The detection and analysis of bi-polar phrases and polarity conflicts. In *Proceedings of 11th International Workshop on Natural Language Processing and Cognitive Science*. Venice, Italy.

Isa Maks and Piek Vossen. 2012. A lexicon model for deep sentiment analysis and opinion mining applications. *Decision Support Systems*, 53(4):680–688.

J. R. Martin and P. R. R. White. 2005. *Appraisal in English*. Palgrave, London.

Rowan Nairn, Cleo Condoravdi, and Lauri Karttunen. 2006. Computing relative polarity for textual inference. In *Proceed. of Inference in Computational Semantics (ICoS 5), Buxton, England*, pages 67–75.

Alena Neviarouskaya, Helmut Prendinger, and Mitsuru Ishizuka. 2009. Semantically distinct verb classes involved in sentiment analysis. In Hans Weghorn and Pedro T. Isaías, editors, *IADIS AC (1)*, pages 27–35. IADIS Press.

Kevin Reschke and Pranav Anand. 2011. Extracting contextual evaluativity. In *Proceedings of the Ninth International Conference on Computational Semantics*, pages 370–374.

Rico Sennrich, Gerold Schneider, Martin Volk, and Martin Warin. 2009. A new hybrid dependency parser for German. In *Proc. of the German Society for Computational Linguistics and Language Technology*, pages 115–124.

Mining HEXACO personality traits from Enterprise Social Media

Priyanka Sinha
Tata Consultancy Services Limited
Indian Institute of Technology Kharagpur
priyanka27.s@tcs.com

Lipika Dey
Tata Consultancy Services Limited
lipika.dey@tcs.com

Pabitra Mitra
Indian Institute of Technology Kharagpur
pabitra@gmail.com

Anupam Basu
Indian Institute of Technology Kharagpur
anupambas@gmail.com

Abstract

In this paper we introduce a novel computational technique of extraction of personality traits (HEXACO) of employees from Enterprise Social Media posts. We deal with challenges such as not being able to use existing survey instruments for scoring and not being able to directly use existing psychological studies on written text due to lack of overlapping words between the existing dictionary and words used in Enterprise Social Media. Using our approach we are able to infer personality traits (HEXACO) from posts and find better coverage and usage of the extended dictionary.

1 Introduction

It is well known that modern organizations rely heavily on unstructured information to capture expertise and knowledge that otherwise exist in the minds of its employees. Understanding the behavior and personality of the employees help in group formation and understanding group dynamics which could help predict project success. Among the many ways in which modern organizational psychology (Ashton et al., 2004) describes human personality, some important attributes that generally emerge can be summarized as follows:

Agreeableness being helpful, cooperative and sympathetic towards others

Conscientiousness being disciplined, organized and achievement-oriented

Extraversion having a higher degree of sociability, assertiveness and talkativeness

Emotionality the degree of emotional stability, impulse control and anxiety

Openness to Experience having a strong intellectual curiosity and a preference for novelty and variety

Honesty-Humility being a good person who is ethical and altruistic

These are collectively known as personality traits in the HEXACO (Honesty-Humility, Emotionality, Extraversion, Agreeableness, Conscientiousness, Openness) personality trait model as described in (Ashton et al., 2004). Intensity and polarity of each trait varies from person to person thereby capturing a person's personality. These traits are measured by trained psychologists using self rating or by being rated by the psychologist. These rating scales such as the HEXACO-PI-R as described in (Lee and Ashton, 2004) contain questions about the person that help in judging their traits. (Ashton et al., 2004) also identifies sets of personality describing words with loading factors that are related to each trait which forms a dictionary of such words.

Written text is a medium of communication within a group, when members communicate through emails and/or social media. Emails originate from individuals and are targeted towards a specified set of people. In social media, there are usually no targeted groups. Rather communication is meant for as many people to see, read and react. While emails are used for confidential information exchange within an enterprise, enterprise social networks are targeted towards rapid disbursement of information across large communities. They also encourage sharing of knowledge and information, flatten hierarchy, and enable speedy resolution through crowd-sourcing.

These text sources are observed to contain very few of the existing personality describing words. In our corpus of an Enterprise Social Media dataset, 0.22% percent of total word usage as well as 152 words out of total 185,251 distinct words

Proceedings of the 6th Workshop on Computational Approaches to Subjectivity, Sentiment and Social Media Analysis (WASSA 2015), pages 140–147, Lisboa, Portugal, 17 September, 2015.

contain personality describing words from the set described in (Ashton et al., 2004). Our dataset has a total of 14,849 distinct users of which only 1,939 users use atleast one of these words atleast once. Whether they are at all used in the context of describing someone's personality or behavior is not studied.

These are a very low number and they do not capture all the implicit expressions in the text describing someone's personality or behavior. We could however infer the presence of personality describing words and other personality expressions from such formal and semi-formal text. As summarized in (Goldbeck et al., 2011a), personality traits are useful in predicting performance and success in enterprise context. Hence, the motivation to explore other techniques to infer personality and behavior expressions about each individual as well as group(s) from enterprise text sources.

2 Literature Survey

There are two different challenges in trying to assess HEXACO traits from enterprise social media as follows:

1. Psychologists have studied the problem of identifying personality traits from language usage. They have used various methods amongst which rating scales, both self reported and administered by trained psychologists are established techniques. The Big Five Factors, HEXACO and other such models of personality traits have been related to language usage by psychologists (Ashton et al., 2004; Tausczik and Pennebaker, 2010). Pennbaker has conducted very many studies relating how people of different demographics in different situations use language and how it relates to human behavioral traits. In particular there are a set of features which are identified as relevant to human behavior. Linking of words to personality traits/behavioral traits has been done by different groups of psychologists. A challenge here is that there are different lists used by different groups.

2. In recent times, phenomenal rise in social media content has given birth to the sub-area of text mining where researchers analyze language usage to infer behavioral traits from social media content. Inferences are usually validated by self appraisal or voluntary revelation of identity or psychologists identify. Since language usage is substantially different in social media and the erstwhile controlled psychoanalytic methods used by psychologists, there has been efforts to generate mappings between social media text and personality traits.

Existing literature in each of the these above areas are reviewed in detail below.

2.1 Review of related work in text analysis for psychoanalysis

These have been used as features in most of the recent work in identifying personality traits from social media text. Most of these works have been validated by trained psychologists. There is not much work that has focussed on text which is from business enterprises where language used is more formal than on websites like Twitter and Facebook.

We discuss below some of the related literature with respect to the challenges mentioned in Section 2.

(Ashton et al., 2004) reports in tabular form a list of adjectives that relate to the each of the HEXACO personality traits. This paper explores the HEXACO personality trait model. It also explores Religiosity as an extra seventh factor and accepts that there may be more factors than six. It notes that the 1982 Goldberg 1,710 adjective set is nearly the entire population of English personality descriptive adjectives. We use the result of this study which results in a reduced set of the 1,710 personality descriptive adjectives in English with loading factor for each of the six factors of the personality trait model. The reduction and identification of the word set seem like an important work for psychologists as it would enable them to work with fewer words which may mean faster and concise analysis. Use of computational power relaxes this restriction. Now even with a much larger dictionary it would be possible to scalably analyze people's personalities using computational models of analysis.

(Tausczik and Pennebaker, 2010) and (Chung and Pennebaker, 2007) describe the LIWC software, its usage and relevance to psychological processes. It summarizes how different parts of speech used by people tell us about them and their behavior. For example, it has been studied that lots of use of first person personal pronouns is an indicator of depression. Content words indicate where the person is focussing such as people thinking about death, sex, money, or friends will refer to them in writing or conversation. People experiencing physical or emotional pain use first person personal pronouns to draw attention to themselves. Greater use of first person personal pronouns correlates with higher rank and higher status. Higher ranked individuals ask fewer questions. First person singular pronoun usage can be used to predict lower status. Greater use of first person plural pronouns show group cohesion. Word count can be a proxy for amount of communication and more communication may promote better group performance. Analysis of tense of verbs indicate temporal focus of attention. "We" signals a sense of group identity. Sometimes "We" also refers to others. When lying, people tend to use more words, more negative words, more motion words, less first person singular pronouns. The use of "You" is important in predicting lower quality relationships.

2.2 Review of related work on text mining of social media content for behavior analysis

(Goldbeck et al., 2011b) gave questionnaires to twitter users to fill out. They used structural properties such as number of followers, number of following, density of social network, number of mentions, hashtags, replies, links. For linguistic features they used LIWC, MRC Psycholinguistic Database and sentiment analysis. Using Weka, regression analysis was done for each feature for personality prediction within 11-18 percent of their actual value. They did not make use of a psychological validation of their results.

(Yarkoni, 2010) reports correlations between LIWC categories and Big Five personality traits. It also reports correlations with lower order facets. 694 participants collected using email or word of mouth were given 100-question and 315-question questionnaires for Big Five, NEO-FFI, NEO-PI-R. Their dataset consists of participants blogs from Google blogger service which may contain more informal text and not enterprise social media. For language usage study, top 5000 unstemmed words (where each blog had more than 50,000 words) in the corpus were ranked with respect to their frequency. These words were correlated with each of the Big Five and other lower order facets. For example, Neuroticism correlated positively with words expressing negative emotion such as awful, lazy, depressing, terrible and stressful; while Extraversion correlated positively with words reflecting social settings or experiences such as bar, restaurant, drinking, dancing, crowd and sang; additionally Openness showed strong positive correlations with words associated with intellectual or cultural experience such as poet, culture, narrative, art, universe and literature. Therefore, we are motivated to explore language use, LIWC to study personality traits.

(Schwartz et al., 2013; Kern et al., 2014; Park et al., 2014) work with the myPersonality dataset which consists of about 19 million Facebook status updates from about 136,000 participants. Their motivation for studying social media as against a psychology lab is that social media language is written in natural social settings, and captures communication among friends and acquaintances. They take two approaches to study language usage in reference to personality traits. One experiment is closed vocabulary study where in for each category for each participant the ratio of sum of frequency of words used by participant in manually created category of language and sum of frequency of words used by participants is noted. Least squares regression is used to link word categories with author attributes, fitting a linear function between explanatory variables (LIWC categories) and dependent variables (such as a trait of personality, e.g. Extraversion). This approach is in some ways similar to earlier approaches. The new approach they take is the open vocabulary approach, where they extract words, phrases(1 to 3 n-grams) and topics (using LDA) via tokenization. The phrases with high pointwise mutual information are retained. Correlation analysis using least squares regression is carried out. They then find categories extending the LIWC category list corresponding to Big Five traits. They also do a predictive evaluation using SVM and ridge regression to predict personality traits using closed/open vocabulary approach. They identify words related to Big Five which are not present in LIWC and any previous analysis. Based on this study, they devise a prediction algorithm to identify personality traits. They do not report whether the myPersonality dataset suffers the challenges of a non-overlapping dictionary with LIWC or personality describing words.

(Banerjee, 2002) describes the lesk similarity algorithm that the software tool (Pedersen et al., 2008) implementation being used as a similarity algorithm is based on. The lesk algorithm uses the information contained in a dictionary to perform word sense disambiguation. Here the dictionary is WordNet. The intuition is that words co occuring in a sentence are being used to refer to the same topic, and topically related senses of words are defined in the dictionary using the same words. It suffers from the fact that lexicographers try to create concise definitions with as few words as possible so even related words may not have common words in their definitions. Using the WordNet relations this is addressed. Every synset in Wordnet has a gloss which is a definition explaining the meaning of the concept of the synset. It also has example sentences. Semantic relationships define a relationship between two synsets. Thus, the glosses of various synset relationships between the word being disambiguated are used as dictionary definitions to the original lesk algorithm. The similarity score between two words is a sum of overlap between the various glosses in Wordnet for each of the two words. The gloss in Wordnet is an approximation of the dictionary definition of the word. Examples of different kinds of glosses used would be example-gloss, gloss-gloss, hypo-gloss.

3 Methodology

Initially we have obtained data from our internal enterprise social network where approximately 300,000 people interact on various topics ranging from technical to work life. This contains different types of posts such as microblogs, blogs, questions, wikis and challenges over a period of 2 years. The other category of content include comments, answers and responses to challenges. Conventional statistical analysis was performed on the data and the following are observed.

One of the ways we identify personality traits is to use a similarity algorithm such as lesk (in Section 2.1) to include adjectives from the dataset that are similar to the adjectives in the HEXACO set for each of the personality traits. In order to increase our yield of personality descriptive words, we include other personality descriptive words similar to the HEXACO set before expanding our set with words similar to those in the dataset. There are 25,553 unique adjectives in the dataset,

Communities	#users	#blog- posts in dataset	#blog- posts of top 50 users	#uBlogs	#uBlogs of top 50 users	#comments per (blog, uBlog)
Technical 1	9,887	9,069	5,301	8,172	5,070	(7, 4)
Technical Sub 1	954	470	322	451	290	(5, 2)
Technical Sub 2	65	43	43	31	31	(3, <1)
Non Technical 1	9,088	2,167	1,053	4,060	2,372	(14, 6)
Non Technical 2	2,442	682	358	350	250	(19, 4)

Table 1: Posting statistics of dataset

Proposed Method	#Words in dictionary	#Words in vocabulary	% unique in dataset	% usage in dataset	% coverage of users
HEXACO	245	152	0.08	0.22	13
HEXACO Extension	2,108	1,999	1.07	3.95	50.18
LIWC	4,487	3,993	2.16	43.77	90.51

Table 2: Coverage statistics of proposed methods

Type	#Unique words	#Total words
Adjectives	25,553	590,910
Nouns	136,592	2,397,410
Pronouns	73	536,813
Verbs	23,033	1,059,940
Total	185,251	4,585,073

Table 3: Part of speech statistics of dataset. Words with different capitalization and spelling are treated as unique.

Trait	Overall % usage	Overall Intensity in dataset	Usage % in Posts	Intensity in Posts	Usage % in Comments	Intensity in Comments
Honesty	0.9	-1424	0.58	-870	0.33	-554
Emotionality	0.66	553	0.45	457	0.21	96
Extraversion	0.96	438	0.58	245	0.39	193
Agreeableness	1.15	-3486	0.75	-2253	0.40	-1233
Conscientiousness	0.75	1539	0.48	958	0.26	581
Openness	0.97	1536	0.67	1071	0.30	464

Table 4: In a work life related community with 7745 people posting 37263 items

Correlation Between	Honesty	Emotionality	Extraversion	Agreeableness	Conscientiousness	Openness
Normalized usage score in posts versus score in feedback	0.0882	0.1770	**0.3362**	**0.3287**	**0.3471**	**0.4005**
Normalized usage score in posts versus positive emotions in posts	-0.0914	0.2040	0.0873	0.0419	**0.3476**	-0.0937
Normalized usage score in posts versus negative emotions in posts	-0.1316	0.1963	-0.0520	-0.0810	**0.2556**	0.0064
Positive emotions in posts versus positive emotions in feedback	**0.3171**	**0.2700**	**0.3844**	**0.4334**	**0.3368**	**0.4689**
Negative emotions in posts versus negative emotions in feedback	**0.3147**	**0.5070**	0.1544	**0.4677**	**0.3845**	**0.3438**

Table 5: Correlations between authored posts and feedback comments received by top users in work life related community of extended HEXACO scores and LIWC emotion categories

	Received Comment Score	+ve Emotion in Posts	-ve Emotion in Posts	+ve Emotion in Received Comments	-ve Emotion in Received Comments
Agreeableness Post Score	0.23	-0.29	-0.58	-0.30	-0.30
Openness Post Score	0.16	0.23	0.54	0.22	0.30
Extraversion Post Score	0.18	0.36	0.43	0.19	0.14
Honesty Post Score	-0.07	-0.35	-0.73	-0.19	-0.48
Conscientiousness Post Score	0.13	0.41	0.21	0.05	0.33
Emotionality Post Score	0.16	0.23	0.54	0.22	0.30

Table 6: Correlations between LIWC processes of emotion in received comments and posted posts in work like related community

which account for 13.79% of the vocabulary. We create a similarity score matrix between the seed set and adjectives in the dataset. In the lesk algorithm using Wordnet, given a set of strings from the gloss' of each word, in order to calculate the overlap score we need the longest common substrings or phrases between them. For each such overlapping substring, the individual score is number of words in the substring squared multiplied by the number of times this substring repeats in the definitions. This score is then weighted with the weight of the type of gloss entry. For example, undemanding is a personality describing adjective of the trait agreeableness and lenient is an adjective in the dataset that has similarity with it and is part of the extended HEXACO set. The words undemanding and lenient have glosses "posing no difficulty requiring little effort" and "demanding little effort not burdensome". The overlapping substring here is "little effort" so the overlap score between these two strings is 2*2*1 = 4. Sum over all the glosses results in a score of 94 for undemanding as an adjective in sense 1. For easy comparison amongst various pairs of words, we normalize the scores by dividing the similarity score of a pair of words with the highest score between the different senses of the pair of words. We threshold the minimum similarity we consider to include the word as similar.

After applying the above algorithm, the earlier list of 245 words was extended to include 2108 words out of which 1,999, i.e., 95% of the words now appeared in the social media content. It was found that 50% of the users have used one of these 1,999 words atleast once. In the next section we propose an algorithm for deriving personality traits of people from their written content based on the usage of this extended set.

We propose a computational means of assigning HEXACO personality trait scores to people based on their posts on enterprise social media. For each person in our dataset, we consider all the posts authored by the person. For each post, for words from the extended HEXACO set, we sum their contribution to the corresponding personality trait and normalize using total words used by the author. Contribution of a word already in the HEXACO set is the loading factor as given in (Ashton et al., 2004). Contribution of a word is the sum of the product of its similarity to a word in a trait and the loading factor of that word in the trait normalized by the total number of words in that trait it is similar to.

4 Observations

From the tables depicting the intensity of each trait in different communities, we can see that openness and agreeableness are well represented and their cummulative intensity in each community is high.

In taking a deeper look into the higher order elements in enterprise social media content we use LIWC2007 (Pennebaker et al., 2007a) on the dataset. 2.1% of our enteprise social media dataset vocabulary are indicative of LIWC processes that account for 43.7% of total enterprise social media content used by 90.51% of the users. This indicates the importance of LIWC processes that are indicative of behavioral traits.

LIWC usage is not directly linked to HEXACO properties, although as reviewed in section 2.1 there have been attempts at using LIWC processes as features that contribute to prediction of Big Five personality traits from web social media. Dataset variability makes it infeasible in many cases to do this mapping as datasets vary in the linguistic features that are indicative of behavior. It is particularly applicable in our case where there are restrained expressions unlike other social media.

We study a subset of users from two communities who have posted atleast a few blogs over the period of 2 years and also have received atleast a few comments so that we may be able to make meaningful observations. We see that openness correlates positively with positive emotion expressed in posts and honesty correlates strongly negatively with negative emotions expressed in posts. We do see that people scoring of their posts on each of the hexaco traits using our method receive near about the same score on the comments they receive indicating that they are possibly perceived as they appear in the posts. From Table 5 and 6, we observe that people's extended HEXACO trait scores on their posts using our methods are strongly correlated with those on the comments they receive, indicating that they are possibly perceived as they appear in their posts. It is slightly lower for Honesty and Emotionality traits but high for Extraversion, Agreeableness, Conscientiousness and Openness. It indicates that people who are more open, agreeable, extraverted, conscientious evoke similar traits from people responding to them in an organization. Another in-

Algorithm 1 Personality scoring algorithm

```
procedure LESK ADAPTATION
    for each trait of HEXACO do
        for each pair of trait adjective and dataset adjective do
            for each sense pair in Wordnet do
                for each pair of gloss do
                    gloss_sim = count number of words in overlapping substring * weight of type of gloss
                end for
                total_gloss_sim = ∑ gloss_sim
            end for
            score = MAX(total_gloss_sim) over all sense pairs
        end for
        sim = score/(MAX(score) over all dataset adjectives)
        threshold sim by minimum similarity (usually greater than 0.9) and add to extended HEXACO trait
    end for
end procedure
procedure LOADING FACTOR
    for each dataset adjective in extended HEXACO set do
        for each trait do
            loading_factor = SUM(similarity with each trait adjective * loading factor of that trait adjective)/total number of trait adjectives
        end for
    end for
end procedure
procedure HEXACO SCORING
    for each employee do
        for each HEXACO trait do
            score = SUM(adjectives used from extended HEXACO set * loading factor of adjective)/number of words used by employee
        end for
    end for
end procedure
```

teresting observation is that there is a low correlation between openness scores of a person posting and the use of emotive words, which indicates that use of positive emotive words or negative emotive words is largely independent of how open and straightforward a person is and evokes that sentiment. We also see that use of a lot of emotion words positive or negative evokes the same kind of emotion in received comments as well.

5 Conclusion and Future Work

Though the set has increased, however, these words still account for only 1.1% of the vocabulary contributing to 3.95% of total word usage. So it can be concluded that though both usage and coverage have gone up still there is a large volume of enterprise social content which remains untapped. Hence, we propose to look at higher order linguistic elements like phrases, interaction patterns and also LIWC processes, as detailed in (Pennebaker et al., 2007b), in text for better coverage.

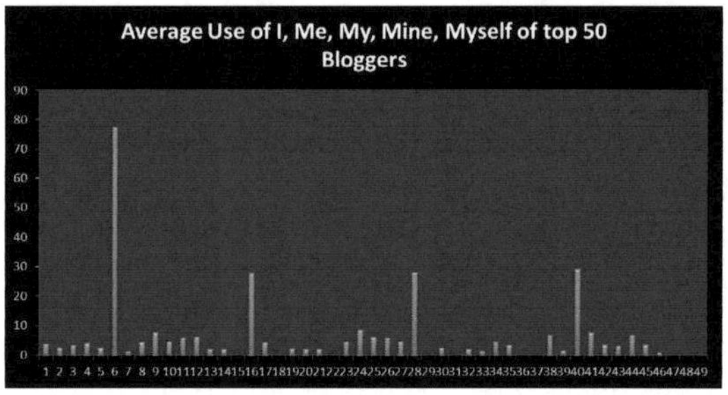

Figure 1: Average usage of first person personal pronouns

Figure 1 is a profile of the average usage of first person personal pronouns by top 50 bloggers. We see that 4 people score significantly higher than others and it is suspected (Tausczik and Pennebaker, 2010; Chung and Pennebaker, 2007) that they are neurotic and depressed. On reading their posts, we find that the highest scorer posts original depressing short stories which have a fan following that encourage the author through positive comments. Therefore, we see that just word usage without communication and other structural aspects do not capture the context in which the words have been used and hence may wrongly identify the author as depressed or neurotic.

As of now we do not have scoring annotations of HEXACO scores using employee completed

(Lee and Ashton, 2004) but we intend to gather text and annotations from employees using surveys to compare our results.

Acknowledgments

We would like to thank Tata Consultancy Services Limited for use of the enterprise social media dataset for research purposes.

References

Michael C. Ashton, Kibeom Lee, and Lewis R. Goldberg. 2004. A hierarchical analysis of 1,710 english personality-descriptive adjectives. *Journal of Personality and Social Psychology*, 87(5):707–721.

Satanjeev Banerjee. 2002. Adapting the lesk algorithm for word sense disambiguation to wordnet. Master's thesis, University of Minnesota.

Cindy K. Chung and James W. Pennebaker. 2007. The psychological function of function words. In *K. Fiedler (Ed.), Social communication: Frontiers of social psychology*, pages 343–359.

Jennifer Goldbeck, Cristina Robles, Michon Edmondson, and Karen Turner. 2011a. Predicting personality from twitter. In *Proceedings of the 3rd IEEE International Conference on Social Computing*, pages 149–156, Boston, Massachusetts, USA.

Jennifer Goldbeck, Cristina Robles, Michon Edmondson, and Karen Turner. 2011b. Predicting personality from twitter. In *IEEE International Conference on Privacy, Security, Risk, and Trust, and IEEE International Conference on Social Computing, 2011*.

Margaret L. Kern, Johannes C. Eichstaedt, H. Andrew Schwartz, Lukasz Dziurzynski, Lyle H. Ungar, David J. Stillwell, Michal Kosinski, Stephanie M. Ramones, and Martin E. P. Seligman. 2014. The online social self: An open vocabulary approach to personality. *Assessment*, 21(2):158–169.

K. Lee and M.C. Ashton. 2004. Psychometric properties of the hexaco personality inventory. In *Multivariate Behavioral Research*, volume 39, pages 329–358.

Gregory Park, H. Andrew Schwartz, Johannes C. Eichstaedt, Margaret L. Kern, Michal Kosinski, David J. Stillwell, Lyle H. Ungar, and Martin E. P. Seligman. 2014. Automatic personality assessment through social media language. In *Journal of Personality and Social Psychology*.

Ted Pedersen, Satanjeev Banerjee, and Siddharth Patwardhan. 2008. WordNet::SenseRelate::WordToSet. `http://www.d.umn.edu/~tpederse/senserelate.html`.

James W. Pennebaker, Roger J. Booth, and Martha E. Francis. 2007a. LIWC2007 for Mac OSX. `http://liwc.net`.

James W. Pennebaker, Cindy K. Chung, Molly Ireland, Amy Gonzales, and Roger J. Booth. 2007b. The development and psychometric properties of LIWC2007. `http://liwc.net`.

H. Andrew Schwartz, Johannes C. Eichstaedt, Margaret L. Kern, Lukasz Dziurzynski, Stephanie M. Ramones, Megha Agrawal, Achal Shah, Michal Kosinski, David Stillwell, Martin E. P. Seligman, and Lyle H. Ungar. 2013. Personality, gender, and age in the language of social media: The open-vocabulary approach. *PLoS ONE*, 8(9):e73791, 09.

Yla R. Tausczik and James W. Pennebaker. 2010. The psychological meaning of words: Liwc and computerized text analysis methods. *Journal of Language and Social Psychology*, 29(1):24–54.

Tal Yarkoni. 2010. Personality in 100,000 words: A large-scale analysis of personality and word use among bloggers. In *Journal of Research in Personality*, volume 44, pages 363–373.

Opinion Holder and Target Extraction for Verb-based Opinion Predicates – The Problem is Not Solved

Michael Wiegand and **Marc Schulder**
Spoken Language Systems
Saarland University
D-66123 Saarbrücken, Germany
michael.wiegand@lsv.uni-saarland.de
marc.schulder@lsv.uni-saarland.de

Josef Ruppenhofer
Dept. of Information Science
and Language Technology
Hildesheim University
D-31141 Hildesheim, Germany
ruppenho@uni-hildesheim.de

Abstract

We offer a critical review of the current state of opinion role extraction involving opinion verbs. We argue that neither the currently available lexical resources nor the manually annotated text corpora are sufficient to appropriately study this task. We introduce a new corpus focusing on opinion roles of opinion verbs from the Subjectivity Lexicon and show potential benefits of this corpus. We also demonstrate that state-of-the-art classifiers perform rather poorly on this new dataset compared to the standard dataset for the task showing that there still remains significant research to be done.

1 Introduction

We present a critical review of previous research in opinion holder and target extraction. *Opinion holders (OH)* are the entities that express an opinion, while *opinion targets (OT)* are the entities or propositions at which sentiment is directed. The union of opinion holders and opinion targets are referred to as *opinion roles*.

In this work we focus on opinion roles evoked by verbs. We examine verbs since opinion role extraction is considered a lexical semantics task and for such tasks verbs are the central focus.

We argue for more lexical resources and corpora that are less biased by domain artifacts. The common practice for producing labeled corpora has so far mostly been extracting contiguous sentences from a particular domain and then labeling those sentences with regard to the entities that were intended to be extracted, i.e. opinion holders and/or opinion targets. In this paper we argue that certain important aspects of the task of opinion role extraction get overlooked if one exclusively considers those corpora that are currently available. We particularly focus on the relationship between opinion roles and their syntactic argument realization. Previous work hardly addressed this issue since either little variation between opinion roles and their syntactic arguments was perceived on the corpora on which this task was examined, or there were other domain-specific properties that could be used in order to extract opinion roles correctly without the knowledge about opinion role realization.

Currently, there exists only one commonly accepted corpus for English containing manual annotation of both opinion holders and targets, i.e. the MPQA corpus (Deng and Wiebe, 2015). Apart from that, not a single lexical resource for that specific task is available. Moreover, there does not exist any publicly available tool that supports *both* opinion holder and target extraction. Typical applications, such as opinion summarization, however, require both components simultaneously (Stoyanov and Cardie, 2011). These facts indicate that there definitely needs to be more research on the task of opinion role extraction.

In order to stimulate more research in this direction, we present a verb-based corpus for opinion role extraction. The difference to previous datasets is that it has been sampled in such a way that all opinion verbs of a common sentiment lexicon are widely represented. Previous corpora have a bias towards those opinion expressions that are frequent in a particular domain. We demonstrate on two opinion holder extraction systems that performance on the new corpus massively drops compared to their performance on a standard dataset. This shows that current systems are not fit for open-domain classification.

2 Opinion Roles and Lexical Semantics

Conventional syntactic or semantic levels of representation do not capture sufficient information that allows a reliable prediction in what argument

Proceedings of the 6th Workshop on Computational Approaches to Subjectivity, Sentiment and Social Media Analysis (WASSA 2015), pages 148–155, Lisboa, Portugal, 17 September, 2015.

positions an opinion role may be realized. This is illustrated by (1) and (2) which show that, even with the PropBank-like semantic roles (i.e. *agent*, *patient*[1]) assigned to the entities, one may not be able to discriminate between the opinion roles.

(1) $[\text{Peter}]^{OH}_{agent}$ **dislikes** $[\text{Mary}]^{OT}_{patient}$.

(2) $[\text{Peter}]^{OT}_{agent}$ **disappoints** $[\text{Mary}]^{OH}_{patient}$.

We assume that it is lexical information that decides in what argument position opinion roles are realized. That is, a verb, such as *dislike*, *believe* or *applaud*, belongs to a group with different linguistic properties than verbs, such as *disappoint*, *interest* or *frighten*. However, the realizations of opinion roles observed in (1) and (2) are not the only possibilities. In (3), there is no explicitly mentioned opinion holder while the target is the agent. Such cases are triggered by verbs, such as *gossip*, *blossom* or *decay*.

(3) $[\text{These people}]^{OT}_{agent}$ are **gossiping** a lot.

Another type of opinion verb is presented in (4) and (5) where two viewpoints are evoked by the same verb in the same sentence. (4) denotes the sentiment view of *Peter* towards *Mary* while (5) represents the sentiment view of *Mary* towards *Peter* (i.e. *Peter* made *Mary* feel better).

(4) $[\text{Peter}]^{OH}_{agent}$ **consoles** $[\text{Mary}]^{OT}_{patient}$.

(5) $[\text{Peter}]^{OT}_{agent}$ **consoles** $[\text{Mary}]^{OH}_{patient}$.

These types of **selectional preferences** (1)-(5) have been observed before including the case of **multiple viewpoint evocation** (4)-(5), most prominently by Ruppenhofer et al. (2008). Yet little research on opinion role extraction has actually paid attention to this issue. One exception is Wiegand and Klakow (2012) who experiment with an induction approach to distinguish cases like (1) and (2). Nonetheless, datasets and lists of types of opinion verbs have not been publicly released.

The above analysis suggests more research on lexical resources is required. In the following, we show that existing resources are not suitable to provide the type of information we are looking for. As a reference of opinion verbs, we use the set of 1175 verbs contained in the **Subjectivity Lexicon** (Wilson et al., 2005). Our main assumption is that the opinion verbs from that lexicon can be considered a representative choice of all kinds of opinion expressions that exists in the English language.

[1]By *agent* and *patient*, we mean constituents labeled as $A0$ and $A1$ in PropBank (Kingsbury and Palmer, 2002).

3 On the Potential of Existing Lexical Resources

In §2, we demonstrated the need for acquiring more lexical knowledge about opinion verbs for open-domain opinion role extraction. This raises the question whether existing general-purpose resources could be exploited for this purpose. If one considers the plethora of different lexical resources developed for sentiment analysis, i.e. sentiment lexicons listing subjective expressions and their prior polarity (Wilson et al., 2005; Baccianella et al., 2010; Taboada et al., 2011), emotion lexicons (Mohammad and Turney, 2013) or connotation lexicons (Kang et al., 2014), one finds, however, that with respect to opinion role extraction there is a gap. What is missing is a lexicon that states for each opinion verb in which argument position an opinion role can be found.

3.1 Sparsity and Other Shortcomings of FrameNet

One resource that has previously been examined for this task is **FrameNet** (Baker et al., 1998). The idea is to identify in frames (which predominantly contain opinion expressions) those frame elements that typically contain either opinion holders or opinion targets. Once this mapping has been established, a FrameNet-parser, such as Semafor (Das et al., 2010), could be used to automatically recognize frame structures in natural language text. By consulting the mapping from frame elements to opinion roles, specific opinion roles could be extracted. Kim and Hovy (2006) followed this approach for a set of opinion verbs and adjectives. Thus, they were able to correctly resolve some problems which cannot be solved with the help of syntactic parsing or PropBank-like semantic roles, such as the role distinctions in (1) and (2). For instance, while the opinion holders in (6) and (7) map to the same frame element *EXPERIENCER*, the PropBank-like semantic roles differ. Unfortunately, the resulting mapping lists from that work are not publicly available.

(6) $[\text{Peter}\ _{EXPERIENCER}\ ]^{OH}_{agent}$ **dislikes** $[\text{Mary}]^{OT}_{patient}$.

(7) $[\text{Peter}]^{OT}_{agent}$ **disappoints** $[\text{Mary}\ _{EXPERIENCER}\ ]^{OH}_{patient}$.

Table 1 shows some statistics of our opinion verbs with regard to matched frames and frame elements. Considering that there are 615 different frame elements associated to the different frames[2]

[2]This count conflates frame elements of the same name that occur in different frames.

# opinion verbs (from the Subjectivity Lexicon)	1175
# opinion verbs with at least one frame	691
# different frames associated with opinion verbs	306
# different frame elements associated with opinion verbs	615

Table 1: Statistics of opinion verbs w.r.t frames and frame elements from FrameNet.

containing at least one of our opinion verbs, it becomes obvious that mapping opinion roles to frame elements is a challenging undertaking.

One major shortcoming of the FrameNet-approach for opinion role extraction is that the current FrameNet (version 1.5) still severely suffers from a data-sparsity problem. For example, approximately 45% of the opinion verbs from the Subjectivity Lexicon are missing from FrameNet (Table 1). Even though there exist ways to expand the knowledge contained in FrameNet (Das and Smith, 2012), there are also conceptual problems with the current FrameNet-ontology (Ruppenhofer and Rehbein, 2012). Since FrameNet is a general-purpose resource, there is no guarantee that frame structures perfectly match selectional preferences of opinion roles. For instance, we found that there are many frames that contain opinion verbs with different selectional preferences. The frame SCRUTINY, for example, typically contains many verbs that take an opinion holder in agent position and an opinion target in patient position (e.g. *investigate* or *analyse*). However, it also contains different verbs, such as *pry*. *Prying* means *to be interested in someone's personal life in a way that is annoying or offensive* (Macmillan Dictionary). Given this definition, we must note that this verb also contains another opinion view (in addition to the one also conveyed by the other verbs in this frame – as exemplified by (8) and (9)), namely that of the speaker of the utterance (condemning the behaviour of the agent of *pry*). As a consequence, the agent of *pry* is also an opinion target while its respective opinion holder is the speaker of the utterance (10).

(8) $[\text{The police}]_{OH}$ **investigated** $[\text{her}]_{OT}$ thoroughly.

(9) $[\text{The press}]_{OH}$ continues to **pry** $[\text{into their affairs}]_{OT}$.

(10) $[\text{The press}]_{OT}$ continues to **pry** into their affairs. *(OH: speaker of the utterance)*

3.2 WordNet Lacking Syntactic Knowledge

At first glance, using **WordNet** (Miller et al., 1990) as a way to acquire knowledge for selectional preferences of opinion verbs seems a better alternative. This resource has a far greater lexical coverage than FrameNet (for example, the set of opinion verbs from the Subjectivity Lexicon are all contained in WordNet). A straightforward solution for using that resource in the current task would be to group opinion verbs that share the same selectional preferences for opinion holders and targets with the help of the WordNet ontology graph. One common way of doing so would be the application of some bootstrapping method in which one defines seed opinion verbs with distinct selectional preferences (for instance, one defines as one group opinion verbs that take agents as opinion holders, such as *dislike*, as another group verbs that take patients as opinion holders, such as *disappoint*, and so on) and propagate their labels to the remaining opinion verbs via the WordNet graph. Such bootstrapping on WordNet has been effectively used for the induction of sentiment lexicons (Esuli and Sebastiani, 2006; Rao and Ravichandran, 2009) or effect predicates (Choi and Wiebe, 2014). It relies on a good similarity metric in order to propagate the labels from labeled seed words to unlabeled words.

We experimented with the metrics in WordNet::Similarity (Pedersen et al., 2004) and found that the opinion verbs most similar to a specified opinion verb do not necessarily share the same syntactic properties. For example, Table 2 lists the 12 opinion verbs most similar to *outrage* and *please*, which are typical opinion verbs that take an opinion holder in patient position and an opinion target in agent position.[3] (They would be plausible candidates for verb seeds for that verb category.) Unfortunately, among the list of similar verbs, we find many opinion verbs which have opinion holder and target in a different argument position, such as *hate* on the list for *outrage*:

(11) $[\text{Mary}]^{OT}_{agent}$ **outrages/appals/scandalizes/...** $[\text{Peter}]^{OH}_{patient}$.

(12) $[\text{Peter}]^{OH}_{agent}$ **hates/fears/loves/...** $[\text{Mary}]^{OT}_{agent}$.

From a semantic point of view, the similarities obtained look reasonable. *rage*, *hate* and *dread* bear a semantic resemblance to *outrage*. However, the syntactic properties, i.e. the selectional (argument) preferences, which are vital for opinion role extraction, differ from *outrage*. WordNet is a primarily *semantic* resource (mainly with a view towards lexical relations rather than valence or argument structure), syntactic aspects that would be necessary in order to induce selectional preferences, are missing. Therefore, we suspect that, by itself, WordNet is not a useful resource for the extraction of opinion roles.

[3]We employ the metric by Wu and Palmer (1994).

outrage: appall, scandalize, anger, rage, sicken, temper, hate, fear, love, alarm, dread, tingle
please: delight, enthral, enchant, gratify, signify, obviate, madden, blind, avoid, despair, disagree, crush

Table 2: The 12 most similar verbs to *outrage* and *please* according to the WordNet::Similarity (underlined verbs do **not** share the selectional preference of the respective target verb).

verbs		adjectives	
tokens	types	tokens	types
252	113	1467	302

Table 3: Comparison of distribution of opinion verbs and opinion adjectives in the Darmstadt Service Review Corpus (DSRC).

4 Text Corpora for Fine-Grained Sentiment Analysis

The previous section suggested that none of those existing lexical resources yield the type of information that is required for opinion role extraction. We now also look at available text corpora and examine whether they reflect opinion verbs in such a way that the problem of opinion role extraction can be appropriately evaluated on them. We start by looking at the review domain.

4.1 Why the review domain is not suitable for studying opinion role extraction for verbs

There has been a lot of research on the review domain, which also means that there are several datasets from different domains allowing cross-domain sentiment analysis. However, for more in-depth opinion role extraction evoked by verb predicates, these types of texts seem to be less suitable – despite the plethora of previous publications on opinion target extraction (Hu and Liu, 2004; Jakob and Gurevych, 2010; Liu et al., 2013b; Liu et al., 2013a; Liu et al., 2014). We identified the following reasons for that:

Firstly, the subtask of opinion holder extraction is not really relevant on this text type. Product reviews typically reflect the author's views on a particular product. Therefore, the overwhelming majority of explicitly mentioned opinion holders refer to the author of the pertaining review.

agent of verb	patient of verb	no (direct) relationship
21.8	44.5	33.8

Table 4: Proportion of relationships between opinion targets and opinion verbs in the Darmstadt Service Review Corpus (DSRC).

Secondly, opinion roles evoked by opinion verbs are less frequent. We extracted all sentences with opinion targets from the *Darmstadt Service Review Corpus (DSRC)* (Toprak et al., 2010)[4] and counted the parts of speech of the corresponding opinion expressions. Table 3 compares the frequency of opinion adjectives and verbs. It shows that adjectives are much more frequent than verbs.

Thirdly, the review domain is typically focused on products, e.g. movies, books, electronic devices etc. This also means that only specific semantic types are eligible for opinion holders and targets, e.g. persons are less likely to be opinion targets. Therefore, much of the research in opinion target extraction relies on entity priors. By that we mean that (supervised) classifiers learn weights for specific entities (typically nouns or noun phrases) of how likely they represent *a priori* an opinion target (Zhuang et al., 2006; Qiu et al., 2011; Liu et al., 2013b; Liu et al., 2014). For example, in the movie domain *Psycho* is very likely to be an opinion target as will be *iPhone* in the electronics domain. However, as such features do not transfer to other domains, they distract research efforts from the universally applicable feature of selectional preferences. Table 4, for example, shows the proportion of different relationships between opinion targets and opinion verbs on DSRC. It shows that there is a considerable number of targets in both agent position (14) and patient position (13) & (15). So, it is not trivial to detect opinion targets here. However, if one looks at typical sentences that fall into these two classes, one finds that entity priors and a few other heuristics would help to solve this extraction problem.

For example, all a supervised classifier would need to learn is that the personal pronoun *I* can never be an opinion target (13) – in the review domain it is typically an opinion holder. (This is a typical entity prior that can be learned.) Otherwise, agents are preferred opinion targets (14) but if the agent is not realized, we simply tag the patient (15). We found that these simple heuristics would manage to correctly identify more than 70% of opinion targets on DSRC (being a dependent of some opinion verb). Under these circumstances, one does not need to know that *recommend* and *stink* have different selectional prefer-

[4]We chose this corpus as a typical representative corpus for sentiment analysis in the review domain.

	MPQA	VERB
# sentences	15753	1073
avg. # mentions of the same opinion verb	6.3	1.1
avg. # (explicit) opinion holders per sentence	0.1	0.7
holders in agent position [in %]	77.4	45.8
holders in patient position [in %]	3.1	13.3
missing explicit holder [in %]	19.6	41.0
multiple viewpoint evocation [in %]	2.6	41.0

Table 5: Statistics of MPQA and VERB.

ences on opinion targets.

(13) I **recommend** [this site]$^{OT}_{patient}$ to anyone.

(14) [Their programs]$^{OT}_{agent}$ **stink**.

(15) **Avoid** [this institution]$^{OT}_{patient}$ if you are a Canadian student!

These heuristics may work on review datasets, but they become misleading when used in a cross-domain setting, since their predictiveness may be confined to specific domains. For example, in a novel written in the first person, the mere occurrence of *I* is not telling. No mention of *I* in Sentence (16) (taken from *Gulliver's Travels*) represents an opinion holder.

(16) When [I] left Mr. Bates, [I] went down to my father: where [...] [I] got forty pounds, and a promise of thirty pounds a year to maintain me at Leyden: there [I] studied physic two years and seven months [...]

4.2 Is the news domain any better?

While we think that the review domain is less suitable for opinion role extraction, the conditions we find on news corpora seem more promising. Typically, news corpora tend to be multi-topic. As a consequence, opinion targets can be of different semantic types. Persons can function both as opinion holders and targets. In other words, corpus artifacts like the ones mentioned in §4.1 are less likely to be helpful in solving the task. The fact that the only corpus with a significant amount of both opinion holders and targets annotated, namely *MPQA 3.0* (Deng and Wiebe, 2015), consists of news text, further lends itself to the usage of that domain. Moreover, we do not have a bias towards adjectives. On the MPQA corpus, for example, we actually found that there are 10% more opinion verb mentions than opinion adjective mentions. This analysis may suggest that the existing MPQA corpus would be suitable for our studies. Yet in the next sections, we show why for the study of opinion roles of opinion verbs, it is advisable to consider yet another corpus.

5 Our New Opinion Verb Corpus

With our new corpus for fine-grained analysis, we mainly pursue three goals that, as discussed above, are not sufficiently met by previous resources:

1. Our corpus is designed for the evaluation of opinion role extraction systems focusing on mentions of opinion verbs.
2. It should widely represent various types of selectional preferences.
3. It should appropriately represent multiple viewpoint evocation.

Our new corpus was sampled from the *North American News Text Corpus* (LDC95T21). The dataset comprising 1073 sentences contains 753 opinion holders, 745 opinion targets and 499 opinion targets of a speaker view (e.g. as in (3)). We sampled in such a way that all opinion verbs from the Subjectivity Lexicon were contained (**Goal 1**). To compare: In the MPQA corpus, almost every second opinion verb is unattested.

In order to demonstrate that our new corpus is a more suitable resource in order to study selectional preferences (**Goal 2**) and multiple viewpoint evocation (**Goal 3**), we prepared some statistics regarding mentions of opinion verbs and their properties in the MPQA corpus and our corpus (denoted by VERB). Due to the unavailability of MPQA 3.0, we had to use MPQA 2.0, whose annotation with regard to opinion targets is incomplete. We therefore compare opinion verbs only with regard to their opinion holders. However, given the strong interrelations between opinion holders and targets (Yang and Cardie, 2013), we think that if it is shown that our corpus better represents the versatility of opinion holders, this should (almost) equally also apply for opinion targets.

Table 5 examines the types of argument positions in which an opinion holder is realized. We distinguish between three different roles (already informally introduced in §2): the holder is in **agent position** (example: *dislike*), the holder is in **patient position** (example: *disappoint*) or the holder is **not an argument at all** (example: *gossip*). The latter are cases in which the speaker (or some nested source) is the opinion holder. Table 5 also shows the proportion of verbs with multiple viewpoint evocation and the average frequency of individual opinion verbs. The table clearly shows that on MPQA opinion verbs selecting opinion holders in an agent position are predominant. We think that this is just an artifact of having a corpus of contiguous sentences whereby frequent verbs predominate. VERB, like MPQA, originates from the news domain. The only difference is that it has been sampled so that all opinion verbs of the Subjectivity Lexicon are equally represented (and not only the frequent ones). A look at our new corpus, which represents the set of opinion verbs of the Subjectivity Lexicon, shows that other types of opinion verbs are actually underrepresented in MPQA. The same can be said about multiple viewpoint evocation. (The number for this latter phenomenon is surprisingly high. We found that the reason of this is that there are many verbs that follow the pattern of *pry* (9)-(10), i.e. conveying both a view of its agent and another view of the speaker, such as *idealize*, *moan*, *overemphasize*, *patronize*, *snub*, *swindle* or *trivialize*.)

We should wonder what impact this bias of opinion role realizations has on building classifiers. If one just focuses on MPQA, then always considering opinion holders in agent position will mean being right in almost 80% of the cases. Similarly, there is no need to consider multiple viewpoint evocation. So, this explains why previous research paid little attention to these issues.

6 Details on Annotation

We followed the annotation scheme of Ruppenhofer et al. (2014). It is based on SalsaTigerXML (Erk and Padó, 2004), an annotation scheme originally devised for representing FrameNet-like semantic roles. On a sample of 200 sentences, we measured an interannotation agreement of Cohen's $\kappa = 0.69$ for opinion holders and $\kappa = 0.63$ for opinion targets. The corpus is going to be made publicly available to the research community.

7 Some Baselines

We now empirically prove that further research on opinion role extraction is needed. For this proof, we consider the two previously discussed corpora, MPQA and VERB. MPQA is chosen as a training set.[5] It is also the largest corpus. We want to show that despite its size, open-domain opinion role extraction requires some information that is still not contained in that corpus. Almost every second opinion verb from the Subjectivity Lexicon is not contained in that corpus.

In this evaluation, we only consider opinion holders. One reason for this is that opinion holders are less controversial to annotate (this also usually results in a higher interannotation agreement (§6)). Another reason is that there is no publicly available extraction system that covers targets.

For our experiments, we use the sequence labeler from Johansson and Moschitti (2013), ***MultiRel***. We chose this classifier since it is currently the most sophisticated system for opinion holder extraction and it is publicly available. *MultiRel* incorporates relational features taking into account interactions between multiple opinion cues. In addition to *MultiRel*, we also consider convolution kernels (***CK***) from Wiegand and Klakow (2012). We include that classifier since it achieved overall better performance than the traditional CRFs on a wide set of experiments (Wiegand and Klakow, 2012) including on cross-domain settings.

[5]The split-up of training and test set on the MPQA corpus follows the specification of Johansson and Moschitti (2013).

Classifier	**MPQA** (train+test)	**VERB** (test)
MultiRel	72.54	44.80
CK	62.98	43.88

Table 6: F-scores of opinion-holder classifiers on the MPQA corpus and the new VERB corpus.

In the evaluation, we only consider the opinion holders of our opinion verbs. Recall that we are only interested in the study of opinion roles associated with opinion verbs.

Table 6 shows the results. *MultiRel* produces the best performance on MPQA, but on VERB suffers from a similar domain-mismatch as *CK*. This drop in performance is not only due to the fact that many opinion verbs do not occur in MPQA, but also because the selectional preferences of these uncovered verbs differ from the majority observed in MPQA (Table 5).

8 Conclusion

We have argued for more research regarding opinion role extraction involving opinion verbs. We showed that with existing corpora, certain problems, such as the differences in selectional preferences among opinion verbs cannot be properly addressed. One cause for this is that corpora available contain opinion verbs with predominantly one selectional preference. Another is that the corpora have certain characteristics that happen to allow inferring opinion roles for specific text types in the corpus (e.g. entity priors in reviews) but which are not transferable to other text types. In order to study the issue of opinion role realization more thoroughly, we have created a small dataset of sentences in which the opinion roles of opinion verbs from the Subjectivity Lexicon have been annotated. With two state-of-the-art classifiers trained on the large MPQA corpus, we could only produce comparatively poor results on opinion role extractions. This shows that further research on that research task is required.

Acknowledgements

We would like to thank Stephanie Köser for annotating parts of the resources presented in this paper. The authors were partially supported by the German Research Foundation (DFG) under grants RU 1873/2-1 and WI 4204/2-1.

References

Stefano Baccianella, Andrea Esuli, and Fabrizio Sebastiani. 2010. SentiWordNet 3.0: An Enhanced Lexical Resource for Sentiment Analysis and Opinion Mining. In *Proceedings of the Conference on Language Resources and Evaluation (LREC)*, pages 2200–2204, Valletta.

Collin F. Baker, Charles J. Fillmore, and John B. Lowe. 1998. The Berkeley FrameNet Project. In *Proceedings of the International Conference on Computational Linguistics and Annual Meeting of the Association for Computational Linguistics (COLING/ACL)*, pages 86–90, Montréal, Quebec, Canada.

Yoonjung Choi and Janyce Wiebe. 2014. +/-EffectWordNet: Sense-level Lexicon Acquisition for Opinion Inference. In *Proceedings of the Conference on Empirical Methods in Natural Language Processing (EMNLP)*, pages 1181–1191, Doha, Qatar.

Dipanjan Das and Noah A. Smith. 2012. Graph-Based Lexicon Expansion with Sparsity-Inducing Penalties. In *Proceedings of the Human Language Technology Conference of the North American Chapter of the ACL (HLT/NAACL)*, pages 677–687, Montréal, Quebec, Canada.

Dipanjan Das, Nathan Schneider, Desai Chen, and Noah A. Smith. 2010. Probabilistic Frame-Semantic Parsing. In *Proceedings of the Human Language Technology Conference of the North American Chapter of the ACL (HLT/NAACL)*, pages 948–956, Los Angeles, CA, USA.

Lingjia Deng and Janyce Wiebe. 2015. MPQA 3.0: An Entity/Event-Level Sentiment Corpus. In *Proceedings of the Human Language Technology Conference of the North American Chapter of the ACL (HLT/NAACL)*, pages 1323–1328, Denver, CO, USA.

Katrin Erk and Sebastian Padó. 2004. A powerful and versatile xml format for representing role-semantic annotation. In *Proceedings of the Conference on Language Resources and Evaluation (LREC)*, pages 799–802, Lisbon, Portugal.

Andrea Esuli and Fabrizio Sebastiani. 2006. SentiWordNet: A Publicly Available Lexical Resource for Opinion Mining. In *Proceedings of the Conference on Language Resources and Evaluation (LREC)*, pages 417–422, Genova, Italy.

Minqing Hu and Bing Liu. 2004. Mining and Summarizing Customer Reviews. In *Proceedings of the ACM SIGKDD International Conference on Knowledge Discovery & Data Mining (KDD)*, pages 168–177, Seattle, WA, USA.

Niklas Jakob and Iryna Gurevych. 2010. Extracting Opinion Targets in a Single- and Cross-Domain Setting with Conditional Random Fields. In *Proceedings of the Conference on Empirical Methods in Natural Language Processing (EMNLP)*, pages 1035–1045, Boston, MA, USA.

Richard Johansson and Alessandro Moschitti. 2013. Relational Features in Fine-Grained Opinion Analysis. *Computational Linguistics*, 39(3):473–509.

Jun Seok Kang, Song Feng, Leman Akoglu, and Yejin Choi. 2014. ConnotationWordNet: Learning Connotation over the Word+Sense Network. In *Proceedings of the Annual Meeting of the Association for Computational Linguistics (ACL)*, pages 1544–1554, Baltimore, MD, USA.

Soo-Min Kim and Eduard Hovy. 2006. Extracting Opinions, Opinion Holders, and Topics Expressed in Online News Media Text. In *Proceedings of the ACL Workshop on Sentiment and Subjectivity in Text*, pages 1–8, Sydney, Australia.

Paul Kingsbury and Martha Palmer. 2002. From TreeBank to PropBank. In *Proceedings of the Conference on Language Resources and Evaluation (LREC)*, pages 1989–1993, Las Palmas, Spain.

Kang Liu, Liheng Xu, Yang Liu, and Jun Zhao. 2013a. Opinion Target Extraction Using Partially-Supervised Word Alignment Model. In *Proceedings of the International Joint Conference on Artificial Intelligence (IJCAI)*, pages 2134–2140, Beijing China.

Kang Liu, Liheng Xu, and Jun Zhao. 2013b. Syntactic Patterns versus Word Alignment: Extracting Opinion Targets from Online Reviews. In *Proceedings of the Annual Meeting of the Association for Computational Linguistics (ACL)*, pages 1754–1763, Sofia, Bulgaria.

Kang Liu, Liheng Xu, and Jun Zhao. 2014. Extracting Opinion Targets and Opinion Words from Online Reviews with Graph Co-ranking. In *Proceedings of the Annual Meeting of the Association for Computational Linguistics (ACL)*, pages 314–324, Baltimore, MD, USA.

George Miller, Richard Beckwith, Christiane Fellbaum, Derek Gross, and Katherine Miller. 1990. Introduction to WordNet: An On-line Lexical Database. *International Journal of Lexicography*, 3:235–244.

Saif Mohammad and Peter Turney. 2013. Crowdsourcing a Word-Emotion Association Lexicon. *Computational Intelligence*, 39(3):555–590.

Ted Pedersen, Siddharth Patwardhan, and Jason Michelizzi. 2004. WordNet::Similarity – Measuring the Relatedness of Concepts. In *Proceedings of the Human Language Technology Conference of the North American Chapter of the ACL–Demonstration Papers (HLT/NAACL)*, pages 38–41, Boston, MA, USA.

Guang Qiu, Bing Liu, Jiajun Bu, and Chun Chen. 2011. Opinion Word Expansion and Target Extraction through Double Propagation. *Computational Linguistics*, 37(1):9–27, March.

Delip Rao and Deepak Ravichandran. 2009. Semi-Supervised Polarity Lexicon Induction. In *Proceedings of the Conference on European Chapter of the Association for Computational Linguistics (EACL)*, pages 675–682, Athens, Greece.

Josef Ruppenhofer and Ines Rehbein. 2012. Semantic frames as an anchor representation for sentiment analysis. In *Proceedings of the Workshop on Computational Approaches to Subjectivity and Sentiment Analysis (WASSA)*, pages 104–109, Jeju, Korea.

Josef Ruppenhofer, Swapna Somasundaran, and Janyce Wiebe. 2008. Finding the Source and Targets of Subjective Expressions. In *Proceedings of the Conference on Language Resources and Evaluation (LREC)*, pages 2781–2788, Marrakech, Morocco.

Josef Ruppenhofer, Julia Maria Struß, Jonathan Sonntag, and Stefan Gindl. 2014. IGGSA-STEPS: Shared Task on Source and Target Extraction from Political Speeches. *Journal for Language Technology and Computational Linguistics*, 29(1):33–46.

Veselin Stoyanov and Claire Cardie. 2011. Automatically Creating General-Purpose Opinion Summaries from Text. In *Proceedings of Recent Advances in Natural Language Processing (RANLP)*, pages 202–209, Hissar, Bulgaria.

Maite Taboada, Julian Brooke, Milan Tofiloski, Kimberly Voll, and Manfred Stede. 2011. Lexicon-Based Methods for Sentiment Analysis. *Computational Linguistics*, 37(2):267 – 307.

Cigdem Toprak, Niklas Jakob, and Iryna Gurevych. 2010. Sentence and Expression Level Annotation of Opinions in User-Generated Discourse. In *Proceedings of the Annual Meeting of the Association for Computational Linguistics (ACL)*, pages 575–584, Uppsala, Sweden.

Michael Wiegand and Dietrich Klakow. 2012. Generalization Methods for In-Domain and Cross-Domain Opinion Holder Extraction. In *Proceedings of the Conference on European Chapter of the Association for Computational Linguistics (EACL)*, pages 325–335, Avignon, France.

Theresa Wilson, Janyce Wiebe, and Paul Hoffmann. 2005. Recognizing Contextual Polarity in Phrase-level Sentiment Analysis. In *Proceedings of the Conference on Human Language Technology and Empirical Methods in Natural Language Processing (HLT/EMNLP)*, pages 347–354, Vancouver, BC, Canada.

Zhibiao Wu and Martha Palmer. 1994. Verb semantics and lexical selection. In *Proceedings of the Annual Meeting of the Association for Computational Linguistics (ACL)*, pages 133–138, Las Cruces, NM, USA.

Bishan Yang and Claire Cardie. 2013. Joint Inference for Fine-grained Opinion Extraction. In *Proceedings of the Annual Meeting of the Association for Computational Linguistics (ACL)*, pages 1640–1649, Sofia, Bulgaria.

Li Zhuang, Feng Jing, and Xiao-Yan Zhu. 2006. Movie Review Mining and Summarization. In *Proceedings of the Conference on Information and Knowledge Management (CIKM)*, pages 43–50, Arlington, VA, USA.

Synthetic Text Generation for Sentiment Analysis

Umar Maqsud
Technische Universität Berlin
Straße des 17. Juni 135, 10623 Berlin, Germany
umar.maqsud@campus.tu-berlin.de

Abstract

Natural language is a common type of input for data processing systems. Therefore, it is often required to have a large testing data set of this type. In this context, the task to automatically generate natural language texts, which maintain the properties of real texts is desirable. However, current synthetic data generators do not capture natural language text data sufficiently. In this paper, we present a preliminary study on different generative models for text generation, which maintain specific properties of natural language text, i.e., the sentiment of a review text. In a series of experiments using different data sets and sentiment analysis methods, we show that generative models can generate texts with a specific sentiment and that hidden Markov model based text generation achieves less accuracy than Markov chain based text generation, but can generate a higher number of distinct texts.

1 Introduction

Text generation is the task of automatically generating texts, which maintain specific properties of real texts. In the context of synthetic text generation, generative models are used to generate test data for benchmarking big data systems (Rabl and Jacobsen, 2012). BDGS (Ming et al., 2014) is a text generator that applies latent dirichlet allocation (Blei et al., 2003) as the text data generation model and BigBench (Ghazal et al., 2013) is a benchmark that provides a text generator based on Markov chain model (Rabiner, 1989).

Sentiment analysis (SA) is a method of processing opinions and subjectivity of a text. The task is to find and extract the sentiment polarity expressed in a text.

The goal of the paper is to demonstrate the ability of different generative models, i.e., latent dirichlet allocation (LDA), Markov chains (MC), and hidden Markov model (HMM), to generate text with a specific sentiment. This is an important problem because the sentiment of a text may be crucial in several applications like extracting the customers reviews about books, movies, or food and classifying them along their sentiment.

The contributions of this paper are as follows. We present a primary study on three different generative models for text generation. LDA and MC are used for text generation in previous work (Ming et al., 2014; Ghazal et al., 2013). We introduce the well known HMM to use it for text generation and compare it with LDA and MC. In a series of experiments, we analyze the scalability, cardinality, and the ability to generate text with a sentiment. For sentiment analysis, we use state-of-the-art methods. The evaluation indicates that the models can generate texts with a specific sentiment. The hidden Markov model achieves a lower accuracy than Markov chains, but can generate more distinct texts.

The remainder of the paper is organized as follows. Sections 2 and 3 provide an overview on generative models and sentiment analysis approaches. In Section 4 the results of the preliminary experiments are presented. Finally, Section 5 presents a summary and discusses directions for future work.

2 Generative Models

We describe in this section the previously mentioned generative models for text generation.

2.1 Latent Dirichlet Allocation

Latent dirichlet allocation (LDA) is a generative probabilistic model and can be applied for text generation (Ming et al., 2014). Documents are modeled as mixtures over latent topics and topics

Proceedings of the 6th Workshop on Computational Approaches to Subjectivity, Sentiment and Social Media Analysis (WASSA 2015), pages 156–161,
Lisboa, Portugal, 17 September, 2015.

are described by a distribution over words. The generation process in LDA has following steps for each document, as described in (Blei et al., 2003):

1. Choose $N \sim$ Poisson(ξ) as the length of a the document.
2. Choose $\theta \sim$ Dir(α) as the mixture of latent topics of the document.
3. For each of N words w_n:
   (a) Choose a topic $z_n \sim$ Multinomial(θ)
   (b) Choose a word w_n from $p(w_n|z_n, \beta)$, a multinomial probability conditioned on the topic z_n.

To learn a LDA model of text documents the library lda-c[1] is used. BDGS (Ming et al., 2014) is used to generate text based on these models.

2.2 Markov Chain

A Markov chain is a sequence of random variables with the Markov property (Rabiner, 1989). Suppose $X = (X_1, X_2 ... X_T)$ is a sequence of random variables and $W = (w_1, w_2 \ldots w_n)$ the state space. Then the Markov property is:

1. Transition probability depends only on the previous state.
   $P(X_t = w_i|X_1, \ldots, X_{t-1}) = P(X_t = w_i|X_{t-1})$
2. Transition probability depends on k previous states (k-order markov chain).
   $P(X_t = w_i|X_1, \ldots, X_{t-1}) = P(X_t = w_i|X_{t-k}, \ldots, X_{t-1})$

A first order Markov chain will only consider the probability of a word appearing after another one. To get more realistic text, higher order n-gram models should be used for generating the text (Ghazal et al., 2013).

2.3 Hidden Markov Model

A hidden Markov model (HMM) is a Markov process with unobserved states and an observable variable (Rabiner, 1989). The hidden states have a probability distribution over the possible observable outputs. Suppose $X = (X_1, X_2 \ldots X_T)$ is a sequence of hidden random variables, $H = (h_1, h_2 \ldots h_n)$ the state space and $O = (o_1, o_2, \ldots o_m)$ an observable variable. Additionally to MC, HMM is defined as:

1. Observation probability depends only on the current hidden state.
   $P(O_t = o_j|X_t = h_i)$

A basic task of HMM is the supervised learning process, where given a set of hidden and observed sequences, the most likely model that produced the observed sequence is searched. A typical application for this problem is part-of-speech tagging, where the observed variables are the words and the hidden states are the part-of-speech tags (Brants, 2000; Cutting et al., 1992).

HMM is used for text generation as follows. First, the text is tagged using a part-of-speech tagger from the Stanford CoreNLP library (Manning et al., 2014). Then, the most likely model that produces those sequences is computed. The hidden state transitions and observations are counted and used as relative frequencies to estimate the transition probabilities.

3 Sentiment Analysis

Two different approaches of sentiment analysis can be identified. The first approach uses lexicons to retrieve the sentiment polarity of a text. This lexicons contain dictionaries of positive, negative, and neutral words and the sentiment polarity is retrieved according to the words in a text. Machine learning uses annotated texts with a given sentiment to build a classification model. Sentiment analysis is implemented as a binary classification problem (Pang et al., 2002).

3.1 SentiWordNet

SentiWordNet (Baccianella et al., 2010) is a widely used lexical resource in sentiment analysis and is based on the English lexical dictionary WordNet (Miller, 1995). This lexical dictionary groups words into synonym sets, which are called synsets, and provides relations between these synsets. SentiWordNet associates each synset with three numeric polarity scores: *positive*, *negative* and *neutral*.

To retrieve the sentiment of a word based on this lexicon, the average scores of all associated synsets of a given word are considered and it is assessed as to be positive, if the average score of the

[1] http://www.cs.princeton.edu/~blei/lda-c

positive polarity is greater than that of the negative. The overall average of all words is calculated to assess the sentiment of a text.

3.2 Supervised Classification

Machine learning can be applied to build a supervised classification model. Text elements are represented by a feature vectors. The features can be the words of the text or their part-of-speech tags.

Support vector machines (SVMs) have been shown to be appropriate for text categorization (Joachims, 1998). In binary classification, the task is to find a hyperplane that separates the document vectors in the two classes and to maximize the margin between them. SVMs are widely used in sentiment analysis (Pang et al., 2002).

For training and testing LibShortText library[2] is used (Fan et al., 2008).

3.3 Stanford Sentiment Treebank

Socher et al. (2013) have introduced a treebank, which includes phrases and sentences annotated with fine-grained sentiment labels. In the five class fine-grained classification task following labels are used: *very negative*, *negative*, *neutral*, *positive*, and *very positive*.

As described in (Manning et al., 2014), sentiment analysis is performed with a model over parse trees. Nodes of a parse tree of each sentence are given a sentiment score. The overall score of the sentence is given at the root node of the parse tree. But it is unclear how to combine the sentiments over many sentences. We count all sentiment representations and take the mean as the overall sentiment of a set of sentences.

4 Experiments

In a series of experiments we analyzed the scalability, cardinality and the ability to generate text with a sentiment.

4.1 Experiment 1: Scalability

In this experiment the scalability of the presented models are measured on data sets of different sizes.

We use the food reviews data set used in (McAuley and Leskovec, 2013) and construct seven sub data sets with 10K, 50K, 100K, 200K, 300K and 500K food reviews respectively. We measure the execution time of the learning algorithms of the models on each of these sub data sets.

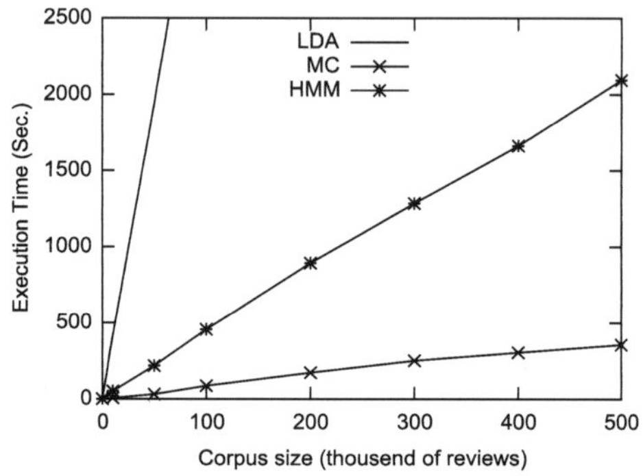

Figure 1: Execution time of LDA, MC and HMM on data sets of different sizes. HMM achieves a smaller execution time than LDA but greater than MC.

Figure 1 shows for each sub data set the execution time of the learning phase. As we can see, MC outperforms the other methods in terms of scalability because it only builds n-grams. HMM has a higher execution time because the data sets have to be tagged using a part-of-speech tagger. LDA performs the worst due to the extensive learning phase.

4.2 Experiment 2: Cardinality

In this experiment the cardinality of the synthetic data sets are measured. The cardinality is defined as the amount of distinct text elements in the generated data set. Two text elements are the same if they have the exact same string. A text element can be an arbitrary type of text, i.e. a sentence or a document. This will show the upscaling behavior in terms of the ability to generate distinct texts.

We use a data set of 10,662 movie reviews used in (Pang and Lee, 2005), which contains an equal number of positive and negative reviews, and divide it into two data sets along their sentiment polarity. On both data sets we build the presented models, which we utilize to scale up by factors of 1, 2, 10, 100 and 1000.

Figure 2 shows that the LDA and HMM models performs best in generating distinct text elements, where almost all text elements are distinct. The MC model generates the smallest amount of distinct text elements, e.g. only 62% distinct text elements using scale up factor 1000. The next word in LDA and HMM only depend on the latent vari-

[2] `http://www.csie.ntu.edu.tw/~cjlin/libshorttext/`

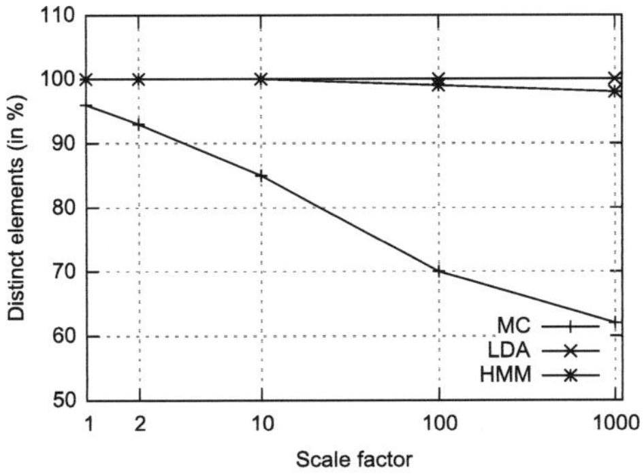

Figure 2: The relative amount of distinct text elements in the synthetic datasets. The synthetic data sets are generated by scale up factors of 1, 2, 10, 100 and 1000. MC generates the smallest amount of distinct text elements, while LDA and HMM generate almost no duplicates.

able and not on the previous words, where in LDA it depends on the latent topics and in HMM on the part-of-speech tags. Therefore, more combinations of words are possible.

4.3 Experiment 3: Sentiment-aware Text Generation

In this experiment it is demonstrated that the models learn high-quality language presented models and are able to generate text with a sentiment.

We use the same data set as in the previous experiment and divide it into two data sets along their sentiment polarity. To build an SVM based classifier we split each data set into a training and test data set. On both data sets we learn the presented models, which we utilize to scale up by factors of 1, 2 and 10. We use (a) SentiWordNet (Baccianella et al., 2010), (b) SVM, and (c) the Stanford sentiment analysis library (Socher et al., 2013) to assess whether the generated reviews have the appropriate sentiment.

Table 1 shows the main experimental results. We see that the HMM is more accurately than LDA but less accurately than the MC. The method (c) outperforms the other methods and achieves an F-measure of 79% for the positive and 79% for the negative class. The basic methods (a) and (b) reveal only a modest difference between the original and synthetic data set, while the advanced method (c) illustrates a significant decrease of the F-measure in the synthetic data sets. One reason why the F-measure have declined is that basic methods work by assessing words in isolation. They give positive scores for positive words and negative scores for negative words and then aggregate these scores. Therefore, the order of words is ignored. In contrast, the advanced method builds a representation of the whole sentence based on the sentence structure using the parse tree. Consequently, MC and HMM perform better than LDA because of their ability to capture the order of words.

	positive			negative		
	(a)	**(b)**	**(c)**	**(a)**	**(b)**	**(c)**
Original	63	75	**79**	57	75	**79**
LDA (1x)	60	73	68	52	71	58
LDA (2x)	62	70	68	52	69	59
LDA (10x)	63	70	69	55	67	59
MC (1x)	62	72	75	54	72	70
MC (2x)	62	73	75	55	**73**	72
MC (10x)	63	74	**76**	56	**73**	72
HMM (1x)	61	69	73	54	68	68
HMM (2x)	61	71	73	54	70	67
HMM (10x)	62	71	73	54	70	67

Table 1: This table shows the F-measures of the original and synthetic data sets for the positive and negative class separately. The synthetic data sets are generated by scale up factors of 1, 2 and 10. The sentiments analysis methods are SentiWordNet (a) SVM (b), and Stanford library (c). The HMM achieves a lower F-measure than MC but a higher than LDA on each scale up factor.

The F-measures of all models and sentiment analysis methods are almost constant on each scale up factor, which indicates a robust upscaling behavior of these models. The HMM achieves a lower F-measure than MC, but can generate a higher number of distinct text elements than MC.

Figure 3 shows the sentiment polarity of the original data set and synthetic data sets. The first column is the original data set tagged by the Stanford library and is classified about 40% as positive, 49% as negative and 11% as neutral. As we can see, the sentiment polarity of the synthetic data set using MC is most similar to the original one, with about 36% tagged as positive, 43% as negative and 21% as neutral. The experiments indicate that the presented models can generate texts with a specific sentiment.

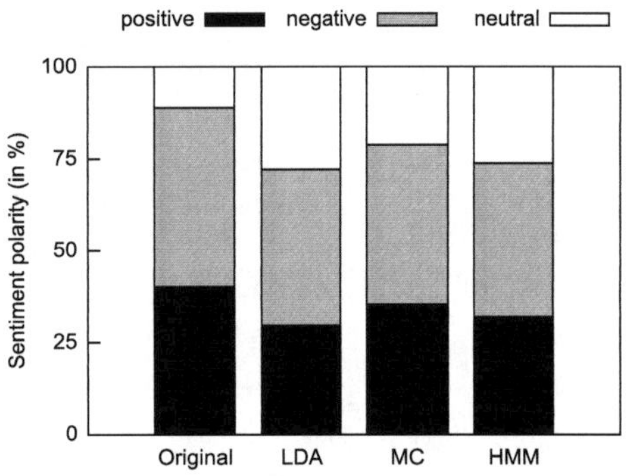

Figure 3: This figure shows the sentiment polarity of the original data set and synthetic data sets. For sentiment analysis the Stanford library is used. The sentiment polarity of the synthetic data set using MC is most similar to the original one.

4.4 Samples from the models

In this section we qualitatively investigate the capabilities of the presented models. The simplest qualitative experiment is to inspect the samples generated by the three models. We use the movie reviews data set and divide it into two data sets along their sentiment polarity. On both data sets we build the presented models, which we utilize to generate the samples.

The samples below were obtained by generating random texts 10 times and selecting the most interesting sample. The samples declared as *negative sentiment*, for example, are retrieved from a model learned on the negative sub data set.

4.4.1 Samples from the LDA model

negative sentiment:

credits i'll emotional uglier camera and can see moore's wanes reason film written to is by her that that that rather

positive sentiment:

simple interdependence particularly and quinn with baran rich questing delicate messenger on wallet comedy-drama such funny check a , . .

4.4.2 Samples from the MC model

negative sentiment:

a little thin , leaving these actors , that it gave me no reason to see the same illogical things keep happening over and over again .

positive sentiment:

often shocking but ultimately worthwhile exploration of the acting , have made to be introverted young men set out to be viewed and treasured for its straight-ahead approach to visualizing nijinsky's diaries is both inspiring and pure of heart , you can't go home again

4.4.3 Samples from the HMM model

negative sentiment:

in his franchise , chou-chou , " the exercise at the love ah-nuld attempted than drama , but pretty predictably , this splitting of the plays to funny routines title of there 's badly the director , and no beautiful life which is someone on a stagy episode .

positive sentiment:

you is hard n't of beautiful updating comedy complex family – be acquainted the usual recipe at every quiet but laughs truly a melodramatic at the in her wholesome , heartwarming david that 's an inevitable bio-pic with museum .

5 Conclusion

In this paper, we presented a primary study on generative models for text generation. A series of experiments indicate that the presented models can generate texts with a specific sentiment. The hidden Markov model achieves a lower F-measure than Markov chain, but can generate a higher number of distinct texts than Markov chains.

In future evaluations the methods will be analyzed within larger and different data sets. Future work will also investigate other generative models for text generation. Grave et al. (2014) introduced a generative model of sentences with latent variables, which takes the syntax into account by using syntactic dependency trees. Sutskever et al. (2011) uses recurrent neural networks to build statistical language models, which can be utilized to generate text.

References

Stefano Baccianella, Andrea Esuli, and Fabrizio Sebastiani. 2010. Sentiwordnet 3.0: An enhanced lexical resource for sentiment analysis and opinion mining. In Nicoletta Calzolari (Conference Chair), Khalid Choukri, Bente Maegaard, Joseph Mariani, Jan Odijk, Stelios Piperidis, Mike Rosner, and Daniel Tapias, editors, *Proceedings of the Seventh International Conference on Language Resources and Evaluation (LREC'10)*, Valletta, Malta, may. European Language Resources Association (ELRA).

David M. Blei, Andrew Y. Ng, and Michael I. Jordan. 2003. Latent dirichlet allocation. *Journal of Machine Learning Research*, 3:993–1022.

Thorsten Brants. 2000. Tnt – A statistical part-of-speech tagger. In *ANLP*, pages 224–231.

Douglas R. Cutting, Julian Kupiec, Jan O. Pedersen, and Penelope Sibun. 1992. A practical part-of-speech tagger. In *ANLP*, pages 133–140.

Rong-En Fan, Kai-Wei Chang, Cho-Jui Hsieh, Xiang-Rui Wang, and Chih-Jen Lin. 2008. LIBLINEAR: A library for large linear classification. *Journal of Machine Learning Research*, 9:1871–1874.

Ahmad Ghazal, Tilmann Rabl, Minqing Hu, Francois Raab, Meikel Poess, Alain Crolotte, and Hans-Arno Jacobsen. 2013. Bigbench: towards an industry standard benchmark for big data analytics. In *Proceedings of the ACM SIGMOD International Conference on Management of Data, SIGMOD 2013, New York, NY, USA, June 22-27, 2013*, pages 1197–1208.

Edouard Grave, Guillaume Obozinski, and Francis R. Bach. 2014. A markovian approach to distributional semantics with application to semantic compositionality. In *COLING 2014, 25th International Conference on Computational Linguistics, Proceedings of the Conference: Technical Papers, August 23-29, 2014, Dublin, Ireland*, pages 1447–1456.

Thorsten Joachims. 1998. Text categorization with support vector machines: Learning with many relevant features. In *Proceedings of the 10th European Conference on Machine Learning*, ECML '98, pages 137–142, London, UK, UK. Springer-Verlag.

Christopher D. Manning, Mihai Surdeanu, John Bauer, Jenny Finkel, Steven J. Bethard, and David McClosky. 2014. The Stanford CoreNLP natural language processing toolkit. In *Proceedings of 52nd Annual Meeting of the Association for Computational Linguistics: System Demonstrations*, pages 55–60.

Julian J. McAuley and Jure Leskovec. 2013. From amateurs to connoisseurs: Modeling the evolution of user expertise through online reviews. *CoRR*, abs/1303.4402.

George A. Miller. 1995. Wordnet: A lexical database for english. *Commun. ACM*, 38(11):39–41, November.

Zijian Ming, Chunjie Luo, Wanling Gao, Rui Han, Qiang Yang, Lei Wang, and Jianfeng Zhan. 2014. BDGS: A scalable big data generator suite in big data benchmarking. *CoRR*, abs/1401.5465.

Bo Pang and Lillian Lee. 2005. Seeing stars: Exploiting class relationships for sentiment categorization with respect to rating scales. In *Proceedings of the 43rd Annual Meeting on Association for Computational Linguistics*, ACL '05, pages 115–124, Stroudsburg, PA, USA. Association for Computational Linguistics.

Bo Pang, Lillian Lee, and Shivakumar Vaithyanathan. 2002. Thumbs up?: sentiment classification using machine learning techniques. In *Proceedings of the ACL-02 conference on Empirical methods in natural language processing-Volume 10*, pages 79–86. Association for Computational Linguistics.

Lawrence R. Rabiner. 1989. A tutorial on hidden markov models and selected applications in speech recognition. *Proceedings of the IEEE*, 77(2):257–286, Feb.

Tilmann Rabl and Hans-Arno Jacobsen. 2012. Big data generation. In *Specifying Big Data Benchmarks - First Workshop, WBDB 2012, San Jose, CA, USA, May 8-9, 2012, and Second Workshop, WBDB 2012, Pune, India, December 17-18, 2012, Revised Selected Papers*, pages 20–27.

Richard Socher, Alex Perelygin, Jean Wu, Jason Chuang, Christopher D. Manning, Andrew Y. Ng, and Christopher Potts. 2013. Recursive deep models for semantic compositionality over a sentiment treebank. In *Proceedings of the 2013 Conference on Empirical Methods in Natural Language Processing*, pages 1631–1642, Stroudsburg, PA, October. Association for Computational Linguistics.

Ilya Sutskever, James Martens, and Geoffrey E. Hinton. 2011. Generating text with recurrent neural networks. In *Proceedings of the 28th International Conference on Machine Learning, ICML 2011, Bellevue, Washington, USA, June 28 - July 2, 2011*, pages 1017–1024.

Detecting speculations, contrasts and conditionals in consumer reviews

Maria Skeppstedt[1,2] **Teri Schamp-Bjerede**[3] **Magnus Sahlgren**[1] **Carita Paradis**[3] **Andreas Kerren**[2]
[1]Gavagai AB, Stockholm, Sweden
{maria, mange}@gavagai.se
[2]Computer Science Department, Linnaeus University, Växjö, Sweden
andreas.kerren@lnu.se
[3]Centre for Languages and Literature, Lund University, Lund, Sweden
{teri.schamp-bjerede, carita.paradis}@englund.lu.se

Abstract

A support vector classifier was compared to a lexicon-based approach for the task of detecting the stance categories *speculation*, *contrast* and *conditional* in English consumer reviews. Around 3,000 training instances were required to achieve a stable performance of an F-score of 90 for *speculation*. This outperformed the lexicon-based approach, for which an F-score of just above 80 was achieved. The machine learning results for the other two categories showed a lower average (an approximate F-score of 60 for *contrast* and 70 for *conditional*), as well as a larger variance, and were only slightly better than lexicon matching. Therefore, while machine learning was successful for detecting *speculation*, a well-curated lexicon might be a more suitable approach for detecting *contrast* and *conditional*.

1 Introduction

Stance taking – including attitudes, evaluations and opinions – has received a great deal of attention in the literature (Hunston and Thompson, 2000; Biber, 2006; Hunston, 2011; Fuoli, 2015), and many studies of speakers' expression of feelings have been carried out in the fields of sentiment analysis and opinion mining with pre-defined or automatically detected categories related to sentiments and opinions. At its most basic level, such analyses use categories of positive, negative or (sometimes) neutral sentiment (Täckström and McDonald, 2011; Feldman, 2013), while other types of analyses use more fine-grained categories of sentiments or attitudes, such as happiness, anger and surprise (Schulz et al., 2013). There are, however, additional aspects or types of stance taking, e.g., contrasting of different opinions (Socher et al., 2013), indications of the degree of likelihood of a conveyed message (Biber, 2006) or expression of conditional statements (Narayanan et al., 2009). Detecting such aspects is an integral part of a high quality sentiment analysis system, as they modify the opinions expressed. In this study, the automatic detection of three such stance categories is investigated:

(1) *Speculation*: "the possible existence of a thing [that] is claimed – neither its existence nor its non-existence is known for sure" (Vincze, 2010, p. 28).

(2) *Contrast*: "Contrast(α,β) holds when α and β have similar semantic structures, but contrasting themes, i.e. sentence topics, or when one constituent negates a default consequence of the other" (Reese et al., 2007, p. 17).

(3) *Conditional*: "describe[s] implications or hypothetical situations and their consequences" (Narayanan et al., 2009, p. 1).

There are previous studies on automatic detection of *speculation* and related stance categories. Results are, however, reported for models trained on large annotated corpora, which are expensive to obtain (Uzuner et al., 2011; Cruz et al., 2015). Here, lexicon-based methods – as well as machine learning models trained on a smaller amount of training data – are instead evaluated for the task of detecting *speculation*, *contrast* and *conditional*. The categories are specifically compared with regards to the following research questions: (a) Are machine learning or lexicon-matching the more suitable method for detecting these three stance categories? (b) How does the amount of used training samples affect the performance of trained machine learning models?

2 Previous research

Speculation has been explored in, e.g., biomedical texts (Vincze et al., 2008; Velupillai, 2012; Aramaki et al., 2014), consumer reviews (Konstantinova et al., 2012), tweets (Wei et al., 2013) and

Proceedings of the 6th Workshop on Computational Approaches to Subjectivity, Sentiment and Social Media Analysis (WASSA 2015), pages 162–168,
Lisboa, Portugal, 17 September, 2015.

Wikipedia texts (Farkas et al., 2010). Biomedical text annotation has also included classification into different levels of uncertainty (Velupillai et al., 2011), as well as into the categories *present*, *absent*, *possible*, *conditional* and *hypothetical* (Uzuner et al., 2011). Some schemes annotate uncertainty markers/cues and their scope (Vincze et al., 2008), while others annotate speculation towards certain types of entities (Velupillai et al., 2011; Aramaki et al., 2014), or categorise text chunks, e.g., sentences or tweets, according to whether they contain speculation or not (Farkas et al., 2010; Wei et al., 2013).

Some systems for automatic detection of *speculation* are modelled as text classification problems, often using support vector classifiers (SVCs) trained on word n-grams (Uzuner et al., 2011; Wei et al., 2013). Others are modelled as named entity recognition systems and use structured prediction for detecting text chunks that function as cues for speculation (Tang et al., 2010; Clark et al., 2011).

The SFU Review corpus, which consists of English consumer generated reviews of books, movies, music, cars, computers, cookware and hotels (Taboada and Grieve, 2004; Taboada et al., 2006), is often used for sentiment analysis. This corpus has been annotated for speculation by Konstantinova et al. (2012), according to a modification of guidelines created by Vincze et al. (2008), in which cues for *speculation* and *negation*, and their scope, were annotated. Inter-annotator agreement was measured on 10% of the corpus, resulting in an F-score and a Kappa score of 89 for the agreement on speculation cues. The same corpus has also been annotated by Taboada and Hay (2008) for Rhetorical Structure Theory categories (Taboada and Mann, 2006, pp. 426–427). A total of 36 different categories were annotated, including *condition*, *contrast* and *concession*[1]. In contrast to the annotations by Konstantinova et al., these annotations were not checked for reliability.

Cruz et al. (2015) trained an SVC to detect the speculation cues annotated by Konstantinova et al., and achieved an F-score of 92. Their lexicon matching approach, which was built on a list of the four most frequent speculation cues, achieved a lower F-score of 70. The SVC was clearly successful, as results slightly better than the inter-annotator agreement were achieved. Since the results were achieved by 10-fold cross-validation on the entire set of annotated data, they were, however, also expensive in terms of annotation effort. The present study, therefore, explores if similar results can be achieved with fewer training samples. In addition, the lexicon matching is here further explored, as it was performed with a very limited lexicon by Cruz et al. (2015).

3 Methods

A lexicon-based and a machine learning-based approach for detecting the three stance categories were compared. The SFU Review corpus annotations by Konstantinova et al. (2012) and by Taboada and Hay (2008) were used for all experiments. These annotations were performed independently and at different times, with Konstantinova et al. segmenting the corpus into *sentences*, while Taboada and Hay used *segments*, which are often shorter. The two segmentation styles were reconciled, by using the sentence boundaries of the Konstantinova et al. corpus, except when the corresponding segment in the Taboada and Hay corpus was longer than this sentence boundary. In such cases, the segment annotated by Taboada and Hay was used as the sentence boundary.[2]

The *speculation* category in the Konstantinova et al. corpus was used for investigating *speculation*, and the *condition* category in the Taboada and Hay corpus for investigating the category *conditional*. Although these categories were somewhat overlapping, since *condition* was included in *speculation*, the categories were employed as defined and annotated in the previous studies. Since the two related categories *contrast* and *concession* are often conflated by annotators (Taboada and Mann, 2006), annotations of these categories in the Taboada and Hay corpus were combined, forming the merged category *contrast*. The speculation classification format previously used in the first of the CoNLL-2010 shared tasks (Farkas et al., 2010) and by Wei et al. (2013) was applied, that is an entire sentence was classified as either belonging to a stance category or not. The procedure used in CoNLL-2010 for transforming the data into this format was adopted, i.e., if either the scope of a *speculation* cue or a segment annotated for *concession/contrast* or *condition* was present

[1]Concession is defined by Mann and Thompson (1983) as "the relationship [that] arises when the speaker acknowledges, in one part of the text, the truth of a point which potentially detracts from a point in another part of the text."

[2]Ill-formed XML files from the Taboada-Hay corpus were discarded, making the corpus used a subset of the original.

and-can and-if anything-else apparently be be-an be-done be-used believe believe-that better but-if buy can can-also can-be
can-do can-get can-go can-have can-only can-say can-you computer could could-be could-have could-not couldn dishwasher don
don-think either even-if extra fear get have-one hope hope-this if if-it if-not if-there if-they if-this if-you it-can it-seemed it-seems
it-still it-would kingdom like-to likely may may-be maybe might might-be must must-say not-be or or-if perhaps
probably re recommend seem seem-to seemed seemed-to seems seems-to should should-be so-if someone
supposed supposed-to that that-can that-could that-would that-you the-extra the-money they-can think think-it think-that think-the think-this
thought to-mind want want-to we-can whether will-probably would would-be would-definitely would-have would-highly would-like
would-recommend wouldn wouldn-be wouldn-recommend you you-are you-can you-could you-don you-like you-may you-might you-must you-re
you-should you-think you-want you-would your your-money

Figure 1: SVC-features selected for *speculation*, displayed in a font size corresponding to their feature weight. (Negative features underlined and displayed in black.)

# sentences	Spec.	Contr.	Cond.	Total
Training	1,184	432	220	5,027
Evaluation	1,217	459	230	5,028

Table 1: Frequencies of categories in data used.

in a sentence, the sentence was categorised as belonging to this category (or categories, when several applied). The sentence list was randomly split into two halves – as training and evaluation data (Table 1).

3.1 Machine learning-based approach (SVC)

A support vector classifier model, the LinearSVC included in Scikit learn (Pedregosa et al., 2011), was trained with bag-of-words and bag-of-bigrams as features. A χ^2-based feature selection was carried out to select the n best features. Suitable values of n and the support vector machine penalty parameter C were determined by 10-fold cross-validation on the training data.

The training and feature selection was carried out for different sizes of the training data; starting with 500 training samples and increasing sample size stepwise with additional 500, up to 5,000 samples. A separate classifier was always trained for each of the three categories, and the categories were evaluated separately.

3.2 Lexicon-based approach (Lexicon)

The lexicon-based approach used three lists of marker words/constructions, one list for each category of interest. Sentences containing constructions signalling any of the three categories were classified as belonging to that category. The lists were created by first gathering seed markers; for *speculation* from constructions listed by Konstantinova et al. (2012) and from a previous resource collected with the aim of detecting speculations in clinical texts (Velupillai et al., 2014), and for *contrast* from constructions listed by Reese et al. (2007). These seeds were then expanded with neighbours in a distributional semantics space (Gavagai, 2015) and from a traditional synonym lexicon (Oxford University Press, 2013). Finally, the expanded lists of candidates for *speculation* and *contrast* markers were manually filtered according to the suitability of included constructions as stance markers. From the list created for *speculation*, a subset of markers signalling *conditional* was selected to create the list for this category.

The final lists contained 191 markers for *speculation*, 39 for *contrast* and 26 for *conditional*.

		Prec.	Recall	F-score
Spec.	SVC	88.59%	95.07%	91.72
	Lexicon	83.41%	78.47%	80.86
Contr.	SVC	54.31%	69.93%	61.14
	Lexicon	43.07%	83.22%	56.76
Cond.	SVC	62.80%	80.00%	70.36
	Lexicon	57.18%	84.78%	68.30

Table 2: Precision, recall and F-score for the two approaches, when using all available training data.

4 Results

Results on the evaluation set for the two approaches (lexicon-matching and the SVC when using all training data) are shown in Table 2. Features selected when obtaining these SVC results are shown in a font size corresponding to their model weight in Figures 1 and 2, and markers found in the evaluation data when using the lexicon-based approach are shown in Figure 3.

Different training data sizes were evaluated with

although although-the but but-it but-the even-though questionable sure

but-if if if-there if-you you you-are you-like you-re

Figure 2: SVC-features selected for *contrast* (first row) and for *conditional* (second row).

bootstrap resampling (Kaplan, 1999). For each data size, 50 different models were trained, each time with a new random sample from the pool of training data. Figure 4 displays all results.

5 Discussion

Both approaches were clearly more successful for detecting *speculation* than for detecting *contrast* and *conditional*. When using the entire training data set, the SVC results for *speculation* were slightly higher than the human ceiling (an SVC F-score of 92, compared to an inter-annotator agreement of 89). The F-scores for *contrast* and *conditional* were, however, considerably lower (approximately 30 points lower and 20 points lower than *speculation*, respectively). The SVC results for the two latter categories also remain unstable for larger training data samples, but stabilise for *speculation* (Figure 4).

The higher F-score for *speculation* than for *contrast* and *conditional*, as well as its higher stability, might be explained by this category being more frequent than the other two. However, there seems to be a much greater variety in the way in which *speculation* is expressed, as shown by the number of SVC-features selected for this category and the number of markers that lead to true positives in the lexical approach, compared to what was the case for the other two categories. Lower recall was also achieved for the lexical approach for detecting *speculation*, despite the many stance markers used for this category. Therefore, it would seem reasonable to hypothesise that, while many training samples would be required for *speculation*, a smaller number of samples should be enough for the other categories. Language is, however, highly contextually adaptable, allowing the same construction to express different phenomena (Paradis, 2005; Paradis, 2015), and frequent English markers for *contrast* and *conditional* seem to be polysemous to a larger extent than *speculation* markers. E.g., 'while' sometimes expresses *contrast*, although it more often has a temporal meaning (Reese et al., 2007), which results in 30 true positives and 70 false positives when it is used as a marker for *contrast* in the lexicon-matching approach. Similarly, 'if' is, by far, the most frequently used marker for expressing *conditional*, as previously observed by Narayanan et al. (2009), and as shown here in the lexical approach, in which 98% of the true positives contained this marker. Despite that, 'if' is also used to indicate indirect questions and as a more informal version of 'whether' (Oxford University Press, 2013), which has a potential to give rise to false positives. In the scheme used by Konstantinova et al., on the other hand, most readings of 'if' were covered by their broad definition of *speculation*.

In addition, it cannot be disregarded that annotations from two different sources were used for the experiment, and that part of the differences in performance, therefore, might be attributed to differences in annotation quality. For the Konstantinova et al. corpus, there is a reliability estimate, which does not exist for the Taboada and Hay corpus. The Taboada and Hay annotation scheme might also be more difficult – as it included 36 annotation categories – and thus more error prone.

Comparing the SVC approach and the lexicon matching, it can be concluded that the only case in which machine learning clearly outperforms lexicon matching is when the SVC for detecting *speculation* is trained on at least 1,500–2,000 training samples. For the categories *contrast* and *conditional*, on the other hand, it can be observed that (1) the machine learning results are unstable, and (2) only very few features – and only positive ones – are used by the models. One point of applying machine learning for text classification is to be able to create models that are complex enough to overcome weaknesses of a lexicon-matching approach, e.g., weaknesses arising from the use of polysemous expressions. Despite being trained on more than 5,000 training samples, only a few features were, however, selected as relevant for *contrast* and *conditional*. Therefore, for automatic detection, it might be more resource efficient to focus the effort on further curation of the lexicons used, rather than on annotation of training data. The complexity of the model for *speculation* seems, however, to exceed what could easily be captured with lexicon-matching, since more features, including negative ones, were used. This further motivates the suitability of machine learning for the task of detecting *speculation*.

It should also be noted that SVC results for

I-think:40 *I-think:4* allegedly:1 almost-certainly:1 *and/or:3* apparently:7 appear:1 *appear:1* as-long-as:2 *as-long-as:3* *assume:2* assuming:2 *assuming:1* *assuming-that:1* believe:20 *believe:12* can-be:25 *chances-are:1* *condition:1* considered:5 *considered:3* could-be:14 doubt:1 *doubt:2* either:19 *either:16* estimate:2 expect:12 *expect:11* feels-like:1 *feels-like:2* *gives-the-impression:1* guess:8 *guess:8* guessing:1 have-a-feeling:1 if:288 *if:19* *implausible:2* *indicate:1* indicated:1 *indicated:1* indicating:1 *indicating:1* it-appears:1 it-can:7 *it-can:1* it-could:7 likely:4 *likely:1* may:43 *may:7* may-be:10 maybe:13 *maybe:3* might:33 *might:1* might-be:5 no-obvious:1 not-sure:6 *not-sure:4* or:220 *or:22* perhaps:15 *plausible:1* *points-to:1* possible:3 *possible:10* possibly:7 potential:4 *potential:3* probably:38 *probably:1* *question:3* seem:17 seemed:28 seeming:1 seems-like:7 should:63 *should:1* shouldn't:4 skeptical:1 *skeptical:2* suggest:9 *suggest:2* suggested:2 suggests:2 *suggests:1* suppose:9 supposedly:1 *supposedly:3* suspect:4 *suspect:1* *suspicion:1* think:66 *think:10* thought:29 *thought:8* *unconvinced:1* *under-the-impression:1* unless:5 *unless:12* unsure:2 *unsure:1* *versus:2* *vs:2* wether:1 whether:9 with-the-understanding-that:1 wonder-if:3 *wonder-why:2* wondering:1 *wondering:4* wondering-if:1 would:175 *would:5*

albeit:1 although:25 *although:9* anyway:1 *anyway:12* *at-the-same-time:3* but:287 *but:249* despite:4 *despite:5* even-if:1 *even-if:13* *even-so:2* however:9 *however:52* *in-contrast:2* in-spite-of:1 *in-spite-of:2* *on-the-contrary:1* on-the-other-hand:4 *on-the-other-hand:8* *regardless:2* still:17 *still:62* *that-said:4* then-again:1 *then-again:1* though:22 *though:28* whereas:2 while:33 *while:70* yet:13 *yet:20*

as-long-as:3 *as-long-as:2* *assuming-that:1* *condition:1* if:192 *if:115* *unless:17* *wether:1* whether:1 *whether:8* *with-the-understanding-that:1*

Figure 3: Constructions leading to true positives (in green) and false positives (in black/italic) for the lexicon-based approach (and number of occurrences as true or false positive). The first group shows constructions for *speculation*, the second group for *contrast* and the third for *conditional*.

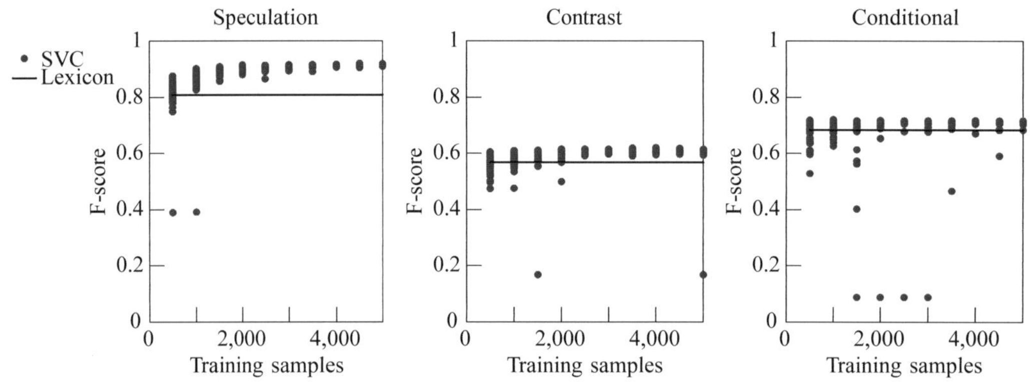

Figure 4: All 50 evaluation results for each random resampling, for each evaluated training data size.

speculation stabilise on high levels already with 3,000 training instances. This shows that results comparable to those of previous studies can be achieved with a smaller amount of training data. For instance, the most closely comparable study by Cruz et al. (2015) achieved the F-score of 92 for detecting speculation cues using 10-fold cross-validation on the entire SFU review corpus. For *contrast* and *conditional* on the other hand, it is difficult to make comparisons to previous studies, as such studies are scarce, but e.g., Clark et al. (2011) achieved an F-score of 89 and 42, respectively, for detecting the related categories *hypothetical* and *conditional*.

In future work, inclusion of additional features for training models for stance detection will be attempted (e.g., syntactic features or distributional features), and the usefulness of applying the detection on extrinsic tasks, such as sentiment analysis (Narayanan et al., 2009), will be further evaluated.

6 Conclusion

For detecting sentences with *speculation*, an SVC trained on bag-of-words/bigrams performed around 10 points better than a lexicon matching approach. When using between 3,000-5,000 training instances, the model performance was stable at an approximate F-score of 90, which is just above the inter-annotator agreement F-score. For detecting *conditional* sentences and sentences including *contrast*, however, the results were lower (an F-score of around 60 for *contrast* and around 70 for *conditional*). On average, the F-score for the machine learning models for these two categories was a few points better than for the lexicon-based methods, but these better results were achieved by models that only used eight features (which were all positive). This, together with the fact that the machine learning models showed a large variance, indicates that a lexicon-based approach, with a well-curated lexicon, is more suitable for detecting *contrast* and *conditional*.

Acknowledgements

This work was funded by the StaViCTA project, framework grant "the Digitized Society – Past, Present, and Future" with No. 2012-5659 from the Swedish Research Council (Vetenskapsrådet).

References

Eiji Aramaki, Mizuki Morita, Yoshinobu Kano, and Tomoko Ohkuma. 2014. Overview of the ntcir-11 mednlp-2 task. In *Proceedings of NTCIR-11*.

Douglas Biber. 2006. Stance in spoken and written university registers. *Journal of English for Academic Purposes*, 5(2):97–116.

Cheryl Clark, John Aberdeen, Matt Coarr, David Tresner-Kirsch, Ben Wellner, Alexander Yeh, and Lynette Hirschman. 2011. Mitre system for clinical assertion status classification. *J Am Med Inform Assoc*, 18(5):563–7.

Noa P. Cruz, Maite Taboada, and Ruslan Mitkov. 2015. A machine-learning approach to negation and speculation detection for sentiment analysis. *Journal of the Association for Information Science and Technology*, pages 526–558.

Richárd Farkas, Veronika Vincze, György Móra, János Csirik, and György Szarvas. 2010. The CoNLL-2010 shared task: Learning to detect hedges and their scope in natural language text. In *Proceedings of the Fourteenth Conference on Computational Natural Language Learning*, pages 1–12, Stroudsburg, PA. Association for Computational Linguistics.

Ronen Feldman. 2013. Techniques and applications for sentiment analysis. *Commun. ACM*, 56(4):82–89, April.

Matteo Fuoli. 2015. A step-wise method for annotating appraisal. (Under review).

Gavagai. 2015. The Gavagai living lexicon. lexicon.gavagai.se.

Susan Hunston and Geoffrey Thompson. 2000. *Evaluation in Text 'Authorial Stance and the Construction of Discourse'*. Oxford University Press, Oxford.

Susan Hunston. 2011. *Corpus Approaches to Evaluation: Phraseology and Evaluative Language*. Routledge, New York and London.

Daniel Kaplan. 1999. Resampling stats in matlab. http://www.macalester.edu/~kaplan/Resampling/ (accessed August 2015).

Natalia Konstantinova, Sheila C.M. de Sousa, Noa P. Cruz, Manuel J. Maña, Maite Taboada, and Ruslan Mitkov. 2012. A review corpus annotated for negation, speculation and their scope. In Nicoletta Calzolari, Khalid Choukri, Thierry Declerck, Mehmet Uğur Doğanur, Bente Maegaard, Joseph Mariani, Jan Odijk, and Stelios Piperidis, editors, *Proceedings of the Eight International Conference on Language Resources and Evaluation (LREC'12)*, Istanbul, Turkey. European Language Resources Association (ELRA).

William C. Mann and Sandra A. Thompson. 1983. Relational propositions in discourse. Technical report, No. ISI/RR-83-115, Marina del Rey, CA: Information Sciences Institute.

Ramanathan Narayanan, Bing Liu, and Alok Choudhary. 2009. Sentiment analysis of conditional sentences. In *Proceedings of the 2009 Conference on Empirical Methods in Natural Language Processing*, EMNLP '09, pages 180–189, Stroudsburg, PA, USA. Association for Computational Linguistics.

Oxford University Press. 2013. Oxford thesaurus of English. Digital Version 2.2.1 (156) on Mac OS X.

Carita Paradis. 2005. Ontologies and construals in lexical semantics. *Axiomathes*, 15(4):541–573.

Carita Paradis. 2015. Meanings of words: Theory and application. In Ulrike Hass and Petra Storjohann, editors, *Handbuch Wort und Wortschatz (Handbücher Sprachwissen-HSW Band 3)*. Mouton de Gruyter, Berlin.

Fabian Pedregosa, Gaël Varoquaux, Alexandre Gramfort, Vincent Michel, Bertrand Thirion, Olivier Grisel, Mathieu Blondel, Peter Prettenhofer, Ron Weiss, Vincent Dubourg, Jake Vanderplas, Alexandre Passos, David Cournapeau, Matthieu Brucher, Matthieu Perrot, and Edouard Duchesnay. 2011. Scikit-learn: Machine learning in Python. *Journal of Machine Learning Research*, 12:2825–2830.

Brian Reese, Julie Hunter, Nicholas Asher, Pascal Denis, and Jason Baldridge. 2007. Reference manual for the analysis and annotation of rhetorical structure. timeml.org/jamesp/annotation_manual.pdf (accessed May 2015).

Axel Schulz, Tung Dang Thanh, Heiko Paulheim, and Immanuel Schweizer. 2013. A fine-grained sentiment analysis approach for detecting crisis related microposts. In *Proceedings of the 10th International ISCRAM Conference*.

Richard Socher, Alex Perelygin, Jean Wu, Jason Chuang, Christopher D. Manning, Andrew Y. Ng, and Christopher Potts. 2013. Recursive deep models for semantic compositionality over a sentiment treebank. In *Proceedings of the 2013 Conference on Empirical Methods in Natural Language Processing*, pages 1631–1642, Stroudsburg, PA, October. Association for Computational Linguistics.

Maite Taboada and Jack Grieve. 2004. Analyzing appraisal automatically. In *Proceedings of the AAAI Spring Symposium on Exploring Attitude and Affect in Text: Theories and Applications*, pages 158–161.

Maite Taboada and Montana Hay. 2008. The SFU review corpus. www.sfu.ca/~mtaboada/research/SFU_Review_Corpus.html (accessed May 2015).

Maite Taboada and William C. Mann. 2006. Rhetorical structure theory: looking back and moving ahead. *Discourse Studies*, 8:423–459.

Maite Taboada, Caroline Anthony, and Kimberly Voll. 2006. Methods for creating semantic orientation dictionaries. In *Proceedings of 5th International Conference on Language Resources and Evaluation (LREC)*, pages 427–432, Genoa, Italy. European Language Resources Association (ELRA).

Oscar Täckström and Ryan McDonald. 2011. Discovering fine-grained sentiment with latent variable structured prediction models. In Paul Clough, Colum Foley, Cathal Gurrin, GarethJ.F. Jones, Wessel Kraaij, Hyowon Lee, and Vanessa Mudoch, editors, *Advances in Information Retrieval*, volume 6611 of *Lecture Notes in Computer Science*, pages 368–374. Springer Berlin Heidelberg.

Buzhou Tang, Xiaolong Wang, Xuan Wang, Bo Yuan, and Shixi Fan. 2010. A cascade method for detecting hedges and their scope in natural language text. In *Proceedings of the 14th Conference on Natural Language Learning*, Stroudsburg, PA. Association for Computational Linguistics.

Özlem. Uzuner, Brett R. South, Shuying Shen, and Scott L. DuVall. 2011. 2010 i2b2/va challenge on concepts, assertions, and relations in clinical text. *J Am Med Inform Assoc*, 18(5):552–556.

Sumithra Velupillai, Hercules Dalianis, and Maria Kvist. 2011. Factuality Levels of Diagnoses in Swedish Clinical Text. In A. Moen, S. K. Andersen, J. Aarts, and P. Hurlen, editors, *Proc. XXIII International Conference of the European Federation for Medical Informatics – User Centred Networked Health Care*, pages 559–563, Oslo, August. IOS Press.

Sumithra Velupillai, Maria Skeppstedt, Maria Kvist, Danielle Mowery, Brian E Chapman, Hercules Dalianis, and Wendy W Chapman. 2014. Cue-based assertion classification for swedish clinical text–developing a lexicon for pyConTextSwe. *Artif Intell Med*, 61(3):137–44, Jul.

Sumithra Velupillai. 2012. *Shades of Certainty – Annotation and Classification of Swedish Medical Records*. Doctoral thesis, Department of Computer and Systems Sciences, Stockholm University, Stockholm, Sweden, April.

Veronika Vincze, György Szarvas, Richárd Farkas, György Móra1, and János Csirik. 2008. The BioScope Corpus: Biomedical texts annotated for uncertainty, negation and their scopes. *BMC Bioinformatics*, 9(Suppl 11):S9.

Veronika Vincze. 2010. Speculation and negation annotation in natural language texts: what the case of BioScope might (not) reveal. In *Proceedings of the Workshop on Negation and Speculation in Natural Language Processing*, pages 28–31, Stroudsburg, PA. Association for Computational Linguistics.

Zhongyu Wei, Junwen Chen, Wei Gao, Binyang Li, Lanjun Zhou, Yulan He, and Kam-Fai Wong. 2013. An empirical study on uncertainty identification in social media context. In *Proceedings of the 51st Annual Meeting of the Association for Computational Linguistics, ACL*, pages 58–62, Stroudsburg, PA. Association for Computational Linguistics.

Using Combined Lexical Resources to Identify Hashtag Types

Credell Simeon
University of Regina
3737 Wascana Parkway
Regina, Sk S4S 0A2
simeon3c@uregina.ca

Robert Hilderman
University of Regina
3737 Wascana Parkway
Regina, Sk S4S 0A2
Robert.Hilderman@uregina.ca

Abstract

This paper seeks to identify sentiment and non-sentiment bearing hashtags by combining existing lexical resources. By using a lexicon-based approach, we achieve 86.3% and 94.5% precision in identifying sentiment and non-sentiment hashtags, respectively. Moreover, results obtained from both of our classification models demonstrate that using combined lexical, emotion and word resources is more effective than using a single resource in identifying the two types of hashtags.

1 Introduction

In recent years, there has been increasing use of microblogs like Twitter where users post short text messages called tweets. One of the most unique and distinctive features found in tweets are hashtags. They are user-defined topics or keywords that are denoted by the hash symbol "#", followed immediately by a single word or multi-word phase joined without spaces (Qadir and Riloff, 2013). A valid hashtag is a community-driven convention that connects related tweets, topics and communties of users. Therefore, they are ideal for promoting specific ideas, searching for and organizing content, tracking customers feedback, and building social conversations. By using hashtags, Twitter users can significantly increase the engagement of their audience (Khan, 2015).

Moreover, hashtags may contain sentiment information. Examples include "#goodluck", "#enjoy", "#wellplayed", and "#worldcupfever". These hashtags can be useful in determining the overall opinion of tweets. Qadir and Riloff (2014) suggest that such hashtags reflect the emotional state of the author, while others (Davidov et al., 2010; Mohammad, 2012) concur that these emotions are not conveyed by the other words in the tweet. By contrast, some hashtags do not contain any sentiment information. Examples include "#soccer", "#USA", "#worldcup", and "#imwatching", respectively. They can be useful in event detection and topic classification of tweets. In our study, hashtags with sentiment information and those without are referred to as sentiment and non-sentiment bearing, respectively.

Because of the heightened interest in the sentiment analysis of tweets, it is important that we are able to identify sentiment and non-sentiment bearing hashtags, accurately. Therefore, in this paper, we propose using existing lexical and word resources to automatically classify these two types of hashtags. We apply a lexicon-based approach to develop two classification models, which use subjective words from different lexical, emotion and word resources. By employing this approach, we intend to demonstrate that using combined resources is more effective than using a single resource for identifying sentiment from non-sentiment bearing hashtags.

Paper organization The rest of the paper is organized as follows: Section 2 outlines related work, Section 3 details the opinion lexicons used, Section 4 describes our proposed methodology, Section 4 discusses our experimental results, and Section 6 presents our conclusion.

2 Related Work

Very few research studies have focused on analyzing hashtags. Wang et al. (2011) proposed that there were three types of hashtags: topic, sentiment-topic and sentiment. Each type refers to the kind of information that is contained within the hashtag such that sentiment-topic hashtags contain both topic and sentiment information. Therefore, there are two types of hashtags with sentiment information, and one type that refer only to topic information. They also classified positive and negative hashtags by using a graph-based approach

Proceedings of the 6th Workshop on Computational Approaches to Subjectivity, Sentiment and Social Media Analysis (WASSA 2015), pages 169–174,
Lisboa, Portugal, 17 September, 2015.

that incorporated their co-occurrence information and literal meaning, and the sentiment polarity of tweets. Experimental results showed that the highest accuracy of 77.2% was obtained with Loopy Belief Propagation with enhanced boosting.

In terms of the most relevant work, Simeon and Hilderman (2015) showed that sentiment and non-sentiment hashtags are accurate predictors of the overall sentiment of tweets. The authors applied a lexicon-based approach to identify the two hashtag types, and then employed supervised machine learning to classify positive and negative tweets containing these hashtags. The experimental results obtained indicated that non-sentiment hashtags are better predictors than sentiment hashtags.

By contrast, Qadir and Riloff (2013) applied a bootstrapping approach in order to automatically learn hashtagged emotion words from unlabeled data. Hashtags were categorized as belonging to one of five sentiment categories: affection, anger/rage, fear/anxiety, joy and sadness/disappointment. Using five hashtags as seed words for each emotion class and a logistic regression classifier, additional hashtags were learned from unlabeled tweets. The learned hashtags were then used to classify emotion in tweets. Experimental results for emotional classification showed that their method achieved higher precision than recall. In a later study, Qadir and Riloff (2014) extended their work to include hashtag patterns and phrases associated with these five sentiments.

In this study, we focus on classifying hashtags into two types: sentiment and non-sentiment bearing. Our main goal is to demonstrate that combining lexical, emotion and word resources is more effective for this classification task than using a single lexical resource. Furthermore, by using this approach, we can reduce dependency on manual annotation, and increase the use of hashtags in the sentiment analysis of tweets.

3 Opinion lexicons

Opinion lexicons are dictionaries of positive and negative terms. For our approach, we employ a number of publicly available lexical resources. They include the manually annotated opinion lexicons of SentiStrength (Thelwall, 2012), AFINN (Nielsen, 2011), Bing Liu (Hu and Liu, 2004), General Inquirer (Stone et al., 1966) and Subjectivity lexicon (Wilson et al., 2005), and the automatically annotated lexicons of SentiWordNet (Baccianella et al., 2010) and NRC Hashtag Sentiment lexicon (Mohammad et al., 2013). They are described below.

1. **SentiStrength** contains over 2500 words extracted from short, social web text. It assigns a score from 1(no positivity) to 5 (extremely positive) for positivity, and -1(no negativity) to -5 (extremely negative) for negativity.

2. **AFINN** is based on Affective Norms for English Words (ANEW) lexicon. It contains 2477 English words, and uses a similar scoring range as SentiStrength. Moreover, it is specifically created for detecting sentiment in microblogs.

3. **General Inquirer** contains over 11,000 words grouped into different sentiment (positive and negative), and mood categories.

4. **Bing Liu Lexicon** contains about 6800 positive and negative words extracted from opinion sentences in customer reviews. It contains misspellings, slangs and other social media expressions.

5. **Subjectivity Lexicon** contains about 8,221 words categorized as strong or weak. For each word, a prior polarity (non-numerical score) is assigned, which can be positive, negative or neutral.

6. **SentiWordNet 3.0** is the largest lexicon containing over 115,000 synsets. A synset is a group of synonymous words with numerical scores for positivity, negativity and objectivity, which sums to a total of one.

7. **NRC Hashtag Sentiment Lexicon** consists of 54,129 unigrams. It is word-sentiment association lexicon that was created using 78 positive and negative hashtagged seed words, and a set of about 775,000 tweets.

4 Proposed Methodology

For this binary classification task, we develop lexicon-based approaches with some modifications. We utilize training and test datasets.

4.1 Overview of the Approach

Initially, tweets are downloaded using the Twitter API. Hashtags are extracted and manually annotated. Tweets containing at least one hashtag of a

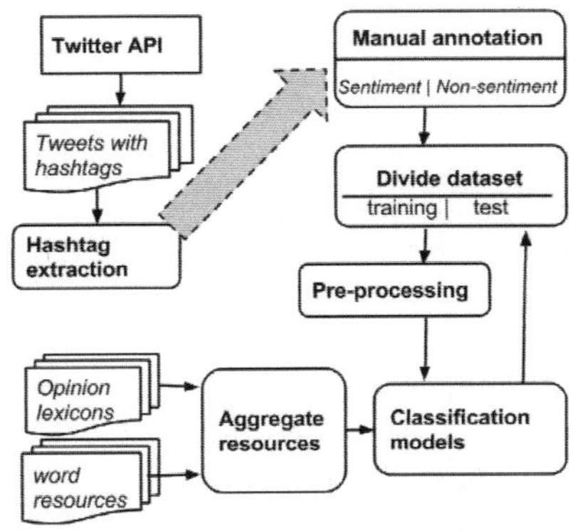

Figure 1: Overview of our approach

particular type are grouped. Then each group is divided into training and test sets. Pre-processing tasks are applied to the training hashtags. Then, classification models are developed and applied to the training hashtags. These models use aggregated lists of opinion words obtained from different lexical and word resources. Finally, each model is applied to the test set.

4.2 Pre-processing

Training hashtags are stripped of their hash symbol, "#". Stemming is applied to the extracted hashtags using a Regrexp stemmer from the Natural Language Processing Toolkit (NLTK) (Loper and Bird, 2002). Using this stemmer, we remove the following suffices:"ed", "ition", "er", "ation", "es", "ness", "ing" and "ment".

For each lexicon, we extract all positive and negative words. However, for a few lexicons, we extract only the strongly subjective words. For SentiStrength Lexicon, we extract positive and negative words with semantic orientations greater than 2.0, and less than -2.0, respectively. For the larger resources we focus only on the adjectives because they are sentiment-bearing (Khuc et al., 2012). As a result, for NRC Hashtag Sentiment Lexicon, we use a POS tagger from NLTK to extract the top 500 adjectives for each sentiment class whereas for SentiWordNet, we consider only the adjectives (as indicated in the lexicon) that have scores for positivity or negativity, which are greater than or equal to 0.5.

4.3 Aggregation of subjective Words

Additionally, we include emotional words from three online resources: Steven Hein feeling words (Hein, 2013) which has 4232 words, The Compass DeRose Guide to Emotion Words (DeRose, 2005) which has 682 words, and SentiSense affective lexicon in which we selected all the adjectives and adverbs in the gloss of the synsets that are categorized as adjectives (de Albornoz et al., 2012). We also include a group of manually identified sentiment-bearing Twitter slangs/acronyms (Fisher, 2012; Nichol, 2014), and some common interjections (Beal, 2014). These words are not typically found in the opinion lexicons. Examples include "fab" for "fabulous", and "OMG" for "Oh my God".

Overall, we use a total of 11 resources. We then combine all the unique words from each of the resources. All duplicates are removed. Then, a total of five aggregated lists of words are created after a series of experiments is performed on the training set to determine the selected combinations. Each aggregated list of words is mutually exclusive. These lists are described below.

1. **(FOW)** (Frequently Occurring Words) list contains the most subjective words. These **542** words have occurred in at least six resources. The threshold of six represents over half of the total number of resources used.

2. **Stems of FOW** contains the stems of all the opinion words in the FOW list. This list contains **522** words.

3. **LDW** (Less Discriminating Words) list consists of opinion words that occur in at least 2 but not exceeding 3 of the 5 larger resources: NRC Hashtag Sentiment, SentiWordNet, General Inquirer, Subjectivity Lexicon and Steven Hein's feeling words. These **1031** words are considered to be the least subjective.

4. **MDW** (More Discriminating Words) list contains words that are strongly subjective. These remaining **7763** words are not FOW or LDW.

5. **Twitter slangs and acronyms** and common interjections, giving a total of **308** words.

4.4 Model Development

We develop two classification models, which use our aggregated lists of subjective words as input.

4.4.1 Model 1

This model uses a binary search algorithm to compare each hashtag with each subjective word. Comparisons are also made between the stem of the hashtag and each subjective word. If a match is found, the search terminates. Otherwise, the search must continue into the second step where substrings of the hashtag are created using two recursive algorithms. The list of substrings contain at least 3 characters and are sorted in descending order of length.

The first algorithm, called *reduce_hashtag*, eliminates the rightmost character from the hashtag after each iteration. The remaining characters form the left substring, whereas the removed character(s) form the right substring. The second algorithm, called *remove_left*, removes the leftmost character from the hashtag after each iteration. After employing both algorithms, the pre-processed hashtag "behappy" has 6 unique substrings: "behapp", "behap", "beha", "beh", "ehappy", and "happy". The resulting substrings of the hashtag are compared to the opinion words in FOW, stems of FOW, and MDW lists because these substrings are smaller representations of the hashtag, and thus, we consider only matches to the most subjective words.

If this search is unsuccessful, we then ascertain if the hashtag contains any non-word attribute in the hashtag that suggests the expression of a sentiment. We consider only the presence of exclamation or question marks (Bakliwal et al., 2012) and repeated characters (at least 3).

Table 1 outlines the eight rules for identifying sentiment hashtags. If none of these rules is found to be true, then the hashtag is determined to be sentiment bearing. Otherwise, the hashtag is non-sentiment bearing.

Rules
Hashtag = opinion word
Hashtag = stem (opinion word)
Stem of the hashtag = an opinion word
Stem of the hashtag = stem of FOW
Max(hashtag substring) = an opinion word
Stem (max(hashtag substring)) = stem of FOW
Max(hashtag substring) = stem (opinion word)
Hashtag contains a sentiment feature

Table 1: Rules for identifying sentiment hashtags

4.4.2 Model 2

In this model, we apply a bootstrapping technique. First, we obtain seed words by using our aggregated lists to find hashtags that are subjective words (including those hashtags that have substrings that are at least 95% in length to a subjective word in our aggregated lists). We then use these seed hashtagged words in order to learn additional hashtags. We employ these four rules: the seed word must be a substring of the hashtag (minimum threshold of 35%) or the stem of the hashtag, and the stem of the seed word must be a substring of the hashtag (minimum threshold of 35%) or the stem of the hashtag. If any of these rules apply, then the hashtag is considered be sentiment bearing. Otherwise, the hashtag is considered to be non-sentiment bearing.

5 Experiment and Results

In this section, we present our experiments that are carried out to evaluate our approach.

5.1 Dataset

Tweets were collected from June 11 to July 2, 2014 during the FIFA World Cup 2014. Tweets were scraped from Twitter using search terms related to the football matches that were being played, in order to capture the opinions of fans. The search terms used were not hashtags as our intention was to acquire a wide variety of hashtags that were created by users. We collected a total of 635,553 tweets containing at least one hashtag. After removing all retweets, hashtags were extracted from the dataset and manually classified. For each hashtag type, we selected the tweets containing at least one hashtag of the respective type. Then, we divided this dataset of tweets equally into training and test sets. Table 2 shows the total number of hashtags in the training and test sets, for each type of hashtag.

Hashtag type	Training	Test	Total
Sentiment	1,368	1,376	2,744
Non-Sentiment	3,070	3,142	6,212

Table 2: Training and test set for each hashtag type

5.2 Experimental setup

In our experiment, we compare the hashtags extracted in the test sets with those from the training set. If the test hashtag is found in the list of training hashtags, the same class label is assigned. Otherwise, we perform similarity testing.

In similarity testing, we compare the stems of the hashtags in the training and test sets. If a match cannot be determined, we ascertain if the test hashtag contains a substring that is at least 95% of the length of one of the training hashtags. If a suitable match is found, the same class label is assigned to the test hashtag. Finally, we compare the predicted class label assigned by the model to that of actual label of the hashtag assigned during manual annotation.

5.3 Results and Discussion

Tables 3 and 4 shows the accuracy (A), precision (P), recall (R), and f-measure (F), metrics (in percent) for Model 1 and 2, respectively. It can be observed from both tables 3 and 4 that our models achieved higher percentages for all four evaluation measures in identifying non-sentiment hashtags than sentiment hashtags. Therefore, we can conclude that it is easier to identify non-sentiment hashtags than sentiment hashtags by combining existing lexical resources. This may be due to the fact that sentiment hashtags contain subjective expressions that are not found in lexical resources. Examples of misclassified sentiment hashtags include "#rootingforyou", "#bringbackourplayers", "needasoccerplayer", and "#historyinthemaking".

Hashtag type	**A**	**P**	**R**	**F**
Sentiment	83.7	86.3	81.2	83.7
Non-sentiment	**84.1**	**94.5**	**85.0**	**89.5**

Table 3: Classification results for Model 1

Hashtag type	**A**	**P**	**R**	**F**
Sentiment	78.7	84.2	72.1	77.7
Non-sentiment	**82.6**	**91.9**	**85.8**	**88.8**

Table 4: Classification results for Model 2

In order to determine the effectiveness of using combined resources, for each model, we substituted the combined resources for a single resource. Figure 2 shows the average accuracy and f-measure scores for using single and combined resources for Model 1 and 2, respectively.

It can be observed in Figures 2 and 3 that by using combined lexical, emotion and word resources, Model 1 and 2 achieve the highest average accuracy and f-measure in identifying sentiment and non-sentiment hashtags when compared to using a single resource. Furthermore, this is more acute for Model 1 than Model 2.

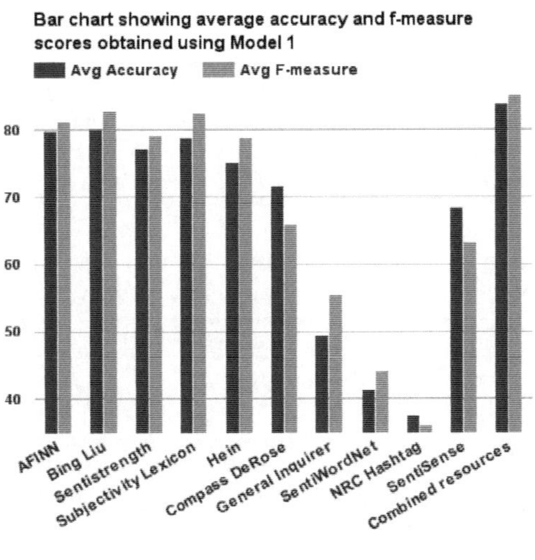

Figure 2: Performance of Model 1

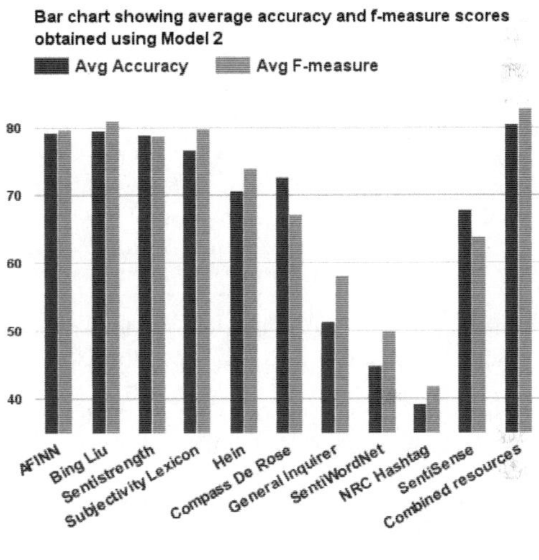

Figure 3: Performance of Model 2

6 Conclusion

In this paper, we applied a lexicon-based approach to identify hashtag types. Our experimental results show that by using combined lexical, emotion and word resources, we can identify non-sentiment hashtags more accurately and precisely than sentiment hashtags. Furthermore, using these combined resources is more effective than using a single resource in identifying hashtag types. In the future, we plan to develop hashtag segmentation algorithms to improve this classification task.

References

Stefano Baccianella, Andrea Esuli, and Fabrizio Sebastiani. 2010. Sentiwordnet 3.0: An enhanced lexical resource for sentiment analysis and opinion mining. In *Proceedings of the Seventh International Conference on Language Resources and Evaluation*, LREC'10, Valletta, Malta.

Akshat Bakliwal, Piyush Arora, Senthil Madhappan, Nikhil Kapre, Mukesh Singh, and Vasudeva Varma. 2012. Mining sentiments from tweets. In *Proceedings of the 3rd Workshop in Computational Approaches to Subjectivity and Sentiment Analysis*, WASSA '12, pages 11–18, Portland, Oregon.

Vangie Beal. 2014. Twitter dictionary: A guide to understanding twitter lingo, August. Retrieved on September 20, 2014.

Dmitry Davidov, Oren Tsur, and Ari Rappoport. 2010. Enhanced sentiment learning using twitter hashtags and smileys. In *Proceedings of the 23rd International Conference on Computational Linguistics: Posters*, COLING '10, pages 241–249, Beijing, China.

Jorge Carrillo de Albornoz, Laura Plaza, and Pablo Gervs. 2012. Sentisense: An easily scalable concept-based affective lexicon for sentiment analysis. In *Proceedings of the Eight International Conference on Language Resources and Evaluation (LREC'12)*, Istanbul, Turkey.

Steven J. DeRose. 2005. The compass derose guide to emotion words. Retrieved on September 20, 2014.

Tia Fisher. 2012. Top twitter abbreviations you need to know. Retrieved on September 21, 2014.

Steven Hein. 2013. Feeling words/emotion words. Retrieved on September 20, 2014.

Minqing Hu and Bing Liu. 2004. Mining and summarizing customer reviews. In *Proceedings of the Tenth ACM SIGKDD International Conference on Knowledge Discovery and Data Mining*, KDD '04, pages 168–177, Seattle, WA, USA.

Jahwan Khan. 2015. How to use hashtags for optimal social media engagement. Online, March. Retrieved on June 26, 2015.

Vinh Ngoc Khuc, Chaitanya Shivade, Rajiv Ramnath, and Jay Ramanathan. 2012. Towards building large-scale distributed systems for twitter sentiment analysis. In *Proceedings of the 27th Annual ACM Symposium on Applied Computing*, SAC '12, pages 459–464, Trento, Italy.

Edward Loper and Steven Bird. 2002. Nltk: The natural language toolkit. In *Proceedings of the ACL-02 Workshop on Effective Tools and Methodologies for Teaching Natural Language Processing and Computational Linguistics - Volume 1*, ETMTNLP '02, pages 63–70, Philadelphia, Pennsylvania.

Saif M. Mohammad, Svetlana Kiritchenko, and Xiaodan Zhu. 2013. Nrc-canada: Building the state-of-the-art in sentiment analysis of tweets. In *Proceedings of the seventh international workshop on Semantic Evaluation Exercises (SemEval-2013)*, Atlanta, Georgia, USA.

Saif Mohammad. 2012. #emotional tweets. In **SEM 2012: The First Joint Conference on Lexical and Computational Semantics – Volume 1: Proceedings of the main conference and the shared task*, pages 246–255, Montréal, Canada.

Mark Nichol. 2014. 100 mostly small but expressive interjections. Retrieved on January 30, 2015.

Finn Årup Nielsen. 2011. A new ANEW: evaluation of a word list for sentiment analysis in microblogs. In *Proceedings of the ESWC2011 Workshop on 'Making Sense of Microposts': Big things come in small packages*, pages 93–98, Heraklion, Crete, Greece.

Ashequl Qadir and Ellen Riloff. 2013. Bootstrapped learning of emotion hashtags #hashtags4you. In *Proceedings of the 4th Workshop on Computational Approaches to Subjectivity, Sentiment and Social Media Analysis*, pages 2–11, Atlanta, Georgia.

Ashequl Qadir and Ellen Riloff. 2014. Learning emotion indicators from tweets: Hashtags, hashtag patterns, and phrases. In *Proceedings of the 2014 Conference on Empirical Methods in Natural Language Processing, EMNLP 2014, A meeting of SIGDAT, a Special Interest Group of the ACL*, pages 1203–1209, Doha, Qatar.

Credell Simeon and Robert Hilderman. 2015. Evaluating the effectiveness of hashtags as predictors of the sentiment of tweets. In *Proceedings of the 18th International Conference on Discovery Science, (DS-2015)*, Lecture Notes in Computer Science, Banff, Alberta. To appear.

Philip J. Stone, Dexter C. Dunphy, Marshall S. Smith, and Daniel M. Ogilvie. 1966. *The General Inquirer: A Computer Approach to Content Analysis*. MIT Press, Cambridge, MA.

Mike Thelwall. 2012. Heart and soul: Sentiment strength detection in the social web with sentistrength. Retreived on April 2nd 2014.

Xiaolong Wang, Furu Wei, Xiaohua Liu, Ming Zhou, and Ming Zhang. 2011. Topic sentiment analysis in twitter: A graph-based hashtag sentiment classification approach. In *Proceedings of the 20th ACM International Conference on Information and Knowledge Management*, CIKM '11, pages 1031–1040, Glasgow, Scotland, UK.

Theresa Wilson, Janyce Wiebe, and Paul Hoffmann. 2005. Recognizing contextual polarity in phrase-level sentiment analysis. In *Proceedings of the Conference on Human Language Technology and Empirical Methods in Natural Language Processing*, HLT '05, pages 347–354, Vancouver, British Columbia, Canada.

Sentiment Classification via a Response Recalibration Framework

Phillip Smith & Mark Lee
School of Computer Science,
University of Birmingham,
Birmingham,
UK

Abstract

Probabilistic learning models have the ability to be calibrated to improve the performance of tasks such as sentiment classification. In this paper, we introduce a framework for sentiment classification that enables classifier recalibration given the presence of related, context-bearing documents. We investigate the use of probabilistic thresholding and document similarity based recalibration methods to yield classifier improvements. We demonstrate the performance of our proposed recalibration methods on a dataset of online clinical reviews from the patient feedback domain that have adjoining management responses that yield sentiment bearing information. Experimental results show the proposed recalibration methods outperform uncalibrated supervised machine learning models trained for sentiment analysis, and yield significant improvements over a robust baseline.

1 Introduction

Probabilistic classifiers are a typically used method for the classification of documents by the sentiment they convey (Pang et al., 2002). Given an unlabelled document, a trained probabilistic model is able to determine an appropriate labelling in relation to a given confidence for the proposed labelling. In the two-class sentiment classification problem a labelling confidence that is greater than 0.5 will lead to a particular sentiment being attached to the input document. However, it is questionable whether a classifier confidence output of 0.51 is sufficiently suitable for the application of any given label. This low confidence poses a problem for sentiment classification, and can often lead to documents being labelled incorrectly, to the detriment of a sentiment analysis system.

A low classifier confidence in sentiment analysis may be produced due to inherent linguistic difficulties that plague systems developed for natural language processing. For example, documents where a sentiment is conveyed implicitly, ambiguously, or in a sarcastic manner can cause problems for machine learning approaches to sentiment classification. Methods have been proposed to deal with such facets of language in sentiment analysis. These tend to focus on hand-crafted lexicons (Balahur et al., 2011) or intra-document contextual cues (Greene and Resnik, 2009) to disambiguate the polarity of a document. We propose a method that takes into consideration related documents in the classification process, and duly adjusts classification output using a *sentiment recalibration framework*.

Our proposed method takes into account external but relevant documents during the sentiment recalibration process. We use these documents to make adjustments to classifier outputs, in an adjustment and correction phase. To our knowledge, this is the first work in sentiment classification to attempt the recalibration of a sentiment classifier given relevant documents. We attribute this ability to the dataset used for our experiments.

The remainder of the paper is structured as follows: in Section 2 we describe the data and annotation experiments devised to observe the relevance of a response to a comment. Section 3 then outlines the motivation for sentiment recalibration, and section 4 details our proposed methodology for the construction of a calibration framework for sentiment classification. Section 5 gives the baseline for evaluation. Section 6 details the results of experimentation with the framework, and discusses the implications. Section 7 describes related work and we conclude and give direction for future work in Section 8.

Proceedings of the 6th Workshop on Computational Approaches to Subjectivity, Sentiment and Social Media Analysis (WASSA 2015), pages 175–180,
Lisboa, Portugal, 17 September, 2015.

2 Data and Annotation

The monologic nature of current datasets for evaluating sentiment classifiers, while valuable to the development of the field, are not applicable to our proposed recalibration framework. Most relevant to our work is the forum post data set (Murakami and Raymond, 2010). However, this is too general for the purposes we are examining due to deviation in discourse topic. Therefore we have developed a dataset for sentiment classification with the related documents that are required for the response recalibration framework. We use patient feedback data provided by the National Health Service (NHS). This has been used before (Smith and Lee, 2014), however author responses were not a feature examined in this work. In this dataset, each feedback item consists of a patient's comment and a response from the NHS. Unlike other online reviews used to investigate the potency of sentiment classification algorithms, this dataset does not contain a user ranking or score to accompany their comment. An annotation phase is therefore required in order to use the documents as an evaluation dataset for our algorithms.

We annotate a subset of 4,059 comments and their related responses for their sentiments expressed and responded to, at the document level. The comments contained 254,611, of which 10,325 were unique. Responses contained 403,315 words, of which 9,115 were unique. Despite a larger average document size, the response vocabulary was smaller that the comment vocabulary. This indicates that the responses given were constrained in nature. An initial pass of the data highlighted that reviews were not merely binary, but often weighed up mixed sentiments before giving a conclusion. Due to this observation, we initially annotate the data with a five-class annotation scheme. This includes, neutral, mixed-positive and mixed-negative categories. The mixed categories denote that varying sentiments are present in the document, but one sentiment is more salient than the other.

Results of this annotation are presented in table 1. Given the annotations, we calculate intercategory agreement using Cohen's kappa coefficient. Between all categories $\kappa = 0.4294$, and observing positive and negative only $\kappa = 0.761$, a good level of agreement. This agreement is indicative of the level to which the sentiment expressed in a comment is mirrored and acknowledged in a related response. Due to this result, we proceed with our experiments using only the positive and negative data.

		$S_{Response}$				
		-2	-1	0	+1	+2
$S_{Comment}$	-2	3	139	6	5	12
	-1	8	2,022	92	33	117
	0	0	153	25	102	44
	+1	4	251	83	671	187
	+2	1	68	1	15	17

Table 1: Comment-response sentiment label confusion matrix.

3 Sentiment Classification Recalibration

This work examines the potential for the outcome of sentiment classifiers to be recalibrated given the presence of a related document. In this work, the response to a sentiment-bearing comment is the related document under consideration. Typical approaches to recalibration may rely on the Platt scaling or binning methods. Platt scaling trains a logistic regression model on the output of an SVM classifier, enabling the production of posterior classification probabilities (Platt and others, 1999). Binning is another calibration method that is particularly effective for classification (Zadrozny and Elkan, 2001). Such recalibration methods focus on statistical methods of recalibrating classifier output. However, when dealing with related natural language documents, we can use inferences from the content of the related text to guide the recalibration process. We therefore propose the use of the response to recalibrate the labelling of the initial comment. This takes a response directed at a comment, and uses the outcome of its classification as a starting point for recalibration. We discuss in further detail the recalibration protocols in the following section.

4 Method

The notion of applying supervised learning methods to classify related documents (Taskar et al., 2001; Jensen et al., 2004) and the post-processing of classification (Benferhat et al., 2014) has been examined in the literature. Based on this, we propose three approaches to leverage the acknowledged sentiment in a response in the recalibration process. The first two methods observe the outcomes of probabilistic classifiers appointed with the role of classifying comment and response sentiment individually. A probabilistic classifier will output a confidence associated with a particular label. Given a confidence greater than .5 a label will be applied. However, a confidence of .51 is probably of no more use than a random guess in the two-class sentiment classification task. Given a complete iteration of the confidence thresholds at .01 confidence intervals, we examine the classifier performance. At each interval, given each instance, where the response label differs to the comment's we assign this label to the review. The third method judges the level of lexical similarity between the comment and response before making a judgement regarding recalibration.

4.1 Probabilistic Threshold Calibration

In classification, the probability of labelling a document with a certain category is just as important as the labelling itself. A classifier may not be overly confident with its initial labelling, and so an external but relevant source of information may help guide and recalibrate the outcome of the initial calibration. Recalibration methods attempt to determine at what threshold the labelling would be most effective. These are typically guided by a line of best fit related to a posterior probability (Zadrozny and Elkan, 2001). We propose a recalibration framework to examine the effects of recalibrating the threshold. The first approach is to iterate over the probabilities at intervals of 0.01, and recalibrate the labelling if the confidence of given labelling is below the threshold. The recalibration is given through the labelling of the response relative to the original comment instance. In the protocol experiments, the confidence of the response classifier is not observed, only the labelling. The label is then commuted to the comment.

The second set of experiments observing probability thresholds imposes the constraint that the response classifier must yield a more confident classification outcome than that of the comment classifier. Both may exhibit the same sentiment, but in order to overcome any confusion due to ambiguous or implicit expressions we commute the response labelling if and only if the confidence output by the response classifier is higher than that of the comment classifier.

4.2 Document Similarity

Classifier confidence is just one potential method of determining cases for instance relabelling where sentiment classifiers may yield incorrect classifications. Another method that deserves consideration is determining the level of lexical similarity between the comment and response. The assumption is made that is that if a response is replying to the content of the original comment, there will be elements of language reuse in the response. Then, the greater the similarity, the more likely the relative document sentiments are homogeneous. We implement the Greedy String Tiling algorithm (Wise, 1993) as a measure of document similarity. The algorithm outputs a score between [0,1], given the level of similarity. As with the previous experiments with relabelling given a classifier confidence, we take the same approach here. Our experiment iterates over varying thresholds, with a 0.01 interval at each step. However, we do not make any adjustments for classifier confidence, only taking the binary labelling as the primary label.

4.3 Baseline

Comments in our dataset receive responses that both acknowledge and concisely respond to the content of the original message. We identify features of these responses that are useful to the sentiment classification process. We employ a rule-based system based on these observations to test the hypothesis that given the presence of these features, the sentiment of the response mirrors that of the original comment. Using a small set of regular expressions for frequent word stems we achieve a recall of .9004. Given the categorisation of the terms we then classify the sentiment of the response and compare the labelling to the gold-standard labelling of the comment. This yields an accuracy of 0.6634. We also cross-validate the three classifiers on the dataset to form another baseline, results of which are shown in Table 2.

	Acc.	Prec.	Recall	F_1
Comment				
NB +1	0. 692	0.502	0.765	0.606
NB -1		0.862	0.659	0.747
MNB +1	0.871	0.784	0.805	0.794
MNB -1		0.911	0.9	0.906
SMO +1	0.856	0.771	0.759	0.765
SMO -1		0.893	0.899	0.896

Table 2: Baseline for sentiment classification (+1 = positive -1 = negative)

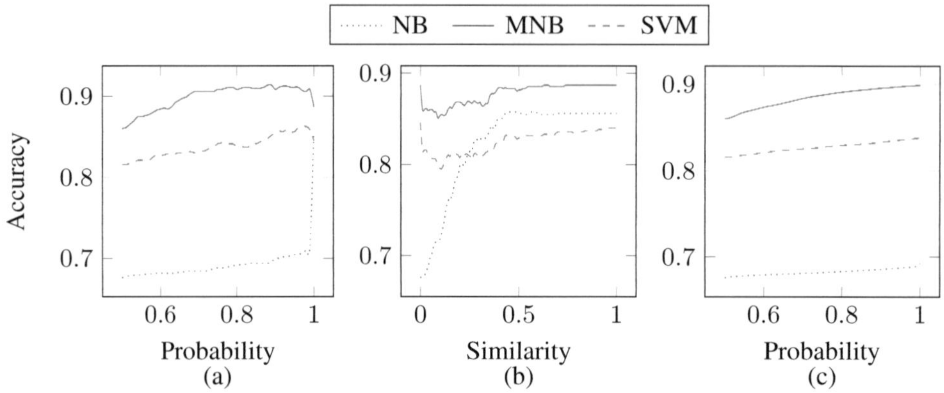

Figure 1: Accuracy comparison graphs for our recalibration methods: (a) confidence threshold (b) similarity threshold (c) confidence threshold where $Pr(R) > Pr(A)$.

5 Results and discussion

Results of the probabilistic relabelling experiment highlight an improvement in classifier accuracy as the probability threshold increases, contrary to expectation. We must look to both Figures 1 and 2 in order to understand this result. One would expect that a classifier outputting a low confidence of classification would yield a higher accuracy given the recalibration process. Results highlight the relative over-confidence of all classifiers when predicting the class of an instance as the number of candidates eligible for relabelling is relatively low. In particular, if we observe the candidates returned for the NB this classifier does not exhibit a great variance in confidence, with the majority of labellings being ≥ 0.99. The hubristic nature of the NB labelling confidence is not beneficial where results are unable to be recalibrated. Given the total relabelling scenario for the NB classifier, whereby all labels from the responses are commuted to annotate the comment, there is a significant increase in classification accuracy of 0.15. In the case of the other two classifiers, such a scenario leads to a decrease in performance. This indicates the poor quality of model initially produced by the NB learner. This also shows the relative strength in model building qualities of the MNB and SVM learners.

The SVM outperforms the NB, but falls short of MNB performance. Figure 2 indicates that potentially poor relabelling choices contribute to this. The success ratio drops dramatically as SVM confidence tends towards 1. This trait is similarly present in both the NB and MNB, also. This is to be expected however, and suggests that a highly confident initial judgement by the comment sentiment classifier should not be altered.

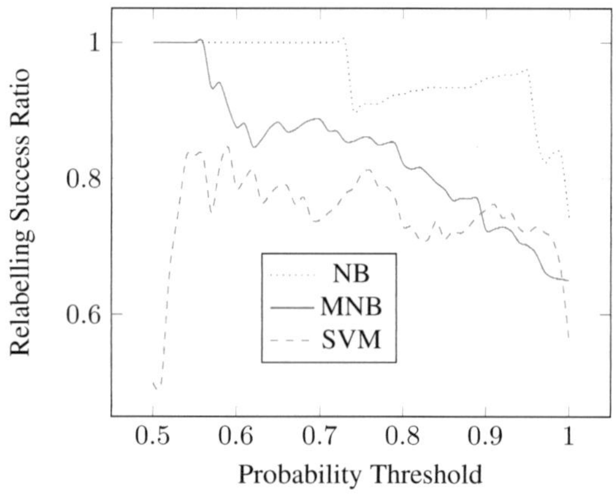

Figure 2: Relabelling success rate given varying classifier confidence thresholds.

Contrasting the probabilistic thresholding results with the similarity threshold relabelling experiments we notice that classifier confidence is a substantially better calibration method. Given the similarity thresholding experiments, decreases in classification accuracy are shown for MNB and SVM. However for NB, significant gains in classifier accuracy are made. This is in contention with the results of the probabilistic thresholding experiments, where gains for NB classification were minimal. We can attribute this to the relaxed string matching method of the implemented similarity measure.

Precision and recall results (although not shown due to space constraints) highlight the dominance of the MNB for in the recalibration framework. Recall increases over all iterations ≤ 0.99, which then yields a drop when full relabelling is applied. Precision peaks at a threshold of 0.78 and decreases following this. The SVM follows suit, however performance degrades almost 0.06 when full relabelling is applied. Precision sees a drop for the negative class, although the NB exhibits reconciling traits. The SVM suffers from a drop in precision of 0.05. The positive class however shows signs of strengthening as the similarity threshold increases. The MNB remains the dominant classifier throughout precision comparison. The recall follows an inverse pattern. As similarity threshold increases for in our negative class experiments, recall gradually increases for MNB and SVM, however makes gains of 0.22 for the NB. The positive recall drops however for all classifiers.

The strong response classification experiments impose a constraint that labelling of the comment can only be commuted from the response classification if and only if the response classifier confidence is higher than that of the comment classification of a given instance. The constraint appears to have a stabilising quality. Comparing graphs (a) and (c) in Figure 1, we see a substantially smoother gradient to the curve of the strong response classification curves in comparison to the general threshold commutation experiments. We do not see the drops in performance for the MNB and SVM classifiers, much to the benefit of the overall classification, but similarly, we do not see the steep climb in classifier accuracy demonstrated by the NB. The precision and recall rates achieved by strong response classification only mimics that of the general probabilistic threshold experiments. Closer comparison of the two shows marginal differences.

Results indicate that there is no requirement for the confidence of the response classifier output to be higher than that yielded for the corresponding instance classified by the model trained on the comment data. Comparing Figure 1 with the comment baseline given in Table 2, accuracy results from the classifiers in the experiments marginally succeed the baseline for the MNB classifier, but for the SVM and NB, accuracy is detrimentally effected. We can conclude that in this case of response relabelling the constraint is too strict.

6 Related Work

Work has observed the useful nature of relationships between documents hen classifying stocks based on the contents of related posts on social networks (Si et al., 2014) and classifying sentiment in posts on online forums based on user relationships, or user stances in online debates (Murakami and Raymond, 2010).

Work on bagging in sentiment classification is somewhat related to our work (Dai et al., 2011; Nguyen et al., 2013). Bagging trains a number of models on a similar set of training data. During classification, each model then classifies the given instance, and a voting protocol labels the instance with the majority label suggested. Our framework however does not train multiple classifiers, although the framework could be extended to incorporate this. Instead, a related document is used to guide and recalibrate the outcome of the initial classification. Our method does not suffer from the issue of low classifier trustworthiness, as we have shown the results of response only classification to be reliable in our baselines. The need for further methods such as stacking is therefore eliminated.

The use of management response in online reviews has been examined to empirically determine the effectiveness in improving a firm's reputation (Proserpio and Zervas, 2014). Analysis has shown moderate improvements where a management response was given. This work did not computationally evaluate the content of reviews, however.

7 Conclusion

We have examined the role of sentiment recalibration in the domain of patient feedback. The proposed classification recalibration method considered acknowledged sentiment in a comment response in order to recalibrate classifier output. Our framework examined three methods for recalibration, two probabilistic and one similarity based. We found that all classifiers exhibited improvements in classification performance when subject to recalibration over varying probability thresholds. Results suggest that the MNB classifier is most suited to the recalibration methods, and yields the best performance, with a 4.2% increase in classification accuracy over our baseline. Our proposed method is suitable where a dataset contains a number of related documents. As the wealth of data for sentiment classification increases, we would like to examine and evaluate our method on additional datasets.

References

Alexandra Balahur, M. Jesús Hermida, and Andrès Montoyo. 2011. Detecting implicit expressions of sentiment in text based on commonsense knowledge. In *Proceedings of the Second Workshop on Computational Approaches to Subjectivity and Sentiment Analysis*, pages 53–60. ACL.

Salem Benferhat, Karim Tabia, Mouaad Kezih, and Mahmoud Taibi. 2014. Post-processing a classifier's predictions: Strategies and empirical evaluation. In *ECAI*, pages 965–966.

Lin Dai, Hechun Chen, and Xuemei Li. 2011. Improving sentiment classification using feature highlighting and feature bagging. In *ICDMW*, pages 61–66. IEEE.

Stephan Greene and Philip Resnik. 2009. More than words: Syntactic packaging and implicit sentiment. In *ACL-HLT*, pages 503–511.

David Jensen, Jennifer Neville, and Brian Gallagher. 2004. Why collective inference improves relational classification. In *ICKDDM*, pages 593–598.

Akiko Murakami and Rudy Raymond. 2010. Support or oppose?: Classifying positions in online debates from reply activities and opinion expressions. In *COLING*, pages 869–875.

Quoc Dai Nguyen, Quoc Dat Nguyen, and Bao Son Pham. 2013. A two-stage classifier for sentiment analysis. In *IJCNLP*, pages 897–901.

Bo Pang, Lillian Lee, and Shivakumar Vaithyanathan. 2002. Thumbs up? sentiment classification using machine learning techniques. In *EMNLP*.

John Platt et al. 1999. Probabilistic outputs for support vector machines and comparisons to regularized likelihood methods. *Advances in large margin classifiers*, 10(3):61–74.

Davide Proserpio and Georgios Zervas. 2014. Online reputation management: Estimating the impact of management responses on consumer reviews. Technical Report 2521190, Boston U. School of Management.

Jianfeng Si, Arjun Mukherjee, Bing Liu, Jialin Sinno Pan, Qing Li, and Huayi Li. 2014. Exploiting social relations and sentiment for stock prediction. In *EMNLP*, pages 1139–1145.

Phillip Smith and Mark Lee. 2014. Acknowledging discourse function for sentiment analysis. In *CICLING*, volume 8404 of *LNCS*, pages 45–52.

Benjamin Taskar, Eran Segal, and Daphne Koller. 2001. Probabilistic classification and clustering in relational data. In *IJCAI*, volume 17, pages 870–878.

Michael J Wise. 1993. String similarity via greedy string tiling and running karp-rabin matching. *Online Preprint, Dec*, 119.

Bianca Zadrozny and Charles Elkan. 2001. Obtaining calibrated probability estimates from decision trees and naive bayesian classifiers. In *ICML*, volume 1, pages 609–616.

Author Index

Association for Computational Linguistics
209 N. Eighth Street
Stroudsburg, Pennsylvania 18360

ISBN 978-1-5108-1189-8

CURRAN ASSOCIATES INC.
proceedings.com